Paradigms of Artificial Intelligence

Springer
Singapore
Berlin
Heidelberg
New York
Barcelona
Budapest
Hong Kong
London
Milan
Paris
Tokyo

Paradigms of Artificial Intelligence

A Methodological & Computational Analysis

Achim Hoffmann

University of New South Wales, Sydney, Australia

 Springer

Dr. Achim Günther Hoffmann
School of Computer Science and Engineering
The University of New South Wales
Sydney 2052
Australia

Library of Congress Cataloging-in-Publication Data

Hoffmann, Achim Günther, 1962-
    Paradigms of artificial intelligence : a methodological and
computational analysis / by Achim Günther Hoffmann
        p.   cm.
    Includes bibliographical references and index.
    ISBN 9813083972
    1.   Artificial Intelligence—Methodology. 2. Paradigm
(Theory of knowledge)   3. Cognition. I. Title.
    Q335.H62   1998
    006.3—dc21   98-19925
                                                            CIP

ISBN 981-3083972

© Springer-Verlag Singapore Pte. Ltd. 1998
Printed in Singapore

Typesetting: Camera-ready by Author
SPIN 10676243   5 4 3 2 1 0

For my parents

Preface

The field of artificial intelligence (AI), formally founded in 1956, attempts to understand, model and design intelligent systems. Since the beginning of AI, two alternative approaches were pursued to model intelligence: on the one hand, there was the symbolic approach which was a mathematically oriented way of abstractly describing processes leading to intelligent behaviour. On the other hand, there was a rather physiologically oriented approach, which favoured the modelling of brain functions in order to reverse-engineer intelligence. Between the late 1960s and the mid-1980s, virtually all research in the field of AI and cognitive science was conducted in the symbolic paradigm. This was due to the highly influental analysis of the capabilities and limitations of the perceptron by Minsky and Papert (1969). The perceptron was a very popular neural model at that time. In the mid-1980s a renaissance of neural networks took place under the new title of *connectionism*, challenging the dominant symbolic paradigm of AI. The 'brain-oriented' connectionist paradigm claims that research in the traditional symbolic paradigm cannot be successful since symbols are insufficient to model crucial aspects of cognition and intelligence. Since then a debate between the advocates of both paradigms is taking place, which frequently tends to become polemic in many writings on the virtues and vices of either the symbolic or the connectionist paradigm. Advocates on both sides have often neither appreciated nor really addressed each others arguments or concerns.

Besides this somewhat frustrating state of the debate, the main motivation for writing this book was the methodological analysis of both paradigms, which is presented in part III of this book and which I feel has been long overdue. In part III, I set out to develop criteria which any successful method for building AI systems and any successful theory for understanding cognition has to fulfill. The main arguments put forward by the advocates on both sides fail to address the methodologically important and ultimately decisive question for or against a paradigm:

> How feasible is the development of an AI system or the understanding
> of a theory of cognition?

The significance of this question is: it is not only the nature of an intelligent system or the phenomenon of cognition itself which plays the crucial role, but also the human subject who is to perform the design or who wants to understand a theory of cognition.

The arguments for or against one of the paradigms have, by and large, completely forgotten the role of the human subject. The specific capabilities and limitations of the human subject to understand a theory or a number of design steps needs to be an instrumental criterion in deciding which of the paradigms is more appropriate. Furthermore, the human subject's capabilities and limitations have to provide the guideline for the development of more suitable frameworks for AI and cognitive science. Hence, the major theme of this book are methodological considerations regarding the form and purpose of a theory, which could and should be the outcome of our scientific endeavours in AI and cognitive science.

This book is written for researchers, students, and technically skilled observers of the rapidly evolving fields of AI and cognitive science alike. While the third part is putting forward my methodological criticism, part I and II provide the fundamental ideas and basic techniques of the symbolic and connectionist paradigm respectively. The first two parts are mainly written for those readers, which are new to the field, or are only familiar with one of the paradigms, to allow an easy grasp of the essential ideas of both paradigms. Both parts present the kernel of each paradigm without attempting to cover the details of latest developments, as those do not affect the fundamental ideas. The methodological analysis of both paradigms with respect to their suitability for building AI systems and for understanding cognition is presented in part III.

I am indebted to the following colleagues and friends for their support, reading of drafts, constructive criticism, and discussions during the long period of writing this book: Paul Compton, Joachim Diederich, Norman Foo, Jim Franklin, Tom Gedeon, Bernd Mahr, Katharina Morik, Peter Slezak, Sunil Thakar, and Fritz Wysotzki. Thanks are also due to Ian Shelley of Springer-Verlag for his support and encouragement in writing this book, to the anonymous reviewers for their feedback, and to May Look for the smooth and pleasant cooperation throughout the production process of this book. Last but not least, I am grateful to my wife Andrea for her patience and understanding, constant encouragement, and help by reading through the manuscript in its final stages. I also thank all other individuals who helped me in various ways in writing this book.

Sydney, May 1998   *Achim Hoffmann*

Table of Contents

Introduction

The field of the fairly young discipline, artificial intelligence (AI), attempts to understand, model and design intelligent systems. AI was formally founded in 1956, the name *artificial intelligence* was created, and the first AI meeting at Dartmouth College took place. The question of what were the principles behind human intelligent behaviour, human reasoning, etc. was addressed much earlier: first by philosophy for more than 2,000 years and more recently by psychology. During the past decades and roughly in parallel to AI, evolved the field of cognitive science, which also studies the nature of human thought. The development of the electronic computer in the middle of the 20th century also raised many speculations about the possibility of an intelligent machine.[1] Currently, AI comprises a wide field of activities, central to it are perception and reasoning methods, as well as learning and natural language processing. Other subfields are rather specific to particular tasks such as playing chess, diagnosing diseases, predicting stock exchange courses, proving mathematical theorems or designing buildings.

The early years of AI began with two different approaches. Some researchers investigated models of neurons starting as early as 1943 (McCulloch & Pitts, 1943) and developed mechanisms on how these simple neural models could show adaptive behaviour. On the other hand, there were mathematically and psychologically minded researchers who set out for the development of algorithms which would correspond rather to the thought processes of man than to the neural processes in human brains. The most influential early work of this group was probably the framing of *physical symbol systems* as a paradigm for developing general intelligent agents by Simon and Newell (1958), Newell and Simon (1963, 1976). Both approaches were competing until in 1969 Minsky and Papert published a book which showed that, although the early neural learning mechanisms could learn anything a neuron could represent, a neuron could represent only very little. After its publication, funding for neural network research was largely cut by government agencies, resulting in a virtual shutdown of all neural network research.

---

[1] The idea of intelligent machines, however, is much older and includes ideas such as that of androids, or the chess machine of Wolfgang von Kempelen, called the *Turk* in 1769. This machine was presented as a fully mechanical chess player. In reality, a person was hiding inside and using levers to control the machine.

Since then, almost all research in AI was conducted in the *symbolic paradigm* of Newell and Simon's physical symbol systems. In the following years, however, most AI researchers reduced their aspirations as well: no longer was a general intelligent agent sought. People were rather content with building application specific intelligent systems. The era of expert systems began. It took until the mid-1980s, before neural networks, under the title *connectionism* were rediscovered as a promising alternative to the symbolic paradigm. The reasons for its re-emergence can be attributed to a variety of developments in physics, in psychology, in AI itself,[2] as well as to the increasing acceptance of Dreyfus philosophical critique at the enterprise of AI. Dreyfus criticised AI since the middle of the 1960s, as an ill-conceived endeavour (Dreyfus, 1965).

After neural networks returned to the stage around 1986, a heated debate began arguing that the symbolic paradigm of AI is to be replaced by the newly emerged *paradigm of connectionism*, the idea of massively parallel and highly connected computer systems of a brain-like architecture. In the following years, connectionism became increasingly popular as an alternative approach to the classical symbolic approach to artificial intelligence. In fact, it was claimed that general intelligent agents have to be built as connectionist systems. On the other hand, even within the traditional symbolic paradigm, announced Nilsson recently the aspiration again to build general intelligent systems (Nilsson, 1995).

The book presents the foundations of both approaches which are often considered to be competitors. Since both approaches represent rather general methods for describing and developing intelligent systems, they are called *paradigms of artificial intelligence*. The term *paradigm* became very popular in the context of scientific frameworks after T.S. Kuhn's book *The structure of scientific revolutions* (Kuhn, 1962). In his book, Kuhn analysed the history of science and developed the notion of *paradigm*. In the scientific context, a paradigm is roughly a set of common assumptions and beliefs among a group of scientists. Kuhn presents a number of examples where such a scientific paradigm was replaced by another paradigm which was historically considered to be a significant scientific progress, i.e. a *scientific revolution*.

Probably the best commonly known example for a scientific revolution is the shift from the Ptolemaic geo-centric planetary theory to Galileo's heliocentric theory. While Ptolemy described the movement of the planets around the earth in complicated epicycles, Galileo's theory described the movements in simpler circles around the sun. The observed epicycles from the earth's point of view were then a derivation of the circular movement of all planets around the sun.

Taking this perspective, proponents of the connectionist approach claimed that a scientific revolution in artificial intelligence and cognitive science is necessary to make further progress; i.e. that the symbolic paradigm has to be replaced by the connectionist paradigm.

---

[2] The achievements were rather disappointing and far behind the earlier predictions.

This book investigates the strengths and weaknesses of both paradigms and will critically assess the claim that a paradigm shift from the symbolic to the connectionist paradigm is needed.

The symbolic approach to artificial intelligence assumes the so-called *physical symbol system hypothesis* which asserts that intelligent systems can appropriately be described as symbol systems. Opposed to that is connectionism, which claims that the idea of symbol systems is insufficient for describing exhaustively truly intelligent systems. The connectionist claim is backed up by philosophical analyses, which indicate that human thought and intelligence rest essentially on 'non-symbolic structures'. In this context, two roles of connectionism can be distinguished: on the one hand, connectionism is considered as a promising foundation for the practical development of AI systems; on the other hand, connectionism is considered as an adequate framework for scientific theories of human cognition.

The following, however, appears to be a strong objection to connectionism. The structure of human thought seems to require a description of substantial complexity. Opposed to that is the human capacity to comprehend complex structures rather limited. A logical consequence of this discrepancy is as follows: a description of complex cognitive processes has to reflect the limitations of the human capability to comprehend such a description. This is opposed to the description's role of reflecting physical or biological principles, which may underlie the natural cognitive processes in some sense.

As a consequence of that, the idea of connectionism seems to bear severe inherent problems, both from a practical point of view as well as from an epistemological point of view. In that context, the following two aspects should be distinguished:

Connectionism as scientific explanation of cognition. Here, an objection seems adequate which resembles an argument by the 18th century German philosopher Immanuel Kant:

> *Symbols are the precondition of the very possibility to comprehend an explanation or description!*

A scientific explanation is required to serve two objectives:

- it has to reflect the phenomena to be explained.
- it has to be comprehensible for the subject which is interested in the explanation.

That means, a scientific description has to be compatible with the cognitive capabilities of a scientist. As long as scientists think in concepts which they denote by symbols - in particular, when communicating with other people - a scientific explanation has to be a symbolic explanation. A non-symbolic description will simply be useless. Presumably, this will not be denied by most advocates of connectionism either. The critical issue is rather the exact notion of *symbol*: Is it the 'syntactical description' of a neural network architecture or is it the 'semantical description' of the cognitive processes?

Connectionism as engineering principle for intelligent systems. Considering connectionism as engineering principle, puts the comprehensibility of the resulting overall design in a less prevailing position than in the first case of a scientific explanation. On the other hand, the requirement that the final design reflects certain principles of human cognitive processes and their biological foundations is relaxed.

In any case, the following question demands an answer:

> In which cases can the process of designing an intelligent system be *easier*[3] in the connectionist paradigm than a design in the symbolic paradigm? Is the design of a certain type of systems easier in the connectionist paradigm - without any symbolic means? Or is the design in the connectionist paradigm easier for engineers with a certain background or with suitable support tools?

These two points represent the core concern of the book. However, the centre of gravity will be on connectionism as an engineering principle, i.e. on the *engineering approach* to AI. The reasoning in this book is supported by computation-theoretic results on learning systems. These considerations will prove that one cannot expect to gain a significant advantage by combining a large number of neurons in a network and by using complex modes of interaction between the neurons. Throughout the book, terms like *intelligence, human intelligence, intelligent behaviour, phenomenon of intelligence, human cognition, cognitive system*, etc., are used. No precise definition will be given; this seems neither possible nor desirable. I believe that the reader will have a sufficient pre-scientific intuitive understanding of it. Where cognition is involved, however, the term will generally refer to human intelligence, while intelligence in general may also refer to an artificial system behaving intelligently. Besides it should be said that this book concentrates on the *behavioural* aspects of intelligence. The philosophical problems associated with consciousness, intentionality, etc., are not touched on at all.

Organisation

The book is divided into three parts: The first part presents the classical symbolic paradigm of AI. The second part presents the connectionist paradigm of AI along with some of the motivations for connectionism. The third part investigates the strengths and weaknesses of each paradigm. These investigations take place partly by epistemological[4] and partly by computational analyses. A more detailed outline of the three parts follows:

Part I. The Symbolic Paradigm. The first part gives an outline of the symbolic approach to AI. It introduces the reader to the *knowledge level*, as

---

[3] ... or requiring less effort ...

[4] Epistemology is a branch of philosophy concerned with the nature of knowledge including its possible and actual genesis, its limitations, etc.

one of the central ideas of the classical AI paradigm in chapter 1. In chapter 2, basic techniques of knowledge representation and reasoning, mainly based on logic, are presented. Further technical details are deferred to the appendix. This is followed by an outline of the principal components and functionalities of expert systems and knowledge-based systems. In chapter 4 follows an outline of typical symbolic learning methods with a few techniques studied in more depth. Chapter 5 summarises the main points of the symbolic paradigm.

Part II. The Connectionist Paradigm. The second part introduces the reader to the basic motivation for and the fundamental ideas of the connectionist paradigm in chapter 6. Neural network models and the associated learning techniques are presented in chapter 7 as exemplifications of the general idea of connectionist systems. One of the central ideas in connectionism is the ability to learn and to adapt incrementally. A number of the more important learning models for neural networks are presented in order to give a more detailed account on how typical learning mechanisms for neural networks work. Chapter 8 presents approaches which seek to integrate symbolic structures into connectionist systems. Part II closes with a summary of the main points of the connectionist paradigm in chapter 9.

Part III. Methodological Analysis of the Two Paradigms. The third part presents the new methodological analysis of both competing paradigms by introducing a new perspective, i.e. by considering the descriptional complexity of the phenomenon to be described, which allows new insights into the debate. More precisely, the question which sort of description is comprehensible at all becomes the focus of the discussions.[5]

The first chapter of part III, chapter 10, introduces the reader to different models of computation, which resemble more or less the two paradigms, and to the formal measure of *algorithmic information theory*[6] which will be the conceptual basis of the formal analyses in chapter 13. Chapter 11 reviews the original connectionist claim as exemplified by Smolensky (1988) in his article *On the Proper Treatment of Connectionism*. An analysis of the notion of *symbol* is presented in chapter 12 which turns out to lie at the heart of the entire debate, as symbols are the keys to communication and understanding. Since connectionism relies essentially on the ability to learn, an analysis of the computational potentials and limitations of neural networks with respect to algorithmic information theory are provided in the following chapter 13. Chapter 14 discusses methodological problems of research in AI and cognitive science. The question of how to conduct research in order to ensure real progress is discussed. This question has received little attention in the literature so far, although its instrumental role for research in AI and cognitive science is obvious. As a consequence of these considerations, chapter 15 discusses *non-factual knowledge*, a partic-

---

[5] This is opposed to the question of what paradigm allows the description of a certain complex functional relationship at all?

[6] Also called Kolmogorov complexity.

ularly problematic type of knowledge, which proves very difficult to integrate systematically into AI systems. The final chapter summarises the main points of the book and presents the conclusions from the analyses given in part III.

Part I

The Symbolic Paradigm

The first part of this book presents an introduction into the symbolic paradigm of AI, which is also referred to as *classical artificial intelligence.*

The historical development in various disciplines resulting in the emergence of the idea of symbol systems is outlined in chapter 1. Furthermore, chapter 1 summarises the central ideas underlying the symbolic paradigm of AI. Chapter 2 presents basic techniques of reasoning, i.e. classical logic as well as some more specialised reasoning techniques to give an impression of the type of research work being conducted in the symbolic paradigm of AI. This is followed by chapter 3, which provides a short introduction to the most important practical outcome of AI so far: expert systems. The penultimate chapter of this part, chapter 4, gives a fairly detailed introduction into the main ideas of machine learning, i.e. into the techniques which allow learning within the symbolic paradigm. This chapter goes into some detail and length, as the topic of learning is of particular importance for the discussion in this book. This is because learning capabilities are absolutely vital to connectionism, the alternative paradigm of AI, which is discussed in part II.

Readers, which are familiar with symbolic AI techniques, can skip chapters 2, 3, and 4 without any loss. Chapter 1 may still be of interest, as it presents material, relevant for the assessment of the paradigm, which is not explicitly discussed in many textbooks on AI. The first part closes with chapter 5 which summarises the main points of the previous chapters on the symbolic paradigm.

1. Foundations of the Symbolic Paradigm

This chapter presents the fundamental ideas of the symbolic paradigm. While these ideas are only sketched here, they will be deepened and illustrated in the following chapters using expositions of specific techniques which are routinely used in the symbolic paradigm of AI. A detailed discussion on the notion of *symbol* itself and the differing views on it in the context of both paradigms is presented in chapter 12 in part III. For the time being, an intuitive understanding of the term should suffice for the following discussion on symbol systems in this introductory chapter.

After the introduction into the historical roots of the symbolic paradigm in section 1.1, this chapter introduces the reader to the idea of symbol systems in section 1.2. The central notion of the *knowledge level* is presented in section 1.3. Section 1.4 summarises the main points of the chapter.

1.1 Introduction

The roots of the intellectual enterprise of AI and cognitive science can be traced back for more than 2000 years to Plato and even before. However, considering the development of the modern digital computer in the 20th century, the more or less immediate intellectual predecessors of AI can be divided into some four or five fields of studies: cybernetics, mathematics and logic, philosophy, psychology, and partly linguistics.

Cognitive psychology in North America before World War II was largely dominated by behaviourism, where only the *observable behaviour* of an individual as a result of stimulation was of interest. All theoretical constructs which would claim certain, from the outside not directly observable, processes going on inside an individual were categorically rejected. Only very few psychologists in North America maintained alternative views since William James in the 19th century. Notably, Tolman (1932) in *Purposive Behavior in Animals and Men* was probably most distant to the dominant stimulus-response position. In an important paper with Brunswik (Tolman & Brunswik, 1935) *The Organism and the Causal Texture of the Environment* he considered man as a goal-seeking organism, whose actual behaviour was shaped by the environment within which the goals were pursued.

Opposed to that, in Europe, psychology developed important ideas on models of human cognition during these decades. Most notably, perhaps. was the work of Bartlett (1932), de Groot (1946), Duncker (1945), Piaget (1929), Selz (1924), and Wertheimer (1945). Bartlett aimed at an understanding of how information was represented 'inside the head' and how such representations are modified and retrieved (Bartlett, 1932). European psychologists maintained a Gestaltist view.[1]

One interesting viewpoint on cognitive psychology in the America of the 1930s can be found in Boring's *The Physical Dimension of Consciousness* (Boring, 1933), where Boring attempts to explain the observable Stimulus-Response behaviour in neurological terms. This may be viewed as an early predecessor of today's connectionism and its role in cognitive science.

In mathematics substantial efforts were devoted on its foundations. As a consequence of a number of problems in the mathematics of the 19th century, including Russell's set-theoretic paradox,[2] the early 20th century saw a tremendous effort being spent on developing formal procedures for mathematical reasoning which would allow to concentrate purely on the rule-governed manipulation of mathematical statements, as opposed to considering the content of those statements. The Hilbert program, whose principal limitations were so famously shown by Gödel (1931), aimed at the formal treatment of proofs, i.e. at precise procedures for manipulating mathematical formulas, which could ensure a logically correct result without any need to consider the meaning of such formulas.[3] One of the important outcomes of this program was the development of the Turing machine (Turing, 1937), a universal framework for the precise description of symbol manipulation procedures.

In the philosophy of science, there also emerged an increasing trend towards a more formal treatment of scientific descriptions and reasoning, which was tagged as *logical positivism*, i.e. the position to base all scientific theories on directly observable facts (see Sarkar (1996) for a review of the developments). A more or less direct reflection of that trend was found in the behaviourism as it was proposed by McDougall (1912) and Watson (1913), as it dominated the North-American psychological landscape for the following decades (see Skinner (1953)). However, the emergence of the Turing machine gave a means into

---

[1] The core of the Gestaltist view is the assumption that singular phenomena cannot be considered independently, but that rather the composition of a multitude of such phenomena have to be considered as a whole. An example which was given by the founder of the Gestaltist view, C.v. Ehrenfels in 1890, is that of the perception of a music. The perception of a singular musical tone takes place on the background of a more complex entity, such as the musical melody comprising a whole sequence of tones. This complex entity is called the Gestalt.

[2] Russell discovered the following problematic definition of a set: let S be the set of all sets which do not contain themselves as an element. Does S contain itself as an element? This showed that the conception of sets was fundamentally flawed at that time and allowed highly problematic definitions. See, e.g., Heijenoort (1967) for more details.

[3] See Hilbert and Bernays (1968) for an exposition of the fundamental ideas of it.

the hands of those, who were seeking an alternative to behaviourism: the idea of viewing a cognitive system as a symbol manipulating system. In fact, this idea gradually emerged through the following decades and was particularly developed by Simon and Newell (1958), Newell and Simon (1972).

Another important development in the late 1940s was the field of cybernetics, founded by Wiener (1948). Cybernetics was concerned with controlling systems through feedback loops. Its further development resulted in today's field of control theory. Both technical and neurological systems were considered under the cybernetic perspective. That is, the functioning of the human and animal brain was viewed as feedback process. This tied in nicely with the behaviourism in psychology, the dominant view in North America before World War II.

All these intellectual predecessors suggested in some sense the idea of AI and cognitive science, i.e. to study the nature of intelligence and to attempt the development of a formal theory of intelligence. As a consequence, a group of largely young scientists gathered at Dartmouth college in 1956, to discuss their ideas about ways to model intelligence.

General Intelligent Agents. The Dartmouth conference of 1956 is widely considered to be the historical event which founded the field of *artificial intelligence*. Its participants included J. McCarthy, M. Minsky, A. Newell, H. Simon, R. Solomonoff, and others. Since these early years of AI and even before, there was the vision of something like a *general intelligent agent*. That is, a system that is capable of performing all sorts of intelligent tasks. The Turing test (Turing, 1950), considered merely a system which was restricted to communication via a telewriter with its environment in order to perform purely intellectual tasks. Opposed to the Turing test setting, general intelligent agents are assumed to have also sensors and effectors to act in the physical world. See the sketch of a general intelligent agent in Figure 1.1. The agent interacts with the outside world through an interface which may resemble human sensors and effectors. However, the agent is assumed to receive certain tasks from the outside world which it attempts to solve. For solving these tasks it has a certain set of methods available which are stored in the '*method box*'. For different tasks possibly different methods have to be employed. Thus, there must be a component which determines which method to be used in which particular situation. The different methods may use general knowledge about the world and about problem solving in order to accomplish the given task effectively. Furthermore, there must be another component which stores the task as well as specific conditions of the outside world in some suitable way. This information is stored in a certain data structure, the *internal representation*. The internal representations are changed by the selected methods and in accordance to given general knowledge. This is done in order to determine the next action and to keep track of new information, potentially indicating changes in the conditions of the outside world. So far the description of the intelligent agent is quite general. One important open question concerns what particular kind of internal

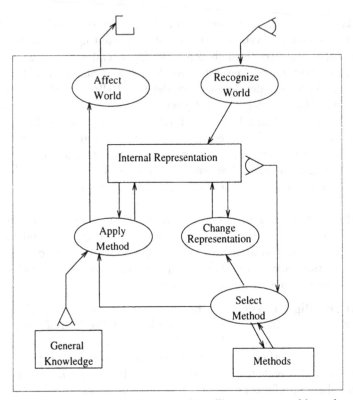

Figure 1.1. The functional units of a general intelligent agent and how they interact.

representation is most suitable to meet the needs of such a general intelligent agent. A certain data structure by itself has no functionality: an interpreting mechanism is always needed. As a consequence, the question concerning the most suitable way of representation must always be considered in the context of potential methods for 'reading' and manipulating these representations. Furthermore, what aspects of a situation or task need to be represented depends on the purpose of the system. Hence, the system's purpose must also be taken into account when determining an appropriate representation. While these are important questions for designing a symbolic representation language for a particular purpose, the following discussion focuses on the principles of the more general framework of symbol systems.

1.2 Physical Symbol Systems

The idea of physical symbol systems was extremely influential throughout most of the work in AI. Hence, we can also speak of the *symbolic paradigm* of AI. According to Newell and Simon (1972, 1976), Newell (1980), a physical symbol system is built from a set of elements, called symbols, which may be composed to form symbol structures by means of a set of relations.

A symbol system has a memory capable of storing, retaining, and retrieving symbols and symbol structures. It has a set of information processes that form symbol structures as a function of sensory stimuli. Furthermore, it has a set of information processes which produce symbol structures which cause motor actions and modify symbol structures in memory in a variety of ways. A symbol system interacts with its environment in two different ways:

- It receives sensory stimuli from the environment which it converts into internal symbol structures.
- It acts upon the environment in ways determined by symbol structures that it produces by internal information processes.

Thus, its behaviour can be influenced by both its current environment through its sensory inputs, and by previous environments through the information it has stored in memory from its experiences.

In general, both symbols and symbol structures are called 'symbols'. Here, symbols are *signs* or tokens which have a certain reference. Although it is not quite clear to what kind of domain the symbols may refer, the idea is roughly that symbols correspond to the content of conscious thought. For example, symbols may refer to physical objects, like 'this house', 'the river over there' etc. Certainly, symbols may also refer to concepts which have no physical manifestation, like the general concept 'house', which refers rather to a *class* of objects (existing and non-existing in the physical world) than to a concrete physical object or group of objects. Furthermore, symbols may even refer to completely abstract concepts, like mathematical concepts, e.g. 'number three' etc.

Symbols are conceived as patterns which may be physically implemented in various ways. In today's computers they are usually patterns of electromagnetism, though their physical nature may differ radically in integrated circuits or vacuum tubes in the computers of the 1940s. Although it is unknown how patterns are represented in the human brain, it is generally assumed that they are represented as neuronal arrangements of some kind.

Newell and Simon's notion of symbol systems is extremely general, so general that symbol systems are actually equivalent to the notion of the Turing machine,[4] i.e. equivalent to the notion of computation. It is important to note at this point, that the driving force for Newell and Simon, in developing their conception of symbol systems, was the idea to develop means for describing the cognitive processes of humans.[5] That is, their concept of physical symbol systems were conceived to form the basis, i.e. a formalism in which to express descriptive operational theories of human cognition. In that sense, the idea of physical symbol systems may be viewed as providing a language in which

---

[4] See section 10.1.
[5] See Newell and Simon (1972).

operational theories of human cognition can be expressed. Newell (1980) formulated the so-called *physical symbol system hypothesis* which claims that physical symbol systems include symbols which correspond to those symbols, humans use:

> ... It becomes a hypothesis that this notion of symbols includes symbols that we humans use everyday in our lives.[6]

The symbol level describes cognition by using symbols as the elementary units and by using rules to manipulate symbols for describing the behaviour of the system. The application of a rule to symbols depends entirely on symbols which are currently present in the system.

This description of physical symbol systems is certainly very abstract. Let us consider high-level programming languages as an example of possible types of symbols and the provided ways of symbol manipulation. The standard data types offered are such as *integer, real, boolean,* and *character.* Moreover, one is allowed to define additional data types and data structures of arbitrary complexity from these primitive types. The methods for manipulating these standard data types are mainly arithmetic operations on the numerical data types and some special operations on the non-numerical data types. These methods appear suitable for elementary problems like accounting etc. However, for complex tasks that we expect to be solved by intelligent agents, these methods seem too simple and not sufficiently abstract.

This poses the question of which level of abstraction is suitable for the physical symbol systems of Newell and Simon? What sort of symbols and their manipulation are needed for solving problems which typically require intelligence. This crucial question is in a sense the main concern of this monograph, and it will be addressed in the following chapters, as well as in part II. A much deeper and principled discussion is presented in part III.

In the symbolic paradigm of AI, a particularly strong variant of a symbolic level of description is very prominent. So-called compositional symbol systems allow new symbol structures to be composed in a way that the meaning, i.e. the reference, of the composed symbol structures, can be derived from the specific rules being used for composing the symbol structure. This requires a strong connection between the rules for composing symbol structures and the domain of reference. Formal logic in the 20th century emphasised exactly this relationship and developed strong foundations for ways of using and manipulating symbol structures in a purely formal but still meaningful way. Consequently, formal logic turned out to play a major role in the symbolic paradigm of AI.[7]

Besides this epistemological aspect of symbols and their relationship to a world in which they can be interpreted, there was another important aspect of symbols: symbols and their correspondence to the content of certain (conscious)

---

[6] In Newell (1980).

[7] See chapter 2 for an introduction to formal logic.

thoughts played a major role in the psychologically oriented part of the AI community.

Symbols were used to describe theories of human cognition. A number of important ideas in AI originated from cognitive psychology, such as the idea of scripts[8] and semantic networks.[9] Another idea derived from considering the human way of memorising information are frames.[10] All these methods represented alternatives to the 'classical' logical approach. They made up the core of the work on *knowledge representation*, one of the main research areas of AI since the 1970s.

To put the presentation of symbol systems into a methodological perspective, the following section discusses various abstract levels of system description, including the so-called knowledge level. The latter one is partly based exactly on the mentioned foundations of formal logic and to another part on the psychologically motivated view on symbols, which will be called *first-person symbols* in part III.

1.3 Abstract Levels of System Description

Considering the characterisation of symbol systems so far, it may have remained unclear in what way they differ from 'plain' Turing machines. In the following, a more methodological view of describing a system using a certain class of descriptive means is taken. Consequently, this section presents different types of descriptions of systems, such as the general intelligent agent of Figure 1.1. In particular, reasons for adopting a certain level of abstraction for describing a certain type of system are discussed. Furthermore, Newell's reasons for proposing the *knowledge level*, as being well-suited for describing intelligent systems will be reviewed.

1.3.1 Traditional Levels of Computer System Description

To begin the discussion, see Figure 1.2 for the traditional levels of abstraction in computer system design. All these levels of description can be used in order to determine the system's overall behaviour in terms of the input-output behaviour of the system from a complete description at the respective level.

---

[8] The idea of scripts is due to Schank, a psychologist at Yale University, to represent the typical structure and aspects of procedural events, such as visiting a restaurant (see e.g. Schank and Abelson (1977)).

[9] See Findler (1979) for an anthology on semantic networks for AI.

[10] Minsky (1975) is accounted as the originator of the idea of frames, i.e. using a record like data structure to allow structured access to all the information which belong to a certain object or situation. This is just like humans would tend to keep all the relevant information associated with an object or situation, such that retrieving that information is facilitated.

1. *Device Level*
2. *Circuit Level*
3. *Logic Level*
    a) *Logic Gate Sub-level*
    b) *Register Transfer Sub-level*
4. *Program Level*
    a) *Machine Code Level*
    b) *Assembler Program Level*
    c) *Problem Oriented Programming Language Level (e.g. Pascal, C, etc.)*

Figure 1.2. Typical levels of increasing degree of abstraction for describing the operation of a computer system.

Each level is characterised by a specific set of elementary functional units. For example, at the device level, there are transistors of various types, resistors, etc.; at the register transfer level, there are registers, multiplexors, decoders, adders, etc; at the programming level, there are arithmetic expressions, assignment statements, etc. These functional units can be combined in certain ways in order to compose a larger and more complex system. By appropriately composing groups of such units, the units at the next higher description level are constructed. Because of this principle, the general possibility of reducing a description at the highest level, to a description at any of the lower levels becomes obvious.

Moreover, at each description level, there are not only the elementary units defined by the respective level, but there is also a certain *medium* which is the 'substance' being used for interaction between the different elementary units. For example, at the device level, the mediums are voltages and currents; at the register transfer level, the mediums are binary scalars or vectors; at the programming level, the mediums are numbers, characters, etc. Finally, in order to give a complete system description at a given level, which allows to derive the system's operation, the particular way of combining a set of elementary units needs to be specified. At the device level, this is the way of wiring different devices together; at the register transfer level, this is the connection of data buses, control signals etc.; at the programming level, this is the sequence of program statements. The different description levels are at the same time different levels of abstraction. A description at the device level reflects physical properties of the involved devices (usually transistors). These properties become increasingly invisible at higher levels of system description. The circuit level disregards certain interconnection patterns between certain devices and considers only compound structures of several devices. Those compound structures have functionalities which are useful for composing even more complex functions. Such more complex functions are the elementary units at the next higher level of description or abstraction. For example, at the logic levels the particular voltages occurring at interconnections between transistors or even between logical gates are ignored. By ignoring such details, the system description - at a more abstract level - becomes more feasible. In designing computer systems, the mentioned levels of abstraction proved useful for simplifying the overall system design task.

Since the more abstract levels of descriptions are essentially simplifications of the descriptions at less abstract levels, it is clearly possible to describe the operation of a complex computer system at the device level. However, this is usually overly difficult. Further, the different levels of abstraction have been designed on purpose to have the characteristic that a computer system can be described at a higher level than the device level, without abandoning important details of its physical implementation. For example, the voltages occurring at certain internal wires can be largely ignored for a description of the input-output behaviour of the computer system. This is due to the modular structure of the logic gates etc. That is, logic gates are constructed in such a way that their functionality is independent of the voltages occurring at the electrical wires inside a logic gate as well as at the gate's interface to other gates.[11]

However, another consequence of this is that certain aspects at the transistor level, such as electric parameters, cannot be described at the symbol level. They are also assumed to be of no interest for the programmer.[12] Each level of description has its own functional description of the available operations. In that sense it is autonomous. Moreover, the operations of each level are implemented by suitably designed operations at the next lower description level. That is, each level can be reduced to the next lower level. For example, the circuit functions are ensured by appropriate arrangement of the involved devices. Similarly, the operations specified at the program level are ensured by a suitable system architecture described at the register transfer level.

1.3.2 The Knowledge Level

In 1982, Newell proposed a certain level of system description suitable for AI systems which he called *knowledge level* and which he located above the program level (Newell, 1982). A knowledge level description uses terms which are assumed to correspond to the *knowledge* humans deal with. The system's behaviour should be predictable based on the system's description at the knowledge level together with the assumption that the system will behave *rationally*.

According to Newell should the *knowledge level* be characterised as follows: The medium of the knowledge level is *knowledge* while the law of behaviour is *rationality*. The components at the knowledge level are *goals*, *actions*, and *bodies*. A body is the physical materialisation of the agent which has a number of actions at its disposition and certain goals it seeks to achieve. See Table 1.1

---

[11] In practice this is not entirely true. Logic gates have fan-in and fan-out values specified which determine the maximal number of gates which can be connected to a given gate in order to not violate the gate's functionality as specified at the logic level due to electrical aspects.

[12] This, however, implies also that, e.g., at the programming level, it is impossible to design the system in order to minimise the power dissipation of the computing system when showing the desired input-output behaviour.

Description Level:	Register Transfer Level	Symbol Level	Knowledge Level
Components:	Registers, Decoders, Multiplexors, etc.	Statements	Goals, Actions, (Physical) Bodies
Behavioural Law:	Logical Operations	Sequential Interpretation	Rationality

Table 1.1. Two defining aspects of computer system levels: components and the behavioural law among those components.

for a comparison. The components at each system description level are the units which are used for expressing a description. The interpretation of these units to obtain the actual function of the system, is reflected by the 'law-of-behaviour', for the respective description level. It should be noted that the increasingly abstract levels of system description are not given by nature. Each level is designed in a way that it provides the basic operations, components, and the behavioural laws of the next more abstract level. Thus, in order to provide a *knowledge level* description of a system, the system at the symbol level must be carefully designed in such a way that the overall system can actually be described at the knowledge level. That is, it must be ensured that the details at the symbol level can be ignored when determining the input-output behaviour of the overall system.

The knowledge level hypothesis: *There exists a distinct computer systems level, lying immediately above the symbol level, which is characterised by knowledge as the medium and the principle of rationality as the law of behaviour.*

Some properties resulting from the idea of rationality as the behavioural law of the knowledge level are discussed below. The basic idea of the general intelligent agent is that the agent will, depending on its goals and its knowledge, determine a particular action to be executed.

The principle of rationality: *If an agent has knowledge that one of its actions will lead to one of its goals, then the agent will select that action.*

A remarkable point is that at the knowledge level, no specific mechanism is considered which may determine the actions to be selected. It is rather an abstract principle which is opposed to the rather bottom-up principles of the lower computer system levels.

The given formulation of the principle of rationality poses the question of how to characterise more precisely the notion of *knowledge*. For example, it is often assumed that if a person knows A and A implies B, then the person knows also that B is the case. This would in practice require a logical inference. From everyday experience, however, it is clear that not all logical inferences are performed by a human. That is, while the ideal of rationality seems very appealing, in practice it is rarely achieved to even generate all logical consequences of the knowledge or assumptions a person has. Besides such logical implications, certain forms of non-deductive reasoning have to be considered to belong to rationality as well, such as reasoning with degrees of uncertainty in assumptions etc.

Whatever a more precise explication of knowledge and rationality may look like, it should be understood that the claim of a law of behaviour at a level of description is also constitutive for the meaning of its medium. That is, there is a circular dependence: what *knowledge* means depends on what *rationality* means. On the other hand, *rationality* depends on how exactly *knowledge* is understood. The notion of knowledge is only very coarsely characterised in Newell (1982), leaving the reader to rely largely on their intuition, i.e., to their pre-scientific conception. While the purpose of *knowledge* is meant to determine a set of selected actions for achieving the given goals, only one of the selected actions will be taken as the next step. The execution of an action depends on a number of preconditions, including the question of whether the execution of an action is physically possible.

The decision as to which of the selected actions should be taken is made using a number of general principles of which some are given below. Those general principles would normally only allow to drop some of the potential actions but would not necessarily result in a single action left over to be taken. For instance, to reduce the set of selected actions, general principles like *minimising the necessary effort, time or energy consumption*, etc. for achieving a set of goals may be applied.

In order to complement this, the following principle states that in the case of multiple goals there should be preference given to those actions which lead to the fulfilment of more than just one goal.

Preference of joint goal satisfaction: *For given knowledge, if goal G_1 has the set of selected actions $\{A_{1,i}\}$ and goal G_2 has the set of selected actions $\{A_{2,j}\}$, then the effective set of selected actions is the intersection of $\{A_{1,i}\}$ and $\{A_{2,j}\}$.*

While this principle potentially reduces the set of selected actions, it is by far too weak to disambiguate the question of which action is to be executed. Furthermore, it leaves an ambiguity among different actions which lead to different sets of goals, where none is a proper subset of the other set of goals.

Another principle mentioned in Newell (1982) states that there is no bias toward a specific action if more than one are acceptable for a given goal. That is, all acceptable actions are to be considered.

The equipotence of acceptable actions: *For given knowledge, if action A_1 and action A_2 both lead to goal G, then both actions are selected.*

It is fairly clear that these principles are not sufficient for giving a complete account on what might be considered as human rationality. Furthermore, so far, it has not been elaborated as to what *knowledge* in this context really means.

In fact, in general the *knowledge level* is not meant to provide a deterministic description of a system's behaviour. A knowledge level description of a system is rather assumed to be *radically* incomplete. That is, sometimes, behaviour of a system can be predicted by a knowledge level description, but often the behaviour *cannot* be predicted. Newell gave the following as a definition of *knowledge* in his original article (Newell, 1982):

Knowledge: *Whatever can be ascribed to an agent, such that its behaviour can be computed according to the principle of rationality.*

In this formulation, knowledge is completely *functionally* characterised. That is, knowledge is characterised in terms of what it does as opposed to being characterised *structurally*, e.g. in terms of objects with particular properties and relations. The idea of the knowledge level can possibly be better explained by considering an agent and an observer of the agent. The observer, attempts to describe the agent at the knowledge level. That means the observer ascribes to the agent certain knowledge, certain goals, and certain possible actions the agent can take. Based on this knowledge about the agent, the observer is able to predict the agent's behaviour. For these predictions, the observer assumes that the agent behaves rationally.[13] Newell considered the knowledge level as particularly useful, because it permits the prediction and understanding of an agent's behaviour without having an operational model of the processing which is actually performed by the agent. The prediction is not made on the basis of knowing the structure of the agent, but merely on the basis of the agent's knowledge of its environment, the agent's goals and its possible actions.

1.4 Summary

This chapter presented the basic ideas behind the symbolic paradigm of AI. It has indicated that the knowledge level plays a central role, as it emphasises the idea of developing systems at an abstraction level which is compatible with that of humans when talking about a domain of expertise and when discussing how to solve problems. Newell hoped to be able to abstract completely from

---

[13] Newell (1982) says that of course all that knowledge of both the agent and the observer, who knows, among other things, what the agent knows..., needs to be represented by symbol structures. However, in the context of the debate on symbolism vs. connectionism, we do not make this claim here.

a particular procedural approach to deal with a domain. He hoped that by representing the relevant knowledge about the domain, a suitable approach of dealing with problems in a procedural way can be automatically derived by the system. In the meantime, however, it became clear that this was too ambitious, as there are too many different types of problems which require specialised approaches in order to exploit the provided domain knowledge successfully. It also became clear that important techniques in the symbolic paradigm must be logical reasoning techniques which allow powerful automatic reasoning. Besides purely deductive reasoning, a large number of alternative reasoning techniques have been developed to cover aspects like reasoning under uncertainty, analogical reasoning, non-monotonic reasoning,[14] etc. The next chapter presents some of the techniques which have been developed to allow a better understanding of the fundamental assumptions behind them. A more general discussion on the problem of developing general reasoning techniques is presented in part III.

---

[14] Non-monotonic reasoning covers reasoning techniques which may allow to derive less inferences if more premises are provided. This is very different to traditional deductive reasoning; non-monotonic reasoning essentially allows some inferences which are not logical consequences of the premises. Additional knowledge may be incompatible with these inferences, and as a consequence, these inferences may no longer be derived when additional knowledge is added to the knowledge base. Thus, the reasoning is *non-monotonic*.

2. Knowledge Representation and Reasoning

For implementing the idea of the *knowledge level*, an operational description of rationality is needed. Logic has always been considered an important aspect of rationality. Logic can be used to generate new knowledge based on given knowledge, or more precisely, using given propositions in order to generate new propositions which have to be true if the given propositions are true. That is, to generate new propositions which are logically entailed by the given propositions. Because of the important role of logic for the notion of rationality, this chapter provides an introduction into the basics of formal logic. Furthermore, section 2.2 discusses other reasoning techniques, which go beyond those of classical logic. This chapter provides an introduction to the fundamental ideas and techniques of automated reasoning. Readers, who are familiar with the field of automated reasoning, can safely skip this chapter.

2.1 Logic

In the following, the reader will be introduced to some of the technicalities of modern symbolic logic as it is also relevant to AI. The exposition starts off with basics which will be known to most readers, and it proceeds to a rather detailed exposition of technical details of resolution proof procedure.

A major distinction is regularly made between propositional logic and predicate logic: Propositional logic deals with *propositions* as atomic units, as the name indicates. This is opposed to predicate logic which can also reflect aspects of the internal structure of propositions.

2.1.1 Propositional Logic

An example, for what conclusions can be drawn by using the laws of propositional logic is as follows:

Given: *If it was snowing throughout the night, the world is white.* **and** *It was snowing throughout the night.*

From these two propositions, it can be inferred that *the world is white.*

The first proposition is a conditional statement. If the condition (*it was snowing throughout the night*) is fulfilled, then the conclusion is true. The second proposition asserts that the condition is true. Thus, it follows *logically* that *the world is white*. In order to determine the 'laws' of logic which describe exactly what conclusions can be drawn, the propositions are broken up into two atomic propositions:

A:*it was snowing throughout the night*
B:*the world is white.*

Using the respective symbolic names A and B for the two atomic propositions, the initial propositions can be restated as follows:

If A, then B. A.

The conclusion to be drawn from that is B. The form of such a logical conclusion is also called *syllogism*. This particular type is one of the most elementary forms of logical reasoning and is known as **Modus Ponens**. The Modus Ponens is often described as

$$\frac{A \rightarrow B, A}{B.}$$

which is to be read as: *Given propositions of the form above the line, the proposition of the form beneath the line can be derived; i.e. B is true, if both, $A \rightarrow B$ as well as A are true.*

Of course, each of the symbols A and B could be substituted by an arbitrary proposition. In fact, whenever a set of propositions are known which match the symbolic form above, the respective conclusion can be drawn, regardless of the meaning of the particular propositions at hand. However, if the condition A is not fulfilled, it is unknown whether the conclusion B is true.

Considering the propositions in the example, which were substituted by A and B, the following is conceivable: Although it was snowing throughout the night, the world is not white at all. (e.g. because the temperature was above $0°C$ and the snow melted as a result.)

Obviously, it is not always true that *the world is white*, if *it was snowing throughout the night*. Hence, the given proposition of the form $A \rightarrow B$ is false. This leads to the *truth table* in Table 2.1, which shows under what circumstances we can say that the conditional proposition '**if A, then B**' is true. The conditional connection of the two propositions A and B is also called *implication* and its usual notation in logic is $A \rightarrow B$ and we say A *implies* B. Depending on the truth values of the propositions A and B, Table 2.1 shows the truth value of the compound proposition $A \rightarrow B$.

Coming back to the example, it may be argued that the conditional proposition $A \rightarrow B$ is true, if the condition part is enhanced by another condition requiring that the outside temperature is below $0°C$. That is, the following assignments to the propositional variables A and B may be made:

Not, And and **Or**

A	B	$\neg A$ not A	$A \wedge B$ (A **and** B)	$A \vee B$ A **or** B
false	false	true	false	false
false	true	true	false	true
true	false	false	false	true
true	true	false	true	true

Implication and Equivalence

A	B	$A \to B$ (if A then B)	$A \leftrightarrow B$ (if and only if A then B)
false	false	true	true
false	true	true	false
true	false	false	false
true	true	true	true

Table 2.1. Truth tables for the five basic logic functions, *not, and, or, implication,* and *equivalence.*

A: *it was snowing throughout the night and the outside temperature is below* 0°C.

B: *the world is white.*

In this example, A bears a meaning which is actually a composition of two atomic propositions: *it was snowing throughout the night* **and** *the outside temperature is below* 0°C. The intuitive meaning of the **and** connective is that the compound proposition is only true, if *both* of its parts are true. That is, we obtain the corresponding truth table in Table 2.1 for the *and* connective. Thus, we may have three atomic propositions as follows:

A_1: it was snowing throughout the night.
A_2: the outside temperature is above 0°C.
B: the world is white.

Suppose, A_1 is true, A_2 is false, and B is true. We can determine the truth value of $A \to B$, where $A = (A_1$ and $A_2)$ by using the given truth tables as follows: first, the truth value of A is determined as a function of the truth values of A_1 and A_2, i.e. the third line in the table for *and* shows the respective truth value 'false' which is to be assigned to A. To determine the overall truth value of '$A \to B$' the second line in the truth table for *implication* matches the given truth values, i.e. the resulting truth value for the entire proposition is 'true'. Instead of using the symbol A above for denoting the composition of the atomic propositions A_1 and A_2, it is usual to write the entire proposition as nested composition of atomic propositions. In our example that means:

$$(A_1 \text{ and } A_2) \to B$$

Using the truth tables of Table 2.1 we can determine the truth value of the overall proposition on the basis of the truth value of each atomic proposition.

For example, assume $A_1 = true$, $A_2 = false$ and $B = true$. Then, we can derive that $(A_1 \text{ and } A_2) = true \text{ and } false = false$. Thus, we have $false \rightarrow true$ which is $true$ according to the truth table for the *implication*.

The fact that the truth value of a compound proposition can be determined as a function of the truth values of all its atomic compounds is known as the *compositionality* of propositional logic.[1]

Analogously, we may want to combine propositions in the sense that the compound proposition is true, if at least one of its two parts is true. The respective logical connective is the **or** and its truth table is also given in Table 2.1. Finally, in some propositions the negation of a proposition may be stated, e.g. 'if it was *not* snowing throughout the night, then the world is *not* white'. Table 2.2 shows the introduced logical connectives together with their notation in logic. Their intuitive meaning is also shown.

	Name of connective Symbol	Formula	Composite sentence with this connective	Meaning
$\neg$	(negation)	$\neg p$	(negation of p)	it is not the case that p
$\wedge$	(conjunction)	$(p \wedge q)$	conjunction of p and q	p and q
$\vee$	(disjunction)	$(p \vee q)$	disjunction of p and q	p or q
$\rightarrow$	(implication)	$(p \rightarrow q)$	p implies q	if p, then q
$\leftrightarrow$	(equivalence)	$(p \leftrightarrow q)$	equivalence of p and q	p if and only if q

Table 2.2. Connectives and their meaning

When we speak in a more technical sense about propositions within the framework of propositional logic, we call propositions *formulas*. Using the logical connectives given above, we can define a formal language L of propositional logic from which all expressions of the language L can be built. To formalise the use of such logical inferences even further, a formal syntax for forming propositions of a language of propositional logic is presented.

Formal Syntax. At least a sufficient number of symbols which represent atomic propositions are needed: these are called propositional variables. As in many textbooks, let us choose as propositional variables the upper case letters beginning with A, B, etc. In order to avoid limitations in the number of atomic propositions we are dealing with, it is advisable to have an infinite set of propositional variables. So let us extend the Latin alphabet $A, ..., Z$ by using integer subscripts of the upper case letters as well. That is, $A, ..., Z, A_0, B_0, ..., Z_0, A_1, ...$Further symbols indicating the order of composition in which a compound proposition, or formula, can be constructed. I.e., we need the symbols $(,), \neg, \wedge, \vee, \rightarrow$.

Thus, our alphabet may be defined as follows:

---

[1] Compositionality holds equally for predicate logic.

$$A_L = \{A, ..., Z, A_0, ..., Z_0, A_1, ..., (,), \neg, \wedge, \vee, \rightarrow, \leftrightarrow\}.$$

Then, we can define, what strings of symbols from the alphabet A_L are considered to be syntactically correct propositions, which are called *well-formed formulas* of L.

Definition 2.1. *Let A_L be an alphabet containing a set of propositional variables. Then, the propositional language L, based on the alphabet A_L contains exactly the following formulas:*

1. *Propositional variables in the alphabet A_L are formulas in L.*
2. *If f is a formula in L, then $\neg f$ is a formula in L too.*
3. *If f and g are formulas in L, then so are $(f \wedge g)$, $(f \vee g)$, $(f \rightarrow g)$, and $(f \leftrightarrow g)$.*
4. *Only what can be generated by the clauses (1)-(3) in a finite number of steps is a formula in L.*

According to this definition, expressions like A, or $(((A \vee B) \wedge (C \rightarrow B)) \rightarrow \neg A)$, or $(A_0 \wedge \neg B_2)$ are formulas of L. Opposed to that, expressions like $A_0(\neg B_1)$, $A \rightarrow \wedge B)$, or $A \vee B$ are not formulas of L. The only thing wrong with the last expression is that parentheses are missing, as required by step 3 of definition 2.1; i.e., $(A \vee B)$ is a formula of L.

Once again, it should be noted that the truth value of any formula f constructed by the given rules can be determined from the truth values of each of the atomic propositions. This can be done by using the respective truth tables for each of the logical connectives used in constructing the formula f.

One may wonder whether these comparably simple laws of logic explain every logical reasoning humans usually perform. For example, reasoning about classes of objects may allow conclusions like the following:

Given:

   All Men are mortal.
   and
   All Greeks are Men.

From these propositions, it can be inferred that

   All Greeks are mortal.

This kind of reasoning relates classes of objects to each other. In particular, since the set of *Greeks* is a subset of the set of *men* and all men have a certain property, one can conclude that all the members of any subset of men, e.g. the Greeks, have the same property (of being mortal). If '*All Men are mortal*' is taken as an atomic proposition it is not visible[2] that an assertion stating a property of all members of a certain class is made. Therefore, the propositional

---

[2] ... on a purely syntactical level. Only when the meaning of these propositions is considered, its structure becomes obvious.

logic framework does not suffice for allowing conclusions drawn like above. The expressive power of propositional logic is too weak. A more powerful framework is offered by *predicate logic*.

2.1.2 Predicate Logic

Aristotle ($\approx 400\ BC$) was already concerned with the problem mentioned above. He introduced his so-called *class logic* which allows to state properties which apply to each member of a class of objects. Aristotle considered statements like '*All men are mortal.*' as a relation between two predicates: The predicate 'Men' and the predicate 'mortal'. He considered the statement above as an assertion on the relation of the members of the two classes of objects: the class of objects to which the predicate '*men*' applies and the class of objects to which the predicate '*mortal*' applies. Aristotle distinguished four different types of linking two predicates A and B. Besides *all A are B*, of which the above is an instance, he considered *some A are B*, *all A are not-B*, and *some A are not-B*.

It took until the 19th century, when G. Frege managed to enhance Aristotle's class logic to what is roughly today's predicate logic (Frege, 1879). The major progress in logic accomplished by Frege was the introduction of relational predicates. Relational predicates are predicates which apply to groups of objects and, hence, allow to describe relations among objects.

An example of the extended expressive power is as follows:

Given: *All Greeks have a mother,* and *The husband of one's mother is one's father,* and *Dimitrios' mother is Helena,* and *Helena's husband is Sokrates.*

The following question may be formulated:

> *Is Sokrates the father of Dimitrios?*

The question can be answered from only using the given propositions and some intuitive logical reasoning. However, Aristotle's class logic does not suffice to infer the answer to that question. This is due to the fact that the class logic has no concept to express the link between Dimitrios, his mother, her husband, and Dimitrios' father.

Modern predicate logic allows to describe the relations above as follows: predicates describing the relation of 'is mother of', 'is husband of', and 'is father of' may be used. Moreover, individual objects to which the relational predicates may apply can be identified.

In modern notation the propositions above could be put as follows:

1. *mother-of*(Dimitrios, Helena).
2. *husband-of*(Helena, Sokrates).
3. *For all persons p, if* there is a person *m such that mother-of(p,m) and there is a person h such that husband-of(m,h), then father-of(p,h).*

This can be written as a first-order predicate logic formula as:

$$\forall p \forall m \; mother-of(p, m) \wedge \forall h \; husband-of(m, h) \rightarrow father-of(p, h).$$

2.1.3 A Formal Language of Predicate Logic

A formal language of predicate logic contains an alphabet and a set of symbols of different types, from which every formula belonging to the language is constructed. Using the symbols of the alphabet, a set of rules for constructing all well-formed formulas of the language are given.

Definition 2.2. *A language L is given by an alphabet $A_L = \{a, b, ..., x, y, ..., f, g, ..., P, Q, ..., (,), \wedge, \vee, \neg, \rightarrow, \exists, \forall\}$ containing names for constants, variables, functions and predicates. Constants are usually denoted by the first lower case letters of the alphabet, such as a, b, ... while variables are denoted by the last lower case letters, such as x, y,.... Functions are usually denoted by lower case letters starting from f, g, etc. Predicates are denoted by upper case letters starting from P, Q, ...*

1. *Terms are defined as follows:*
   a) *Constant or variable symbols in L are terms.*
   b) *If f is an n-ary function symbol in L, and each of $t_1, \ldots, t_n$ is a term in L then $f(t_1, ..., t_n)$ is a term in L too.*
   c) *Only what can be generated by the rules 1a and 1b is a term in L.*
2. *If π is an n-ary predicate symbol in L, and each of $t_1, \ldots, t_n$ is a term in L, then $\pi(t_1, \ldots, t_n)$ is a formula in L.*
3. *If ϕ is a formula in L, then $\neg \phi$ is a formula in L too.*
4. *If ϕ and ψ are formulas in L, then so are $(\phi \wedge \psi)$, $(\phi \vee \psi)$, $(\phi \rightarrow \psi)$, and $(\phi \leftrightarrow \psi)$.*
5. *If ϕ is a formula in L and x is a variable, then $\forall x \phi$ and $\exists x \phi$ are formulas in L.*
6. *Only what can be generated by the clauses (2)-(5) in a finite number of steps is a formula in L.*

The rules for forming a formula of a language of predicate logic correspond to the largest possible extent to the rules for constructing all formulas of a language of propositional logic according to Definition 2.1. Rule 2 generates the *atomic formulas* in L. The formulas generated by rule 5 are called *universal* and *existential* formulas, respectively.

Definition 2.3. *If $\forall x \psi$ (or $\exists x \psi$) is a sub-formula of ϕ, then ψ is the **scope** of this particular occurrence of a quantifier $\forall x$ (or $\exists x$) in ϕ.*

Definition 2.4. *a) An occurrence of a variable x in the formula φ (which does not belong to the scope of a quantifier) is called* **free** *in φ if this occurrence of x does not fall within the scope of a quantifier (∀x or ∃x) occurring in φ.*
b) If ∀xψ (or ∃xψ) is a sub-formula of φ and x is free in ψ, then this occurrence of x is said to be bound *by the quantifier ∀x (or ∃x).*

Definition 2.5. *A closed formula in L is a formula which contains no free variables. This is also called a* **sentence**.

2.1.4 Interpretations

An interpretation assigns a *meaning* to all 'non-logical' symbols in a formula. These 'non-logical' symbols are terms and predicates in a language of predicate logic. Generally speaking, an interpretation I of a language L of predicate logic consists of

a) a domain of discourse, i.e. a set of objects D,
b) an assignment of constant names to some of the objects,
c) an assignment of each n-ary function symbol to a mapping from n-tuples of the domain of objects onto that same domain of objects D, i.e. functions refer always to an object of the domain.
d) an assignment of each n-ary predicate symbol to the subset of n-tuples of objects of D for which the predicate is said to be true.

Given an interpretation, the truth value of any closed formula (sentence) can be determined. For the simpler case, where no variables occur, this is done by evaluating each individual predicate to either true or false. For doing that, it is necessary to determine the objects to which the terms of the predicate refer. That is, one has to evaluate all functions occurring as arguments of predicates. After the truth values of all atomic propositions have been determined, the overall truth value can be determined by using the corresponding truth tables given in the section on propositional logic according to the construction of the entire sentence.

Example

Consider the following alphabet: A_L = {*loves, hat-of,* John, *red-hat,* Mary, ...}. Consider the following formulas:
loves(John, Mary), ¬*loves(John, red-hat)*, and ¬*loves(John, hat-of(Mary))*.
Assume the following interpretation of the used symbols *John, Mary, loves(.,.), hat-of(.), red-hat.* (See also Figure 2.1.) A domain D of objects may be given by
D = {John, Mary, green-hat, red-hat, table, 'nil-hat'}.[3] The function 'hat-of' may be a function as follows:

---
[3] 'nil-hat' is included in the set of objects just for the purpose of allowing a completely defined function 'hat-of'. It is not meant to refer to an object in any physical world.

hat-of(John)	=	red-hat
hat-of(Mary)	=	green-hat
hat-of(table)	=	'nil-hat'
hat-of(green-hat)	=	'nil-hat'
hat-of(red-hat)	=	'nil-hat'
hat-of('nil-hat')	=	'nil-hat'

The predicate *loves(.,.)* may be interpreted as being true only for the following subset of all pairs of objects from D:

(1)   loves(Mary, John)
(2)   loves(John, Mary)
(3)   loves(John, red-hat)

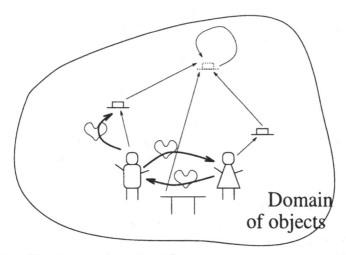

Figure 2.1. The drawing shows the different objects to which the names of our example language may refer. The thin arrows indicate how the 'hat-of' function can be interpreted as a mapping from each of the objects to another object. The thick arrows with the heart in their middle show the interpretation of the two-argument predicate 'loves' as a relation between selected ordered pairs of the domain.

Assuming this interpretation of the elements of the language L, i.e. the terms and predicates, the sentences above can be evaluated as follows:

1. *loves(John, Mary)*: This proposition is true since 'loves' is true for its arguments according to the interpretation above.
2. *¬loves(John, red-hat)*: This proposition is false, since according to the interpretation above it is true that *loves(John,red-hat)*. According to the truth table for the negation it follows that *¬loves(John, red-hat)* is false.
3. *¬loves(John, hat-of(Mary))*: To determine the truth value of this proposition, it is necessary to determine the object to which *hat-of(Mary)* refers. According to the interpretation of the function *hat-of*

it refers to the object *green-hat*. Thus, we have to determine, whether the predicate *loves* applied to the pair *(John,green-hat)* is true? Looking up the table above, it turns out that the predicate is not true for this pair of objects, hence the proposition ¬*loves(John, hat-of(Mary))* is true.

Things become a bit more complicated if quantified variables occur in the propositions. As an example, suppose the following proposition has been stated in addition to the propositions considered so far:

$$(4) \quad \forall x \exists y \; \text{loves}(x, y).$$

In natural language this means: *Everything loves something*. The truth value of this sentence has to be determined in the following way: for all possible values of the variable x it has to be determined whether the proposition $\exists y \; \text{loves}(x, y)$ is true. Only if that proposition is true for *all* possible values of x, the entire sentence is true. However, in order to determine whether $\exists y \; \text{loves}(x, y)$ is true, a value for y has to be found such that the proposition 'loves(x, y)' is true.

Considering our interpretation, we can determine whether the proposition is true by:

1. Assuming the value 'John' for x, we can find the value 'Mary' for y such that 'loves(x, y)', i.e. 'loves(John, Mary)' is true.
2. Assuming the value 'Mary' for x, we can find the value 'John' for y such that 'loves(x, y)', i.e. 'loves(Mary, John)' is true.
3. Assuming the value 'green-hat' for x, we cannot find any value for y such that 'loves(x, y)', i.e. that 'loves(green-hat, y)' is true.

The last consideration shows that the proposition '$\exists y \; \text{loves}(\text{green-hat}, y)$' is false, since there is no object which is loved by the 'green-hat'. Consequently, we discovered one value for the variable x, namely 'green-hat', for which the proposition '$\exists y \; \text{loves}(x, y)$', i.e. '$\exists y \; \text{loves}(\text{green-hat}, y)$' is false. This implies that the proposition '$\forall x \exists y \; \text{loves}(x, y)$' is false as well.

In the situation above, we assumed that we know our world exactly. i.e. we know all what is the case and all what is not the case. Unfortunately, in general the 'current state of the world' is not exactly known. Instead, just a set of propositions may be given which are assumed to be a true and partial description of the 'current state of the world'. Therefore, we are interested in what conclusions can be drawn based on an incomplete description of the world. For that purpose, it is important to analyse, which 'current state of the world' is possible, assuming the given description is true. For example, in the case above, a proposition saying that '*Mary's hat is green*' would still allow a world in which *John* has a *red hat* or a *green hat* or ... or a *blue hat* and ... We do not know enough to say what *hat* John has and we don't know many other things. The 'worlds' that are possible, given a set of formulas are true, are called *models* of these formulas. See for more details appendix A.1.

A **theory** of a set of propositions S is the set of all propositions which are true in all models of S. The set S of propositions is often also called axioms of the theory.

A theorem T of a set of axioms S is a proposition which is a logical consequence of S, i.e. a proposition which is true in all models of S.

In the following, a technique is presented which allows to work out for any proposition T, whether it is a logical consequence of a set of axioms S or not. This is also called a theorem prover.

2.1.5 Resolution

Resolution is a technique for proving theorems[4] introduced by Robinson (1965), which is particularly well suited for computers. It is a uniform procedure performing a single *resolution step* at a time. Resolution is a complete proof procedure. that is, it will find a proof of a theorem if a proof exists. Moreover, resolution is *sound*, i.e. it will never say, a proposition θ is a theorem of a set of sentences S, if in fact θ is not a theorem of S.

Resolution proves theorems by detecting contradictions. That is, the negation $\neg T$ of the candidate theorem T is added to the set of propositions S of which T is tested to be theorem. If the set $S \cup \{\neg T\}$ contains a contradiction, then the proposition T is a theorem of S.

To do this, the set of propositions $S \cup \{\neg T\}$ is transformed into a set of clauses. A clause is a disjunction of literals. A literal is a single predicate or its negation. The resolution process on a set of clauses is fairly simple, as sketched in Figure 2.2. For more technical details on the procedure, see appendix A. It

---

1. Find a pair of clauses C_1 and C_2 which contain matching literals L_1 and L_2. Matching literals are literals of the same predicate, exactly one of them negated. The arguments of the two literals need to match as well. If variables occur in the arguments, they can possibly be replaced by other, more specific, terms which match the arguments of the corresponding literal. This is done by a specific *unification algorithm* as it can be found in the appendix A.
2. Form a new clause C' containing all the literals of C_1 and C_2, but neither L_1 nor L_2. If C' does not contain any literal, then a contradiction is found. That is, T is a theorem of S and the resolution process stops.
3. Goto step 1.

Figure 2.2. A sketch of the resolution process for proving theorems by contradiction. Resolution tries to find a contradiction in a set of clauses.

contains a more formal and more detailed description of the process of transforming a set of predicate logic formulas into clause form and of the resolution

---

[4] A theorem T of a set of propositions S is a logical consequence of that set of propositions S. Thus, whenever the set of propositions S is true, then the Theorem T must be true as well.

procedure itself. As the following examples show, resolution can also be applied to propositional logic, where literals are simply a propositional variable or its negation.

Examples

Several examples for the resolution process are shown. Figure 2.3, 2.4, and 2.5 show propositional examples while Figure 2.6 gives an example of the predicate logic case.

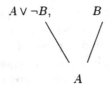

Figure 2.3. *A* can be derived by resolution.

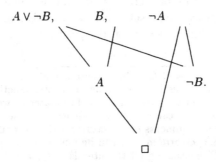

Figure 2.4. A contradiction can be proved by resolution.

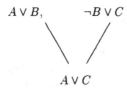

Figure 2.5. Deriving a clause from two parent clauses using resolution.

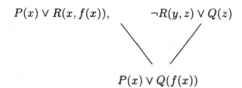

Figure 2.6. Deriving a predicate clause from two parent clauses using resolution.

2.2 Beyond Classical Logic

This section discusses the limitations of classical logic as it was sketched in
section 2.1 and 2.1.2. A number of developments in the symbolic paradigm of
AI are pointed out, which aim at overcoming these limitations. While it is an
important achievement of classical logic to devise techniques of symbol manipulation which result in provably correct conclusions, there are still problems
left, including the following:

- The knowledge that can be represented in a logical language is always certain.
  It is assumed that all propositions are true. There is no concept of probability,
  vagueness, or other modalities like possibility etc.
- Because the inferences which logical calculi allow us to derive are guaranteed
  to be sound, they are also very 'conservative' in what can be derived. That
  is, they do not accommodate for processes of guessing or what is often called
  common sense.

For example, one may state the following general rule:

All birds can fly,

which can be put in first-order predicate logic as:

$$\forall x\ Bird(x)\ \rightarrow\ Flies(x).$$

This may work quite nicely for certain purposes. For more advanced applications, however, it may be necessary that existing exceptions are noted. For
example, *All birds except ostriches can fly.*

$$\forall x\ Bird(x)\ \wedge\ \neg Ostrich(x)\ \rightarrow\ Flies(x).$$

However, there are more exceptions: For example, penguins cannot fly, birds
with a broken wing cannot fly, dead birds cannot fly, etc. Of course, it is not
easy to see an end of the list of exceptions, if it becomes important to be
comprehensive. There are plush birds, sick or even dead birds, injured birds,
birds in narrow cages etc. In the context of AI this problem is often called the
qualification problem. It is often difficult to precisely define what objects
would really qualify as a bird in the sense it was meant above. In human
practice, our common sense helps to sort out many of those problems. When
building AI systems, we have to make explicit what our common sense knows.

A similar problem occurs if we want to describe the knowledge needed to
perform a sequence of actions. For such a purpose, the agent, e.g. a robot, needs
a sufficient description of the environment, the task to be achieved and about
what effects an action may have. If all that knowledge is properly described,
an agent can use logical reasoning to determine which of a number of possible
actions will achieve the set task. Unfortunately, it is often extremely difficult

to completely describe the environment and the consequences of an action. For example, when a robot moves an object from A to B, does it move all the object stacked on top of that object as well? Is it possible that the stack of those objects collapses while moving the bottom object? How does such a collapse affect the state of the environment? What about the dust which adheres to the moved object? What about other agent's actions? If a robot touches accidentally or intentionally a ball, does the ball move? How far does it move? Can it change other objects' state or location as well? ...

There is virtually no end to the possible effects of actions or to the changes of the environment which may not even be triggered by the agent itself. However, if any of these possibilities is not explicitly described, the agent runs the risk of doing the wrong thing. This problem is also known as the **frame problem**.

Means which have been developed to get a better grip on these problems are on the one hand heuristics and on the other hand formalisms which allow the explicit statement of suitable policies to handle ambiguities etc. One well-known heuristic is the closed-world assumption (CWA),[5] assuming that all facts which are not explicitly stated are not the case. This has relevance in many situations and in everyday situations our common sense often assumes it. For example, assume

John asks Mary whether she has any brothers or sisters.
Mary answers that she has a sister Anne.

John will assume that Mary has in fact only one sister and no brothers. He will assume that, although Mary did not say that explicitly. However, John could argue that if Mary had another brother or sister, she would have told him.

Another such heuristic is used in belief revision. This is an area where techniques are developed to maintain a set of propositions, considered as beliefs. If a new proposition is added, this may cause a contradiction with existing beliefs. As these are considered mere beliefs, as opposed to knowledge, some of the beliefs may be revised in order to achieve consistency within the entire set of beliefs. Usually, there are many ways of altering a set of propositions to make them consistent with a newly arrived proposition.

Example

- (1) Tweety is a bird.
- (2) All birds can fly.
- (3) Tweety cannot fly.

In this case, (3) may be recently learnt. That is, either (1) or (2) or both need to be revised, but there is no purely logical ground on which it can be decided what to revise.

---

[5] See e.g. Nilsson and Genesereth (1987).

Indeed, the logician Quine maintains even that in principle, any statement of a set of statements can be chosen to be held as 'true', if only suitable adjustments to the rest of the set of statements are made (Quine, 1951, 1953). One prominent heuristic to decide on what to do, is to perform those revisions which result in the minimal change.[6] Whereby, there are different ways of measuring what a minimal change might be. Is it the minimal loss of information? But then, what exactly do we mean by information? Different notions of information have been proposed and more may be proposed in the future.

Means of addressing the mentioned problems explicitly includes default logics as well as other techniques which allow other types of reasoning, such as probabilistic reasoning, Bayesian networks, fuzzy sets, and others.

2.2.1 Default Theories

The CWA, discussed above, negates simply every fact which is not known to be true. In contrast to that, it is often helpful to have rules which assert a limited set of positive facts if the contrary is not known. If Peter knows that Tweety is a bird, he may, by default, assume that Tweety can also fly. A general mechanism that asserts facts related to some existing knowledge unless evidence for the contrary is known is provided by default rules. Early work on the idea is found in Reiter (1980). A default rule is an inference rule used to augment a set of sentences S under certain specified conditions. If D is a set of default rules, the augmentation of S with respect to D is denoted by $\varepsilon[S, D]$. Default rules are written in the following form:

$$\frac{\alpha(x) : \beta(x)}{\gamma(x)}$$

Where x stands for a single variable or a tuple of variables while α, β and γ are (possibly empty) formulas of the underlying (predicate logic) language L in use. The default rule

$$\frac{\alpha(x) : \beta(x)}{\gamma(x)}$$

is interpreted as follows: If $\alpha(x)$ is a logical consequence of $\varepsilon[S, D]$ for some x and $\beta(x)$ does not contradict $\varepsilon[S, D]$ then $\varepsilon[S, D]$ includes $\gamma(x)$.

Example

Let D contain the following default rule:

$$\frac{Bird(x) : Flies(x)}{Flies(x)}$$

---

[6] One rationale for it is that information is generally not for free and changing more than necessary would throw away the information previously contained in the changed knowledge base. See Gardenförs and Rott (1995) for a much deeper discussion of these issues.

That means, if x is a bird and it is consistent with the augmented set of sentences $\varepsilon[S, D]$ that x flies, then it is assumed that x flies. (x can fly by 'default'.) Assume, it is known that *Tweety is a bird* and that *Ostriches cannot fly*. That is, $S = \{Bird(Tweety), Ostrich(x) \rightarrow \neg Flies(x)\}$. The default augmentation of S with respect to D includes the assumption that *Tweety can fly*, i.e. $\varepsilon[S, D] = \{Flies(Tweety)\} \cup S = \{Bird(Tweety), Flies(Tweety), Ostrich(x) \rightarrow \neg Flies(x)\}$.

Opposed to that, assume it is known, in addition to S, that *Tweety is an ostrich*. That is, if $S_1 = S \cup \{Ostrich(Tweety)\}$, then

$$\varepsilon[S_1, D] = \{Ostrich(Tweety), Bird(Tweety), Ostrich(x) \rightarrow \neg Flies(x)\}$$

does not contain $Flies(Tweety)$. Since S_1 is a superset of S, the default augmentation is **non-monotonic**, i.e. when the set of propositions is extended, the set of propositions which can be derived may actually shrink. This is not possible in classical logic. The form of the example is a special case of the general form of default rules, since the proposition $\beta(x)$ which must not contradict the current theory is the same as the added assumption $\gamma(x)$. Sometimes, it may be desirable to use a more general $\beta(x)$ than the assumption added to the theory. For example, a default rule like *if x is an animal*, then *if x is not known to have more than two feet* it is assumed that *x can fly*.

In non-monotonic reasoning, it may be necessary that conclusions which have been generated, e.g. by the execution of a default rule, are retracted later. As an example, assume A has seen B driving a Rolls Royce. A may have concluded 'by default' that B owns the Rolls Royce and furthermore that B is rich. Suppose A learns later that B is actually the driver of the owner of the Rolls Royce, A should retract his conclusion that B owns the Rolls Royce and, furthermore, that B is rich. A system which maintains a set of propositions in such a manner, is usually called a *Truth Maintenance System* (TMS). Several approaches to 'Truth Maintenance' have been developed, where Doyle (1979) and Kleer (1986) represent the early work on the topic. See Russell and Norvig (1995) for a recent survey.

2.2.2 Further Types of Logic

Besides the presented classical and non-classical types of logic there are further types of logic which have been developed outside of AI; namely in mathematics and philosophy. In the following two selected types of logic are briefly mentioned without going into technical details.

Higher-Order Logic. The description of a world in a language of first order predicate logic was in some sense restricted. We were able to describe different objects by stating that a number of predicates applies to them, while other predicates do not apply to them. It was not possible to make any statements about predicates itself. For example, it was not possible to assert that all *symmetric* predicates are *transitive* predicates. To express a statement like that, we had to quantify over the set of predicates as opposed to quantify over the set of objects.

Predicate logic which allows the quantification over predicates and allows for 'predicate-predicates' is called *second-order predicate logic*. Analogously, the framework which allows to quantify over 'predicate-predicates', etc. is called 'third-order predicate logic'.

Modal Logics. Besides the development of mathematical logic as partially introduced in early sections of this chapter, there was also work going on towards the development of a *modal logic*. A modal logic deals with modes of statements like *possible, necessary*, etc. The idea is to deal with statements like 'it is possible that Peter loves Mary'. Or statements like 'Water is necessarily a liquid'. Neither propositional nor predicate logic can deal with such modes. The distinction between a possibly false and a necessarily false statement like 'In year 2001 we all will turn into angels' and '2+2=5' cannot be expressed in the classical logic frameworks.

Modal logic has been developed in the 20th century. Until the 1960s there were a number of different modal logics around but none of them was clearly better than the others. The most important difference to mathematical logic was the absence of a clear definition of semantics. In 1959, Kripke (1959) managed to introduce a semantic analysis of a modal logic which found general acceptance. Kripke's key notion was that of a *possible world*. The intuitive idea behind this notion is to think of a way things may have been as opposed to the way things *actually are* in the only 'real world'. Technically, it is an unanalysed notion. It is dealt with by assuming simply a set of '*possible worlds*, one of them being our 'real world'. If a statement is true in all possible worlds, it is necessarily true. If it is only true in some of the possible worlds, it is possibly true, etc.

2.3 Reasoning with Uncertainty

While reasoning with uncertainty is another important area of ongoing research, it provides already valuable techniques for practical applications. Coming back to the *qualification problem*, one could say that the difficulty lies in completely specifying exactly the circumstances under which a certain statement is true, or under which circumstances an object falls under a certain category. In practice, to give a complete specification is often not feasible.

However, using degrees of uncertainty for statements, like *all birds can fly*, one could try to capture all the unknown or unspecified exceptions by a suitable degree of uncertainty. Using classical probability theory, one could possibly say with probability of 0.9, a given bird can also fly. This could not only capture ostriches and penguins but also all sorts of other reasons for not being able to fly, without enumerating all of them. Thus, reasoning under uncertainty could significantly ease the process of knowledge acquisition, i.e. the development of a suitable knowledge base as well as it could enhance the applicability of methods for AI systems.

In this section, we just give a short introduction to one of the most important techniques, to those of Bayesian reasoning. Bayesian reasoning is based on classical probability theory. So, the formal grounds of probability theory follow first.

- Event algebra. The basic idea of the event algebra is to define, what events can be formulated on the basis of a set of elementary events.

  Let $\Omega = \{A_0, A_1, A_2, ...\}$ be a set of pairwise disjoint elementary events. A set of elementary events could be the outcome of throwing a dice. In that case, $\Omega = \{1, 2, 3, 4, 5, 6\}$.

  $\Sigma \subseteq 2^{\Omega}$ is an event algebra on Ω if
  1. $\emptyset \in \Sigma \wedge \Omega \in \Sigma$
  2. $\forall_{i \in I} A_i \in \Sigma \Rightarrow \quad (\bigcup_{i \in I} A_i) \in \Sigma$ for any countable index set I.
  3. $\forall_{i \in I} A_i \in \Sigma \Rightarrow \quad (\bigcap_{i \in I} A_i) \in \Sigma$ for any countable index set I.
  4. $A, B \in \Sigma \Rightarrow A \setminus B \in \Sigma$

According to the event algebra Σ the case that an odd number is the outcome of the dice throw is also an event, i.e. the event $\{1, 3, 5\}$. Based on the event algebra, we can now define a probability measure on Σ which has to satisfy the following conditions, which are known as the the Kolmogorov axioms:

1. $P(\Omega) = 1$.
2. $P(A \cup B) = P(A) + P(B)$, for A and $B \in \Sigma$, if $A \cap B = \emptyset$.
   $\Rightarrow P(\overline{A}) = 1 - P(A)$.[7]

It follows from the axioms that
$P(\emptyset) = 0$, as well as
$P(A \cup B) = P(A) + P(B) - P(A \cap B)$, which is more general version of the second axiom above.

One particularly interesting quantity is the probability of an event to occur, if we already know or assume that another event occurred. Suppose, we are told that an odd number was the outcome of the dice throw. Then, what is the probability that it was the number 5? Intuitively, assuming one has an ideal dice, where all numbers have the same probability to occur, it should be $\frac{1}{3}$, while each number has the probability of $\frac{1}{6}$, not knowing or assuming the occurrence of any event. This probability of an event A to occur given that another event B occurred, is called **conditional probability** and is defined as follows:

$$P(A|B) = \frac{P(A \cap B)}{P(B)}$$

In our case, we would have $A = \{5\}$ and $B = \{1, 3, 5\}$ and $A \cap B = A = \{5\}$. Consequently for an ideal dice we have $P(A) = \frac{1}{6}$ and $P(B) = \frac{1}{2}$.

---

[7] $\overline{A}$ denotes $\Omega \setminus A$.

Thus, we calculate $P(A|B) = \frac{P(A \cap B)}{P(B)} = \frac{\frac{1}{6}}{\frac{1}{2}} = \frac{1}{3}$.

Another important notion is the **independence of events**. Two events A and B are said to be **independent events** if

$$P(A|B) = P(A).$$

Intuitively, that means that the fact that the event A occurred has no impact on the probability of the event B. In the dice example, this may be the case for A being the event of an odd number and B being the event of a number less than 3, i.e. $A = \{1,3,5\}$ and $B = \{1,2\}$. Then, we have

$$P(A|B) = \frac{P(A \cap B)}{P(B)} = \frac{P(\{1\})}{P(\{1,2\})} = \frac{\frac{1}{6}}{\frac{1}{3}} = \frac{1}{2},$$

which is the same as $P(A) = \frac{1}{2}$. From the independence of two events A and B, it follows also that

$$P(A \cap B) = P(A) \times P(B).$$

The following **Theorem of Bayes**, tells us how to compute the conditional probability $P(A|B)$ from the reverse conditional probability $P(B|A)$ and the a priori probabilities $P(A)$ and $P(B)$:

$$P(A|B) = \frac{P(B|A) \, P(A)}{P(B)}$$

This is often useful, as the reverse conditional probability together with the a priori probabilities may be easily available. One typical domain, where this can be used is medicine. What is often unknown is the probability that a patient has a particular disease D, given the patient shows symptom S. However, estimates of how frequent D is in general may be available as well how frequent D is in cases where symptom S is observed. Furthermore, even if accurate statistical data is unavailable, a doctor can usually estimate much more accurately the conditional probability that symptom S occurs, given the patient has disease D.

As a consequence, the Theorem of Bayes can be used to calculate the probability of the disease D, when the symptom S is observed. The probabilities for calculating the probability for D under a number of different symptoms may be available given only one of these symptoms is observed. Unfortunately, there is no simple way of determining the probability for D given that more than one symptom is observed, as there may be arbitrary interactions between two or more symptoms. The simultaneous occurrence of two symptoms may mean a cancellation of both, or they may amplify the probability for D, or they may be essentially the same symptom not increasing the probability for the disease if only one of them was observed, or anything in between may be the case.

What is needed to calculate the probability is information about the interaction of the symptoms. As a consequence, the conditionalised version of the

Theorem of Bayes is given below, which allows to calculate the probability for an event, given that two other events occurred simultaneously:

$$P(A|B \cap C) = \frac{P(B|A \cap C)\,P(A|C)}{P(B|C)}$$

It is obvious from this theorem that much more information is needed to compute the conditional probability. In fact, the number of probabilities or their estimates increases exponentially with the number of events under consideration (or for that purpose, the number of symptoms). This is because the number of potential interactions between events (symptoms), i.e. the number of possible combinations, increases exponentially.

The required probabilities can greatly be reduced if certain conditional independence assumptions can be made. That is, if the conditional probability of the occurrence of event A given event B is not changed by the occurrence of the third event C, then it is said that A and C are **conditionally independent**, given B.

$$P(A|B \cap C) = P(A|B).$$

The conditional independence of A and C would allow the following simplified calculation of $P(B|A \cap C)$:

$$P(B|A \cap C) = P(B)\frac{P(A|B)}{P(A)}\frac{P(C|B)}{P(C|A)}.$$

Knowing the probabilities of $P(A|\neg B)$ and $P(C|\neg B)$ in addition to the probabilities of $P(A|B)$, $P(C|B)$, and $P(B)$, would allow to eliminate the denominator, as we can use the same formula for the complementary conditional probability

$$P(\neg B|A \cap C) = P(\neg B)\frac{P(A|\neg B)}{P(A)}\frac{P(C|\neg B)}{P(C|A)}$$

and we know from the Kolmogorov axioms that $P(B|A \cap C) + P(\neg B|A \cap C) = 1$. This is the theoretical basis for Bayesian networks which are outlined below.

Bayesian networks. Based on the fact that the acquisition of reasonable estimates of simple conditional probabilities is often possible and that conditional independence assumptions are plausible in many circumstances, it is possible to develop useful knowledge bases, containing probability assessments and to have reasoning procedures which handle the involved uncertainties.

A framework which gained substantial interest and credibility in recent years is that of **Bayesian networks**, which are also called **belief networks**.

An outline of the basic idea follows together with the basic reasoning procedure. For more details, see Pearl (1988), Heckerman (1991), or Russell and Norvig (1995). Figure 2.7 shows an example of a Bayesian network. Each of the ellipses represent a possible event of interest. The arrow between the events represent possible causal relations among the events. For example, the arrows between *lightning struck house* and *house at fire* indicate that lightning that struck the house may set it at fire. As this will not always happen, but only with a certain probability, the associated probability tables to each of the events indicate the probability that the event occurs, depending on whether the potential causes occurred or not. The given network reflects the fact that the event *feel heat* and *smell smoke* are considered to be independent of each other. Opposed to that are the causing events setting the house at fire not considered to be independent factors. This is reflected in the conditional probability table associated to *house at fire*.

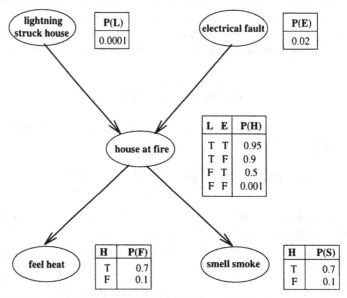

Figure 2.7. A typical Bayesian network with the conditional probabilities annotated. The letters L, E, H, F, S stand for the events *lightning struck house, electrical fault, house at fire, feel heat*, and *smell smoke* respectively.

Based on the conditional probabilities given in the network, it is possible to calculate the probability of the joint occurrence of any combination of the involved events. If we consider each event as an independent random variable X_i[8] then the joint consideration of the outcomes of all events is denoted by $P(X_1 = x_1, X_2 = x_2, ..., X_n = x_n)$, where x_i stands for a particular value of the corresponding random variable, i.e. for a particular outcome or occurrence

---

[8] In the example case above they are boolean random variables, but they can also be any other type of random variable. A random variable has an associated probability measure over its range of possible values and assumes a value according to its probability measure.

vs. non-occurrence of the event. The probability can be calculated according
to the following formula:

$$P(X_1 = x_1, ..., X_n = x_n) = \prod_{i=1}^{n} P(x_i|Parents(X_i)),$$

where $Parents(X_i)$ refers to the state of all parents of the variable X_i. For example, in Figure 2.7 $Parents(house\ at\ fire)$ are the random variables *lightning
struck house* and *electrical fault*.

According to that formula, the probability of the joint occurrence of the
combined event that lightning strikes the house and there is an electrical fault,
but the house is not set at fire, no smoke is smelled but heat is felt is as follows:

$$P(L \wedge E \wedge \neg H \wedge F \wedge \neg S)$$

$$= P(F|\neg H)P(\neg S|\neg H)P(\neg H|L \wedge E)P(L)P(E)$$

$$= 0.1 \times 0.9 \times 0.05 \times 0.0001 \times 0.02 = 0.000000009.$$

The development of such a Bayesian network, or belief network, is often
feasible, as the causal structure of a domain is often approximately known, and
not more than an approximate understanding is required that reflects most
of the cases occurring in practice. In a second step, once the topology has
been developed, the conditional probabilities are either estimated by domain
experts, such as doctors, or they can be estimated by statistical data collections.
For more details, see Pearl (1988), Heckerman (1991), Heckerman, Breese, and
Rommelse (1995), or Russell and Norvig (1995).

2.4 Complexity of Reasoning

As discussed above, it seems that the knowledge which a system requires to
be able to perform sensibly in a 'real-world' environment is difficult to provide
and tends to require a very large number of rules to be stated explicitly. This is
not only a practical problem for the development of a proper knowledge base,[9]
but it also poses a major problem for the effective processing of such a large
knowledge base. The computational complexity[10] of processing the encoded

---

[9] See also 3.3 for further discussion of the issue.

[10] See Garey and Johnson (1979) for a good treatment of computational complexity.
Being **NP**-complete for this problem means roughly speaking, that the number
of computing steps increases exponentially in the worst case with the number of
propositions involved. This represents a major practical problem even with today's
fast computers, as the required computing time reaches very quickly the order of
magnitude of days or even years. With even faster computers which we may have
in the future, the size of feasible problems will only increase marginally. Thus,
NP-completeness of problems will continue to represent a very severe obstacle.

knowledge effectively is often high, i.e. requiring algorithms to take unacceptable computing times when they attempt to utilise all of a knowledge base's content. For example, the problem to determine whether a proposition is a logical consequence of a set of propositions, is already **NP**-complete in propositional logic. Taking the full expressive power of first-order predicate logic, it becomes even worse. It is semi-decidable, i.e. there is no algorithm which will always terminate and will produce the correct answer. Although substantial effort has been put into alleviating the computational complexity of reasoning in practical situations, it is still a major hurdle for developing useful knowledge-based systems, which are able to reason in acceptable periods of time.

Typical ways of reducing the computational complexity of reasoning problems is to introduce a stronger structure into the knowledge representation. The simplest thing for a predicate logic language, is probably to introduce typed variables. That is, to have different sub-domains, or types of objects under consideration. When types are assigned to each place of a variable in a predicate, it will reduce dramatically the possible variable instantiations a reasoning algorithm needs to consider. Another approach is to restrict the type of propositions that can be expressed in a knowledge representation language, or the type of queries that can be made. For example, the above mentioned problem, of determining whether a proposition is a logical consequence of a given set of propositional logic sentences, is also called the satisfiability problem of propositional logic.[11] Satisfiability for clauses with three or more literals has been shown to be **NP**-complete Garey and Johnson (1979). However, if only clauses are considered that contain less than three literals, the satisfiability problem can be solved in time quadratic in the number of clauses.

It is an important research area to investigate the computational complexity of existing knowledge representation languages and to develop new or modified knowledge representation languages that allow a more efficient processing of the knowledge. See e.g. Nebel (1990) or Fagin et al. (1995) and the proceedings of the *Knowledge Representation and Reasoning* Conferences as well as the proceedings of the major general AI conferences for work on that.

---

[11] The relation between logical consequence and satisfiability is demonstrated by the resolution proof procedure. Resolution attempts to determine whether the set of clauses is satisfiable or not, i.e. whether the set of clauses contains a contradiction or not.

3. Expert Systems

Applications of the techniques developed in the symbolic paradigm span over a wide field of diverse domains, problems and tasks. They range from high-powered chess programs[1] or world-champion level backgammon programs (Tesauro, 1995) to systems that partly understand natural language, help in designing pieces of engineering (see Gero and Sudweeks (1996)); find good solutions to complex optimisation problems, such as scheduling problems, (see Smith, Parra, and Westfold (1996)); assist in detecting money laundering activities (Senator et al., 1995); or to construct complex mathematical proofs.[2] However, it is probably fair to say that the most important class of applications of AI techniques so far, is the development of expert systems.

Historically, the emergence of expert systems was a further development of the early symbol manipulation approaches to AI. Solving complex difficult problems has always been considered as the core of AI. In the early years of AI, work was concentrated on the development of general purpose problem-solving techniques, e.g. Newell and Simon (1963), Fikes and Nilsson (1971). The conclusion at which AI researchers arrived in the late 70s and early 80s, however, was that *knowledge* is instrumental for the development of successful AI systems. This was opposed to the earlier belief that clever search techniques would be the key to designing intelligent systems. Further, the focus in the development of expert systems was to develop useful systems with a limited scope of intelligent behaviour. This was opposed to the earlier hopes to develop principles, e.g. the General Problem Solver (GPS) Simon and Newell (1958), Newell and Simon (1963), which would lead to systems of general intelligence. Expert Systems were conceived to adopt substantial aspects of human (expert) reasoning as well as to capture the relevant knowledge of the domain of expertise in order to produce sensible advice. In a sense, expert systems also came closer to

---

[1] Deep Blue, the world's strongest chess program defeated the human World Chess Champion Garry Kasparov in a match of 6 games 3.5:2.5 in early May 1997! While the performance of Deep Blue is extremely impressive indeed, it may be argued that this is only partly due to the AI techniques involved. Overall it represents a highly sophisticated piece of (software and hardware) engineering work.

[2] One of the spectacular achievements of automated Theorem proving was the proof of the Four-colour-map problem, a long-standing open problem in graph theory, which was solved with the assistance of an automated Theorem prover (Appel & Haken, 1977).

conventional software as their purpose and functionality became much clearer. However, there are some distinctive features of an expert system which sets it apart from conventional software. Figure 3.1 shows the characteristic difference between an expert system and conventional software. In expert systems, there is a clear division of the domain specific knowledge and the mechanism which uses that knowledge in order to derive the desired conclusions.

Expert systems were initially thought to simulate expert behaviour in a restricted domain. Later, it was found that it is often very difficult to ensure a system's performance at the expert level. Further, since many applications are safety critical, today's expert systems are often considered to be rather an assistant to an expert who is checking the result produced by an expert system. Expert systems may also have merely an advisory role, more like 'sophisticated handbooks' with an automatic search and inference facility. In the following, ex-

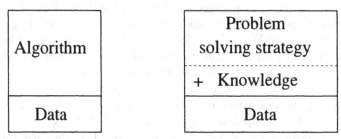

Figure 3.1. Comparison of expert systems and a conventional program.

pert systems are discussed in some more detail along with a critical assessment of the practical problems in developing an expert system application. Problems with building expert systems are mentioned and the consequences they had for the development of the field are indicated in section 3.2 and in 3.3.

3.1 Rule-Based Expert Systems

The idea of building expert systems was accompanied by the idea that the knowledge needed could be acquired from experts who can already solve the tasks in question.[3] As a consequence, expert systems were developed which tackled quite demanding tasks such as medical diagnosis (Buchanan & Shortliffe, 1984), geology (Davis et al., 1971; Duda, Gaschnig, & Hart, 1979), and the configuration of computer systems (McDermott, 1982).

The knowledge of these early expert systems was usually obtained by interviewing experts about how they solved the tasks. Asking experts to obtain the knowledge was done by a *knowledge engineer*, who encoded the knowledge obtained in the form of *heuristic, empirical* or *associational* rules-of-thumb.

---

[3] See Puppe (1993) for a textbook and survey on the topic.

Those rules-of-thumb presented basically a plain mapping from observable problem characteristics to the conclusions. For example, in medical diagnosis, MYCIN (Buchanan & Shortliffe, 1984) employed rules like 'if a certain symptom is observed, then there is evidence for a particular disease'. Based on a (possibly large) number of such rules, the early expert systems chained rules together in order to come to a final conclusion which was presented to the user. Consequently, the early expert systems had a simple uniform control structure and a similarly simple form of representation for the expert-provided knowledge. These were fairly simple production rule systems.[4]

What is now called 'first generation of expert systems' were exactly such production rule systems, or simply 'rule-based systems'. Rule based systems have a rule base which contains the problem-specific part of the system and a rule inferencing mechanism which checks which rules are applicable and chains rules together in order to arrive at a desired conclusion. Rules are of the form

If A and B ... then R.

where R is the result which can be assumed if the condition part of the rule is satisfied by the current content of the working memory.[5] The working memory contains initially the description of the problem instance, the system is supposed to solve. The two basic methods of combining a number of rules is *forward chaining* and *backward chaining*. During the problem solving process using *forward chaining*, the rule based system applies rules and adds the respective results to the problem description into the working memory.

Backward chaining attempts to find a chain of rule applications in reverse order. That is, it first identifies those rules which could immediately lead to the desired result. If the condition part of such a rule R_i is not satisfied by the current problem description in working memory, the system attempts to find other rules whose application would result in assertions which would satisfy the condition part of rule R_i. This process is continued until a complete chain of rule applications is found, which produces the desired result from the given problem description.

The architecture of expert systems

In the following, characteristic features of expert systems, which have already been found in the first-generation expert systems of the early 1980s will be presented. A typical architecture of such an expert system is shown in Figure 3.2. The various components are explained below.

Problem Solving Strategies: The problem solving strategies are general purpose methods which use the provided domain knowledge together with the

---

[4] These simple production rule systems actually resembled very much Post's production rule formalism as he introduced it in Post (1943) as an explication of the notion of computation. See chapter 10 for more details.

[5] If $A, B,...$, and R are all atomic propositions, this type of rules are also called *Horn clauses*.

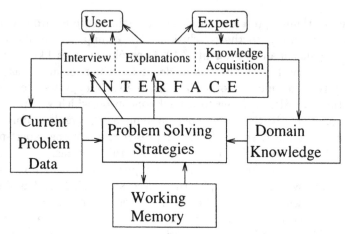

Figure 3.2. Structure of an expert system.

available data about the current problem case to find a solution. This part of the expert system is often also called the *inference engine*. During that process, additional information may be acquired from the user and/or explanations of the conducted problem solving process may be provided.

Domain Knowledge: Domain knowledge is the application specific part of the expert system. The domain knowledge resides in the *knowledge base* and describes rules or knowledge relevant to the application at hand.

Working Memory: During the problem solving process, the working memory is filled with intermediate results generated by the inference engine (problem solving component).

Current Problem Data: This data describes the problem instance being presented to the expert system. For example, this may be patient data for a medical expert system on which a diagnosis should be based.

Interface: The interface of an expert system usually comprises three parts.

The *knowledge acquisition component* allows to specify the domain knowledge to be represented in the knowledge base. The expert, normally mediated by a knowledge engineer, provides the knowledge. During the development process, the domain knowledge is verified by giving the expert system test problems. If the system arrives at an unintended conclusion, the expert requires an explanation in order to locate the errors and/or gaps in the provided knowledge and in order to repair the knowledge base. An update of the knowledge base may also be necessary after the system has been used, since the application domain may change to a certain extent or because an enhanced class of problems should be handled by the expert system.

The *explanation component* generates explanations of how the system arrived at its conclusions. In the simplest case, such an explanation is merely a trace of the rules being used for deriving the conclusion. More sophisticated forms may explain the system's actions in more abstract terms which may reduce the amount of data in the produced explanation and which may also facilitate the interpretation of the explanations. The purpose of the explanation component is twofold: On the one hand it provides an explanation for the user to increase the confidence in the solution and/or to allow the user to reject a solution on well-reasoned grounds. On the other hand, the explanation component is important for the development process of the system for supporting the knowledge acquisition process.

The *interview component* is solely conceived to interact with the user when the system is in routine use. The interview component requests some case information from the user or presents the expert system's result to the user.

Problems and further developments

The expert's knowledge was typically represented at a single level of abstraction in first-generation expert systems (rule-based systems). There was no explicit distinction between knowledge about *how* to do the task, knowledge about the *domain* or knowledge about *why* certain things are the way they are. Initially, having such a uniform knowledge representation was hoped to make the development of expert systems particularly easy. Unfortunately, in the subsequent years, it turned out that the lack of structure in the knowledge being employed caused a number of severe practical problems. Substantial difficulties were encountered with knowledge acquisition, maintainability of a rule base, and brittleness of the expert system's performance. The explanatory power of these systems turned out to be unsatisfactory as well (see Davis (1982) or Clancey (1983)).

Knowledge acquisition turned out to be much more of a hurdle than initially assumed. Experts are often unable to adequately explain how *they solve* their problems. They either did not give precise rules at all or they gave rules which are rather rationalisations[6] of their behaviour than an operational description of it. But an operational description is exactly what is needed for a simple expert system which can at least mimic the expert's behaviour, even without being able to explain what it is doing or why it makes sense.

Since the early expert systems were essentially simple production rule systems, their ability to explain a conclusion was basically limited to providing information on the trace of the rules being executed. Furthermore, it could be shown that more adequate explanations can be generated by using more abstract information. For example, while the rule-based expert system MYCIN (Buchanan & Shortliffe, 1984) was accomplishing different subtasks by executing different rules, it could not tell about these different subtasks.

---

[6] That is, rules which appear plausible to the experts and/or their social environment.

MYCIN performed subtasks like the gathering of information about the problem case at hand, or it differentiated between possible hypotheses. By explicitly distinguishing such subtasks and using a terminology which is user understandable, the explanatory power of expert systems can substantially be improved (see Swartout and Moore (1993)).

Related to the reasons for the rule-based expert systems for not giving satisfactory explanations is their brittleness and the fact that they do not have knowledge about the limitations of their competence. Human experts know where their field of expertise lies and they realise when they cross the boundaries of their competence. Humans would rather say 'I don't know' then give a senseless answer. Further, human expertise degrades rather gracefully as opposed to rule-based expert systems when a task does not lie in the core of the expertise. A further problem was that sometimes very complex interactions exist between the provided rules. This makes it difficult to extend the competence of the system by merely adding a few further rules. Experience showed that there are often negative interactions between rules which cause the overall performance to degrade. So, adding new rules could easily result in the degradation of the system's performance in cases which were not considered when designing the new rules.

A third consequence of the unstructured representation of knowledge in more or less uniform rules is the low maintainability (see Soloway, Bachant, and Jensen (1987)). It is not only the extension of the rule base which is difficult, but it is also because the validation of a given rule base is not supported. This is because the knowledge, about different aspects of the task, are distributed over the entire rule base. A better organisation of the knowledge could, for example, allow the systematic analysis of the consistency of the provided domain knowledge. Such domain knowledge could, for example, describe the physics of a system to be diagnosed. A further consequence of the unstructured representation of knowledge is that it is very difficult to reuse parts of the knowledge being employed by an existing expert system when building a new system.

The role of the knowledge level in expert systems

While the early expert systems, the first generation expert systems, could only very crudely be characterised by their application domain or by their way of using rules, e.g. backward or forward chaining, it was virtually impossible to provide more detailed insight into the functioning of a system.

In later expert systems, this changed because of the emphasis on the distinction between the *knowledge level* and the implementation level. This distinction allows to describe an expert system in more useful terms like classification, data abstraction, abduction, etc. The knowledge level allows a more principled system design. The focus is rather on how the problem can be solved as opposed to how the system can actually be implemented. This change also has its effect on the process of knowledge acquisition: it gives more guidance for what knowledge needs to be newly acquired and what knowledge can be reused from an already existing system which is solving a similar task.

The later expert systems, also referred to as 'second-generation expert systems', showed a number of distinct architectural features which set them apart from the first generation of expert systems. The following section discusses some of the main features of the *second-generation expert systems*.

3.2 Second-Generation Expert Systems

Second-generation expert systems[7] differ from first-generation expert systems in a number of ways. The most important characteristic is probably that *knowledge* is considered to be the core of a second-generation expert system. Nowadays, its importance has generally been acknowledged due to the problems encountered when maintaining, adapting and extending a rule base of *first-generation expert systems*.

It has been recognised that different models and problem-solving methods are needed and that the choice of the used models and methods plays a major role for the efficiency and the competence of the expert system being built. Another typical characteristic of second-generation expert systems is that it is more clearly distinguished between what knowledge is used and the way it is implemented. This amounts to the distinction between the *knowledge level* and the *symbol level*. One could roughly say that in the meantime expert systems researchers have gained an increased understanding of what knowledge is required to solve problems and how that knowledge can effectively be encoded.

In second-generation expert systems, the knowledge used is better structured. Different types of knowledge are explicitly distinguished. As a consequence, there was a need for developing techniques to represent and use different types of knowledge.

The explicit distinction between different types of knowledge and the use of specialised reasoning techniques can be viewed as a defining characteristic of second-generation expert systems. It turned out to be useful to partition different sets of rules which, for example, advocate conflicting conclusions. There was also a need for having a tailored control mechanism for the execution of the partitioned rules. As a consequence, a clear distinction between domain knowledge and control knowledge was being implemented (see Stefik (1981) or Clancey (1983)).

While control knowledge was made explicit, the domain knowledge was diversified further. Different types of domain knowledge were identified and separated. Experts, e.g. doctors, cannot only find a diagnosis based on a set of symptoms, but they also understand, to a certain degree, the physiological processes in the human body. Based on that observation was the idea to develop

---

[7] See David, Krivine, and Simmons (1993) for an extensive discussion of the issue.

reasoning techniques from 'first principles'(Davis, 1982; Reiter, 1987).[8] Instead
of only using knowledge that describes how to solve the particular *task* at hand,
it also turned out to be very useful to use knowledge about the *domain*. This
allows to give better explanations, to increase the re-usability of knowledge,
and to reduce the difficulty of analysing the validity of the provided knowledge.
The most advanced applications of this type are probably the model-based
diagnostic systems (see Kleer (1994)). Qualitative representations of physical
systems and processes have also been developed (see, e.g., Bratko, Mozetič, and
Lavrač (1989), Kleer (1994), Werthner (1994)). These models make reasoning
about complex physical systems much easier by providing a higher abstraction
level than the classical quantitative models in physics and engineering. Today, a
large number of expert systems are constructed every year in a large number of
application areas, ranging from engineering, environmental sciences, economic
and business applications, manufacturing, medicine to chemistry and other
sciences. In recent years more than 500 scientific Journal papers are reporting
each year on the development of new expert systems. Primarily devoted to the
development and application of expert systems are journals like *Expert Systems
with Applications, Expert Systems, IEEE Expert, Engineering Applications of
Artificial Intelligence, AI Applications,* or *Journal of Intelligent Manufacturing.*

3.3 Practical Difficulties: The Knowledge Acquisition Bottleneck

Substantial research has been conducted on the problem of knowledge acquisition, which was recognised as a major bottleneck in the development of expert systems. Knowledge acquisition is widely considered as a modelling activity (Schreiber, Wielinga, & Breuker, 1993; Schreiber, Wielinga, Akkermans,
van de Velde, & de Hoog, 1994; Shaw & Gaines, 1993). What is modelled is the
expertise of a domain expert. Such a model is attempted to be described at the
Knowledge level (Newell, 1982). Most of the Knowledge Acquisition approaches
to build knowledge-based systems, e.g. Aussenac, Frontin, Riviere, and Soubie
(1989), Schreiber et al. (1993, 1994) or Chandrasekaran (1986), Dieng, Giboin,
Tourtier, and Corby (1992), Shadbolt and Wielinga (1990), support a prob-
lem/knowledge analysis by the expert, the knowledge engineer, general system
analysts, ... or some combination of them. This may involve steps like developing a conceptual model of the knowledge being used by an expert, distinguishing
different subtasks to be solved, different types of knowledge to be distinguished
during reasoning processes, etc. Eventually, such a knowledge engineering approach either results in a model of the expertise which is easy to turn into an

---

[8] However, the knowledge actually used may not really represent the *first* principles,
   i.e. the knowledge may not exactly reflect the physiological processes in a human
   body which underlie the disease to be diagnosed. The knowledge may rather describe more abstract processes which correspond roughly, or merely metaphorically,
   to physiological processes.

operational program manually, or even an automatically generated operational program comes out of the process.

Another recent development are Ripple-Down Rules (Compton & Jansen, 1990; Compton, Kang, Preston, & Mulholland, 1993) which have been used for building very large knowledge bases (2000 rules) for the medical expert system PEIRS (Edwards et. al., 1993) which is in routine use. Ripple-Down Rules, (see Kang, Compton, and Preston (1995), Richards and Compton (1997), Martinez-Bejar, Shiraz, and Compton (1998), Beydoun and Hoffmann (1997), Kaspar and Hoffmann (1997) for recent extensions and applications of the basic method), have the significant advantage that they allow an incremental knowledge acquisition process, where earlier system performance is never reduced due to changes to the knowledge base. This is a major problem with other knowledge acquisition approaches: that amendments to a knowledge base may have adverse effects on previously demonstrated performance of the system due to complex and unforeseen interactions of the different rules in the knowledge base. Despite these efforts, knowledge acquisition is still a major problem in developing expert systems. The knowledge experts are actually employing when solving problems is apparently much less accessible to them then initially assumed. Also, it seems very difficult to integrate a large body of knowledge properly and to allow human-like reasoning over that knowledge. The CYC project, (see Lenat (1995)), was about developing a very large knowledge base of everyday knowledge, which targeted at a knowledge-based system which would be able to enhance itself from, e.g., normal textual knowledge sources just as humans are capable to do. This project also experienced the problems of integrating a large body of knowledge and achieving a 'common sense' performance of an AI system. The SOAR project also targeted at a general architecture for cognition and intelligence (Newell, 1990; Rosenbloom, Laird, & Newell, 1993). However, similar to expert systems, SOAR requires suitable domain knowledge in order to solve problems. The provision of the domain knowledge in SOAR is also a fairly laborious task.

As a consequence of the practical problems of knowledge acquisition, it is hoped that machine learning will provide at least assistance in the knowledge acquisition process, by allowing rules for a knowledge base to be automatically generated based on available case data. Machine learning is treated in detail in chapter 4. Although machine learning techniques enjoyed a tremendous growth in interest in recent years as providing techniques for knowledge discovery in databases, machine learning cannot be considered the perfect solution for building knowledge bases, as the required training data is often not sufficiently available.

The unsatisfactory experiences in the early years of expert systems were supported by an alternative view of the phenomenon of human intelligence, which was opposed to the view of the traditional paradigm of physical symbol systems. The philosopher Dreyfus (1972), Dreyfus and Dreyfus (1986), Dreyfus (1992) criticised traditional AI for a long time based on philosophical arguments. He essentially claimed that human intelligence rests to a large extent on tacit knowledge which cannot be implemented in a physical symbol system. Dreyfus' view received strong support by the publication of the book *Understanding Computers and Cognition: A new Foundation for Design* by Winograd and Flores (1986), as Winograd himself was once a key figure of the symbolic paradigm! As a consequence, connectionism[9] was welcomed as an alternative approach to the development of intelligent systems. One of the striking features being that connectionist systems are supposed to learn the desired behaviour by themselves.

---

[9] See Part II for a detailed treatment of connectionism. Chapter 11 provides a more detailed discussion on the mentioned philosophical grounds.

4. Symbolic Learning

The purpose of this chapter is to present fundamental ideas and techniques of machine learning. Since learning is clearly one of the very demanding abilities of intelligent beings, attempts to have machines learn was always at the heart of AI. For the connectionist paradigm, the learning capabilities of neural networks represented the most important feature to gain interest and credibility for a distinct paradigm allowing to build truly intelligent systems. Since literature on machine learning is vast, it is impossible to give a complete account on the work which has been done. This chapter contains some of the most influential ideas and concepts in symbolic machine learning research in order to give the reader a basic insight into the field. After the introduction in 4.1, section 4.2 gives general ideas of how learning problems can be framed. The section provides useful perspectives to better understand what learning algorithms actually do. Section 4.3 presents the Version space model which is an early learning algorithm as well as a conceptual framework that provides important insight into the general mechanisms behind most learning algorithms. In section 4.4, a family of learning algorithms, the AQ family for learning classification rules is presented. The AQ family belongs to the early approaches in machine learning. The following section 4.5 presents the basic principles of decision tree learners. Decision tree learners represent the most influential class of inductive learning algorithms today. Finally, a more recent group of learning systems are presented in section 4.6, which learn relational concepts within the framework of logic programming. This is a particularly interesting group of learning systems since the framework also allows to incorporate background knowledge which may assist in generalisation. Section 4.7 contains a summary and outlook on the potential of machine learning in the future.

4.1 Introduction

Symbolic approaches to learning have been developed for a large variety of possible applications. While learning for classification is prevailing, other learning tasks have been addressed as well which include tasks such as learning to control dynamic systems, general function approximation, prediction as well as learning to search more efficiently for a solution of combinatorial problems.

For different types of applications specialised algorithms have been developed. Although, in principle, most of the learning tasks can be reduced to each other. For example, the control of a dynamic system can be reduced to a classification problem by classifying system states according to which control action has to be taken.[1] Similarly, a prediction problem can be reduced to a classification problem by defining classes for each of the possible predictions.[2] A classification problem can be reduced to a prediction problem, etc.

The learner's way of interaction. Another aspect in learning is the way of how a learning system interacts with its environment. A common setting is to provide the learning system with a number of classified training examples. Based on that information, the learner attempts to find a general classification rule which allows to classify correctly both, the given training examples as well as unseen objects of the population. Another setting, *unsupervised learning*, provides the learner only with unclassified objects. The task is to determine which objects belong to the same class. This is clearly a much harder task for a learning algorithm than if classified objects are presented. See chapter 7.7 for unsupervised neural learning approaches. Interactive learning systems have been developed, which allow interaction with the user while learning. This allows the learner to request further information in situations, where it seems to be needed. Further information can range from merely providing an extra classified or unclassified example that has been randomly chosen, to answering specific questions which have been generated by the learning system. The latter way allows the learner to acquire information in a very focused way. Some of the ILP systems in section 4.6 are interactive learning systems.

Another more technical aspect concerns how the gathered information is internally processed and finally organised. According to that aspect the following types of representations are among the most frequently used for supervised learning of classifiers:

- decision trees
- classification rules (production rules) and decision lists
- PROLOG programs
- the structure of a neural network[3]
- Instance-based learning (nearest neighbour classifiers etc.)[4]

---

[1] However, the training data may not tell directly for which system state what action should be taken, it may just provide an evaluation of a longer sequence of actions. See e.g. Sutton and Barto (1998) for more details.

[2] In prediction problems there is a sequence of values given, on which basis the next value of the sequence is to be predicted. The given sequence, however, may usually be of varying length. Opposed to that are many classification problems based on a standard representation of a fixed length. However, exceptions exist here as well.

[3] This is discussed in part II.

[4] That means gathering a set of examples and a similarity function to determine the most similar example for a given new object. The most similar example is being used for determining the class of the presented object. Case-based reasoning is also a related technique of significant popularity, see Kolodner (1993), Leake (1996).

The focus of the considerations will be on learning classification functions. A major part of the considerations, however, is applicable to a larger class of tasks, since many tasks can essentially be reduced to classification tasks. Although the focus will be on *concept learning*, which is a special case of classification learning, it also attempts to find representations which resemble in some way concepts humans may acquire. While it is fairly unclear, how humans actually do that, the following discusses the attempt to find a 'comprehensible'[5] representation of a classification function.

4.2 Preliminaries for Learning Concepts from Examples

In this section a unified framework will be provided, in which almost all learning systems fit in. This includes neural networks, that also learn classifiers from examples. The following components can be distinguished to characterise concept learning systems:

- a set of examples
- a learning algorithm
- a set of possible learning results, i.e. a set of concepts.

Concerning the set of examples, it is an important issue to find a suitable *representation*. In fact, it has been recognised that the representation of examples has a major impact on success or failure of learning.

4.2.1 Representing Training Data

The representation of training data, i.e. of examples for learning concepts, has to serve two ends: On the one hand, the representation has to suit the user of the learning system, in that it is easy to encode the given data in the representation form. On the other hand, the representation has to suit the learning algorithm. Suiting the learning algorithm again has at least two facets: firstly, the learning algorithm has to be able to digest the representations of the data; secondly, the learning algorithm has to be able to find a suitable concept, i.e. a useful and appropriate generalisation from the presented examples.

The most frequently used representation of data is some kind of attribute or feature vectors. That is, objects are described by a number of attributes.

The most commonly used kinds of attributes are one of the following:

- Unstructured attributes:

---

[5] Unfortunately, this term is also quite unclear. However, some types of representations are certainly more difficult to grasp for an average human than others. For example, cascaded linear threshold functions, as present in Multi-Layer Perceptions, seem fairly difficult to comprehend as opposed to, e.g., boolean formulas.

- Boolean attributes, i.e. either the object does have an attribute or it does not. Usually specified by the values $\{f, t\}$, or $\{0, 1\}$, or sometimes in the context of neural networks by $\{-1, 1\}$.
- Discrete attributes, i.e. the attribute has a number of possible values (more then two), such as a number of possible colours $\{red, blue, green, brown\}$, shapes $\{circle, triangle, rectangle\}$, or even numbers where the values do not carry any meaning, or any other set of scalar values.
- Structured attributes, where the possible values have a presumably meaningful relation to each other:
  - Linear attributes. Usually the possible values of a linear attribute are a set of numbers, e.g. $\{0, 1, ..., 15\}$, where the ordering of the values is assumed to be relevant for generalisations. However, of course also non-numerical values could be used, where such an ordering is assumed to be meaningful. For example, colours may be ordered according to their brightness.
  - Continuous attributes. The values of these attributes are normally reals (with a certain precision) within a specified interval. Similarly as with linear attributes, the ordering of the values is assumed to be relevant for generalisations.
  - Tree-structured attributes. The values of these attributes are organised in a subsumption hierarchy. That is, for each value it is specified what other values it subsumes. This specification amounts to a tree-structured arrangement of the values. See Figure 4.5 on page 72 for an example.

Using attribute vectors of various types, it is fairly easy to represent objects of manifold nature. For example, cars can be described by features such as colour, weight, height, length, width, maximal speed, etc.

4.2.2 Learning Algorithms

Details of various learning algorithms are given later in this chapter. However, generally speaking, we can say that every learning algorithm searches implicitly or explicitly in a space of possible concepts for a concept that sufficiently suits the presented examples. By considering the set of concepts and their representations through which a learning algorithm is actually searching, the algorithm can be characterised and its suitability for a particular application can be assessed. The following subsection discusses how concepts can be represented.

4.2.3 Objects, Concepts, and Concept Classes

Before discussing the representation of concepts, some remarks on their intended meaning should be made. In concept learning, concepts are generally understood to subsume a certain set of objects. Consequently, concepts can formally be described with respect to a given set of possible objects to be classified. The set of *possible objects* is defined by the kind of representation chosen for representing the examples. Considering for instance attribute vectors for describing objects, there is usually a much larger number of *possible objects* than the number of objects which may actually occur. This is due to the fact that in the case of attribute vectors, the set of possible objects is simply given by the Cartesian product of the sets of allowed values for each of the attributes. That is, every combination of attribute values is allowed, although there may be no 'pink elephants,' 'green mice,' or 'blue rabbits'.

However, formally speaking, for a given set of objects X, a concept c is defined by its extension in X, i.e. we can say c is simply a subset of X. That implies that for a set of n objects, i.e. for $|X| = n$ there are 2^n different concepts. However, most actual learning systems will not be able to learn all possible concepts. They will rather only be able to learn a certain subset. Those concepts which can potentially be learnt, are usually called the *concept class* or *concept space* of a learning system. In many contexts, concepts which can be learnt are also called *hypotheses* and *hypothesis space* respectively. Later, more formal definitions will be introduced. Also, in the rather practical considerations to machine learning a slightly different terminology is used than in the more mathematically oriented considerations.

However, in general it can be said that an actual learning system L, given n possible objects, works only on a particular subset of all the 2^n different possible concepts which is called the concept space C of L. For C, both of the following conditions hold:

1. For every concept $c \in C$ there exists training data, such that L will learn (or output a description of) c.
2. For all possible training data, L will learn (or output the description of) some concept c, such that $c \in C$. That is, L will never learn a concept $c \notin C$.

Considering a *set of concepts* there is the huge number of 2^{2^n} different sets of concepts on a set of n objects. To give a numerical impression: looking at 30 boolean features describing the objects in X under consideration, would amount to $n = 2^{30} \approx 1000000000 = 10^9$ different possible objects. Thus, there exist $\approx 2^{1000000000}$ different possible concepts and $\approx 2^{2^{1000000000}} \approx 10^{10^{300000000}}$ different concept spaces, an astronomically large number.

Another characteristic of learning algorithms, besides their concept space, is the particular order in which concepts are considered. That is, if two concepts are equally or almost equally confirmed by the training data, which of these two concepts will be learnt?

In the following section, the two issues are treated in more detail in order to provide a view of learning which makes the similarities and dissimilarities among different algorithms more visible.

4.2.4 Consistent and Complete Concepts

In machine learning some of the technical terms describing the relation between a hypothesis of how to classify objects and a set of classified objects (usually the training sample) are used differently in different contexts. In most mathematical/theoretical considerations a hypothesis h is called *consistent* with the training set of classified objects, if and only if the hypothesis h classifies all the given objects in the same way as given in the training set. A hypothesis h' is called *inconsistent* with a given training set if there is an object which is differently classified in the training set than by the hypothesis h'. There may be more than two object classes.

Opposed to that is the terminology following Michalski (1983a). Firstly, he considers only two classes of objects: one is the class of *positive* examples of a concept to be learned and the remaining objects are *negative* examples. Secondly, a hypothesis h for a concept description is said to *cover* those objects which it classifies as positive examples. Following this perspective, it is said that a hypothesis h is *complete* if h covers all positive examples in a given training set. Further, a hypothesis h is said to be *consistent* if it does not cover any of the given negative examples. The possible relationships between a hypothesis and a given set of training data are shown in Figure 4.1.

4.3 Generalisation as Search

In 1982, Mitchell introduced the idea of the *version space*, which puts the process of generalisation into the framework of searching through a space of possible 'versions' or concepts to find a suitable learning result (Mitchell, 1982).

The version space can be considered as the space of all concepts which are consistent with all learning examples presented so far. In other words, a learning algorithm considers initially, before any training data has been presented, the complete concept space as possible outcomes of the learning process. After examples are presented, this space of still possible outcomes of the learning process is gradually reduced.

Mitchell provided data structures which allow an elegant and efficient maintenance of the version space, i.e. of concepts that are consistent with the examples presented so far.

Example

> To illustrate the idea, let us consider the following set of six geometrical objects *big square, big triangle, big circle, small square, small triangle,* and *small circle,* and abbreviated by *b.s, b.t, ... , s.t, s.c* respectively. That is, let $X = \{b.s, b.t, b.c, s.s, s.t, s.c\}$.
>
> And let the set of concepts C that are potentially output by a learning system L be given by:
> $C = \{\{\}, \{b.s\}, \{b.t\}, \{b.c\}, \{s.s\}, \{s.t\}, \{s.c\}, \{b.s, b.t, b.s\}, \{s.s, s.t, s.s\}, \{b.s, s.s\}, \{b.t, s.t\}, \{b.c, s.c\}, X\}.$
>
> That is, C contains the empty set, the set X, all singletons and the abstraction of the single objects by relaxing one of the requirements of having a specific size or having a specific shape.

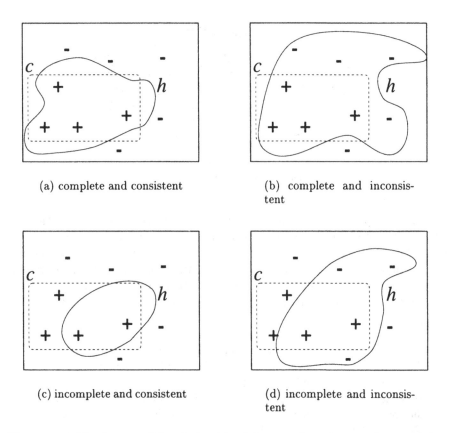

(a) complete and consistent

(b) complete and inconsistent

(c) incomplete and consistent

(d) incomplete and inconsistent

Figure 4.1. The four possible relationships between a hypothesis and a set of classified examples. The correct concept c is shown as dashed line. The hypothesis h as solid line. A *consistent* hypothesis covers all positive examples. A *complete* hypothesis covers no negative example.

In Figure 4.2 the concept space C is shown and the partial order between the concepts is indicated by the dashed lines. This partial order is the key to Mitchell's approach. The idea is to always maintain a set of *most general concepts* and a set of *most specific concepts* that are consistent and complete with respect to the presented training examples.

If a most *specific* concept c_s contains some object x, which is given as a positive example, then c_s as well as all concepts which are supersets of c_s are consistent with the positive example x. Similarly, if a most *general* concept c_g does not contain some object x, which is given as a negative example, then all concepts which are subsets of s_g do not contain the negative example, i.e. are consistent with the negative example as well as c_g itself.

In other words, the set of consistent and complete concepts which exclude all presented negative examples and include all presented positive examples is defined by the sets of concepts S and G being the most specific and most

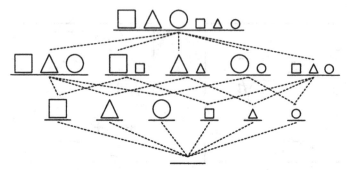

Figure 4.2. The partial order of concepts with respect to their coverage of objects.

general concepts consistent and complete with respect to the data. That is, all concepts of C which lie between S and G are complete and consistent as well. A concept c lies between S and G, if and only if there are two concepts $c_g \in G$ and $c_s \in S$ such that $c_s \subseteq c \subseteq c_g$. An algorithm that maintains the set of consistent and complete concepts is sketched in Figure 4.3. Consider the following example to illustrate the use of the algorithm in Figure 4.3:

Example

> Let us denote the various sets S and G by S_n and G_n respectively after the n-th example has been processed. Before the first example is presented we have $G_0 = \{X\}$ and $S_0 = \{\{\}\}$.
>
> Suppose a big triangle is presented as positive example. Then G remains the same, but the concept in S has to be generalised. That is, we obtain $G_1 = G_0\{X\}$ and $S_1 = \{\{b.t\}\}$.
>
> Suppose the second example is a small circle and is a negative example. Then S remains the same, but the concept in G has to be specialised. That is, we obtain $G_2 = \{\{b.s, b.t, b.c\}, \{b.t, s.t\}\}$ and $S_2 = S_1 = \{\{b.t\}\}$. Note that G_2 contains two different concepts which neither contain the negative example but which are both supersets of the concept in S_2.
>
> Suppose the third example is a big square and is a positive example. Then in G we remove the second concept since it does not contain the new positive example and the concept in S has to be generalised. That is, we obtain $G_3 = \{\{b.s, b.t, b.c\}\}$ and $S_3 = \{\{b.s, b.t, b.c\}\}$.
>
> That is, $S_3 = G_3$ which means that there is only a single concept left which is consistent and complete with respect to all presented examples. That is, the only possible result of any learning algorithm that learns only concepts in C that are consistent and complete is given by $\{b.s, b.t, b.c\}$.

In general, the learning process can be stopped if S equals G meaning that S contains the concept to be learned. However, it may happen that $S \neq G$ and an example is presented which forces either S being generalised or G being specialised but there is no generalisation (specialisation) possible according to the definition in Figure 4.3.

Given: A concept space C from which the algorithm has to choose one concept as the target concept c_t. A stream of examples of the concept to learn. (The examples are either positive or negative examples of the target concept c_t.)

begin

    Let S be the set of most specific concepts in C; usually the empty concept.

    Let G be the set of most general concepts in C; usually the single set X.

    while there is a new example e **do**

        if e is a positive example

        then Remove in G all concepts that do not contain e.

            Replace every concept $c_o \in S$ by the set of

            most specific generalisations with respect to e and S.

        endif

        if e is a negative example

        then Remove in S all concepts that contain e.

            Replace every concept $c_o \in G$ by the set of

            most general specialisations with respect to e and G.

        endif

    endwhile

end.

Note: The set of **most specific generalisations** of a concept c with respect to an example e and a set of concepts G are those concepts $c_g \in C$ where $c \cup \{e\} \subseteq c_g$ and there is a concept $c_G \in G$ such that $c_g \subseteq c_G$ and there is no concept $c_{g'} \in C$ such that $c \cup \{e\} \subseteq c_{g'} \subset c_g$.

The set of **most general specialisations** of a concept c with respect to an example e and a set of concepts S are those concepts $c_s \in C$ where $c_s \subseteq c \setminus \{e\}$ and there is a concept $c_S \in S$ such that $c_S \subseteq c_s$ and there is no concept $c_{s'} \in C$ such that $c_s \subset c_{s'} \subseteq c \setminus \{e\}$.

Figure 4.3. An algorithm for maintaining the version space.

This fact would indicate that there is no concept in C which is consistent with the presented learning examples. The reason for this is either that the concept space did not contain the target concept, i.e. C was inappropriately chosen for the application domain. Or that the examples contained noise, i.e. that some of the presented data was incorrect. This may either be a positive example presented as a negative or vice versa or a positive example inaccurately described, owing to measurement errors or other causes. For example, the positive example *big triangle* may be misrepresented as the positive example *big square*.

If the concept space C does not contain all possible concepts on the set X of chosen representations, the choice of the concept space presumes that the concept to be learned is in fact in C, although this is not necessarily the case. Utgoff and Mitchell (1982) introduced in this context the term *inductive bias*. They distinguished *language bias* and *search bias*. The language bias determines the concept space which is searched for the concept to be learned (the target concept). The search bias determines the *order* of search within a given concept space. The proper specification of inductive bias is crucial for the success of a learning system in a given application domain.

In the following sections, the basic ideas of the most influential approaches in (symbolic) machine learning are presented.

4.4 Learning of Classification Rules

There are different ways of learning classification rules. Probably the best known ones are the successive generation of disjunctive normal forms, which is done by the AQ family of learning algorithms, which belongs to one of the very early approaches in machine learning. Another well-known alternative is to simply transform decision trees into rules. The C4.5 program package (Quinlan, 1993a), for example, also contains a transformation program, which converts learned decision trees into rules.

4.4.1 Model-Based Learning Approaches: The AQ Family

The AQ algorithm was originally developed by Michalski (1969), and has been subsequently re-implemented and refined by several authors (e.g. Michalski and Larson (1983)). Opposed to ID3[6] the AQ algorithm outputs a set of 'if...then...' classification rules rather than a decision tree. This is useful for expert system applications based on the production rule paradigm. Often it is a more comprehensible representation than a decision tree. A sketch of the algorithm is shown in Figure 4.1. The basic AQ algorithm assumes no noise in the domain. It searches for a concept description that classifies the training examples perfectly.

The AQ algorithm. The operation of the AQ algorithm is sketched in Table 4.1. Basically, the algorithm generates a so-called *complex* (i.e. a conjunction of attribute-value specifications). A *complex* covers a subset of the positive training examples of a class. The complex forms the **condition** part of a production rule of the following form:

'If **condition** then predict **class**'.

The search proceeds by repeatedly specialising candidate complexes until a complex is found which covers a large number of examples of a single class and none of other classes. As indicated, AQ learns one class at a time. The process for learning a single concept is outlined below.

---

[6] C4.5, the successor of ID3 actually contains facilities to convert decision trees into *if ... then ... * rules.

Procedure AQ(POS, NEG) returning COVER:

Input: A set of positive examples POS and a set of negative examples NEG.

Output: A set of rules (stored in **cover**) which recognises all positive examples and none of the negative examples.

let COVER be the empty cover;
while COVER does not cover all positive examples in POS
    select a SEED, i.e. a positive example not covered by COVER;
    call procedure STAR(SEED, NEG) to generate the STAR, i.e. a set of
        complexes that cover SEED but no examples in NEG;
    select the best complex BEST from the star according to
        user-defined criteria;
    add BEST as an extra disjunct to COVER;
return COVER.

Procedure STAR(SEED, NEG) returning STAR:

let STAR be the set containing the empty complex;
while there is a complex in STAR that covers
        some negative example $E_{neg} \in$ NEG,
   Specialise complexes in STAR to exclude E_{neg} by:
        let EXTENSION be all **selectors** that cover SEED but not E_{neg};
   % **selectors** are attribute-value specifications
   % which apply to **seed** but not to E_{neg}.
        let STAR be the set $\{x \wedge y | x \in$ STAR$, y \in$ EXTENSION$\}$;
        remove all complexes in STAR subsumed by other complexes in STAR;
   Remove the worst complexes from STAR
        until size of STAR is $\leq$ the user-defined maximum ($maxstar$).
return STAR.

Table 4.1. The AQ algorithm: Generating a cover for class C

Learning a single class. To learn a single class c, AQ generates a set of rules. Each rule recognises a subset of the positive examples of c. A single rule is generated as follows: first, a 'seed' example E from the set of positive examples for c is selected; second, it tries to generalise the description of that example as much as possible. Generalisation means here to abstract as many attributes as possible from the description of E.

AQ begins with the extreme case that all attributes are abstracted. That is, AQ's first rule has the form 'if true **then** predict class c'. Usually, this rule is too general. However, beginning with this rule, stepwise specialisations are made in order to exclude more and more negative examples. For a given negative example neg covered by the current rule AQ searches for a specialisation which will exclude neg. A specialisation is obtained by adding another condition to the condition part of the rule. The condition to be added is a so-called *selector* for the seed example. A selector is an attribute value combination which applies to the seed example but not to the negative example *neg* currently being considered.

This process of searching for a suitable rule is continued until the generated rule covers only examples of class c and no negative examples, i.e. no examples of other classes.

Since there is generally more than one choice of including an attribute-value specification, a set of 'best specialisations so-far' are retained and explored in parallel. In that sense, AQ conducts a kind of beam search on the hypothesis space. This set of solutions which is steadily improved is called a *star*. After all negative examples are excluded by the rules in the star, the best rule is chosen according to a user-defined evaluation criterion. By that process, AQ guarantees to produce rules which are *complete* and *consistent* with respect to the training data, if such rules exist. AQ's only hard constraint for the generalisation process is not to cover any negative example by a generated rule. Soft constraints determine the order of adding conditions (i.e. attribute value specifications).

Example

Consider again the training examples given in Figure 4.2. Learning rules for the class of pleasant weather would work as follows:

A positive example E is selected as a seed, say example 4 having the description $E = [(a = true) \land (b = false) \land (c = true) \land (d = false)]$.

From this seed, initially *all* attributes are abstracted, i.e. the first rule is

if true then pleasant.

Since this rule clearly also covers weather situations which are known as unpleasant, the rule has to be specialised. This is done, by re-introducing attribute-value specifications which are given in the seed example. Thus, each of the four attributes is considered. For every attribute, it is determined whether its re-introduction excludes any of the negative examples. Considering attribute a:

The condition $(a = false)$ is inconsistent with example 1 and 2, which are both negative examples. Condition $(b = false)$ excludes the examples 1 and 2, which are negative and it excludes the positive example 3 as well. Condition $(c = true)$ excludes the positive example 5 and the negative example 6. Finally, condition $(d = false)$ excludes three negative examples 2, 6, and 7, while it does not exclude any positive example.

Intuitively, specialising the rule by adding condition $(d = false)$ appears to be the best.

However, the rule

if $(d = false)$ then pleasant

still covers the negative example 1. Therefore, a further condition has to be added. Examining the three possible options leads to the following:

The condition $(a = false)$ is inconsistent with example 1 and 2, which are both negative examples, i.e. adding this condition would result in a consistent and complete classification rule.

Condition $(b = false)$ excludes the examples 1 and 2, which are negative
and it excludes the positive example 3 as well. After adding this condition
the resulting rule would no longer cover the positive example 3, while all
negative examples are excluded as well.
Condition $(c = true)$ excludes the positive example 5 and the negative
example 6 and is thus of no use.
Again, it appears natural to add the condition $(a = false)$ to obtain a
satisfying classification rule for pleasant weather:
if $(a = false) \wedge (d = false)$ then pleasant

4.4.2 Non-Boolean Attributes

Figure 4.4. Linear Attributes.

In many practical applications of machine learning, objects are not represented
by a set of boolean attributes.

The example given above considered the simplest case where the objects
were described by boolean attributes only. Considering further types of attributes, as mentioned in section 4.5.3, some extensions to the demonstrated approach are necessary. Basically more attribute-value specifiers as in the boolean
case have to be considered. In the boolean case the possible specifications were
$(a = false)$ or $(a = true)$.

- For discrete attributes without any particular relation among its different
  values, the attribute specifications can easily be extended from only boolean
  values to the full range of attribute values. That is, the possible specifications
  are $(A = v_1)$, $(A = v_2)$, ..., $(A = v_n)$. Also, subsets of values can be used for
  constructing selectors, i.e. for including the seed example and excluding the
  negative examples. These are called *internal disjunctions*.
- Internal disjunctions. Disjunctions which allow more than one value or interval for a single attribute. Since the disjuncts concern the same attribute, the
  disjunction is called *internal*. Examples are '(colour = red *or* green *or* blue)'.
- For linear attributes, see Figure 4.4. A linear attribute is an attribute where
  an example has a particular value within a range of linearly ordered values.
  Concepts are defined by defining an admissible interval within the linearly
  ordered attribute values, as e.g. $(A < v_1)$, $(A \geq v_1)$, ..., $(A < v_n)$, $(A \geq v_n)$.
  Also 'two-sided' intervals of attribute values like $(v_1 < A \leq v_2)$ can be
  handled by AQ (Michalski, 1983a).
- For continuous attributes, the specifications are similar to the case of linear
  attributes, except that instead considering the value range of the attribute,
  the values that actually occur in the given positive and negative examples are

considered and ordered to be $v_1, v_2, ..., v_k$. Subsequently as thresholds, the
values of $\frac{v_i+v_{i+1}}{2}$ are calculated and used as in the case of linear attributes.

- Tree-structured attributes, see Figure 4.5. Tree-structured attributes replace
  the linear ordering of the attribute value range by a tree-structure. The value
  of a node n in the tree structure is considered to cover all values which are
  either assigned directly to one of n's successor nodes or are *covered* by one
  of n's successor nodes.

  The defined partial ordering is used to specify attribute values: every possible
  attribute value is considered. Some attribute values do not subsume other
  values; these are treated as in the case of the discrete attributes. Those values
  which subsume other values are used to group meaningful attribute values
  together. For example, $(a = polygon)$ would subsume all values down the
  tree, i.e. triangle, square, etc.

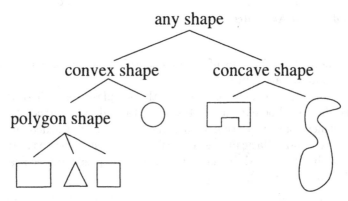

Figure 4.5. An example of a tree-structured attribute 'shape'.

The advanced versions of the AQ family (see Michalski (1983a)) of learning
algorithms deal with all these different attribute types by determining selectors
as *minimal dominating atoms*. A minimal dominating atom is a single attribute
with a specified admissible value range. This is that value range, which excludes
the given negative example and covers as many positive examples as possible.
That is, in the case of value ranges for linear or continuous attributes, an
interval is determined by excluding the values of as many negative examples as
possible and by including the values of the positive examples.

4.4.3 Problems and Further Possibilities of the AQ Framework

Searching for Extensions of a Rule. The search for specialising a too
general classification rule is heuristic in AQ due to the computational complexity

of finding specialisations.[7] A kind of greedy approach is conducted by adding one constraint at a time to a rule. Since there is usually more than one choice to add a further constraint to a rule, all such ways of adding a constraint are tried, by adding all new rules to the so-called *star*. The star contains only a pre-specified maximum number of rule candidates.

If after new rules are added to the star, the number of rules in the star exceeds the specified maximum number, rules are removed according to a user-specified preference or quality criterion. As quality function, typically heuristics are used by the AQ system like

'Number of correctly classified examples divided by total number of examples covered.'

Learning multiple classes. In the case of learning multiple classes AQ generates decision rules for each class in turn. Learning a class c is done by considering all examples with classification c as positive examples and considering all others as negative examples of the concept to learn. Learning a single class occurs in stages. Each stage generates a single production rule, which recognises a part of the positive examples of c. After creating a new rule, the examples that are recognised by a rule are removed from the training set. This step is repeated until all examples of the chosen class are covered. Learning the classification of a single class, as above, is then repeated for all classes.

Learning relational concepts using the AQ approach. The approach presented has also been extended to learn relational concepts, containing predicates and quantifiers instead of just fixed attributes. For more details, see Michalski (1983a).

Extending AQ. Various extensions to the basic AQ algorithm presented above have been developed. One important class of extensions addresses the problem of noisy data, e.g. the CN2 algorithm, see Clark and Niblett (1989). For the application of systems based on the AQ algorithm to real-world domains, methods for handling noisy data are required. In particular, mechanisms for avoiding the *overfitting* of the learned concept description to the data are needed. Thus, the constraint that the induced description must classify the training data perfectly has to be relaxed.

AQ has problems to deal with noisy data because it tries to fit the data completely. For dealing with noisy data, only the major fraction of the training examples should be covered by the learning rules. Simultaneously a relative simplicity of the learned classification rule should be maintained as a heuristic for obtaining plausible generalizations.

---

[7] Note that the set cover problem is known to be **NP**-complete (Garey & Johnson, 1979), which is very related to various quality criteria one may have in mind for a rule discriminating between negative and positive examples. That is, for many quality measures, the task to find the *best* rule will be **NP**-hard.

4.5 Learning Decision Trees

Decision trees represent one of the most important class of learning algorithms today. Recent years have seen a large number of papers devoted to the theoretical as well as empirical studies of constructing decision trees from data. This section presents the basic ideas and research issues in this field of study.

4.5.1 Representing Functions in Decision Trees

There are many ways for representing functions, i.e. mappings from a set of input variables to a set of possible output values. One such way is to use decision trees. Decision trees gained significant importance in machine learning. One of the major reasons is that there exist simple yet efficient techniques to generate decision trees from training data.

Abstractly speaking, a decision tree is a representation of a function from a possibly *infinite* domain into a *finite* domain of values. That is,

$$D : X \to C,$$

where X is the possibly infinite set of objects and C the set of classes assigned to the objects by the function D realized by a decision tree.

The representation of such a function by a decision tree is at the same time also a guide for how to efficiently compute a value of the represented function. Figure 4.6(a) shows a decision tree of a simple boolean function. The decision tree is a tree in which all leaf nodes represent a certain function value. In order to use a decision tree for determining the function value for a given argument, one starts in the root node and chooses a path down to one leaf node. Each non-leaf node in the tree represents a decision on how to proceed the path, i.e. which successor node is to be chosen next. The decision criterion is represented by associating conditions[8] with each of the edges leading to the successor nodes. Usually, for any non-terminal node n a single attribute is used to decide on a successor node. Consequently, that successor node is chosen for which the corresponding condition is satisfied. In Figure 4.6(a) the decision in the root node depends solely on the value of the variable a. In the case of $a = F$ the evaluation of the tree proceeds at the left successor node, while being $a = t$ would result in considering the right successor node. In the latter case the evaluation had already reached a leaf node which indicates that $f(t,t) = f(t,f) = T$. In the case of $a = f$ the value of b determines whether the left or the right successor node of node 2 has to be chosen, etc.

4.5.2 The Learning Process

The learning of decision trees is one of the early approaches to machine learning. In fact Hunt, Mairn, and Stone (1966) developed his *Concept Learning System*

---

[8] normally mutually exclusive conditions...

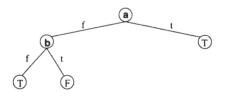

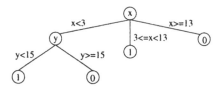

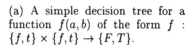

(a) A simple decision tree for a function $f(a, b)$ of the form f : $\{f, t\} \times \{f, t\} \to \{F, T\}$.

(b) A function $f(x, y)$ of the form $f : N \times N \to \{0, 1\}$.

Figure 4.6. Two decision trees on different domains.

Number	a=sunny	b=hot	c=humid	d=windy	class=$f(a, b, c, d)$
1	true	true	true	false	U
2	true	true	true	true	U
3	false	true	true	false	P
4	false	false	true	false	P
5	false	false	false	false	P
6	false	false	false	true	U
7	false	false	true	true	U

Table 4.2. A set of examples for the concept of pleasant weather. 'P' indicates pleasant weather, while 'U' indicates unpleasant weather.

CLS in the 1960s, which was already a decision tree learner. A decision tree representation of a classification function is generated from a set of classified examples.

Consider the examples in Table 4.2. Assume, we want to generate a decision tree for the function f which determines the value P only for the examples $3-5$.

The learning algorithm can be described at an abstract level as a function from sets of feature vectors to decision trees. Generalisation occurs indirectly: the input example set does not specify a function value for the entire domain. Opposed to that a decision tree determines a function value for the entire domain, i.e. for *all* possible feature vectors.

The basic idea of Quinlan's ID3 algorithm (Quinlan, 1979), which evolved later to program package C4.5 (Quinlan, 1993a), is sketched in Figure 4.8. The general idea is to split the given set of training examples into subsets such that the subsets eventually obtained contain only examples of a single class. Splitting a set of examples S into subsets is done by choosing an attribute A and generating the subsets of S such that all examples in one subset have the same value in the attribute A. In principle, if an attribute has more than two values, two or more groups of values may be chosen such that all examples which have a value in the attribute A that belongs to the same group are gathered in the same subset. In order to cope with noise, it is necessary, to stop splitting sets

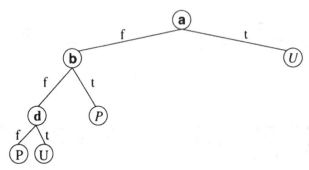

Figure 4.7. A decision tree representing the boolean function partially defined in the Table above. (The italic P (and U) represents the inclusion of undefined function values which are set to P (or to U respectively) by default.)

of examples into smaller and smaller subsets before all examples in one subset belong to the same class.

Therefore, a decision tree learning algorithm has the two following functions that determine its performance:

- A *termination condition* which determines when to refrain from further splitting of a set of examples.
- An *evaluation function* which chooses the 'best' attribute on which the current set of examples should be split.

Input: A set of examples E, each consisting of of m attribute values corresponding to the attributes $A_1, ..., A_m$ and class label c. Further, a termination condition $T(S)$ is given, where S is a set of examples and an evaluation function $ev(A, S)$ where A is an attribute and S a set of examples. The termination condition is usually that all, or almost all, the examples in S have the same class value.
Output: A decision tree.

1. Let $S := E$.
2. If $T(S)$ is true, then **stop**.
3. For each attribute A_i determine the value of the function $ev(A_i, S)$. Let $A_j = \max_{i \in \{1,...,m\}} ev(A_i, S)$. Divide the set S into subsets by the attribute values of A_j. For each such subset of examples E_k call the decision-tree learner recursively at step (1) with E set to E_k. Choose A_j as the tested attribute for the node n and create for each subset E_k a corresponding successor node n_k.

Figure 4.8. An outline of the ID3 algorithm

The termination condition: $T(S)$. As indicated in Figure 4.8, the termination condition $T(S)$ plays an important role in inducing decision trees. The simplest form of a termination condition says 'stop' when all examples in S have the same class.

More sophisticated versions of the termination condition stop even when not all examples in S have the same class. This is motivated by the assumption that either the examples in the sample contain noise and/or that only a statistical classification function can be expected to be learned.

The evaluation function: $ev(a, S)$. The ID3 algorithm as shown in Figure 4.8 performs only a one level lookahead to select the attribute for the next decision node. In that sense it is a greedy algorithm. Quinlan introduced in his early paper (Quinlan, 1979) an information theoretic measure, which performs fairly well. Other heuristic proposals for a selection criterion include pure frequency measures as in CLS (Hunt et al., 1966), or the *Gini index* as used in CART (Breiman, Friedman, Olshen, & Stone, 1984) or a statistical test as in CAL5 (Müller & Wysotzki, 1996). See also Bratko (1990) for a discussion of these measures and simple implementations in PROLOG. An exhaustive search for finding a minimal size tree is not feasible in general, since the size of the search space is too large (exponential growth).

Quinlan's entropy measure[9] estimates how many further splits will be necessary after the current set of examples is split (by using the splitting criterion being evaluated). Consider a set of examples E, a set of classes $C = \{c_i | 1 \leq i \leq n\}$, and an attribute A with values in the set $\{v_j \mid 1 \leq j \leq m\}$. The information in this distribution needed to determine the class of a randomly chosen object is given by:

$$info(C) = - \sum_{i \in \{1,...,n\}} p_i \log_2 p_i \qquad (4.1)$$

where p_i is the probability of an example falling into class c_i. The probability P_i will be estimated by the relative frequency of an example in E falling into class i. That is, p_i will be estimated as $\frac{|E_i|}{|E|}$. After splitting on an attribute, some further information may still be needed, depending on the subset of examples associated to each of the branches. That is, after a split, the information needed on average can be computed by computing the information needed for each of the subsets according to formula 4.1 and by weighting the result by the probability, for taking the respective branch of the decision tree. Then, the following gives the information needed on average to determine the class of an object *after* the split on attribute A_j:

$$info(C|A) = - \sum_{j \in \{1,...,m\}} \sum_{i \in \{1,...,n\}} p_{ij} \log_2 p_{ij} \qquad (4.2)$$

---

[9] The entropy measure has been first formulated in Shannon and Weaver (1949) as a measure of information. The intuition behind it is that it gives the average number of bits necessary for transmitting a message using an optimal encoding. In the context of decision trees the number of bits required for transmitting a message corresponds to the number of splits required for determining the class of an object.

where p_{ij} denotes the probability for an object to have attribute value v_j and falling into class i. This is the measure proposed by Quinlan (1979). Again p_{ij} will be estimated by the relative frequency of an example in E of having attribute value v_j and falling into class i. Intuitively, the amount of information needed on average after a split on a particular attribute should be as small as possible. The choice of a splitting attribute *minimises* on this measure.

Quinlan defines the inverse, the information gain achieved by a split as follows:

$$Gain(E, A) = info(E) - info(E|A) \qquad (4.3)$$

As a consequence, the objective is then to maximise the information gain by choosing a splitting criterion.

Example

Considering the examples given in Table 4.2 and assuming the relative frequency of examples in the given sample equals their probability, the following values would be computed:
Initially the required information needed to determine the class of an example is given by:

$$info(E) = -(\frac{4}{7}\log_2 \frac{4}{7} + \frac{3}{7}\log_2 \frac{3}{7}) \approx 0.98$$

Considering the complete set of seven objects and splitting on a:

$$info(E|a) = -(\frac{2}{7}(1\log_2 1) + \frac{5}{7}(\frac{3}{5}\log_2 \frac{3}{5} + \frac{2}{5}\log_2 \frac{2}{5})) \approx 0.69$$

and splitting on b:

$$info(E|b) = -(\frac{3}{7}(\frac{2}{3}\log_2 \frac{2}{3} + \frac{1}{3}\log_2 \frac{1}{3}) + \frac{4}{7}(\frac{1}{2}\log_2 \frac{1}{2} + \frac{1}{2}\log_2 \frac{1}{2})) \approx 0.96$$

and splitting on c:

$$info(E|c) = -(\frac{5}{7}(\frac{3}{5}\log_2 \frac{3}{5} + \frac{2}{5}\log_2 \frac{2}{5}) + \frac{2}{7}(\frac{1}{2}\log_2 \frac{1}{2} + \frac{1}{2}\log_2 \frac{1}{2})) \approx 0.978$$

and splitting on d:

$$info(E|d) = -(\frac{3}{7}(1\log_2 1) + \frac{4}{7}(\frac{1}{4}\log_2 \frac{1}{4} + \frac{3}{4}\log_2 \frac{3}{4})) \approx 0.46$$

Hence, splitting on attribute d requires on average the smallest amount of further information for deciding the class of an object. In fact, in three out of seven cases the class is known to be *unpleasant* weather after the split. The remaining four examples are considered for determining the next split in the respective tree branch. That is, for the following step only the subset of examples shown in Table 4.3 has to be considered.

Number	a=sunny	b=hot	c=humid	d=windy	class=$f(a,b,c,d)$
1	true	true	true	false	U
3	false	true	true	false	P
4	false	false	true	false	P
5	false	false	false	false	P

Table 4.3. The reduced set of examples after splitting on attribute d and considering only those examples with the attribute value $d=false$.

Then, we get the following values for the required information after splitting on attribute a:

$$info(E|a) = -(\frac{1}{4}(1\log_2 1) + \frac{3}{4}(1\log_2 1)) = 0$$

and splitting on attribute b:

$$info(E|b) = -(\frac{1}{2}(1\log_2 1) + \frac{1}{2}(\frac{1}{2}\log_2\frac{1}{2} + \frac{1}{2}\log_2\frac{1}{2})) = 0.5$$

and splitting on attribute c:

$$info(E|c) = -(\frac{1}{4}(1\log_2 1) + \frac{3}{4}(\frac{2}{3}\log_2\frac{2}{3} + \frac{1}{3}\log_2\frac{1}{3})) \approx 0.688$$

Consequently, the next attribute chosen to split on is attribute a, which results in the decision tree shown in Figure 4.9.

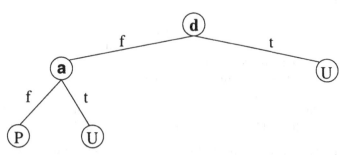

Figure 4.9. The decision tree obtained using Quinlan's information-theoretic measure. In fact, the decision tree is the shortest possible for the given example set.

Practical experience has shown that this information measure has the drawback of favouring attributes with many values. Motivated by that problem, Quinlan introduced inC4.5 (Quinlan, 1993a) a normalised Entropy measure, the gain ratio, which takes the number of generated branches into account. The gain ratio measure (Quinlan, 1993a), considers the potential information that may be gained by a split of E into $E_1, ..., E_k$, denoted by $Split(E, A)$. The potential information is that each branch has a unique class assigned to it, i.e. it can be defined as follows:

$$Split(E, A) = - \sum_{i=1}^{k} \frac{|E_i|}{|E|} \log_2 \frac{|E_i|}{|E|} \qquad (4.4)$$

where A splits the set of examples E into the disjoint subsets $E_1, ..., E_k$.

The gain ratio measure, then, is defined as follows:

$$Gainratio(E, A) = \frac{Gain(E, A)}{Split(E, A)}$$

In the release 8 of C4.5 (Quinlan, 1996b), the gain ratio computed for binary splits on continuous attributes is further modified in order to improve predictive accuracy.

Good and Card (1971) provide a Bayesian analysis of the diagnostic process with reference to errors. They assume a utility measure $u(i, j)$ for accepting class c_j when the correct class is actually c_i. Based on that they developed a selection criterion which takes the optimisation of utility into account.

4.5.3 Representational Aspects in Decision Tree Learning

Continuous Attributes. Quinlan's original ID3 algorithm handles attributes with discrete values only. Unfortunately, many problem domains contain continuous descriptors, such as height or weight, which are difficult to handle discretely. The ID3 algorithm does not utilise the implicit information contained in the fact that the values of an attribute are (meaningfully) ordered. As a consequence, the original ID3 algorithm has been extended in C4.5 (Quinlan, 1993a) to handle continuous attributes as well. Quinlan's model trees (Quinlan, 1993b) can also generate continuous output functions. The basic idea is to find a binary split on the value range. For that purpose all values $v_1, ..., v_m$ that occur in the actually given examples are considered and ordered according to their values. Subsequently every possible split by choosing a threshold between v_i and v_{i+1} for all $i \in \{1, ..., m-1\}$ are considered and the best split is chosen.

Unknown Attribute Values. In a number of applications it may happen that an example is not completely described, i.e. that some of its attribute values are missing. This may be due to missing measurements of certain attributes, errors in or incompleteness of reports etc. For example, when dealing with large historical databases, often some values for attributes are unknown. In medical cases, not every patient has a specific test taken, hence, it is rather normal that some values are missing. However, one standard approach to cope with the problem of unknown values is to estimate the value using the given examples which have a specified value. This approach is taken in, e.g., ASSISTANT (Cestnik, Kononenko, & Bratko, 1987) as well as in C4.5 (Quinlan, 1993a).

However, one can actually distinguish at least the following reasons for the missing values which suggest different treatments: missing because not important (don't care), missing because not measured, and missing because not applicable (e.g. a question like 'Are you pregnant' is not applicable to male patients). These reasons could be very valuable to exploit in growing a tree or in concept learning in general.

Splitting strategies. It is interesting to note that if an attribute has more than two values it may still be useful to partition the value set only into two subsets. This guarantees that the decision tree will contain only binary splits. The problem with a naive implementation of this idea is that it may require 2^{n-1} evaluations where n is the number of attribute values. It has been proved by Breiman et al. (1984) that for the special case of only two class values of the examples, there exists an optimal split with no more than $n - 1$ comparisons. In the general case, however, heuristic methods must be used.

One simple idea to deal with that problem is as follows: examples are ordered by the values of the attribute in question and then the best split is chosen, which divides the examples into two disjoint sets according to their ordering relation. This idea has been implemented, e.g. in CART (Breiman et al., 1984) and in C4.5 (Quinlan, 1993a).

4.5.4 Overfitting and Tree Pruning

From a statistical point of view, the decision tree learning algorithm of Figure 4.8 has the drawback that it tends to overfit the data. That is, the learned tree is too large and, as a consequence, classifies less accurate than a smaller tree would do. This is basically due to noise in the training data. Two main methods have been studied to overcome this problem:

1. Modify the evaluation function to terminate search when no attribute is considered to provide *significant* information about the class (see e.g. Quinlan (1986)).
2. Prune the obtained decision tree to reduce its complexity while keeping its classification accuracy at a reasonable level (see Breiman et al. (1984), Quinlan (1993a), Weiss and Indurkhya (1994), or Weiss and Kulikowski (1991)).

It is widely assumed that pruning after generating the full decision tree is the more effective method (Breiman et al., 1984). A number of pruning techniques have been proposed. Pruning may occur in different ways:

- The tree may be pruned beginning with its leaf nodes (see Quinlan (1987)).
- Pruning may take place by merging intermediate nodes of the tree together. *Weakest link pruning* (Breiman et al., 1984) is an example for that.

Pruning, beginning with its leaf nodes, can be done as follows (see Quinlan (1987)): ascending in the tree beginning in its leaf nodes and testing at every non-leaf node whether replacing the subtree of node n by one of its leaf nodes would improve the classification accuracy. For determining the classification accuracy statistical tests have to be used on a separate set of test examples. These test examples must be statistically independent from the training examples used for learning the decision tree to be pruned. If a sufficient number of test examples are not easily available, this may cause a problem. One approach to deal with that problem is using cross validation (Breiman et al., 1984).

4.6 Inductive Logic Programming

Inductive Logic Programming (ILP) is a method to construct logic programs describing a target concept based on examples of this target concept. Although, ILP has limited practical applications so far, its potential seems promising. The ILP framework allows to incorporate flexibly domain knowledge into the learning process. Furthermore, ILP can learn relational concepts which can, for example, compare different attributes with each other in a concept definition. This is opposed to, e.g. decision tree learners like C4.5 , which tests one attribute at a time and compares the attribute rather with a constant value than with another attribute.

The term *Inductive Logic Programming* is motivated by the idea of considering the hypothesis space being the set of logic programs. Then, the result of learning will be a particular logic program. If the learning process is an inductive process, i.e. generating a more general logic program from a given set of examples, then the generation of a *logic program* takes place in an *inductive* way. The field of inductive logic programming comprises a number of techniques and implemented systems which can be subsumed under this idea. One particularly appealing idea in this field is that background knowledge can easily be incorporated into the framework. That is, the hypothesis space can be shaped by describing certain knowledge known to the user a priori, by giving a partial logic program. Then, the input to the learning system is both, training examples as well as a partial logic program. The output is a completed logic program. Since the hypothesis space is the set of logic programs, or at least a subset of these, the descriptional power of what can be learned is substantially larger than that of propositional learners like the decision tree learner of section 4.5. In the following, the central ideas of inductive logic programming will be presented.

One of the very early systems which incorporated relational background knowledge into the generalisation process was Michalski's INDUCE(Michalski, 1983b). Inspiring for many of the current approaches was the work on model inference by Shapiro (1983), Plotkin's work on least general generalisation (Plotkin, 1969), the work by Emde, Habel, and Rollinger (1983) on MOBAL and its predecessors, and the work by Sammut and Banerji (1986) on the interactive learning system MARVIN.

4.6.1 A Categorisation of ILP Systems

ILP systems can be categorised according to a number of dimensions, just as general inductive learning systems.

- Batch learning vs. incremental learning
  either are all examples presented at the beginning of the learning process or they are provided piece by piece.
- Interactive vs. non-interactive learning.
  That is, if a learning system may consult the user/expert during its learning process for, e.g. obtaining feedback on the correctness of its (intermediate) conclusions, the learner is called *interactive*.
- Learning from scratch vs. using background knowledge.
  That is, learning systems which only take the presented examples into account vs. learning systems which consider further knowledge in addition to training examples. In the ILP context, the background knowledge is usually a partial program (or theory of the domain) which is completed or altered based on the provided examples. If the program is substantially modified in order to fit the given examples, the learning system is also called a *theory revisor*.

Interactive ILP systems include the MIS system (Shapiro, 1983), MARVIN (Sammut & Banerji, 1986), CLINT (De Raedt & Bruynooghe, 1989, 1992), CIGOL (Muggleton & Buntine, 1988), MOBAL (Morik, Wrobel, Kietz, & Emde, 1993) and others. Work on systems based on inverting resolution include Rouveirol (1991), Muggleton and Buntine (1988), Buntine (1989).

Interactive ILP systems typically learn multiple predicates from a small set of examples and by interaction with the user. The user interaction often implies the learning of multiple predicates, since for learning a complex concept, the user gives often hints using less complex concepts which, however, need in turn to be learned since they are initially unknown to the learning system.

Empirical Inductive Logic Programming. A number of ILP systems target at learning a single predicate from a large set of examples. These systems are called *empirical ILP systems* in De Raedt (1992). Examples of such systems are FOIL (Quinlan, 1990), mFOIL (Džeroski & Lavrač, 1991; Džeroski & Bratko, 1992), GOLEM (Muggleton & Feng, 1990), LINUS (Lavrač, Džeroski, & Grobelnik, 1991), MARKUS (Grobelnik, 1992) and others.

Definition 4.1. *Given background knowledge B, a hypothesis h and a set of examples E, the hypothesis h is said to cover an example $e \in E$ with respect to the background knowledge B, if $B \cup h \models e$. That is, a function 'covers' can be defined as follows:*

$$covers(B, h, E) := \{e \in E | B \cup h \models e\}.$$

In practice, this definition of coverage involves the problem that it may be difficult or even algorithmically impossible[10] to determine whether a particular example is entailed by the given background knowledge and a chosen hypothesis.

Most often, e.g. in the systems MIS (Shapiro, 1983) or CIGOL (Muggleton & Buntine, 1988), the SLD-resolution proof procedure[11] with bounded or unbounded depth is used for testing whether an example is entailed by a hypothesis h and the given background knowledge B.

Usually there are two types of background knowledge distinguished: *extensional* background knowledge and *intensional* background knowledge. The *extensional background knowledge* is restricted to be a set of ground facts; i.e. background knowledge is extensional if it contains single literals with constants as arguments only. This is obviously a fairly strong constraint on the expressive power of background knowledge.

Opposed to that is *intensional background knowledge* allowed to contain non-ground clauses as well. That is, it may contain Horn clauses of more than a single literal and a clause may contain variables as well. Most of the empirical ILP systems are using the extensional notion of coverage. Interactive ILP systems, on the other hand, are mostly adopting the idea of intensional coverage.

In the following, ways of generalisation in the ILP framework will be discussed. For that purpose, a few more technical terms are defined.

Definition 4.2. *Given a language L, a* **generalisation operator** ρ *maps a clause c to a set of (more general) clauses $\rho(c)$ which are generalizations of c. That is,*

$$\rho(c) = \{c' \in \mathcal{L} |]' \succ]\},$$

where $\succ$ is the 'more general than' relation.

There are basically two possible ways to generalise a given clause:

- Substitute the involved terms by more general terms. For example, replace a constant by a variable.
- Remove a literal from the body of a clause.

Relative least general generalisation. Plotkin Plotkin (1969) developed his notion of *least general generalisation*. The least general generalisation considers two clauses c_1, c_2 and produces a third clause c_3 which is the clause that is least more general than both of the clauses c_1 and c_2 together.

For defining exactly what this means, we define a least general generalisation *(lgg)* for the parts of a clause first. That is, we define *(lgg)* for terms, atoms, and literals.

---

[10] It may be algorithmically impossible, if the used language is not decidable.
[11] See Lloyd (1987) for details.

Definition 4.3. *The **least general generalisation** $lgg(e_1, e_2)$ of two syntactical expressions e_1, e_2 is defined as follows. For e_1 and e_2 being*
terms: *$lgg(t_1, t_2)$ is given by*

1. $lgg(t, t) = t$,
2. $lgg(f(s_1, ..., s_n), f(t_1, .., t_n)) = f(lgg(s_1, t_1), ..., lgg(s_n, t_n))$,
3. $lgg(f(s_1, ..., s_m), g(t_1, ..., t_n)) = V$, *where $f \neq g$, and $V_{f(s_1,...,s_m),g(t_1,...,t_n)}$ is a variable,*
4. $lgg(s, t) = V_{s,t}$, *where $s \neq t$ and at least one of s and t is a variable.*

atoms:

1. $lgg(p(s_1, ..., s_n), p(t_1, ..., t_n)) = p(lgg(s_1, t_1), ..., lgg(s_n, t_n))$, *if atoms have the same predicate symbol p,*
2. $lgg(p(s_1, ..., s_m), q(t_1, ..., t_n))$ *is undefined if $p \neq q$.*

literals:

1. *if L_1 and L_2 are atoms, then $lgg(L_1, L_2)$ is computed as defined above,*
2. *if both L_1 and L_2 are negative literals, $L_1 = \overline{A_1}$ and $L_2 = \overline{A_2}$, then $lgg(L_1, L_2) = lgg(\overline{A_1}, \overline{A_2}) = \overline{lgg(A_1, A_2)}$,*
3. *if L_1 is a positive and L_2 a negative literal, or vice versa, $lgg(L_1, L_2)$ is undefined.*

clauses: *let $c_1 = \{L_1, ..., L_m\}$ and $c_2 = \{K_1, ..., K_n\}$. Then $lgg(c_1, c_2) = \{L_{ij} = lgg(L_i, K_j) | L_i \in c_1, K_j \in c_2$ and $lgg(L_i, K_j)$ is defined$\}$.*

Example

For each of the given types of syntactical expressions follow examples:
terms: $lgg(a, a) = a$. $lgg(a, b) = V_{a,b}$. It is important to note that if a variable is introduced for a pair of terms, then for every occurrence of this pair, the *same* variable is introduced. For example, $lgg(f(a, a), f(b, b)) = f(lgg(a, b), lgg(a, b)) = f(V_{a,b}, V_{a,b})$.
atoms: $lgg(p(a), p(b)) = p(lgg(a, b)) = p(V_{a,b})$.
$lgg(q(f(a, b), c), q(a, c)) = q(lgg(f(a, b), a), lgg(c, c)) = q(V_{f(a,b),a}, c)$.
$lgg(p(a), q(a, a))$ is undefined.
literals: $lgg(q(a, b), \overline{q(a, a)})$ is undefined.
clauses: $lgg((p(a, b) \leftarrow q(a, c), r(c, b)), (p(d, e) \leftarrow q(d, f), r(f, e))) = p(V_{a,d}, V_{b,e}) \leftarrow q(V_{a,d}, V_{c,f}), r(V_{c,f}, V_{b,e})$.

Now we are ready for the definition of *relative least general generalisation* (rlgg) as follows:

Definition 4.4. *The **relative least general generalisation** of two clauses c_1 and c_2 is their least general generalisation $lgg(c_1, c_2)$ relative to background knowledge $\mathcal{B}$.*

That means for $\mathcal{B}$ being a collection K of ground literals and c_1, c_2 being two atoms A_1, A_2 respectively:

$$rlgg(A_1, A_2) = lgg((A_1 \leftarrow K), (A_2 \leftarrow K)).$$

Inverse resolution. Muggleton and Buntine (1988) introduced *inverse resolution* as a general technique to ILP. The basic idea is to invert the normal resolution step of the resolution proof procedure.[12]

Resolution of predicate logical clauses involves the substitution of general terms by less general terms. Usually, variables are turned into constants of functions of variables. For inverse resolution, this process needs to be inverted. For example, constants are replaced by variables. The inverse process, however, involves a slight complication compared to the usual substitution process: It requires that the substitution process of constants by variables keeps a record of which occurrence of a constant is replaced by which variable. See the following example:

Example

Let $A_1 = p(f(V_1), V_2)$ be an atom being substituted by $\theta\{V_1/a, V_2/a\}$. That is, $A_1\theta = p(f(a), a)$. Clearly, there should be an inverse substitution θ^{-1} which, applied to $A_1\theta$, results in A_1.

Therefore, $\theta^{-1} = \{(a, \langle 1 \rangle)/V_1, (a, \langle 2, 1 \rangle)/V_2\}$ where the index after the term to be replaced indicates which occurrence of the term is to be replaced by the following term.

In the following, inverse resolution is less formally treated and rather examples are given than lengthy formal definitions.

Example

Assume the following background knowledge:
$B = \{b_1 = father(paul, peter), b_2 = youngster(peter)\}$.
Assume the current hypothesis $h = \emptyset$ and the following positive example $e_1 = childof(peter, paul)$ is presented.
Inverse resolution attempts to generalise from the given knowledge by assuming the given example had been derived from the background knowledge. That is, by assuming the example e_1 is the result of a resolution step. If e_1 is the result of a resolution step, there must be a clause c as follows: $c = (e_1 \leftarrow b_1)$ or $c = (e_1 \leftarrow b_2)$. This, however, would not yet constitute a generalisation. The mentioned clauses can rather be deductively derived from B and e_1. In order to introduce a generalisation process, inverse substitution is used.
That is, in the positive example e_1 a constant is turned into a variable by choosing an inverse substitution like $\theta^{-1} = \{paul/x\}$. This results in the clause $c_1 = (e_1\theta^{-1} \leftarrow b_1\theta^{-1}) = (childof(peter, x) \leftarrow father(x, peter)$.
This first generalisation step resulting in clause c_1 may be followed by a second one, again taking the available background knowledge B into account. In order to derive c_1 by a resolution step involving the second part of the background knowledge, a clause like $c_2 = \{e_1\theta^{-1} \leftarrow$

---

[12] See chapter 2, appendix A, Lloyd (1987), Nilsson and Genesereth (1987) or (Russell & Norvig, 1995) for details on the resolution proof procedure.

$(b_1\theta^{-1}, b_2)\}$ or a more general one is needed. A more general clause than c_2 can be obtained by applying another inverse substitution θ_1^{-1} to c. Thus, for $\theta_1^{-1} = \{peter/y\}$ we obtain: $c_2 = c\theta_1^{-1} = childof(y, x) \leftarrow (father(x, y), younster(y))$.
c_2 is a fairly strong generalisation of the initially given facts in $\mathcal{B}$ and e_1.

This demonstrates the generalisation power of inverse resolution. However, it should also be noted that the same generalisation power poses the practical problem to contain the taken generalisation steps to those which are desired. That is, by using these syntactical operations, many clauses can be generated which do not make any sense. From the given example it can be seen that in the process of inverse resolution, there were two operations involved which are inherently *non-deterministic*.

- The choice of the emerging clause, i.e. which part of the background knowledge is used in order to derive the example or an intermediately generated clause, such as c_1 in the example above. In most cases, there are many options to choose from.
- The other choice regards which particular inverse substitution θ^{-1} is used. The most conservative choice for θ_{con}^{-1} in the example above had been the empty substitution. This, however, had led to no generalisation but rather to a mere deductive derivation of the following clauses:
  $childof(peter, paul) \leftarrow father(paul, peter)$ and
  $childof(peter, paul) \leftarrow (father(paul, peter), youngster(peter))$. On the other hand, the most general inverse substitution for obtaining the first clause had been $\theta_g^{-1} = \{peter/x, paul/y\}$, which replaces both involved constants by variables.

The above used a generalisation operator for generating a new clause and is called the *absorption operator* (the **V** operator). It was already used in the early ILP systems MARVIN (Sammut & Banerji, 1986) and CIGOL (Muggleton & Buntine, 1988).

CIGOL uses also several other operators. One important operator among them is *intra-construction*, which is an instance of the **W** operator. A **W** operator combines two **V** operators and thereby introduces a new predicate. The process of introducing new predicates which are not available in the background knowledge or in the examples is called *predicate invention*.

A unified framework, introduced in Muggleton (1991), for relative least general generalisation and inverse resolution proposes to use the *most specific inverse resolution* for each step in the generalisation process.

Example

Considering the example for the inverse resolution the most specific inverse resolution would choose the empty set for every inverse substitution step. That is, $\theta_1^{-1} = \emptyset$ and $\theta_2^{-1} = \emptyset$ which results in the clauses $(childof(peter, paul) \leftarrow father(paul, peter))$ and

$(childof(peter, paul) \leftarrow father(paul, peter), youngster(peter))$ respectively.

In GOLEM and CIGOL are relative least general generalizations implemented which use the most specific linear derivations. More details are given in Muggleton (1991).

The relative least general generalisation can be considered as bottom-up generalisation, i.e. starting from the ground facts and becoming more general step by step. Opposed to that also a top-down approach can be taken. That is, starting with general hypotheses and becoming more specific step by step. For that purpose, we have to consider ways of systematically specialising hypotheses in the ILP framework.

Specialisation techniques. For specialisation we are interested in operators which can be applied step by step to a given hypothesis. Usually, the operators for specialisation are called *refinement operators*.

Definition 4.5. *Given a language bias* $\mathcal{L}$*, a* **refinement operator** ρ *maps a clause c to a set of clauses* $\rho(c)$ *which are specialisations (or refinements) of c:*

$$\rho(c)\{c'|c' \in \mathcal{L}, c \succ c'\}.$$

A refinement operator determines normally only the set of minimal specialisations (the most general specialisations) of a clause. For doing that, a specialisation operator can make use of the following two types of syntactical operations:

- Apply a substitution to a clause. This makes the terms occurring in the clause less general, hence the corresponding predicates apply to less objects or tuples of objects respectively.
- Add a literal to the body of a clause. This introduces an additional condition to the body of the clause and hence makes it less general.

After considering the processes of both, the generalisation and the specialisation of a given clause, the general structure of most of the ILP systems can be sketched by giving a simplified view of the model inference system (MIS) (Shapiro, 1983); see Figure 4.10.

In principle, in the *specialisation loop* as well as in the *covering loop* different stopping criteria are possible. This may be of interest for the following two reasons:

- for handling noisy data; i.e. not all positive examples have necessarily to be covered and there may be negative examples which could possibly be covered by the hypothesis.
- to control the hypothesis generation process beyond the requirement of being complete and consistent with the given examples. This can be considered to represent a search bias.

Initialise hypothesis h to a (possibly empty) set of clauses in $\mathcal{L}$.
repeat
   Read the next example e
     /* *specialisation loop* */
     if e is a negative example and e is covered by some clause in h
     then delete all incorrect clauses in h
     endif
     /* *generalisation loop* */
     if e is a positive example and e is not covered by h
     then generate a clause c which covers e,
        but none of the negative examples presented so far
     endif
   until h is complete and consistent.
   output hypothesis h as result.
forever

Figure 4.10. A simplified skeleton of the model inference system (MIS).

Initialise hypothesis $h := \emptyset$ to the empty set.
Let E be the set of all (positive and negative) examples.
Initialise $c := T(x_1, ..., x_n) \leftarrow$.
while *there is a positive example $e_{pos} \in E$ which is not covered by h* **do**
   while *there is a negative example $e_{neg} \in E$*
       which is covered by a clause $c \in h$ **do**
   remove c from h: $h := h \setminus \{c\}$.
   repeat
     determine (heuristically) the best refinement $c_{best} \in \rho(c)$.
     $c := c_{best}$.
   until *c does not cover e_{neg}.*
   Add c to h: $h := h \cup \{c\}$.
   endwhile
   Remove all positive examples from E which are covered by h.
endwhile

Figure 4.11. The general structure of an ILP learning algorithm which learns by stepwise specialisation. (a top-down ILP algorithm.)

Besides the hypothesis generation process sketched in Figure 4.11, ILP systems, such as FOIL (Quinlan, 1990), may also have an additional pre-processing of the examples. This pre-processing handles missing data and it may supplement negative examples to the training examples by using the *closed-world assumption*. Further, ILP systems may do some post-processing with the generated hypothesis. Such post-processing may include a pruning process, like in FOCL (Pazzani, Brunk, & Silverstein, 1991) (In FOIL such pruning is done after a single clause is generated.) Further post-processing may concern the removal of irrelevant literals from particular clauses in the hypothesis or even the removal of entire clauses from the hypothesis. Reason for the removal of

- **clauses** may be that after the hypothesis has been completely generated, those positive examples covered by a clause c may also be covered by the other clauses in h. Hence, the coverage of the positive examples of h and $h \setminus \{c\}$ may be the same.
- **literals** may be that the additional condition the literal imposes on the applicability of the clause, does not exclude any of the negative examples in the training set. Such a case may occur if the literal was added to a clause in order to not cover negative examples. However, these negative examples may also be excluded by literals which have been subsequently added to the clause.

In general, such post-processing can also be used to cope with noisy domains to avoid overfitting the data. For noisy domains, the literals and clauses to be removed would not clearly be irrelevant. Instead other criteria of rather statistical nature need to be used to determine what to remove from the generated hypothesis.

4.6.2 Some ILP Systems

In the following, an incomplete selection of ILP systems is characterised by the hypothesis language they use as well as by special features they exhibit.

FOIL. FOIL (Quinlan, 1990) uses a hypothesis language which is restricted to function-free program clauses. Both, the training examples as well as the background knowledge are function-free ground facts. Successor developments of FOIL, like FOIL2.0 (Quinlan, 1991) and FOIL4 (Cameron-Jones & Quinlan, 1993) allow, however, to specify types for each of the arguments of the predicates. This can drastically reduce the search space. As an example, consider a predicate like *likes-car-of-make(Fred, Mercedes)*. For these predicates the second argument will always be a car make and the first argument will be a person. Replacing such constants by variables should not imply that instead of *Fred* there may appear *VW* or *Ford*.

As a heuristic to find the 'best' specialisation, FOIL uses the criterion called *weighted information gain* based on the measures used in Quinlan's attribute-based decision tree learners, ID3 and C4.5 (Quinlan, 1993a).

GOLEM. In GOLEM (Muggleton & Feng, 1990), similar to FOIL, both training examples as well as the background knowledge, are restricted to ground facts. However, in contrast to FOIL, GOLEM can handle functions. Further, background knowledge can be provided using non-ground Horn clauses. These are converted by GOLEM into a collection of ground facts, using SLD-resolution up to to a fixed depth h. GOLEM is based on the notion of *relative least general generalisation* as introduced by Plotkin (1969). Thus, GOLEM is a cautious generaliser.

MOBAL. The MOBAL system (Morik, 1991; Morik et al., 1993) which is based on earlier developments, such as the BLIP system (Morik, 1989) is an integrated knowledge acquisition and learning system. The entire system consists of a number of tools, including a *model acquisition tool* which generates abstract rule models from a set of particular rules given. Further, MOBAL contains a *sort taxonomy tool* which generates taxonomies of constant terms occurring in predicates. That is, a restricting set of types is generated. These types are used when generalisations are made by using typed variables for the different arguments of a predicate. By this process, not only the search space is reduced, also the accuracy of the constructed generalizations can significantly be improved.[13]

The ILP learner in MOBAL is RDT (Kietz & Wrobel, 1992) which learns multiple predicate definitions. MOBAL also contains an inference engine which is used to generate new facts upon RDT's induction of new predicate definitions.

The training examples for MOBAL are function-free ground facts. The used predicates are typed, either user-provided types or automatically generated ones.

The *rule models* used in MOBAL serve as templates for those predicate definitions which are allowed to be generated based on the training examples. The rule models represent a further strong language bias on the hypothesis language and can either be user specified or automatically generated.

A *rule model* uses first and second order variables as follows: a rule model R has the form $T \leftarrow L_1, L_2, ..., L_m$, where T is the target predicate to be defined. Each L_i is a *literal schema*. A literal schema is given by

$$L_i = Q_i(Y_1, ..., Y_{n_i})$$

or by

$$L_i = \neg Q_i(Y_1, ..., Y_{n_i})$$

All Y_j variables are first order variables which are assumed to be all-quantified. The variable Q_i is a (second order) predicate variable that can only be instantiated by predicates of the respective arity n_i (.i.e, predicates with n_i places).

Example

In order to learn a predicate definition like

$$(childof(x, y) \leftarrow father(y, x), youngster(x))$$

a rule model like

$$Q(x, y) \leftarrow Q_2(y, x) \wedge Q_3(x)$$

is necessary.

---

[13] Provided that appropriate sort taxonomy was generated.

The system is normally supplied with a number of different rule models. In searching for suitable predicate definitions, the system tries all supplied rule models to find an instantiation which allows to generate a rule which fits the training examples. An instantiation of a rule model is not only required to match the specified arity of each of the involved predicate variables. Also the type of the predicate's arguments have to match the type of the variables which are assumed with an already instantiated predicate variable. For example, if the target predicate comes with type restrictions for its arguments, these type restrictions are imposed on all those predicates in the body of the rule, which contain these variables.

Although the idea of rule models is very powerful in restricting the search space, in practice the constrained hypothesis space left to be searched is often still substantial.

GRENDEL. A similar idea is behind the ILP system GRENDEL (Cohen, 1992). GRENDEL allows the specification of an antecedent description grammar, which describes the set of allowed clauses. Thereby, such grammar may specify particular predicates which have to occur in a clause, or classes of predicates which may be used alternatively and similar options are given for the arguments of the predicates.

Example

The following grammar may be specified:

```
body(file-attack(A,B,C,D,E,F)) -> rels(A,B,C,D,E,F).

rels(A,B,C,D,E,F) -> [].
rels(A,B,C,D,E,F) -> rel(A,B,C,D,E,F),rels(A,B,C,D,E,F).

rel(A,B,C,D,E,F) -> pred2(X,Y)
                    where subset ([X,Y],[A,B,C,D,E,F]).
...
pred2(X,Y) -> [X=Y].
pred2(X,Y) -> [adj(X,Y)].
pred2(X,Y) -> [not(adj(X,Y))].
...
```

Where 'body' stands for the body of the clause to be learned. Each expression on the left side can be replaced by the corresponding right side. Atomic predicates are only '=', 'adj' and 'not'. All non-terminal symbols have to be replaced by terminal symbols (atomic predicates).

By such a grammar, the user has a powerful mean to constrain GRENDEL's search for a hypothesis which fits the given data. Cohen demonstrates, how GRENDEL allows to specify a grammar to emulate FOIL (Quinlan, 1990) or FOCL (Pazzani et al., 1991).

LINUS. LINUS (Lavrač et al., 1991; Lavrač, Džeroski, Pirnat, & Križman, 1993; Lavrač & Džeroski, 1994) is a learning system, which can learn relational concepts by transforming relations into (propositional) attributes. It is essentially an attribute-based propositional learner which can be extended to learn relations by incorporating background knowledge. The examples are given by an attribute-value based description. This description can be optionally extended by additional 'derived' attributes which are generated as functions of the original attributes. Background knowledge is used to define such additional attributes. The new attributes may be based on functions or predicates which apply to one or more of the original attributes of the training examples.

The operation of LINUS is divided into three stages:

1. Pre-processing:
   LINUS extends the attributes of the training examples by additional attributes which are determined by the user specified set of *utility predicates and functions*. Predicates may be relations among attribute values, which are represented as binary attribute.

2. The pre-processed examples are fed into an attribute-value learner. LINUS contains three different attribute-value learning algorithms. CN22 (Clark & Boswell, 1991) is a further development of the AQ algorithms. ASSISTANT (Cestnik et al., 1987) is a top-down inductive decision tree learner which is a refinement of the ID3 algorithm.

3. Post-processing of the learned *if-then rules*. The post-processing which transforms the generated if-then rules on an attribute-value basis into logic programming notation. That is, into a set of deductive hierarchical database clauses.

4.6.3 Discussion on Inductive Logic Programming

Inductive Logic Programming (ILP) has been covered in relative length compared to other learning techniques. Reason being that the flexible integration of domain knowledge appears very promising. In part III it will be argued that effective learning approaches need to utilise available domain knowledge in order to improve their performance: that is to allow learning from fewer examples and to improve the reliability of the learning result. While ILP allows a truly flexible formulation of domain knowledge, the types of domain knowledge that can be specified are still fairly restricted. For example, uncertainties cannot be easily incorporated. Incorporating 'numerical learning primitives,' such as performing a regression analysis among certain attributes is becoming available in systems, such as PROGOL (Muggleton, 1995).

On the other hand, the ILP framework introduces a huge number of potential generalisations by considering all sorts of relations among attributes. For many applications those relations may be largely irrelevant, which implies for those cases that the ILP framework requires much more training examples or complementing domain knowledge, than less powerful (attribute-value based) learners. However, in many systems, the complementing knowledge can be considered as providing additional attributes for the examples. That is, the space of potential generalisation is simply increased. This may be seen most pronounced perhaps in the system LINUS (Lavrač & Džeroski, 1994).

In other words, mechanisms are needed where domain knowledge can be used to dramatically restrict the search space for generalisations as well as ways of controlling the search order are needed. The system GRENDEL (Cohen, 1992) uses grammars to determine the shape of possible generalizations. Similarly, the system MOBAL (Morik et al., 1993) allows to provide templates for the learning result. See also Lavrač and Džeroski (1997) or Nienhuys-Cheng and Wolf (1997) for more recent work on ILP.

4.7 Discussion on Learning

As we have seen, a large number of approaches have been proposed on how to construct symbolic descriptions of concepts, classification rules or, more generally speaking, functions and relations from a number of instances of the learning target. A number of these approaches have been usefully employed, while many others are still in the realm of research and will hopefully lead to useful applications at a later stage. Some of these approaches have been presented in this chapter.

Whether a learning algorithm has been successfully employed depends on a number of factors. Firstly, it depends on whether the learning algorithm was applied to a suitable domain at all. This is a less trivial issue than it may seem: on the one hand, individual researchers who develop a particular learning algorithm have often only very limited access to application domains.[14] On the other hand, it is usually very difficult to judge in advance whether a domain is suitable for a particular learning algorithm. Secondly and more generally speaking, the success and failure of a learning attempt for a given problem depends crucially on choosing a suitable representation of the training data and choosing a suitable learning technique that searches within a reasonably restricted set of potential learning targets. The representation of the training data as well as the choice of the learning technique may actually prevent the learner from being able to express a suitable concept or function as the learning result. Conversely, if the space of potential target concepts is too large, the available data may not suffice to rule out all those candidate concepts which do not represent acceptable solutions to the learning task.

---

[14] This situation has been alleviated to a certain degree by the establishment of the University of California at Irvine Machine Learning repository, which holds a fairly large number of data sets which have been used by Machine Learning researchers in the past as well as a number of Machine Learning algorithms. All the data is globally accessibly via FTP or the World Wide Web at the address "http://www.ics.uci.edu/~mlearn/Machine-Learning.html".

There are a number of other research directions not discussed in this section. Those include model selection, i.e. the idea of splitting the hypothesis space into multiple sub-hypothesis spaces and then to apply certain techniques to pick a good sub-hypothesis space for searching for a most consistent hypothesis (see Kearns, Mansour, Ng, and Ron (1997) or Kohavi and John (1997)). Another issue is combining multiple classifiers which were learned from multiple training data sets, which are obtained by resampling techniques. That is, by constructing new data sets from a given data set, e.g. by choosing subsets of the original data set. The combination of multiple such classifiers has been demonstrated to substantially improve the accuracy of the combined classifier in many domains (see Quinlan (1996a), Breiman (1996)). Other approaches to learning include Bayesian learning and lazy learners. Bayesian learning creates probabilistic classifiers based on the frequency distribution of the attribute values for each class of objects. (See section 2.3, or Heckerman (1991), Heckerman, Geiger, and Chickering (1995), Suzuki (1996), or Singh and Provan (1996) for more details.) Lazy learners merely store the data they receive without processing. Only when a demand to classify or react in other ways occurs, lazy learners start processing their stored data to find an answer. Nearest neighbour classifiers and case-based reasoning[15] are probably the best-known class of algorithms of this kind (see Aha (1997) for a recent survey). Other research is devoted to problems of sequential decision making where feedback from the environment may be received only in a delayed fashion. That is, only after a possibly large number of decisions has been made, the overall sequence is evaluated. A robot on the search for a new power supply may be scenario for that. Reinforcement learning techniques, e.g., Temporal difference learning (Sutton, 1988) or Q-learning (Watkins, 1989) and further refinements of those have been developed to deal with such problems (see Kaelbling (1996), Sutton and Barto (1998)).

Progress on the integration of learning techniques with already available data and knowledge in a system is needed. A relatively new area of significant interest became known under the title *knowledge discovery and datamining* (KDD). The objective here is to integrate databases with learning techniques or with other, more traditional, techniques of data analysis, primarily with statistics (see Fayyad, Piatetsky-Shapiro, Smyth, and Uthurusamy (1996), Weiss and Indurkhya (1997) or Simoudis, Han, and Fayyad (1996), Heckerman, Mannila, Pregibon, and Uthurusamy (1997) for the proceedings of the recent KDD conferences).

So far, most of the learning techniques result in decision trees, logical expressions, or combinations of linear threshold functions, i.e. neural networks as discussed in part II. However, there is no reason to believe, that there are no more alternative ways of expressing functions or relations, which may be more suited to certain types of problems.

Yet another aspect of human learning which is not well matched by machine learning techniques is the fact that humans learn many concepts in parallel.

---

[15] See Kolodner (1993) or Leake (1996).

Humans refine and sharpen their understanding of concepts continuously; they advance on learning multiple concepts in parallel. They integrate their learning into their entire body of knowledge and reasoning capabilities. See also chapter 15 for further discussion on human knowledge and its acquisition. A recent exposition of many learning techniques is found in Mitchell (1997). Current research on symbolic learning is reported at many places, among them the International Conference on Machine Learning, the European Conference on Machine Learning, the major general conferences on AI, the *Machine Learning Journal* and a number of other journals often covering not only symbolic learning, such as the journal *Intelligent Data Analysis*.

5. Summary of the Symbolic Paradigm

A large body of research has been conducted in the symbolic paradigm of AI. The symbolic paradigm, today, embraces a large number of ideas, approaches and techniques addressing a wide variety of different problems. Hence, it is difficult to select a few techniques which would justly represent the techniques assembled in the symbolic paradigm. However, by and large, all the presented techniques had in common that they assumed, to a varying degree, a declarative representation of either what can be called task knowledge,[1] expertise, or a more or less declarative description of a domain in which an AI system should function. The latter is often called domain knowledge.[2]

Although, in a symbol system, knowledge has to use symbol structures, knowledge is not really representable by structures at the symbol level only. The symbols need to be complemented by appropriate processes which deal with the symbols, which perform some sort of interpretation.[3] The idea of the knowledge level allows a splitting of the symbol level into two sub-levels: the knowledge and the remainder, which is still called 'symbol level'. This split is expected to support the systematic development of both.

The various reasoning techniques presented in chapter 2 all assumed that a body of *knowledge* is represented in a respective formalism; hence they support the implementation of the idea of the knowledge level. The reasoning techniques provide means of automatically manipulating such represented knowledge in order to produce new 'pieces of knowledge'. Furthermore, those reasoning techniques endeavoured to ensure that the newly derived 'pieces of knowledge' are as valid as the knowledge from which they are derived. As mentioned above,

---

[1] Task knowledge refers only to knowledge of how to perform the task. This is opposed to knowledge about, e.g. the environment, which may rather serve as indirect means to perform the task.

[2] Furthermore, it should be noted that the term *knowledge* becomes less clear the more one thinks about it. Can we humans express all our knowledge, e.g. in language? What about subconscious thought processes? How do we distinguish knowledge from mere beliefs or opinions? It belongs rather to the realm of philosophy to discuss these issues. For introductions into this area, see books on epistemology, e.g. Musgrave (1993) or Lucey (1996).

[3] Even if the interpretation is only reflected in what is done with those symbols, i.e. *how* these symbols are manipulated or used to manipulate other symbols ..., as opposed to an explicit interpretation of symbols expressed in other symbols of some meta-language, such as logical languages, etc.

such reasoning techniques have been developed in philosophy as early as by the ancient Greeks. In AI, however, it was realised that classical logic[4] is by far not sufficient for modelling human reasoning processes. In particular, so-called non-demonstrative reasoning has not yet seen suitable formalisations. Approaches like those under the title non-monotonic reasoning or similar, are attempts to rectify that situation. However, scrutinising the topic of *knowledge* further, reveals that much deeper problems exist: There seems to be no clear boundary of what knowledge needs to be explicitly stated to precisely characterise human common sense. This difficulty led to the coining of terms like the *frame problem* or the *qualification problem.*

Besides these problems, which result in extensive explicit descriptions of the relevant knowledge for an AI system, there is another major problem: The computational complexity of processing the encoded knowledge effectively within a practically feasible time frame. To determine whether a proposition is a logical consequence of a set of propositions, is already **NP**-complete in propositional logic.[5] Taking the full expressive power of first-order predicate logic makes it much worse. First-order predicate logic is semi-decidable, i.e. there is no algorithm which will always terminate and will produce the correct answer! Although substantial effort has been put into alleviating the computational complexity of reasoning in practical situations, it is still a major hurdle for developing useful knowledge-based systems, which are able to reason in acceptable periods of time. Besides reasoning techniques, substantial effort has been devoted to the development of learning techniques, which produce knowledge to be represented in a declarative way and which is amenable to reasoning techniques as those mentioned before. Furthermore, it has also been indicated that substantial successes in limited application domains have been achieved with approaches of the symbolic paradigm, most notable, the development of expert systems and knowledge-based systems for a wide variety of applications.

Besides these successes, one has to concede that even the development of limited AI applications is normally still very labour-intensive, as the proper modelling of an expert's knowledge and the peculiarities of an application domain are not at all straightforward with current techniques. In that context, it should be emphasised that the appealing idea of the knowledge level had only limited success. reason being that there is still a substantial gap between the knowledge an expert can easily express and the requirements of the formalisms for representing and processing knowledge developed thus far in the symbolic paradigm. Indeed, substantial areas of human knowledge are still not systematically addressed, as discussed in chapter 14. Besides the successes with handling

---

[4] Which roughly comprises both, propositional and predicate logic.

[5] That means, roughly speaking, that the number of computing steps increases exponentially in the worst case with the number of propositions involved. This represents a major practical problem even with today's fast computers, as the required computing time reaches very quickly the order of magnitude of days or even years.

specific AI applications, a general intelligent agent is still not in sight.[6] Hence, the debate whether that can be achieved in the symbolic paradigm at all is still going on.

---

[6] Although Nilsson (1995) is calling for targeting at the general intelligent agent again after AI research was content with application specific systems for a long time.

Part II

The Connectionist Paradigm

The second part of this book presents an introduction to the main ideas of neural network models, the technical vehicles of connectionism, which represents the major alternative to the classical, or symbolic paradigm of AI.

Chapter 6 presents the historical reasons for the re-emergence of neural networks under the title *connectionism* as an alternative approach to AI in the mid-1980s. In chapter 7, a collection of important connectionist computing and learning models are presented. This is not an exhaustive collection, but it should give a sufficiently clear picture of what types of ideas have been developed and it should convey the general 'flavour' of the paradigm.

However, these neural network models should not be equalled with connectionism as such. The term connectionism refers rather to the idea of understanding cognition and building large-scale intelligent systems using neural-network style computing models. Chapter 8 presents ideas for approaches that seek to accommodate symbols within a connectionist model. One such class of models are called *structured connectionist models*, which concern the (structured) arrangement of a large number of nodes and their interaction, rather than specific models of a single neuron.

Opposed to that are neural networks often used for a very specific technical application, e.g. they are used as general function approximator where a number of values of the target function are supplied as training data. Thus, the general term of *neural networks* refers mostly to the technical instrument as opposed to a general framework for understanding cognition and building intelligent systems. The more philosophical ideas behind connectionism will be treated in depth in part III.

6. Foundations of the Connectionist Paradigm

The re-emergence of neural networks, under the title *connectionism* as a paradigm for building intelligent systems, can probably be attributed to several sources that gained increasing influence simultaneously during the 1980s and culminated in the work of Rumelhart, McClelland, and the PDP Research Group (1986), which marks the beginning of the era of connectionism.

Section 6.1 presents the most important forces which lead to the re-emergence of neural networks under the title *connectionism*. It should be noted that there are two issues to be distinguished: neural networks as useful engineering devices for building, e.g., pattern classifiers; and connectionism which seeks to use neural network-like structures on a massively parallel basis in order to model, understand, and build intelligent systems. Section 6.2 provides basic concepts of the biological aspects of neural networks.

6.1 The Emergence of Connectionism

The re-emergence of the idea of neural networks as a general framework for building intelligent systems in the mid 1980s can probably be attributed to a number of developments which took place in adjacent fields around that time. The five most important reasons for the popularity neural networks enjoyed in the past are discussed below:

Development in micro-electronics. Advances in very large scale integration (VLSI) have made it much easier to build massively parallel machines, such as the Connection Machine (Hillis, 1985, 1987; Thiel, 1994), of *Thinking Machines Corp.*, which was the first commercial massively parallel computer expressly devoted to simulate intelligence and life. See Alspector and Allen (1987) for more general developments in that time, and Mead (1989) for fundamentals of the VLSI[1] design of neural networks. In the following years there was an increasing interest in neural network-like models of computation. While the limited processing power of conventional sequential machines was increasingly considered a major obstacle to more powerful computers, the area of parallel processing gained in interest. Thus, neural network models gave the hope to find effective ways to exploit parallelism in machines, as the biological

---

[1] VLSI stands for Very Large Scale Integration of electronic circuits.

role-model of the human brain apparently manages to use parallel processing for such marvellous performances.

Philosophical objections to symbolic AI. Strong support for connectionism also came from philosophical observations of human thought. Dreyfus (1972), Dreyfus and Dreyfus (1986), Dreyfus (1992), Winograd and Flores (1986), and others took the philosophy of Heidegger as a powerful argument against the possibility of (symbolic) AI.[2] They took Heidegger's investigations as evidence for the claim that a *description* of the human *thought* is totally different from symbolic structures. Dreyfus' main point was: Human cognition and understanding is based on social interaction. As a consequence, intelligent systems have to be embedded in a context in order to assign proper meaning to symbols and to adapt to changes. Dreyfus employs the Heideggerian phenomenological concept of *breakdown* to argue that the particular frame of mind of a person determines when and what particular objects come into one's mind. This shows, according to Dreyfus, that human thought does not use a fixed representation of the agent's environment. Depending on what has happened, human intelligence 'creates on the spot' an appropriate representation of what might be relevant for the intended course of action. Dreyfus also claims that human values and goals are only *implicitly* contained in the way people act within their environment.

The objects which constitute the outer world can change along with their properties. The values which are only implicitly contained in the particular course of action of an individual can completely change as well. Dreyfus claims that such a kind of profound change, which happens within the *ultimate context*, cannot be simulated by machines. The *ultimate context*, as Dreyfus (1972) calls it, is the backbone on which these profound changes happen. The changes are only understandable on the basis of some *ultimate context*, which is responsible for all the changes in behaviour, goals, intentions, values, etc., which human beings may encounter throughout their lives. The *ultimate context* according to Dreyfus, is in some sense *infinite* which implies that it cannot be represented by symbols at all.[3] In contrast to all that are computers, which *have* to represent values and goals as well as their 'view' of the world *explicitly* by symbols. Therefore, computers cannot behave like humans. See chapter 11 for more details.

Practical experiences in the symbolic paradigm. The practical experiences in AI until the mid-1980s, when work in AI was still almost exclusively in the symbolic paradigm, indicated rather severe difficulties in almost all areas of AI. The development of useful intelligent systems turned out to be much more difficult than initially expected.

---

[2] See chapter 11 for a more detailed presentation of the philosophical objections. This chapter also presents a more principled discussion of the symbol level and its weaknesses.

[3] At least it cannot be represented by a finite number of symbols.

While in the early years of AI, researchers hoped to succeed with developing general purpose heuristics which could deal with almost all types of problems, people realized later that systems need to be equipped with a substantial body of 'knowledge' to deal with a complex domain.

However, the process of knowledge acquisition turned out to be much more difficult than initially expected. Domain experts proved to have substantial problems in articulating their knowledge. Even describing a way of solving a given single problem with sufficient precision to be programmable, proved to be very hard. These experiences suggested, for some researchers, that the idea of symbol systems may be inappropriate after all.

The physiological metaphor. While human brains are capable of complex tasks, such as recognising faces very quickly, computers have severe problems of solving such tasks, although their computing speed may be much higher than the processing speed of a neuron. Clearly, the human brain works on a massively parallel basis, which is most likely responsible for the brain's astonishing performance. Thus, the idea of developing massively parallel computer systems in the style of an artificial neural network appeared promising.

The appeal to engineers. Many engineers welcomed the neural network models and the associated learning procedures, as they dealt with continuous values and the mathematical foundations of the techniques were continuous mathematics. This was the type of mathematics they were familiar with from their own discipline. This contrasted largely with the learning techniques which had been developed in the symbolic paradigm. Furthermore, the metaphor of brain-like computing attracted much more interest outside the immediate field of computer science than functionally comparable developments in the classical symbolic paradigm of AI. As a consequence, many engineering applications have been tried with neural network learning models. These experiments in turn drove the development of refined learning techniques for neural networks. Engineers often look at neural networks rather as general function approximators than as a paradigm for the development and understanding of comprehensively intelligent systems.

The following section presents some of the basics on biological neural networks. Artificial neural network models are presented in chapter 7.

6.2 Biological Neural Networks

Considering a natural intelligent system, e.g. a human being, it may be instructive to investigate the physiological basis of it. Nature my be a valuable source of inspiration for designing AI systems, though a complete 'reverse engineering' approach seems out of the question due to the overwhelming anatomical complexity of the human brain.

The human brain is made up of a vast network of neurons coupled with receptors and effectors. The input to the network is provided by millions of receptors while the output of the brain is transformed into effects on our body and the external world via effectors. The receptors continually monitor changes in the internal and external environment. Hundreds of thousands of cells control the effectors, such as muscles and the secretion of glands.

The human brain is made up of thousands of millions of neurons. A typical estimate is about 10^{10} to 10^{11}, i.e. 10 to 100 billion neurons. Many neurons have between 1,000 and 10,000 connections to other neurons in the brain. There are thousands of different types of neurons in the brain.[4] This includes neurons whose purpose has been identified as being specialised to the processing of sensory information. Those specialised neurons which deal directly with the signals coming from sensors, which are receptors for light, sound, touch, etc., are called sensor neurons. Other neurons are responsible to control our muscles and are, therefore, called motor neurons.

The brain can hardly be considered as a simple stimulus-response chain from receptors to effectors. The vast network of billions and billions of neurons is rather interconnected in extremely complex and diverse ways, including simple loops as well as complex feedback cycles. Thus, signals coming from the receptors are mixed with signals already travelling in this vast network resulting in a change of the signals travelling inside the network as well as to yield signals for controlling the effectors.

In that way, the brain, or Central Nervous System (CNS), manages to generate actions which depend on both the current stimulation as well as on some residue of past experiences. Past experiences may be reflected in current activities of the network, i.e. certain signals travelling inside the network as well as in the current pattern of connections.

As a consequence of the large variety of neurons in the brain,[5] it is impossible to speak of *the typical neuron*. However, a model of a neuron is sketched below, which captures some of the basic features and functionality found in many different types of neurons.

Today, more than forty properties of biological neurons are known to influence the neurons information processing capability. One distinguishes three different parts in biological neurons: a soma, axons, and dendrites (see Figure 6.1). Biological neurons are connected with each other. Their connections are called *synapses*. The axon may be considered as the output channel of the neuron which conveys its activation level to the synaptic connections with other neurons. The ends of the axons are called nerve terminals or *endbulbs*. The dendrites on the other hand act as the neuron's input receptors for signals coming from other neurons. They convey the input potential to the neuron's soma, i.e. to the neuron's body. The input potential in that case is also called post-synaptic potential. The neuron's soma, in particular where it connects to

---

[4] See e.g. Arbib (1989), Heimer (1994) for a more detailed outline of the anatomy of the human brain.

[5] There are more than 1,000 different types of neurons estimated to occur in the human brain.

the axon, i.e. in the *axon hillock*, acts as an accumulator of input potentials and/or as an amplifier of these signals.

The tips of the branches of the axon impinge upon other neurons or upon other effectors. The locus of interaction between an endbulb and the cell upon which it impinges is called a *synapse*, and we say that the cell with the endbulb *synapses upon* the cell with which the connection is made. In fact, we now know that axonal branches of some neurons can have many 'endbulbs' that allow them to make synapses along their lengths as well as their ends.

Although conduction of signals can go in either direction on the axon, most synapses tend to communicate activity to the dendrites or soma of the cell they synapse upon, when activity passes to the axon hillock and then down the axon to the terminal aborisation. The axon can be very long. For instance, a neuron that controls the big toe is rooted in the spinal cord and thus has an axon that runs the complete length of the leg. This enormous length of an axon contrasts sharply with what must be the very small size of many of the neurons in our heads, with over ten billion of them in such a small space. Small cells exist in the retina of our eyes, called amacrine cells, whose branchings cannot appropriately be labelled dendrites or axons, because they are extremely short and may well communicate activity in either direction, serving as local modulators of the surrounding neurons.

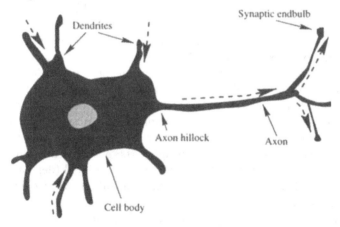

Figure 6.1. A schematic view of a neuron. The activity coming from receptors or from other neurons changes the membrane potentials on the dendrites and cell body (soma). The effects of these stimulations accumulate at the axon hillock where, for appropriate spatio-temporal patterns of stimulation, a threshold is reached which triggers a pulse of membrane potential to be propagated along the axon. This pulse is carried via the branching of the axon to the synaptic endbulbs, which in turn stimulate the membrane potential of the neurons or muscle fibres to which the synaptic endbulbs are connected.

Dynamics of biological neurons. Neural activations are mostly circularly stimulated. A neuron is activated by other neurons to which it is connected. In turn, its own activation stimulates other connected neurons to activation.

If an impulse is started at any one place on the axon, it propagates in both directions. However, if we start the pulse at one end of the axon (normally the axon hillock), it can only travel away from that end, since once a section has been triggered it becomes refractory until well after the impulse has passed out of range. An impulse travelling along the axon triggers new impulses in each of its branches, which in turn trigger impulses in their even finer branches. Axons come in two kinds: myelinated and unmyelinated. A myelinated fibre is wrapped in a sheath of myeline, a sequence of Schwann cells wrapped tightly around an axon with small gaps, called nodes of Ranvier, between adjacent segments. Instead of the somewhat slow active propagation down an unmyelinated fibre, the nerve impulse in a myelinated fibre jumps from node to node, thus speeding passage and reducing energy requirements. When an impulse arrives at one of the endbulbs, after a slight delay it yields a change in potential difference across the membrane of the cell upon which it impinges. The membrane on the endbulb is called the *pre-synaptic membrane*, and the membrane of the surface upon which the endbulb impinges is called the *post-synaptic membrane*. It may surprise that at most synapses the direct cause of the change in (electrical) potential of the post-synaptic membrane is not electrical but chemical. There are some exceptional cell appositions that are so large or have so tight coupling that the impulse affects the polarisation of the post-synaptic membrane without chemical mediation. However, the normal process is that the electrical pulse that reaches the endbulb causes the release of *transmitter* molecules from little packets called *vesicles* through the pre-synaptic membrane. The transmitter then diffuses across the very small *synaptic cleft* to the other side. When the transmitter reaches the post-synaptic membrane, it causes a change in the polarisation of this membrane. The effect of the transmitter may be of two basic kinds: either *excitatory*, tending to move the potential difference across the post-synaptic membrane in the direction of the threshold (depolarising the membrane), or *inhibitory*, tending to move the polarisation away from threshold (hyper-polarising the membrane).

The many small changes in potential differences across the membrane of a neuron, owing to the activity of many or all the synapses which impinge upon it, propagate - in most cases - passively through the membrane of its dendrites and its cell body, decaying as they propagate. At the axon hillock, many different and often small potential changes converge, so that the total contribution by which excitation exceeds inhibition may be quite large. In other words, the transmitter released when the impulse of a single synapse arrives at the endbulb, and generally causes a change in the post-synaptic membrane, which is not large enough to trigger it. Nonetheless, the cooperative effect of many such sub-threshold changes may yield a potential change at the axon hillock that exceeds threshold, and if this occurs at a time when the axon has passed the refractory period of its previous firing, then a new impulse will be fired down the axon. For more details on the findings in neurobiology, see Arbib (1989, 1995), Arbib, Erdi, and Szentagothai (1997), Bower (1997), Parks, Levine, and Long (1998) or Journals such as the *Journal of Neurobiology*, *Journal of Neurophysiology*, *Biological Cybernetics*, and others.

7. Connectionist Computing Models

The area of connectionism and neural networks has evolved into a very large and active area in recent years. Many neural network types have been developed or are currently under development. It is impossible to give here a comprehensive account of the entire field. Thus, in the following only some of today's most important artificial neural network models are discussed. A critical examination of the underlying assumptions and hopes of connectionism as the idea of using such neural networks, mainly associated with learning methods, on a large scale to develop complex intelligent systems follows in part III.

First of all, a brief historical survey is given on the development of artificial neural networks in section 7.1 as well as a general classification of the various neural network models. It should be noted that neural networks are often used for pattern classification tasks and other engineering problems, which is quite different from the connectionist claims that connectionist systems, composed of a large number of neurons, are suitable for building complex intelligent systems. See part III for an in-depth discussion on the issue. Section 7.2 introduces the reader to the classical neural learning model, the *Perceptron*. This is followed by the even more important model of the Multi-Layer Perceptron in 7.4, which consists of a number of cascaded Perceptrons. In fact, it was the Multi-Layer Perceptron which stimulated so strongly the recent re-emergence of neural networks as a general model for intelligence. While Multi-Layer Perceptrons are feed-forward networks, i.e. one layer of Perceptron units feeds the next layer of Perceptron units, also other topologies have been proposed, most notably, topologies which include cycles in the network, as is presented in 7.5. Section 7.6 presents a network structure which was essentially motivated from physics and is used not only as classification technique but also as an optimisation technique for combinatorial problems, namely constraint satisfaction problems. This is followed by self-organising networks in section 7.7. These are networks which are trained from unclassified data as opposed to the network models presented earlier in this chapter. The final section 7.8 summarises the chapter and emphasises the important points to be kept in mind for part III.

7.1 Short History of Artificial Neural Networks

McCulloch and Pitts (1943) introduced the fundamental idea of threshold units of a weighted sum of input activities for modelling neural activity. Also, the early ideas of negative feedback loops in cybernetics and control theory (see Wiener (1948)), inspired the development of theories of learning in neural networks. Another important pioneer of neural networks is Hebb (1949), who promoted the idea that long-term memory in humans and animals works by permanent alterations in the synapses. Minsky's doctoral dissertation (Minsky, 1954) is another early work exploring the possibilities of neural networks. In 1957, Rosenblatt (1957) introduced the 'modern' Perceptron-style type of networks which is composed of a number of threshold units. Widrow and Hoff (1960) and Widrow (1962) introduced similar units, called 'adalines' (for adaptive linear). Guides to the early period of neural networks are Rosenblatt (1962), or Nilsson (1965). In 1969, Minsky and Papert published their book *Perceptrons*, which resulted in virtually abandoning the entire field of neural networks. Minsky and Papert showed the inherent limitations of threshold-based computing units. While they analysed only networks without hidden layers, their book was considered to prove the inappropriateness of the entire approach for building intelligent machines.

The collection of papers in Hinton and Anderson (1981) can be considered as initiating the renaissance of neural networks, which became known under the title *connectionism*. However, only after the 'bible' of connectionism, the two volume PDP (Parallel Distributed Processing) book by Rumelhart et al. (1986) was published, connectionism began to enjoy wide-spread interest inside and outside the AI community. After 1986, the general interest in connectionism steadily grew and more and more models, often variations or extensions of the basic models presented in the 'bible,' were developed. New Journals and large conferences were set up to accommodate the needs of the emerging scientific community. A short classification scheme according to which most of the currently proposed neural network types can be classified is presented below.

A classification of artificial neural network models. Today's most important artificial neural networks can roughly be classified according to the following three criteria: the *architecture*, the *mode of operation* and the *style of learning*. Table 7.1 gives an overview of this classification. The first aspect, **the architecture**, refers to the topological organisation of a collection of neurons. Most networks are organised in layers, where one layer of neurons is connected with the next following layer, often in a feed-forward fashion; i.e. the output signals of the previous layer of neurons is provided as input signals to the neurons of the next layer. If there are connections from higher layers back to lower layers, signals are fed back. Such networks are often called *recurrent networks*. Some networks have connections between their neurons which are bidirectional, i.e. that activities can spread in both directions. However, most artificial neural networks have unidirectional connections where there is only the output signal from one node travelling to the input of another node.

The second aspect concerns the **mode of operation** of a system. That aspect refers to what sort of activities are going on when the network computes. Some networks are dynamic, i.e. there is a constant change in the activation, even when the same stimulus has been presented for a long time. Most networks, however, behave rather static after a new stimulus is provided, certain activity signals are triggered and remain until the stimulus changes.

The last but not least aspect concerns the **style of learning**. There are those networks which correct successively possible errors in their performance with respect to the provided training data. This requires supervised training input, as the system needs to be provided with target signals, which it is supposed to reproduce. For example, in the case of classification learning, the input needs to contain the correct class of an input pattern. Opposed to that are the correlational learners, which work with unclassified training data.[1] These systems attempt to detect a meaningful structure in the presented data, such as clusters, which may be used for classification or for data reduction, i.e. a dimensional reduction of the presented data. The following will give illustrative examples for each of the mentioned aspects of artificial neural networks.

Architecture	
Number of Layers:	1–10 layers
Directionality:	Feedforward/feedback
Reciprocality:	Unidirectionality/bidirectional
Mode of Operation	
Equilibrium:	Static/dynamic
Style of Learning	
Type:	Error correcting/Correlational
Inputs:	Supervised/Unsupervised

Table 7.1. A categorisation of artificial neural networks.

7.2 Perceptron: Learning Linear Threshold Functions

The Perceptron is one of the very early neuron-like computing models for which a reliable learning method, the so-called *delta rule*, has been developed. This is not only historically of particular importance. A subsequent extension of the original Perceptron was part of the reason for the renaissance of neural networks in the 1980s. The development of the so-called generalised delta rule for the Multi-Layer Perceptron (MLP). Before the technical details of the delta rule

---

[1] They are often called *Hebbian learners* as the idea can be traced back to Hebb (1949).

are presented, we need to lay down how the input data to our neural network models are presented. Data involves both training data, which is used by the neural network to learn, as well as data for which the outcome of the neural network has to be computed, i.e. data on which the neural network performs its learned function. The following presentation of typical data representations hold not only for Perceptrons and MLPs, but for virtually all types of neural networks.

7.2.1 Representing Data for Learning in Connectionist Systems

Most of the neural network models presented in this chapter are usually applied to pattern recognition tasks. As a consequence, the following presents the standard way of representing patterns to be processed by most types of neural network models. See also the discussion in section 4.2 on symbolic learning for a comparison.

Pattern recognition is an essential process of almost all intelligent systems whether natural or artificial. A pattern recognition task occurs in areas such as reading, interpreting visual images, recognising voices and understanding what they are saying. Pattern recognition not only takes place in such physical domains, but also abstract patterns may be the objective of pattern recognition processes. For example, an isomorphism between two different graphs, the creation of analogies or the understanding of metaphors, etc. To take a closer look at the issues involved, one can distinguish

a) the *description* or representation of patterns
   and
b) the *classification* of descriptions, or representations, of patterns.

Representation of Patterns. The most frequently used type of pattern description is the description by a set of features. On the one hand, this type of representations is simple and on the other hand it appears to be sufficiently expressive for most application areas. Each pattern is described by its respective values for each of the features. In the context of neural networks, patterns are usually represented as vectors of numerical values, often real-valued numbers in a given interval, e.g. $[0, 1]$, or $[-1, 1]$.

Formally speaking, a vector (an ordered set) of features is considered. For each feature x_i a pre-specified range r_i of values is admissible. Thus, by defining the feature vector together with the set of admissible values for each feature, the complete set of possible representations of patterns is defined. More precisely: Given is a feature vector $\mathbf{x} = \langle x_1, \ldots, x_n \rangle$ and a range $r_i \subseteq \Re$ for each feature $x_1, \ldots, x_n$. Thus, the set $\mathbf{X}$ of possibly occurring patterns is given by the Cartesian product of the ranges of all features. That is,

$$\mathbf{X} = r_1 \times \ldots \times r_n \subseteq \Re^n$$

Hence, the patterns can be regarded as points in the n-dimensional Euclidean space. See Figure 7.1. Once, a pattern representation has been chosen, the classification of patterns can be treated in a formal manner.

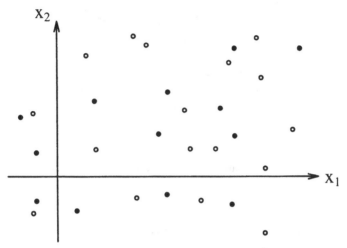

Figure 7.1. An example pattern space as a subset of $\Re^2$. The filled and unfilled circles belong to two different classes respectively.

Linear Threshold Functions. A linear separation function f is given as follows:

$$f(\mathbf{x}) = \begin{cases} 1 & \text{if } \sum_{i=1}^{n} w_i x_i > \theta \\ 0 & otherwise. \end{cases}$$

That is, if the weighted sum of the feature values exceeds a certain threshold θ, the function value switches from 0 to 1. In Figure 7.2 the graphical representation of a linear threshold function is given. Linear threshold functions have been extensively studied in pattern recognition in the 1960s. See Duda and Hart (1973) for a survey. The geometrical interpretation of a linear threshold function is in the case of a two-dimensional feature space is a separating line, dividing the plane into two classes (Figure 7.2). Such a separation is the simplest case of classification which divides the set of pattern representations, or shorter patterns, into two disjoint subsets. In the n-dimensional feature space, the separating linear threshold function can be imagined as a hyper-plane dividing the feature space into two separate areas. A simple algorithm for determining an appropriate linear threshold function is known as the *Perceptron algorithm*, which was developed by Rosenblatt (1959). It is an implementation of the so-called *delta rule*.

The Delta Rule. To motivate and formulate the delta rule, let us consider the following quantities of a linear threshold function. Note that first the function

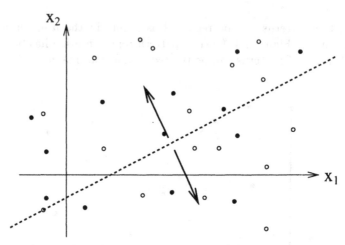

Figure 7.2. The threshold θ adjusts the graph of $f(\mathbf{x})$ by a parallel move.

$$f(\mathbf{x}) = \sum_{i=1}^{n} w_i x_i$$

is considered which gives a continuous output value and does not involve a threshold which decides on a boolean output value.

- A pattern $\mathbf{x}$ is a vector of input signals. That is, $\mathbf{x} = \langle x_1, ..., x_n \rangle$.
- The weight vector $\mathbf{w} = \langle w_1, ..., w_n \rangle$ is the set of weights which are used to compute the linear threshold function on the input signals.
- The output value o of the linear threshold function is given by $o = \sum_{i=1}^{n} w_i x_i$.
- t denotes the target output value of the linear threshold function.
- $\delta = o - t$ denotes the error, i.e. the difference of the actual output value o and the desired target output value t.

The change of weights is the instrument at hand to improve the function towards producing the desired target values. Thus, the following examines how the change in a weight improves or deteriorates the function computed using the weight vector. Consider the impact of the change of a single weight w_j on the resulting error of the output signal δ:

$$o = (\sum_{i=\{1,...,n\}\setminus\{j\}} w_i x_i) + w_j x_j. \tag{7.1}$$

For brevity, we set the constant a by

$$a = (\sum_{i=\{1,...,n\}\setminus\{j\}} w_i x_i) - t.$$

Then, the error δ can be rewritten as

$$\delta = a + w_j x_j.$$

In order to reduce the error, it is appropriate to increase the weight w_j, if δ is negative and to decrease w_j if δ is positive; provided the input value x_j is positive. If x_j is negative, w_j must be changed in the opposite direction.

7.2.2 Linear Decision Functions

Input: A set of positive and negative examples P^+ and P^-.
Output: A weight vector $\mathbf{w} = \langle w_1, ..., w_n \rangle$ for the linear threshold function that classifies the examples in P^+ and P^- accordingly, if such a weight vector exists.

    begin
(1)   Initialise-weights $w_1, \ldots, w_n$ to 0.
(2)   Choose an $\mathbf{x}$ from $P^+ \cup P^-$;
(3)   **if** $(\mathbf{x} \in P^+$ and $\mathbf{wx} > 0)$ or $(\mathbf{x} \in P^-$ and $\mathbf{wx} \leq 0)$
        then goto step 2;
      endif
(4)   **if** $X \in P^+$ and $\mathbf{wx} \leq 0$
(5)   **then** $\mathbf{w} := \mathbf{w} + \mathbf{x}$; **goto** step 2;
      endif
(6)   **if** $\mathbf{x} \in P^-$ and $\mathbf{wx} > 0$
(7)   **then** $\mathbf{w} := \mathbf{w} - \mathbf{x}$; **goto** step 2;
      endif
    end.

Figure 7.3. The classical Perceptron learning algorithm. The appropriate weights and the threshold value θ are successively adjusted. Rosenblatt proved that the algorithm always finds a separating linear threshold function if one exists.

The algorithm's convergence towards the target function (which is a linear threshold function) is illustrated in Figure 7.4. The modifications in the weights and the threshold value is given in Table 7.2. However, the distribution of the patterns in the feature space does not always allow the separation of the two classes by a linear threshold function. In simple cases, this is due to noise in the feature values. In other cases, it is due to the fact that a linear threshold function is simply not adequate for separating the respective pattern classes. In such cases, more appropriate and in most cases more complex separation functions have to be employed. However, in the following, further separation functions are presented although they are still quite simple. Figure 7.5 shows a linear threshold function which separates the given patterns approximately correct.

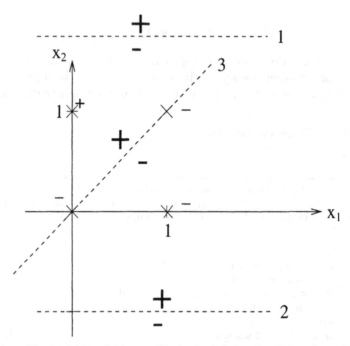

Figure 7.4. The initial line '1' is actually in the infinite classifying the entire area as negative. After the only positive example (0,1) is presented, the Perceptron algorithm moves the dividing line to position '2'. After the presentation of the negative example (1,0) Perceptron moves the dividing line to position '3'. Note that the points on the line are negatively classified.

Pattern to learn:

x_1	x_2	t
0	0	0
0	1	1
1	0	0
1	1	0

Learning process:

x_1	x_2	x_3	w_1	w_2	$w_3 = \theta$	o	t	$\Delta = 0 - t$	operation	line no.
0	0	-1	0	0	0	0	0	0	none	1
0	1	-1	0	0	0	0	1	-1	$w := w + x$	1
1	0	-1	0	1	-1	1	0	1	$w := w - x$	2
1	1	-1	-1	1	0	0	0	0	none	3
0	0	-1	-1	1	0	0	0	0	none	3
0	1	-1	-1	1	0	1	1	0	none	3
1	0	-1	-1	1	0	0	0	0	none	3
1	1	-1	-1	1	0	0	0	0	none	3

Learning process stopped, because the response o was correct for all four patterns, i.e. all patterns were correctly learned.

Table 7.2. The table shows the weight modification by the Perceptron learning rule. The last column indicates to what line the weights correspond in Figure 7.4.

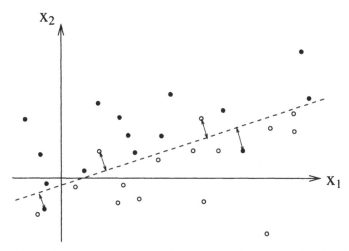

Figure 7.5. The shown patterns cannot be separated by a linear-threshold function. The dashed line shows the optimal linear approximation with respect to the least square criterion. That is, the distance to the incorrectly classified objects would be minimised. The area above the line can be classified as • and the area beneath the line as o.

7.3 Limitations of Linear Threshold Functions

Unfortunately, linear threshold functions are fairly limited in their ability to divide a feature space into two different areas. For many classes of sets of patterns an appropriate separation cannot be achieved by a linear threshold function. Even reasonable approximations may not exist as linear threshold functions.

However, in the extremely influential book *Perceptrons* by Minsky and Papert (1969) the limitations of linear threshold functions has been studied in depth. Minsky and Papert proved severe limitations. Among these limitations is the Perceptrons inability to perform the logical XOR function (i.e. $(x_1 \wedge \neg x_2) \vee (\neg x_1 \wedge x_2)$.) See Figure 7.6.

In order to be able to enhance the expressibility of the single linear separation functions, combinations of linear separation functions have been investigated. One simple form of that are the stepwise linear separation functions. Stepwise linear separation functions divide the feature space into multiple segments. Each segment then is divided by an own linear separation function into two different regions. See Figure 7.7 for an example. However, even the stepwise linear separation functions are not capable to perform the XOR function. For realising an XOR function, one has to cascade linear separation functions. That is, the input features to the finally deciding linear threshold functions are the outputs of linear threshold functions. Such cascaded Perceptrons are discussed in the next section.

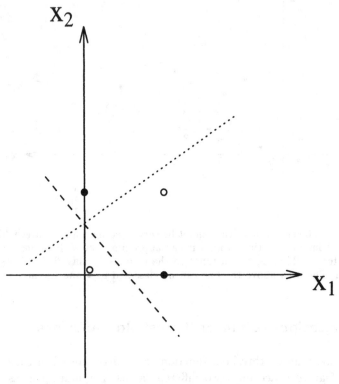

Figure 7.6. The XOR function cannot be achieved by dividing the feature space by a single line. Both dashed lines would produce an incorrect value for one input pair.

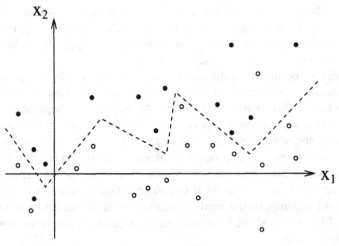

Figure 7.7. A stepwise linear separation function.

7.4 Multi-Layer Perceptron

How can the inability of the standard Perceptron to model non-linear functions, such as the XOR function, be overcome? One way is to use multiple Perceptrons, where each of them discriminates a subset of the patterns of a class c. The various subsets have to be merged together in order to cover the entire set of patterns belonging to c. Figure 7.8 shows how this works. However, the train-

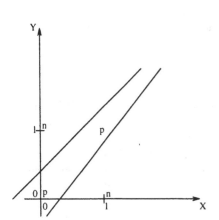

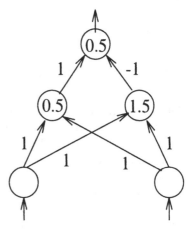

(a) Positive examples are given between the two lines and negative examples outside of this area.

(b) Two input units feed a composition of three Perceptrons that compute the XOR function.

Figure 7.8. Merging the area above the upper line with the area beneath the lower line in (a) can be done by three Perceptrons connected as shown in (b).

ing of a combination of Perceptrons appears much harder than the training of a single Perceptron. In general it is not clear how to distribute the responsibility to cover a given set of patterns by a particular Perceptron node. Because of this difficulty, Minsky and Papert did not investigate layered combinations of Perceptrons in their famous *Perceptron* book.

Another critical issue is the exact shape of the threshold function. That is, whether the function changes its value rather smooth or not. In Figure 7.9 the graphs of the normal linear threshold function and two smoother versions are shown.

7.4.1 The Generalised Delta Rule

The generalised delta rule, also known as the *backpropagation rule*, has been introduced into the context of the MLP, in Rumelhart, Hinton, and Williams

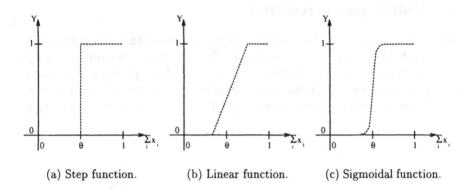

(a) Step function.   (b) Linear function.   (c) Sigmoidal function.

Figure 7.9. Three possible threshold functions.

(1986). It is a general learning rule, which allows to find even in an MLP a more or less appropriate set of threshold values and input weights for each neuron. It may be noted that Parker (1985) as well as Werbos (1974) had obtained similar results, and it has even to be attributed to Bryson and Ho (1969). However, Rumelhart and McClelland are credited for reviving the Perceptron since in addition to their independent development of the generalised delta rule, they showed how to use it for training multi-layer networks.

Similarly to the ordinary Perceptron learning algorithm, the operation of the backpropagation in MLPs is also based on presented patterns and iteratively adjusting the weights and thresholds of each neuron depending on whether the produced output is as desired or not. The problem of the Perceptron learning algorithm for use in MLPs is the following: The decision as to which of the hidden units should operate in which way cannot easily be made.

By the use of the sigmoidal function or any other continuous and differentiable output function for each neuron, the MLP network becomes capable to propagate an occurring error in the output signal to the units of earlier layers in the network. This amounts to a decreasing error in the output signal for the next time. The idea is as follows: Just as the simple delta rule, the generalised delta rule compares the actual value of the output signal with the desired value, and evaluates the difference in order to modify the weights and threshold of the output unit so that the difference will be reduced the next time. Moreover, this difference is also used in order to be *back-propagated* to the previous units which may influence the output signal; hence the name *backpropagation rule*. As a consequence, not only for the output unit but also for the intermediate layers, a desired output is determined for each unit. Based on the desired output values for the intermediate layer units, obtained by the backpropagation rule, the actual behaviour of intermediate units is modified as well to approach the respectively desired output value. More precisely, the backpropagation rule modifies the weights in direct proportion to the error in the units to which it is connected.

7.4.2 The Mathematical Formulation of the Generalised Delta Rule

The following will show that the generalised delta rule performs a steepest descent procedure on the error surface in the weight space of the respective network. Consider the network in Figure 7.10. The input signals to the net-

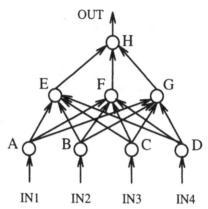

OUT

Figure 7.10. The topology of a Multi-Layer Perceptron.

work are given by the input vector $\mathbf{I} = \langle i_1, ..., i_n \rangle$. The vector of output units is denoted by $\mathbf{U_o}$. In Figure 7.10, $\mathbf{U_o} = \{H\}$. Every node in the network computes a linear threshold function of the input signals to that node and the weights associated with each of the input signals. Let us denote the input vector carrying the pattern $\mathbf{p}$ by $\mathbf{I^p}$. Every node j computes the following output function:

$$f_j(\mathbf{I}) = \sum_{i=1}^{n_j} (w_{ji} i_{ji})$$

for the input vector $\mathbf{I_j} = \langle i_{j1}, \ldots, i_{jn_j} \rangle$ to node j.
Furthermore,

E_p denotes the error of the output value of the MLP in question given the
   pattern p as input.
t_{pj} denotes the target output value of unit j for pattern p, while
o_{pj} denotes the actual output value. Finally, let
w_{ji} denote the weight of the link from output of node i to the input of node j.

   To avoid having positive and negative error measures, let us define the error E_p to be proportional to the square of the difference between desired and actual output value. Let us denote the difference by $\delta_{pj} := t_{pj} - o_{pj}$. That is,

$$E_p = \frac{1}{2} \sum_{j \in U_o} (t_{pj} - o_{pj})^2 = \frac{1}{2} \sum_{j \in U_o} (\delta_{pj})^2 \qquad (7.2)$$

For a set of patterns P we can define the overall error of the network E as follows:

$$E = \sum_{p \in P} E_p. \tag{7.3}$$

Moreover, the change of weight w_{ji} upon applying pattern p as input to the network is denoted by $\Delta_p w_{ji}$. Then, we define

$$\Delta_p w_{ji} := \eta \delta_{pj} o_{pi}. \tag{7.4}$$

This is the delta rule which will be used in order to perform a steepest descent on the error surface in the weight space. The introduced constant η will be used as a scaling factor for controlling the speed of the steepest descent on the error surface.

In order to show that this rule performs in fact a steepest descent, it has to be examined, how the error E_p is influenced by a change in a particular weight w_{ji}. Thus, firstly equation 7.2 is rewritten in order to show the influence of w_{ji} on the left side:

$$E_p = \frac{1}{2} \sum_{k \in U_\circ} (\delta_{pk})^2 = \frac{1}{2} \sum_{k \in U_\circ \setminus \{j\}} (\delta_{pk})^2 + \frac{1}{2}(\delta_{pj})^2 \tag{7.5}$$

For brevity we set

$$a := \frac{1}{2} \sum_{k \in U_\circ \setminus \{j\}} (\delta_{pk})^2.$$

Then, we can rewrite equation 7.5 by

$$E_p = a + \frac{1}{2}(\delta_{pj})^2 = a + \frac{1}{2}(t_{pj} - o_{pj})^2 = a + \frac{(t_{pj})^2}{2} - t_{pj} o_{pj} + \frac{(o_{pj})^2}{2} \tag{7.6}$$

At next we have to decompose the actual output value o_{pj} in a respective way. That is, first we set

$$b := \sum_{k \in I_j \setminus \{i\}} w_{jk} o_{pk}$$

again for brevity. Then, we can decompose o_{pj} as follows:

$$o_{pj} = \sum_{k \in I_j} w_{jk} o_{pk} = \left(\sum_{k \in I_j \setminus \{i\}} w_{jk} o_{pk} \right) + w_{ji} o_{pi} = b + w_{ji} o_{pi} \tag{7.7}$$

Now, we plug equation 7.7 into equation 7.6 and obtain

$$E_p = a + \frac{(t_{pj})^2}{2} - t_{pj} o_{pj} + \frac{(o_{pj})^2}{2} = a + \frac{(t_{pj})^2}{2} - t_{pj}(b + w_{ji} o_{pi}) + \frac{(b + w_{ji} o_{pi})^2}{2}$$

$$\Leftrightarrow E_p = a + \frac{(t_{pj})^2}{2} - t_{pj} b - t_{pj} w_{ji} o_{pi} + \frac{b^2 + 2b w_{ji} o_{pi} + (w_{ji})^2 (o_{pi})^2}{2} \tag{7.8}$$

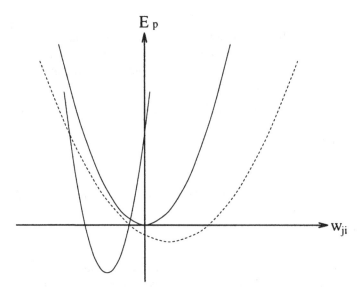

Figure 7.11. Graphs of quadratic error functions E_p for pattern p depending on the weight w_{ji}. Although the slopes and locations vary, the direction towards the minimum is clear.

Equation 7.8 is actually a simple quadratic equation of the form

$$E_p(w_{ji}) = c_1(w_{ji})^2 + c_2 w_{ji} + c_3$$

for adequately chosen constants c_1, c_2, c_3. Thus $E_p(w_{ji})$ can be represented by a graph as in Figure 7.11. At next, equation 7.8 can easily be differentiated in w_{ji} as follows:

$$\frac{\partial E_p}{\partial w_{ji}} = -t_{pj}o_{pi} + o_{pi}b + w_{ji}(o_{pi})^2 \tag{7.9}$$

This can be rewritten as

$$\frac{\partial E_p}{\partial w_{ji}} = -t_{pj}o_{pi} + o_{pi}\Big(\sum_{k\in I_j\backslash\{i\}} w_{jk}o_k\Big) + w_{ji}(o_{pi})^2 = -t_{pj}o_{pi} + o_{pi}\Big(\sum_{k\in I_j} w_{jk}o_{pk}\Big)$$

$$\Leftrightarrow \quad \frac{\partial E_p}{\partial w_{ji}} = -t_{pj}o_{pi} + o_{pi}o_{pj} = -o_{pi}\delta_{pj} \tag{7.10}$$

With the following equation it becomes obvious that not only the error for pattern p is reduced by changing w_{ji} according to equation 7.4. For the overall error E a steepest descent is implemented by this rule as well. That is, consider the derivative of the overall error function (equation 7.3) in w_{ji}.

$$\frac{\partial E}{\partial w_{ji}} = \sum_{p\in P}\frac{\partial E_p}{\partial w_{ji}} = -\sum_{p\in P}(o_{pi}\delta_{pj}) \tag{7.11}$$

In order to find a minimum on the error surface in the weight space the weights have to be changed in sufficiently small steps. The factor for scaling the change of the weights depending on the current error is the constant η in equation 7.4. So far, we considered only the weight adjustment for the output layer using a linear output function.

Semi-linear output functions. Let us generalise that to semi-linear output functions of each unit:

We set first

$$net_{pj} = \sum_{i \in I_j} w_{ji} o_{pi} \tag{7.12}$$

and assume a function f_j which is nondecreasing and differentiable which computes the output value of unit j depending on the linear sum above. That is,

$$o_{pj} := f_j(net_{pj}) \tag{7.13}$$

It should be noted that linear threshold functions are not covered by the class of functions above, since their derivative at the threshold is infinite.

To get the correct generalisation of the delta rule, we must set

$$\Delta_p w_{ji} \propto -\frac{\partial E_p}{\partial w_{ji}} \tag{7.14}$$

It is still useful to split this derivative into two parts to reflect the change in error as a function of change in the net input to the unit's output function, and the effect of changing a particular weight on the net input. This is given in the following:

$$\frac{\partial E_p}{\partial w_{ji}} = \frac{\partial E_p}{\partial net_{pj}} \frac{\partial net_{pj}}{\partial w_{ji}} \tag{7.15}$$

According to equation 7.13 we can see that

$$\frac{\partial net_{pj}}{\partial w_{ji}} = \frac{\partial}{\partial w_{ji}} \sum_{k \in \{I_j\}} w_{jk} o_{pk} = o_{pi} \tag{7.16}$$

At next, let us define

$$\delta_{pj} := -\frac{\partial E_p}{\partial net_{pj}}. \tag{7.17}$$

Note that this is consistent with our previous definition of δ_{pj} before equation 7.2 for linear units, since $o_{pj} = net_{pj}$, if unit u_j is linear. This results, however, in rewriting equation 7.15 as

$$-\frac{\partial E_p}{\partial w_{ji}} = \delta_{pj} o_{pi}. \tag{7.18}$$

This equation indicates that implementing a gradient descent in E requires weight changes according to the same rule as in the standard delta rule:

$$\Delta_p w_{ji} = \eta \delta_{pj} o_{pi}. \tag{7.19}$$

The problem still to be solved is to compute δ_{pj} for every unit, also for those units on the hidden layer. The following shows that δ's can be easily determined for the hidden units by simple recursive computations. To compute δ_{pj} from equation 7.17, we use the chain rule to rewrite the partial derivative reflecting two factors: one factor reflecting the change in error as a function of the output of the unit; and one factor reflecting the change in the output as a function of changes in the input. That is, we write

$$\delta_{pj} = -\frac{\partial E_p}{\partial net_{pj}} = -\frac{\partial E_p}{\partial o_{pi}} \frac{\partial o_{pj}}{\partial net_{pj}}. \tag{7.20}$$

Using equation 7.13 we have

$$\frac{\partial E_p}{\partial o_{pj}} = f_j'(net_{pj}) \tag{7.21}$$

for the second factor, which is simply the derivative of the output function $f_j(net_j)$ for unit j. To determine the first factor, we have to distinguish two different cases: unit u_j being an output-layer unit and being a hidden-layer unit. First we consider unit u_j being an output layer unit. Then it follows immediately from the definition of E_p that

$$\frac{\partial E_p}{\partial o_{pj}} = -(t_{pj} - o_{pj}), \tag{7.22}$$

which is the same as for the standard delta rule. By substituting the two factors in equation 7.20, we obtain for any output unit u_j

$$\delta_{pj} = (t_{pj} - o_{pj}) f_j'(net_{pj}). \tag{7.23}$$

The case, where u_j is not an output unit, the considerations are slightly more complicated:

$$\sum_{k \in U_o} \frac{\partial E_p}{\partial net_{pk}} \frac{\partial net_{pk}}{\partial o_{pj}} = \sum_{k \in U_o} \frac{\partial E_p}{\partial net_{pk}} \frac{\partial}{\partial o_{pj}} \sum_{i \in I_j} w_{ki} o_{pi}$$

$$= \sum_{k \in U_o} \frac{\partial E_p}{\partial net_{pk}} w_{kj} = -\sum_{k \in U_o} \delta_{pk} w_{kj} \tag{7.24}$$

Thus, the hidden-layer version of the substitution of the two factors in equation 7.20 yields

$$\delta_{pj} = f_j'(net_{pj}) \sum_{k \in U_o} \delta_{pk} w_{kj} \tag{7.25}$$

whenever u_j is not an output unit. The equations 7.23 and 7.25 give a recursive procedure for computing the δ's for all units in the network. These in turn are used to determine the weight changes for all network weights according to equation 7.19.

Hence, we arrived at the procedure of the generalised delta rule for training a MLP with semi-linear activation functions for each unit. Figure 7.12 shows the backpropagation learning algorithm in pseudo code, which employs the generalised delta rule.

Input: A set of positive and negative examples P^+ and P^-. An untrained Multi-Layer Perceptron.
Output: A trained network that classifies the given examples with minimal error.

    begin
(1)   Initialise all weights and thresholds
          with individually and randomly chosen values from $[0, 1]$.
(2)   Choose an **x** from $P^+ \cup P^-$
(3)   Compute all output values o_i for all network units.
(4a)   Use equation 7.19 and 7.23 to update the weights w_{ji} of
          the output units.
(4b)   Use equation 7.19 and 7.25 to update the weights w_{ji} of
          the hidden layer units.
(5)   **Stop**, if overall error E is smaller then allowed maximum error,
          or if updates are insignificant.
(6)   **Goto** step 2.
    end.

Figure 7.12. The backpropagation learning algorithm. The appropriate weights and the threshold values θ_i are successively adjusted for all adjustable nodes in the network. (All nodes except the nodes of the input layer.)

7.4.3 Applications of Multi-Layer Perceptrons

During the past ten years or so, a large number of applications have been developed using neural computing models, many of them using some type of MLPs. The following two case studies present an impression of what connectionist systems are capable of.

NETTalk. The system NETTalk was designed by Sejnowski and Rosenberg (1987) for the task of learning to correctly pronounce written English language. The pronunciation task was essentially to map a stream of written English language into a sequence of phonemes. Phonemes are the basic 'sound units' humans produce when speaking. The produced sequence of phonemes is then fed into an electronic sound generator allowing the synthetic speech generation. The task is non-trivial because in English, the pronunciation of a letter clearly depends on its context, such as the letter c, for example, is pronounced differently in *cat* and in *cinema*. The letter *k* is even ignored in words like *knight*, while in words like *kernel*, it is pronounced as the *c* in *cat*.

The design of NETTalk provided a stream of 7 characters to the neural network when the middle character was to be mapped into phonemes. That is, a context of the three previous and the three following characters was known to the system of allowing an informed decision. For each character, there were 29 inputs to the neural network, activating exactly one input at a time. That is, there were 26 inputs for each character in the alphabet and three additional inputs for blank, period, and other punctuation. The NETTalk system eventually[2] used 80 hidden units and was trained on a set of 1,024-word text, which was manually mapped into a stream of phonemes.

After the training period of 50 passes of the training data, NETTalk managed to pronounce 95% of the words correctly. It did not achieve 100% because for some words the pronunciation depended on a wider context than the seven character window, i.e. it depended on the surrounding words as well. Less impressively, though, the accuracy of NETTalk on unseen data was only 78%, which is not too bad but worse than conventional software.

Nevertheless, the performance of NETTalk had its impact. Not so much because of its achieved accuracy, but rather because its gradual learning process and its improvement in pronunciation appeared to many people to resemble the process of a child learning to speak. Starting off with babbling sound and gradually becoming clearer and more understandable.

ALVINN. The system *Autonomous Land Vehicle In a Neural Network* (ALVINN), as described in Pomerleau (1993), Jochem and Pomerleau (1996), is a neural network approach to steering a vehicle along a road. ALVINN was surprisingly successful in doing this job. It was used to steer the NavLab vehicles of the Carnegie Mellon University (a Chevy van and a US Army personnel carrier).

The vehicles were equipped with a number of sensors including a colour stereo vision system as well as a scanning laser range finder and radar. The vehicles had a computer-controlled steering, acceleration, and braking. The pixel signals form the video system were pre-processed and fed into the input units of the neural network (a MLP) as an array of 30 × 32 grid of input signals. The output layer of the network had 30 output units, each for each direction of steering. The output unit with the highest activation level is chosen to determine the steering direction to be taken. The hidden layer of the fully connected MLP contained 5 units.

ALVINN was trained by the data produced from observing a human driver. In order to obtain data from rather critical situations which a human driver does not often encounter during a normal driving session, additional data was generated as follows: The actually obtained images were also turned by a few degrees to both sides in order to mimic situations where the vehicle tends to

---

[2] This is the version which was published. Different networks were tried before the published variant was found.

go slightly off the track and the corresponding steering signal was generated accordingly.

As a result, ALVINN managed to keep the vehicles on their tracks on certain types of roads for which it was trained. It managed to drive up to a speed of 75mph for a distance of 90 miles. However, ALVINN had problems when other vehicles were involved or lighting conditions were poor or changed, etc.

7.5 Recurrent Networks

Feedforward networks compute a function on the current input signals. This is not always sufficient for technical applications. Furthermore, in biological systems, previous input signals also have their effect on the computed function value.

Recurrent networks address this shortcoming of feedforward networks: in recurrent neural networks, some or even all output signals are fed back to units which lie before the output units. Hence, their network topology contains loops, i.e. such networks have at least one neuron N whose output signal is fed back into a 'previous' neuron which partly or even completely determines one or more input signals to N. Such networks can provide information on the network's state at the previous time step. Consequently, those units are often called *context units*. Hence, recurrent networks are typically used for learning of time series and similar domains with sequential data, where certain structures in these sequences are to be discovered. Recurrent networks are often used for forecasting, where they have been used with considerable success on a number of time series problems. The Elman networks (Elman, 1990), for example, were used to learn context-free grammars. See Figure 7.13 for an example of a recurrent network Elman (1990), Servan-Schreiber, Cleeremans, and McClelland (1989). The idea is to use the same or a slightly adapted learning algorithm as back-propagation. During training, such a recurrent neural network compresses historical information in order to find a good representation of the structure of the past data. Usually, recurrent networks are employed for problems, where the relevant time series data does not span too long a distance, as it becomes difficult for the network to discover structure among data items of great distance in time. Figure 7.14 shows an Elman-Tower, a recurrent network, which allows to memorise a larger number of time steps. The number layers on the right side can be chosen according to the needs of the application. These layers serve as storage of the content of the original hidden layer i time steps before. Since all this information is available at the hidden layer on the left, the previous values can be used to determine a suitable output function. Besides the Elman recurrent networks, there have also been a number of other proposals for networks which can handle time series data, such as Waibel (1989) or Mozer (1992). Frasconi, Gori, and Soda (1995), Frasconi, Gori, Maggini, and Soda (1995) developed an approach to integrate prior knowledge into the learning

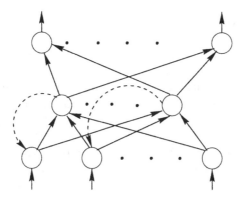

Figure 7.13. A simple recurrent network to learn context sensitive grammars. The dashed lines are connections which feed activity signals back into neurons at a lower layer.

process of the recurrent network. The following presents alternative network types, which do not rely on the idea of the delta rule for minimising error.

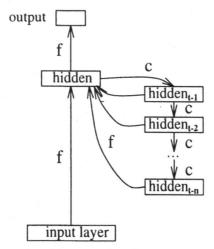

Figure 7.14. The schematic architecture of an Elman tower. The connections labelled 'f' are fully connected layers. The connections labelled 'c' are mere copies of the activity levels of the 'source layer' at the previous time step.

7.6 Hopfield Networks

Hopfield (1982, 1984) and Hopfield and Tank (1985, 1986) introduced a computational paradigm for using a neural network style architecture as an auto-associative memory. Hopfield networks belong to the early architectures in the early 1980s, when neural networks re-emerged under the title connectionism. Since it functions according to different principles than the previous network types, Hopfield networks are discussed in more detail.

A Hopfield network is basically a set of simple threshold units which are fully interconnected with each other. That is, in the case on n neurons there are n^2 interconnections among them. That means also that the interconnections between two units i and j are directed, i.e. there are actually two interconnections, one going from i to j and another one going from j to i. See Figure 7.15. The

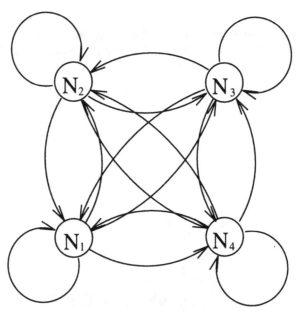

Figure 7.15. The structure of a small Hopfield Network. All units are connected with each other.

output signal of each unit depends on a (non-linear) function of the weighted sum of its input signals. In order to ensure that the output signal of a unit does not directly depend on its previous value the weight of the interconnection of a unit with itself is generally set to 0. In their approach Hopfield and Tank define the following variables which characterise the state of the network of n nodes:

For $i \in N = \{1, \ldots, n\}$ we consider

o_i : the output state of the ith neuron,

α_i: the activation threshold of the ith neuron,
w_{ij} the interconnection weight, that is the strength of the connection from
neuron j to neuron i. w_{ii} is always set to 0.

Thus, the total input value to neuron i is given by $\sum_{j \in N} w_{ij} o_j$. Generally
the weights w_{ij} are assumed to be real valued, although certain restrictions may
be useful, e.g. restricting weights to binary values. Every interconnection weight
may assume the value 0 indicating that there is <u>no</u> actual interconnection. In
general, Hopfield networks have heavy interconnections. i.e. in practice the
interconnection weight matrix is rarely sparse.

7.6.1 The Hopfield Unit Output and Update Functions

There are a number of different proposals for the output function of the Hopfield
neurons. One simple function is given by the stepwise linear threshold function:

$$o_i = \begin{cases} 1 & \text{if } (\sum_{j \in N} w_{ij} o_j) > \alpha_i \\ 0 & \text{otherwise} \end{cases} \qquad (7.26)$$

Often the threshold α_i is set to 0.

State propagation. Considering the dynamic aspect of the Hopfield network,
we denote the output value of a neuron i at time t by $o_i(t)$. Thus, the output
value $o_i(t + 1)$ of a neuron i at the next time step after t is determined by
equation 7.26 using the output values of the neurons at time t.

Considering the quadratic matrix $\mathbf{W}$ of n rows and columns, which contains all interconnection weights of the n-neuron network, we can formulate
the output transition rule for each of the neurons as follows:

$$o_i(t + 1) = \mu_s(\sum_{j \in N} w_{ij} o_j(t) + i_i), \qquad (7.27)$$

where i_i is some additional input bias to neuron i, in order to change the actual
threshold value of the neuron. The output function μ_s may vary from network
to network. One simple function, however, is the following binary function:

$$\mu_s(x) = \begin{cases} 1 & x > 0 \\ 0 & x \leq 0 \end{cases} \qquad (7.28)$$

Network updating strategies. Although it is suggestive to update the neurons' output values synchronously, it has been found by experiments that also
partial updates of the network may be useful. That is, only some of the neurons'
output value are recomputed for the next time step.

In the case of $\alpha_i = 0$ for all $i \in \{1, ..., n\}$, stable states of an entire Hopfield network are characterised by a (local) minimum of the following function,
metaphorically also called the *energy function*:

$$E = -\frac{1}{2} \sum_{i \in N} \sum_{j \in N} w_{ij} o_i o_j \tag{7.29}$$

This energy function together with the output function 7.26 and a set of desired stable network states O^s, $s \in \{1, \ldots, m\}$ leads to the following function for determining the initial weight values of the network:

$$w_{ij} = \sum_{s=1}^{m} (2O_i^s - 1)(2O_j^s - 1) \quad i \neq j \tag{7.30}$$

Note that equation 7.30 implies a symmetry among the network weights, since it holds

$$w_{ji} = \sum_{s=1}^{m} (2O_i^s - 1)(2O_j^s - 1) = w_{ij} \tag{7.31}$$

7.6.2 Application Areas of Hopfield Networks

Hinton in Hinton and Anderson (1981) proposed to use Hopfield networks for solving constraint satisfaction problems. Thereby, the energy function of the network is to be interpreted as to what extent the current network activation pattern satisfies the specified constraints. The lower the energy, the better the constraints are met.

While Hopfield networks are suitable for constraint satisfaction problems, they can also be applied to pattern recognition problems. An example for that is given below.

Using Hopfield networks for pattern recognition. Hopfield networks can be used for pattern recognition in the following way: The idea is to assign to each pattern class a different stable state of the network. The pattern recognition process consists of applying the pattern to be classified as output value pattern for the neurons of the network. Due to the pre-adjusted weights the network will go through a number of state transitions in order to reach eventually one of the stable states which have been assigned to each of the possible pattern classes. However, a stable state is not always reached. Thereby, in which state the network will stabilise determines the classification of the pattern. The process of passing through a number of unstable states corresponds to the computation of a similarity between the input pattern and the patterns corresponding to the stored stable states. For that purpose, the network weights are initially adjusted according to equation 7.30.

However, it might happen that the network stabilises in an undesired state after applying a certain pattern for classification. This is particularly likely, if (in binary applications) the Hamming distance between two stable states, i.e. the number of neurons whose output signals differ in both states, is relatively small.

An example for storing and retrieving patterns as stable states in a Hopfield network follows:

Example

Consider a binary output value network with four neurons and a neuron
threshold $\alpha_i = 0$ for all $i \in N$.
Let the network require to store the following pattern vector as a stable
state:

$$O^s = \begin{pmatrix} 0 \\ 1 \\ 0 \\ 1 \end{pmatrix} \qquad (7.32)$$

First the neuron interconnection weights are determined according to equation 7.33:
The weights representing the desired stable states have to be preset according to

$$w_{ij} = (2O_i^s - 1)(2O_j^s - 1) = w_{ji} \qquad (7.33)$$

where

$$O^s = \begin{pmatrix} O_1^s \\ O_2^s \\ O_3^s \\ O_4^s \end{pmatrix} = \begin{pmatrix} 0 \\ 1 \\ 0 \\ 1 \end{pmatrix} \qquad (7.34)$$

Thus, we obtain $w_{12} = (2O_1^s - 1)(2O_2^s - 1) = (0-1)(2-1) = -1 = w_{21}$
and similarly

$$\begin{aligned}
w_{13} &= (0-1)(0-1) = +1 = w_{31} \\
w_{14} &= (0-1)(2-1) = -1 = w_{41} \\
w_{23} &= (2-1)(0-1) = -1 = w_{32} \qquad (7.35) \\
w_{24} &= (2-1)(2-1) = +1 = w_{42} \\
w_{34} &= (0-1)(2-1) = -1 = w_{43}
\end{aligned}$$

Since the weights of the interconnections of each neuron to itself are set
to zero the calculations result in the following weight matrix:

$$W = \begin{pmatrix} 0 & -1 & +1 & -1 \\ -1 & 0 & -1 & +1 \\ +1 & -1 & 0 & -1 \\ -1 & +1 & -1 & 0 \end{pmatrix} \qquad (7.36)$$

And with this weight matrix the network state is propagated by

$$O(t+1) = \begin{pmatrix} 0 & -1 & +1 & -1 \\ -1 & 0 & -1 & +1 \\ +1 & -1 & 0 & -1 \\ -1 & +1 & -1 & 0 \end{pmatrix} O(t) \qquad (7.37)$$

This propagation equation together with equation 7.28 for defining the
output function μ_s yields a stable state for the intended input pattern
in 7.32. That is, we obtain for O^s the following output values:

$$W \ O^s = \begin{pmatrix} -2 \\ 1 \\ -2 \\ 1 \end{pmatrix} \tag{7.38}$$

It is interesting to see how the network behaves if other input patterns are supplied as initial output values of the neurons and how or whether the network will end up in a stable state. Consider the following input patterns:

$$O^1(t) = \begin{pmatrix} 1 \\ 0 \\ 0 \\ 1 \end{pmatrix} \qquad O^2(t) = \begin{pmatrix} 0 \\ 0 \\ 0 \\ 1 \end{pmatrix} \qquad O^3(t) = \begin{pmatrix} 1 \\ 0 \\ 1 \\ 0 \end{pmatrix} \tag{7.39}$$

Supplying the network with $O^1(t)$, its subsequent state at $t+1$ will be given by

$$O^1(t+1) = \mu_s(W \ O^1(t)) = \mu_s \begin{pmatrix} -1 \\ 0 \\ 0 \\ -1 \end{pmatrix} = \begin{pmatrix} 0 \\ 0 \\ 0 \\ 0 \end{pmatrix} \tag{7.40}$$

This new output vector will in turn yield in the next time step $t+2$:

$$O^1(t+2) = \mu_s(W \ O^1(t+1)) = \mu_s \begin{pmatrix} 0 \\ 0 \\ 0 \\ 0 \end{pmatrix} = \begin{pmatrix} 0 \\ 0 \\ 0 \\ 0 \end{pmatrix} \tag{7.41}$$

That is, the initial output vector O^1 resulted in a new stable state of the Hopfield network. This stable state, however, was not explicitly stored as such initially.
For $O^2(t)$ we obtain:

$$O^2(t+1) = \mu_s(W \ O^2(t)) = \mu_s \begin{pmatrix} -1 \\ 1 \\ -1 \\ 0 \end{pmatrix} = \begin{pmatrix} 0 \\ 1 \\ 0 \\ 0 \end{pmatrix} \tag{7.42}$$

This yields for the subsequent time step $t+1$ to:

$$O^2(t+2) = \mu_s(W \ O^2(t+1)) = \mu_s \begin{pmatrix} -1 \\ 0 \\ -1 \\ 1 \end{pmatrix} = \begin{pmatrix} 0 \\ 0 \\ 0 \\ 1 \end{pmatrix} = O^2(t) \tag{7.43}$$

The network is caught in a cycle. It does not find a stable state but ends up in an infinite transient phase.

Finally let us consider $O^3(t)$ for which we obtain:

$$O^3(t+1) = \mu_s(W\ O^3(t)) = \mu_s \begin{pmatrix} 0 \\ -1 \\ 1 \\ -1 \end{pmatrix} = \begin{pmatrix} 1 \\ 0 \\ 1 \\ 0 \end{pmatrix} \qquad (7.44)$$

The vector obtained in equation 7.44 is exactly the initially stored stable state. Hence, the system has 'recognised' its stored pattern.

An interesting point of Hopfield networks is that stable states may be developed which have not been initially used for determining the initial set of network weights. For more details, see e.g. Fiesler and Beale (1997).

7.7 Unsupervised Learning in Neural Networks

A quite different type of learning approach pursue a class of neural networks which are often called *self-organising systems*. Less spectacularly, they may also be considered as unsupervised learning systems. Unsupervised learning means to find 'natural' regularities among unclassified objects or patterns. The learning system is not provided with the information of how to classify a particular pattern or whether two patterns belong to the same class.

The unsupervised learning system has to determine whether two input patterns belong to the same class, based purely on the similarity or dissimilarity among the provided input patterns. This 'cluster discovery' capability of such systems is also referred to as an ability to 'self-organisation'. Another related but possibly more important application is that of modelling the distribution of patterns. That is, the self-organising system learns with what probability a particular pattern can be expected to occur. Needless to say, the learning process also involves substantial generalisation beyond the actually presented training data. In neural networks the term of 'self-organising neural networks' is rather popular, probably because of the idea that a system is exposed to a natural environment and it learns to survive in it by organising a respective internal structure by itself.

The best known self-organising neural network approaches are the *Adaptive Resonance Theory* by S. Grossberg and the *Self-Organising Feature Maps* by T. Kohonen. The following subsection 7.7.1 presents the basic idea of the ART networks. This is followed by another well-known class of self-organising networks in subsection 7.7.2: The Kohonen feature maps.

7.7.1 Adaptive Resonance Theory

Grossberg (1976), and Carpenter and Grossberg (1987a, 1987b, 1990)) proposed networks based on the adaptive resonance theory (ART). Such networks consist of two interacting subsystems and an entity which controls the interaction between both subsystems. Figure 7.16 shows the coarse system structure of ART1. There have been subsequent developments of the basic ART idea, which are known as ART2 Carpenter and Grossberg (1987b) and ART3 Carpenter and Grossberg (1990). The subsystem FA is responsible for receiving and pro-

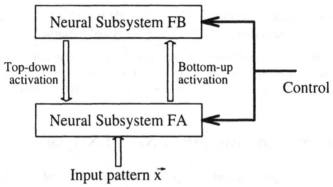

Figure 7.16. Survey of the structure of the ART1 network.

cessing the input patterns. Subsystem FB, on the other hand, is responsible for acquiring patterns which are to be activated by suitable input patterns. In that sense, the neurons of FB are supposed to act as long-term memory. The control signals are used to regulate the system's operational mode, as described below, and distinguish the ART approach from Hopfield Networks.

Details of Neuronal Layers. Figure 7.17 shows a more detailed diagram of the neural subsystems shown in Figure 7.16. Both subsystems FA and FB are

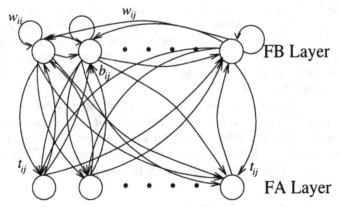

Figure 7.17. Interlayer connections in the ART1 network.

fully interconnected with each other. The output of each neuron of FA is fed as input to each neuron of FB and vice versa. This layer interconnection is thought to support 'resonance' when a match between a stored pattern and an input pattern occurs. This is typical for an ART1 architecture.

The FA subsystem serves two purposes:

- It holds the input pattern,
- forms the FB layer excitation through its bottom-up weights b_{ij}.

The FB layer contains basically 'grandmother' cells, each representing a class of patterns.[3] The neuronal activation of the FB neurons is fed back to the FA layer through the interlayer interconnections t_{ij}. The most characterising point of the FB neurons are their intra-layer interconnections. The neurons of the FB layer are mutually interconnected so that they behave self-exciting, competitive and neighbour-inhibiting. That means:

- Each FB neuron reinforces its own output through a positive interconnection between its output and one of its inputs.
- Each FB neuron maintains a negative (inhibitory) connection to every other neuron in the FB layer.
- Since each unit has both of the above properties, they are called to behave competitive.

A Sample Design of an ART1 Network. A sample implementation of the FA–FB structure discussed above, is as follows: Let us define the interconnection weights w_{ij} where both neurons i and j are in FB by:

$$w_{ij} = \begin{cases} 1 & \text{if } i = j \\ -\epsilon & \text{otherwise} \end{cases} \qquad (7.45)$$

These weight assignments can be interpreted as an 'on-centre, off-surround' interconnection strategy. The intra-layer interconnection weight values t_{ij}, where i corresponds to neurons in the FA layer will be described later. The competition, or inhibition, parameter ϵ is a design parameter with the constraint:

$$\epsilon < \frac{1}{N_{FB}} \qquad (7.46)$$

N_{FB} is hereby the number of neurons in layer FB. Moreover, the competitive character of the FB layer can be modelled by

$$o_i(N+1) = f_i[o_i(N) - \epsilon \sum_{i \neq k} o_k(N)] \qquad i, k = 1, 2, \ldots, N_{FB} \qquad (7.47)$$

where $o_i = f_i(net_i)$ and the function $f_i()$ is a neuron activation output mapping function which is only required to be monotonically non-decreasing for

---

[3] The term 'grandmother cell' comes from the idea that a single cell represents a concept such as the concept 'grandmother.'

positive values of net_i and zero if net_i is negative. This requirement implies that only one neuron, or one stored class of patterns, is supposed to 'win' the competition if the overall network will converge for a given input pattern. This property somewhat resembles the idea of Kohonen's self-organising feature maps discussed in 7.7.2.

Network Dynamics in ART1. Owing to the feedback structure already outlined, the dynamical network behaviour is not only crucial for learning but also for the recognition of an input pattern belonging to an already stored pattern class. These actions are steered by the additional control signals as indicated in Figure 7.16 which put the network into two different modes of operation:

- The *attention phase* employs the neurons of the FA layer only when an input pattern is presented.
- The *orientation phase* subsequently determines which of the neurons in layer FB will eventually 'win' the competition for single activation. If no single 'winner neuron' turns out, a so far uncommitted FB layer neuron is engaged for representing an apparently new pattern class to which the current input pattern belongs.

Actual ART1 network operation. When an input pattern is presented, the ART network does both, recognition *and* learning.

If the input pattern is one that is sufficiently similar to one which has been previously memorised, the network will only recognise. Hereby, one possible modification of the FB layer may be that of reinforcement of the respectively activated neuron. This recognition process is an iterative one. At first, an adaptive[4] filtering through the input neurons of the FA layer takes place. The filtered signals are conveyed to the FB layer where the competition for the selection of one of the stored pattern classes takes place. The result of this competition is fed back to the FA layer until a consistent result at FA is achieved, i.e until the neurons of the FA layer produce stable output signals.

The feedback from the FB layer to the FA layer of the activation of the neuron, which won the competition on FB, may be considered as encoded expectations or learned expectations. Here the idea of resonance becomes visible. The resonance between the two layers FA and FB represents a search through the 'encoded' or memorised patterns in the overall network. If no resonance can be found between FA and FB then there is so far no appropriate pattern stored. Thus, the network should 'learn' the new class of patterns, by creating a new node in the FB layer which represents the new pattern class.

A Concrete ART1 Algorithm. Actually the ART1 represents an entire class of systems or learning and recognition algorithms. An example of an ART1 implementation is presented below. The process contains six steps:

---

[4] 'Adaptive' since the weights b_{ij} may change with each iteration. More details on that will be given subsequently.

1. Select parameters ϵ and ρ and initialise the interlayer connection weights as follows:

$$t_{ij}^0 = 1 \qquad \forall i, j \qquad (7.48)$$

$$b_{ij}^0 = \frac{1}{1+n} \qquad (7.49)$$

Here, the two equations above are special cases of general restrictions on the initialisation of the network interlayer connection weights given in Carpenter and Grossberg (1987a). Equation 7.48 satisfies the *template learning inequality*, while equation 7.49 satisfies the *direct access inequality*.

2. Present the input pattern as a vector of length d with values from $\{-1, +1\}$ to the FA layer.

3. Compute the activations of the FB layer neurons, i.e. each neuron i in FB has the activation given by:

$$net_i = \sum_j b_{ij} x_j \qquad (7.50)$$

4. Determine a 'winner', i.e. a neuron with the maximum activation in the FB layer by applying equation 7.47. All neurons of FB compete hereby, as long as more than one neuron are active in FB. Let the output value of the winning neuron be denoted by:

$$o_j^{FB_{WIN}} = \max_{o_k \in FB} \{o_k^{FB}\} \quad k = 1, ..., N_{FB} \qquad (7.51)$$

5. Now, the verification phase begins which is basically a search for an adequate resonance. Using the winner from step 4 the feedback to the FA layer via the top-down interconnections is weighted by t_{ij}. That is, we obtain:

$$net_i^{FA} = t_{ij} o_j^{FB_{WIN}} \qquad (7.52)$$

The new resulting FA output values are compared with the given input vector. This may be considered as an attempt to confirm the winning neuron in the FB layer determined in step 4.

Hereby, as criterion of comparison a number of different measures may be used. For example the following formula may be used in the case of binary input vectors:

$$\sum_i net_i^{FA} > \rho ||X|| \qquad (7.53)$$

In ART1, $||X|| = \sum_i |x_i|$ is used. As mentioned in step 1 the parameter ρ has been set as a design parameter. ρ determines how critically the match should be evaluated.

6. If the test of step 5 succeeds, the b_{ij} and t_{ij} weights are updated to account for the new input vector X by using the slow learning dynamics equations:

$$\dot{t}_{ij} = \alpha_1 m(j)[-\beta_1 t_{ij} + f_i(x_i)].\tag{7.54}$$

Again, t_{ij} is the weight or strength of the interconnection *from* neuron j *to* neuron i in FA. α_1 is a positive parameter that controls the learning rate, and β_1 is a positive constant that allows gradual forgetting or decay. $f_i(x_i$ is the output function of neuron i in FA using x_i as activation. The function $m(j)$ is described below.

It should be noted that the intra-layer weights of FB are <u>not</u> adjusted by 7.54. So far, only the interconnection weights *from* the FB layer *to* the FA layer are adjusted. Next, the interconnection weights from FA to FB are adjusted according to the following equation:

$$\dot{b}_{ji} = \alpha_2 m(j)[-\beta_2 b_{ji} + f_i(x_i)].\tag{7.55}$$

Again, b_{ji} is the interconnection weight for the connection *from* neuron i in FA *to* neuron j in layer FB. As for equation 7.54, α_2 and β_2 are analogous parameters controlling learning and forgetting.

The function $m(j)$ in both of the above equations is used to restrict the updating of weights to those involving only the winning class $o_j^{FB_{WIN}}$ as defined in 7.51, using:

$$m(j) = \left\{ \begin{array}{ll} 1 & \text{if } o_j = o_j^{FB_{WIN}} \\ 0 & \text{otherwise} \end{array} \right.\tag{7.56}$$

However, if the comparing test of step 5 fails, this neuron is ruled out and step 4 is repeated as long as no winner is found and there are still remaining candidates.

Possible application domains. Typical applications are clustering of vectors, e.g. for pattern recognition purposes - often for preprocessing, such as feature extraction. See Kischell et al. (1995) for an application in medical imaging or Kim, Kim, and Kim (1996). The following presents another important self-organising system architecture, Kohonen's self-organising feature maps.

7.7.2 Self-Organising Feature Maps

Kohonen proposes an alternative neural learning structure Kohonen (1982a, 1982b, 1984, 1987), Kangas, Kohonen, and Laaksonen (1990) or Kohonen (1997). The basic idea is to have networks that perform dimensionality reduction through conversion of the feature space. The goal is to obtain *topologically ordered* similarity graphs or clustering diagrams. Additionally, a lateral unit interaction function is used to implement a form of local competitive learning.

Topological Neighbourhoods. Once a topological dimension is chosen, the concept of an equivalent dimension neighbourhood around each neuron has to be determined. Figure 7.18 shows an example of a 2-D map. The neighbourhood of each neuron u_a, denoted by N_a is centred around neuron u_a while the cell or neighbourhood size may vary over time, which is typical during the training phase. For example, initially N_a may start as the entire 2-D network, and the radius of N_a shrinks as iteration proceeds; as described below.

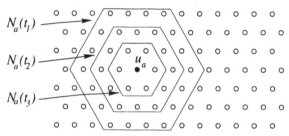

Figure 7.18. Example of a topological neighbourhood N_a of neuron unit u_a. The corresponding neighbourhood is shrinking with increasing number of training iterations n_i.

Due to the discrete nature of the 2-dimensional net the neighbourhood of a neuron may be defined in terms of nearest neighbours. For example, the four nearest neighbours of a unit u_a may be its N, S, E, and W neighbours. The eight nearest neighbours would include the corners in NE, SE, SW, and NW direction as well.

The Learning Algorithm. All neurons receive the complete input vector I as input. Each single input signal has an individual weight associated for each of the neurons. The goal of the learning process is to find clusters of similar input vectors within a large number of presented unlabelled input vectors.

The weight vector for a neural unit u_i is usually denoted by $M_i = (w_{i1}, w_{i2}, \ldots, w_{id})^T$. A useful viewpoint is to consider each neural unit as a filter that tries to match the input vector in competition with the other neurons. The overall structure of a self-organising feature map may then be considered as:

> an array of matched filters, which competitively adjust unit input weights on the basis of the current weights and degree of match.

In the following, the approach is presented in more quantitative detail: The network's weights are normally initialised with random values. Then, for the input vector $X(k)$ at time k the distance $d(X(k), M_i)$ between $X(k)$ and the weight vector M_i for each neuron u_i is computed according to some distance measure d. d may be an inner product measure (correlation), Euclidean distance, or another suitable measure. For example, let us proceed with the Euclidean distance. At first, through a matching phase the most similar neural unit u_s is determined by using:

$$\|X(k) - M_s(k)\| = \min_i \{\|X(k) - M_i(k)\|\} \tag{7.57}$$

That is, at iteration k, given the input vector X, u_s is the neuron whose weight vector matches best the input vector. Through the subsequent network updating phase, this affects *all* neurons in the currently defined cell or cluster $N_s(k)$ surrounding u_s as follows:

$$M_i(k+1) = \left\{ \begin{array}{ll} M_i(k) + \alpha(k)[X(k) - M_i(k)] & i \in N_s(k) \\ M_i(k) & i \notin N_s(k) \end{array} \right. \qquad (7.58)$$

The updating strategy in 7.58 corresponds to a discretised version of the differential adaptation law given in the following:

$$\frac{dM_i}{dt} = \alpha(t)[X(t) - M_i(t)] \qquad i \in N_s(t) \qquad (7.59)$$

$$\frac{dM_i}{dt} = 0 \qquad i \notin N_s(t) \qquad (7.60)$$

Equation 7.59 clearly shows that the distance between $X(t)$ and the weight vector M_i decreases by the given updating strategy. Thus after updating, the weight vectors in N_s are closer to the input vector $X(t)$. Weight vectors of neurons outside N_s remain unchanged. The fact that units inside N_s are relatively closer to the input vector after the training step than the weight vectors of units outside of N_s reveals the competitive nature of the algorithm. Hereby, the parameter α is a possibly iteration-dependent design parameter.

Properties of the Training Algorithm. As can be deduced from the updating rules the resulting accuracy of the mapping depends on the choices of N_s, $\alpha(k)$, and the number of updating iterations. Kohonen mentions numbers of $10,000$ to $100,000$ iterations as typical. Furthermore, $\alpha(k)$ should generally start with a value close to 1.0, and gradually decrease with k. The neighbourhood size $N_s(k)$ deserves careful consideration as well. Too small a choice of $N_s(0)$ may lead to maps without topological ordering. Thus, it appears reasonable to let $N_s(0)$ be rather large and to shrink $N_s(k)$ with k growing to the fine-adjustment phase, where N_s consists only of the nearest neighbours of unit u_s. The limiting case is, of course, where $N_s(k)$ comprises only a single unit.

Applications. Kohonen's self-organising maps are mainly used for pattern recognition purposes, often for pre-processing, such as feature extraction. See Manhaeghe, Lemahieu, Vogelaers, and Colardyn (1994), or Kischell et al. (1995), for an example in medical pattern recognition, Miller and Coe (1996) for astronomy, or Luckman, Allinson, Ellis, and Flude (1995) for face recognition. Also a special-purpose hardware implementation on a single chip has been designed for Kohonen maps and the associated learning algorithm Macq, Verleysen, Jespers, and Legat (1993).

7.8 Summary

This chapter presented a variety of neural network models along with corresponding learning techniques. Although the presented network types were quite diverse, they represent only a fraction of the neural network models proposed in the literature. The literature on the technical aspects of neural networks and their application, which lie mostly in engineering and pattern recognition, is vast and to give a comprehensive account is neither feasible nor desirable for the purpose of this book. The presented models were motivated partly by biological models, but were largely the result of studying the structure behind the mathematical functions a network can represent. In other words, the presented learning models are <u>not</u> accurate reflections of biological neurons or the physiological processes in the brain. They are rather inspired in a metaphorical sense by certain aspects of biological brains, such as the massive interconnection between neurons, the threshold functions of neurons, etc. Furthermore, a large number of network models have been developed in the literature to serve purely certain engineering needs, as opposed to reflect biological aspects of the brain. See, for example, radial basis functions Wei and Hirzinger (1997) or the 'Mixture-of-Experts' structure of networks, Jordan and Jacobs (1994), Xu and Jordan (1996). However, for the general understanding of the debate between the symbolic and connectionist paradigm of AI, one does not need to go into the details of the latest developments in neural networks and their learning procedures. The models presented in this chapter reflect the general flavour of the field fairly well. Thus, the material in this chapter certainly equips the reader well enough with the technical background for appreciating the discussions in part III of this book. The interested reader may consult the proceedings of the major conferences on the topic for more details, among them the *Neural Information Processing Symposium*, the *International Conference on Artificial Neural Networks*, the *International Conference on Neural Information Processing*, the *International Conference on Neural Networks*, the *International Conference on Cognitive Science*, as well Journals on the topic, including *IEEE Transactions on Neural Networks*, *Neural Computation*, *Neurocomputing*, *Connection Science*, and others.

8. Integrating Symbols into Connectionist Models

Fodor and Pylyshyn (1988) argued against connectionism because it cannot handle apparent cognitive abilities which can easily be handled in the symbolic paradigm. These abilities are those of systematicity, compositionality and other structure-sensitive capabilities. They refer to abilities of understanding and construction of sentences like 'Paul loves Emma' and 'Emma loves Paul.' It seems that once one understands the relation 'loves' one can replace the subject and the object of the sentence by arbitrarily chosen persons. Furthermore, the order of the persons matters. That is, whenever there is an internal representation of 'Paul' being used, there must also be a mechanism which ensures which role this representation will take in the relationship 'loves'. Fodor and Pylyshyn call such properties of representations *structure-sensitive*. See chapter 11 for a much deeper discussion of these and related issues.

What is of interest here, is the fact that there have been a few constructive responses to the critique of Fodor and Pylyshyn. The following presents two approaches to address the systematicity and compositionality problem. The first one goes under the title *Structured Connectionism*, while the second one is called *Integrated Connectionist/Symbolic Architecture*. Finally, we will briefly mention approaches to convert symbolic structures into connectionist structures and the other way round. Besides the work presented here, there are other approaches to integrate symbolic and connectionist aspects in systems, including Thrun (1996).

8.1 Structured Connectionism

Work in *structured connectionism* differs in the type of networks being considered as well as in some of the underlying assumptions from the 'unstructured connectionism'.[1] One of the underlying assumptions of structured connectionism is that useful networks need to have an appropriate structure *built-in*. This has a number of important implications. One important implication is,

---

[1] *Unstructured connectionism* means those connectionist approaches which attempt to use a general purpose network which is then trained for any particular problem in question, and thus, is tailored towards its application essentially by training only.

that there is no such thing as a general purpose network structure which can easily be adapted to whatever purpose one likes. Often, the Multi-layer Perceptron is viewed as general purpose network structure which merely needs to be trained to function properly in a given application domain. One of the leading researchers in structured connectionism, J. Feldman, writes:

> "The belief that weight adaptation in layered or other unstructured networks will suffice for complex learning is so wrong-headed that it is hard to understand why anyone professes it."[2]

Accepting the view that the search for general purpose networks is misguided implies that connectionist networks need to be pre-structured for a given application. That is, every network to be used needs to be 'engineered' first, just as software needs to be designed for every application specifically. Learning, then, has the role of adapting or fine-tuning a given structured network towards the domain conditions at hand. This is opposed to considering learning as tailoring a general-purpose network towards a specific application. These assumptions are fairly untypical for the flavour of connectionism as discussed so far. In fact, structured connectionism may appear to be closer to a particular style of traditional software engineering than to the idea of connectionism in the sense of dealing with subsymbols, etc.[3]

The philosophy behind structured connectionism is to gain insight from biological systems that do complex tasks very effectively, which is still difficult to do with current computer technology. Such tasks include the recognition of complex visual or acoustic patterns, etc. Considering that the neurons in the human brain have a comparably low processing speed, (around 1ms) and the quick performance of the overall system for classifying images, etc., implies that it takes the brain not much more than a few hundred processing steps. On the search for artificial connectionist structures as well as algorithms for computer vision these constraints imposed on natural systems could be used as a guideline to rule out approaches which could not meet the constraint of taking not more than several hundred computing steps in a massively parallel connectionist system. A proposal by Shastri and Ajjanagadde (1993) is outlined below, which epitomises the work under the heading of *structured connectionism*. Note that generally in structured connectionism, as well as in the following proposal, it is not assumed that one node in a structured connectionist architecture corresponds 1:1 to a biological neuron. Those nodes are to be viewed as macros, i.e. corresponding to an assemblage of biological neurons.

Shastri and Ajjanagadde's Architecture Shastri and Ajjanagadde (1993) proposed a model for communication among different units in a connectionist system, which accounts for the phenomenon of symbolic reasoning by communicating pulse codes between different parts of a connectionist architecture.

---

[2] See Feldman (1993):302.
[3] See chapter 11 for a discussion of the issue of subsymbols.

The following presents some technical details of their proposal. For more details see Shastri and Ajjanagadde (1993).

The basic idea is that the pulse codes serve as symbols communicated between different units. If two pulse codes are in synchrony, they encode the same symbol. See the pulse diagram in Figure 8.1 for an example. The following gives

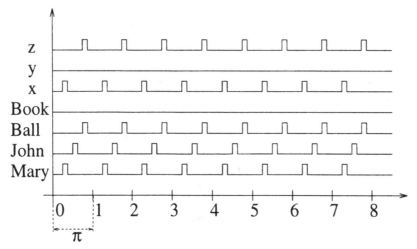

Figure 8.1. The basic idea of pulse codes is to assign differently phased pulses to different symbols. That is, in this diagram, *John, Mary* and *Ball* are activated but have differently phased activation pulses. The constant *Book* is not activated. The activation pulse of the variable x is in phase with the pulse of John. As a consequence, The variable x is bound to the constant *John* as long as their pulse codes are in phase. That is, for a predicate, say $give(x, y, z)$ the three argument places can be bound to constants by activating each of the argument places with a distinct pulse code which is in phase with the pulse code of the corresponding constants. In the diagram, only x is instantiated with *John* and z with *Ball*. Note that the variable y is not activated. This amounts to y being an unbound variable and, as will be seen in the text, amounts to an all-quantified variable in queries.

examples of how pulse codes can be used to retrieve knowledge from a long-term knowledge base, which is encoded statically by a fixed wiring of nodes and how it can be used to perform symbolic reasoning tasks.

In Figure 8.2 a fraction of a network is shown which is able to store and retrieve simple facts, like *John gives Mary a ball*. The building blocks of such a 'mini-network' are the three pentagon-shaped nodes denoted *e:give, c:give,* and *F1* on the one hand and the activation inhibiting connections to the links between nodes on the other hand. A node *e:predicate-name* is responsible to enable the predicate, while a node *c:predicate-name* is responsible to collect the answer of a query. The enabler-node produces a 'full-period activity pulse signal' as shown in Figure 8.2 in the timing diagram on the right for the internal evaluation of the query to the predicate.

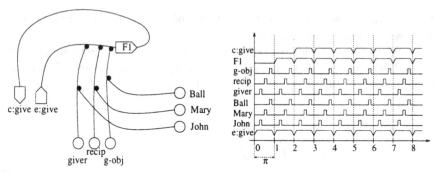

Figure 8.2. The shown 'mini-network' encodes the fact *give(John, Mary, Ball)*, i.e. John gives Mary a Ball. The retrieval of that knowledge works as explained in the text.

The node *F1* is a so-called τ-and node, which produces an active output signal over the entire pulse period π of the system if and only if it receives an uninterrupted full-period input signal. That is, a τ-and node generates an active output signal only if the activity signal from the enabler-node reaches the τ-and node undisturbed.

The only sources of a potential disturbance are the wires connected to the link from the enabler-node to the τ-and node. That is, for each argument of a predicate there is one wire, whose active signal would result in an inhibiting effect on the signal transmitted on the link between the enabler-node and the τ-and node (see Figure 8.2). That is, each argument of the predicate being activated by some pulse code would inhibit the enabler signal, and thus would inhibit the τ-and node to emit an activity signal. This inhibition of the τ-and node can only be avoided, if for an argument carrying a pulse code signal σ an inhibiting signal arrives at that argument wire, which is in phase with σ, thus resulting in a cancellation of σ.

The retrieval in Figure 8.2 works as follows: The enabler-node *e:give* is activated, and produces a full-period pulse signal as shown in the timing diagram on the right. This signal will activate the *F1* τ-and node if it is transmitted to *F1* undisturbed. An active signal emitted by *F1* will cause an activity signal by the collector node *c:give* indicating a 'yes'-answer. The potential candidates to disturb (inhibit) that signal are the connections from *giver*, *recip*, and *g-obj* to that link. If any of these wires carries an activity signal, it will inhibit the propagation of the activity signal from *e:give* to *F1*, thus preventing the activation of *F1*. In order to instantiate an argument of the predicate *give*, a pulse code will be provided for each of the argument places. This pulse code would normally inhibit the activity signal travelling from *e:give* to *F1*, unless a synchronous pulse signal is provided by any inhibitory link from one of the constant nodes on the right side. That is, if *giver* and *John* carry a pulse signal synchronous to each other, the signal coming from *John* will inhibit the signal travelling from *giver*, resulting in not disturbing the activity signal travelling from *e:give* to *F1*. As a result, *F1* will emit an activity signal only if the pulse codes for each of the arguments of the predicate coincide with the pulse codes provided by the 'constant nodes' shown in the diagram. That is, only if the arguments are instantiated with the constants as connected in the network, a 'yes'-answer will be generated. Assuming a delay time of one pulse period, *F1* and finally *c:give* will emit their signals as indicated in the timing diagram on the right.

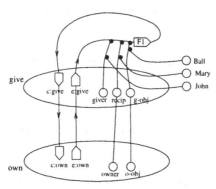

Figure 8.3. This 'mini-network' encodes the fact $give(John, Mary, Ball)$, i.e. John gives Mary a Ball as well as $\forall x, y, z \; give(x, y, z) \rightarrow own(y, z)$. If the arguments of the predicate *own* are instantiated by some pulse code, that pulse code is propagated to the *give* predicate. Similarly, if the collector node *c:give* sends an activity signal (i.e. a 'yes'-answer), then this is propagated to the *own* predicate. That is, whenever the *give* predicate is true, the *own* predicate will be true as well. Thus, the network implements effectively the all-quantified proposition above.

In Figure 8.3 a simple network is shown that represent the all-quantified proposition $\forall x, y, z \; give(x, y, z) \rightarrow own(y, z)$. It also allows to perform corresponding inferences: All arguments provided for the *own* predicate are propagated to the corresponding arguments of the *give* predicate. If the *give* predicate is evaluated to 'true', i.e. if the *c:give* node is activated, its activation is propagated to the *c:own* node, indicating that the predicate *own* is evaluated to 'true' too. One should imagine that the long-term memory would not only hold the fact that *John gives Mary a Ball*, but that there are many more such facts stored by the corresponding connections of the constants to the respective wire for each argument. As a result, if each of the possible arguments issues a different pulse code, the node *F1* will only be activated, if all the argument fillers are cancelled by a synchronous pulse code coming from the constants. Note that in this network, it is not possible to recall the all-quantified proposition as such, but only its meaning reflected in the answers to queries regarding the *own* predicate. However, in Shastri and Ajjanagadde (1993), other network structures are presented which would also allow such meta-level retrieval of knowledge.

More examples and a few more types of nodes are presented in Shastri and Ajjanagadde (1993), effectively demonstrating how pulse-coded symbols can be passed around in a huge network and can be used to perform symbolic reasoning within a relatively few pulse periods. It is also shown, how uninstantiated variables can be instantiated as a result of a query; e.g. questions like 'What gave John to Mary?' can be answered using additional types of nodes. Another issue being shown, is how conceptual hierarchies stored in the long-term knowledge base, i.e. stored by hard-wiring, can be integrated into the reasoning system.

A particularly appealing aspect of this proposal is that it represents a model which takes current knowledge about the brain physiology into account. That is, in particular the idea of pulse-coded messages being transmitted in the brain is supported by neurological findings, such as those by von der Malsburg (1981, 1986), von der Malsburg and Schneider (1986) or Abeles (1982, 1991) and others.

8.2 Smolensky's Integrated Connectionist/Symbolic Architecture

Smolensky (1995) proposes an architecture which shows both, the attractive features of traditional connectionist architectures as well as such structure-sensitive properties, as emphasised in the critique by Fodor and Pylyshyn (1988), are maintained with distributed representations of, e.g. 'Paul', 'Emma', etc. The basic idea is outlined below:

The state of many parallel and distributed processing systems, such as MLPs or similar neural network models, can be characterised by a vector or, in most cases more appropriately, by multi-dimensional vectors, such as a matrix of weights $\mathbf{W}$, one weight for each of its interconnections between two neurons, together with a vector $\mathbf{a}$ of activation levels of each of the neurons. Furthermore, the processing can be described as vector operations, where the next activation level vector $\mathbf{a}^{t+1}$ is determined by applying a suitable vector operation on $\mathbf{a}^t$ and $\mathbf{W}$. In many cases this will be a vector multiplication, possibly followed by simple scalar transformations for each of the elements of the to be newly formed activation vector $\mathbf{a}^{t+1}$. Smolensky proposes to use the tensor product for encoding structural information when combining vector representations (see also Smolensky (1990b)). The tensor product of two vectors $\mathbf{a} = \langle a_0, a_1, ..., a_n \rangle$ and $\mathbf{b} = \langle b_0, b_1, ..., b_m \rangle$ is defined as follows:

$$a \otimes b = \begin{pmatrix} a_0 b_0 & a_0 b_1 & a_0 b_2 & ... & a_0 b_m \\ ... & ... & ... & ... & ... \\ a_n b_0 & a_n b_1 & a_n b_2 & ... & a_n b_m \end{pmatrix}.$$

This has the consequence that the tensor product multiplies the number of elements of each operand. While this results in a dramatic increase of elements, it also allows to encode structure-sensitive information. For example, Smolensky proposes that a sentence like 'Paul loves Emma' could be represented in a symbolic fashion by $loves(Paul, Emma)$, or shorter even by $L(P, E)$ This can be turned into a LISP-like structure where all symbol structures are possibly recursive lists of two elements as follows:

$$[Loves, [Paul, Emma]].$$

A structure like that can be represented as the following connectionist activity vector:

$$p = r_0 \otimes L + r_1 \otimes [r_0 \otimes P + r_1 \otimes E].$$

The vectors r_0 and r_1 serve as encoders for the fact that the corresponding vector was the left or the right part respectively. In this case, short vectors would do such as $r_0 = \langle 0, 1 \rangle$ and $r_1 = \langle 1, 0 \rangle$. The important point is merely that the vectors are linearly independent. from each other. With r_0 and r_1 defined this way, each tensor product operation would double the number of vector elements in the resulting vector. The tensor product $r_0 \otimes L$ results in a two-dimensional vector where the first row contains zeros only. Similarly, the tensor product $r_1 \otimes E$ results in a matrix where the second row contains zeros only. By such a mechanism, the structural information can be preserved even after vectors are added up, etc. It allows to really keep track of recursive expressions etc no matter how involved they might be. Recursive structures result in correspondingly higher-dimensional vectors. The interested reader will find more details, in Smolensky (1990b, 1995).

The important point for the current exposition is the idea that really structural information, as it is used in symbolic systems, can be encoded in a connectionist system as well. In general, one can think of other ways of encoding such structural information, but the required processes to maintain and use this information may not be standard vector operations.

8.3 Relating Symbolic Rules to Connectionist Networks

There has been a body of research produced on extracting symbolic rules from trained neural networks as well as on providing symbolic rules as a priori structure for a neural network which is trained subsequently. That is, translations in both directions, from symbols to neural networks and from neural networks into symbols have been studied.

8.3.1 Rule-Extraction from Neural Networks

The main motivation for extracting symbolic rules from trained neural networks lies in the desire to have explanatory capabilities besides the pure performance. That is, it is often not enough, if a neural network has learned to perform a certain task. An explanation of what it has learned is often needed in order to increase the confidence of users in the trained neural networks. Usually, the obtained rules are only approximations of the function the neural network has learned.

In general, to extract a rule from a neural network involves usually a substantial search process through the space of rules which possibly match the network's performance best. It has been pointed out that the number of rules that can be extracted from a trained neural network is potentially exponential in the number of inputs used Gallant (1988). A number of search techniques for finding rules have been proposed in the literature. Gedeon, Ramer, Padet, and Padet (1995) present a taxonomy of different rule extraction techniques based on how the problem of combinatorial explosion is avoided. They distinguish four aspects: 1) how the search space for rules is reduced, 2) whether the learning algorithm is modified, 3) how the search is carried out, and 4) whether the network is treated as a black-box.

Many techniques reduce the search space by clustering. Often the weights are clustered, see Craven and Shavlik (1993), or the hidden units are clustered, see Fu (1992, 1994). For these techniques, often the employed backpropagation learning algorithm is modified by modified cost functions to influence the iterative adjustments of weights in order to ensure the feasibility of extracting rules from the trained network.

Rule extraction from a black-box view of the neural network is usually not satisfactory. Approaches which use only the weight matrix have been successful in specific domains. Gedeon (1997) has shown that complementing the use of the weight matrix by considering the typical inputs to the neural networks can improve the rule-extraction process. There are a number of other approaches such as Craven and Shavlik (1997), who construct decision trees from neural networks trained on time series data or Alexander and Mozer (1995) who use templates for rule extraction. See also Andrews and Diederich (1996), Tickle, Andrews, Golea, and Diederich (1998) for a collection of recent work on rule extraction.

8.3.2 Providing Symbolic Structure to a Neural Network A Priori

There are different approaches to incorporate some symbolic knowledge into a neural network before training. One approach constructs a special purpose network architecture which reflects the symbolic rules, e.g. (Towell & Shavlik, 1994).

Another approach is to predefine the weights of a standard MLP network. Training is then normally only conducted briefly in order to ensure that the provided a priori structure is reasonably maintained. This second approach has the following advantage over the first approach: When using longer training periods, the a priori provided knowledge can be overwritten, if the training data suggests to do so.

Providing rules to structure a network initially, can also have the benefit, of an easier rule extraction after training of the network took place. This is, because it can be expected that a similar rule to the initially provided rule will be extracted. Hence, the search space for finding a suitable rule to extract, can be dramatically reduced (see Towell and Shavlik (1993, 1994) for more details).

9. Summary of the Connectionist Paradigm

Starting in the 1940s, and after receiving a strong boost in the mid-1980s, a substantial body of research has been conducted in the connectionist paradigm of AI. A large number of neural network models have been developed, besides those which have been presented in the previous chapters. Many of them are not biologically plausible. The reasons for this vary. One main point is that there is a substantial interest in neural network-style continuous function approximators. That is, for this purpose, the biological role models are not of particular interest; instead it is the fact that a multitude of computing units can be combined in order to compute smooth continuous functions of a possibly large number of variables.

Another reason is the interest to exploit the massive parallelism of distributed computing in order to gain speed. Again, the biological resemblance is largely limited to the fact that the neural network models have a large number of interconnected computing units which process their inputs in parallel.

The greatest interest in neural networks, from a practical point of view, can be found in engineering, where high-dimensional continuous functions need to be computed and approximated on the basis of a number of data points. That is, training a neural network on those data points would result in a continuous function which at least approximates the function values for the given data points. Furthermore, because the functions represented by neural network models are generally smooth, there is some optimism that the learned function can be used. Indeed, if enough data is available, which is often the case for low-dimensional functions, the learned function is often of reasonable use. Nevertheless, there is often still a certain mistrust in the reliability of what neural networks learn, as it is usually difficult to understand exactly, what function has been learned or to anticipate what function will be learned on the basis of available data. As a consequence, neural networks are still largely used in experimental settings, in research labs, etc. They have been used in a number of commercial applications, but they still struggle to win the trust and confidence of the more conservative engineering community. This, however, will be important to disseminate the technology to routine use at a larger scale.

There a numerous books available and regular international conferences, including *Neural Information Processing Systems* of which the proceedings are published as *Advances in Neural Information Processing Systems* by MIT Press,

International Conference on Artificial Neural Networks, International Conference on Neural Information Processing, International Conference on Neural Networks, International Symposium on Artificial Neural Networks, etc., are being held to present neural networks as a technology for many application areas, ranging from pattern recognition, over control, to financial prediction. However, it should be noted that these rather technical applications of neural networks are not to be confused with the grand hope of connectionism as it is discussed here:

> To provide a new paradigm for understanding and building large-scale intelligent systems.

To date, successful applications of the neural network technology are relatively small-scale applications. This is opposed to the hope for general intelligent agents. In the context of these practical applications, there is also significant research being devoted to the integration of neural networks with other techniques, such as fuzzy sets (Da Ruan, 1997), or genetic algorithms (Pearson, Albrecht, & Steele, 1995). Generally, during recent years, there has also been an increasing interest in providing either neural networks with a certain a priori structure such as knowledge expressed in terms of fuzzy sets or production rules. Interest in the opposite direction, i.e. in generating symbolic rules, which explain what a neural network has learned, has also increased in recent years.[1]

---

[1] See section 8.3.2 for more details.

Part III

Methodological Analysis of the Two Paradigms

While the first two parts of this book had largely the character of a review, which can be found elsewhere in more detail, part III contains a new in-depth analysis comparing both paradigms. The content of this third part provides a deeper understanding of the underlying assumptions of both paradigms and its implications.

More importantly, however, this part argues that the debate about the paradigms of AI has to look at the paradigms from a completely different angle to make sense. The question about what is, in principle, the proper paradigm is shifted towards a more quantitative issue. Instead of deciding whether the functionality of a system can be described within a paradigm at all, the focus is shifted to the following question:

> How difficult is it to provide an operational description of the functionality of an intelligent system? How difficult is it to understand such a description?

Answers to these questions will also depend on the descriptional complexity of intelligence or human-level cognition. In the first chapter of this part, chapter 10, the computational foundations of the following analysis are presented, which includes the explication of the concept of algorithm, as well as the definition of the notion of algorithmic information theory (Kolmogorov complexity). Chapter 11 presents the conflicts between the symbolic and connectionist paradigm in more detail. In particular, the crux of the connectionist claims and their justifications are presented. Chapter 12 presents a deeper analysis of the difference in the conceptions of the notion of *symbol* in both paradigms. It is argued that different conceptions are at least partly responsible for the heated debate about the appropriateness of either paradigm. In chapter 13 the learning capabilities of connectionist networks are investigated, specifically with respect to the acquisition of complex[2] functions from training data. Chapter 14 presents a discussion about a suitable research methodology for AI and cognitive science. There has not been much discussion on the topic from such a principled point of view yet. However, the existence of the AI debate shows that this is much needed. As a consequence of the considerations in chapter 14, chapter 15 discusses non-factual knowledge which requires particular attention to deal with it in AI systems and to account for it in cognitive theories. Finally, chapter 16 summarises the main points of the analyses in part III and derives an assessment of the potential of both paradigms.

---

[2] with respect to descriptional complexity.

10. Formal Foundations

This chapter covers the basic formal notions which are used for the following analyses. The fundamental concepts are universal computing models and are presented in the following section 10.1. Computational universality refers to the expressive power of a paradigm, i.e. to the general limitations of what sort of functions can be expressed at all in a paradigm. This is followed in section 10.2 by a presentation of the notion of *algorithmic information theory* or, synonymously, *Kolmogorov complexity*, which is based on the notion of the Turing machine. In the last section of this chapter, the point is made that the description of intelligent behaviour is likely to require a large amount of algorithmic information. That is, even the shortest possible operational description is still of very substantial length.

10.1 The Notion of Algorithm

In the development of the notion of algorithm, a remarkable convergence can be observed. (Turing, 1937) introduced his Turing machine as explication of the intuitive notion of algorithm.[1] It should be noted that the notion of algorithm, as developed by Turing and a few contemporary mathematicians was not thought to describe in a formal way what today's computers can do. It was rather to clarify, what sort of 'computing procedures' can be precisely defined at all. That is, in a way that a person,[2] a mathematician, can effectively execute the procedure and effectively arrive at the result of the such defined function. Moreover, a conjecture has been stated by Church and Turing, known as the Church-Turing thesis, that the intuitive notion of algorithm is actually explicated by the formal notion of the Turing machine.[3] This implies that it is not expected that any more powerful formalisation of the intuitive notion of algorithm will ever be developed. In this context it should be noted that the

---

[1] Around the same time other approaches, like Church's λ-**calculus** (Church, 1936) or Post's production systems (Post, 1943) had been developed. Finally, however, it could be proved that all these different formalisms are equivalent with respect to the set of functions which they describe.

[2] Which was the 'computer' in Turing's original article (Turing, 1937).

[3] See Davis (1982) for a discussion on this thesis.

notion of algorithm is the most general, the most powerful kind of description mankind has ever developed.

10.1.1 The Turing Machine

The Turing machine is briefly described as follows (see Figure 10.1 for a basic variant of the Turing machine): The Turing machine has a finite number of internal states. A tape on which the Turing machine can read and write symbols from a finite alphabet via its read/write head is unlimited on both sides. The Turing machine starts its operation in a particular internal state and terminates its operation in another particular state. The read/write head will focus on the first square on the tape where the input string (in consecutive squares) to its computation is provided. The Turing machine will execute a sequence of operations. Each of these operations depends on the current symbol under the read/write head and its internal state. The operation may erase the old symbol on the tape in the square under the read/write head and replace it by another symbol. Furthermore, the Turing machine may change its internal state and move (optionally) its read/write head one square to the left or to the right. The entire computation terminates when the Turing machine gets into the special internal termination state. The result of the computation is found at a pre-specified location on the tape relative to the position of the read/write head. Which operation is executed depends on the internal state and the current symbol under the read/write head is specified in the corresponding Turing table. An example is shown in Figure 10.1 beneath the Turing machine.

Interestingly, it has been proved that there are some problems, e.g. the decision problem of first order logic, the halting problem, etc. no Turing machine can solve.[4] Although the Turing machine is usually considered to be a theoretical model of real computers, it should be noted that no physical machine will ever have the computational power of a Turing machine. Neither will a physical tape be of potentially infinite length nor will a machine run a program of arbitrary complexity. In the section on *algorithmic information theory* a restricted version of the notion of algorithm will be presented.

10.1.2 Production Rules

Post (1943) developed another explication of algorithms or effective procedures. The basic idea was to consider the process of proving Theorems. One begins

---

[4] Lucas (1961) and others have argued that exactly these results can be used for proving the freedom of the human mind. Actually, Dreyfus's argument that the human mind does not follow rules is a similar line of thought. Both, Lucas and Dreyfus, argue that the human mind is able to transcendent any rule schema as it is given by the notion of algorithm.

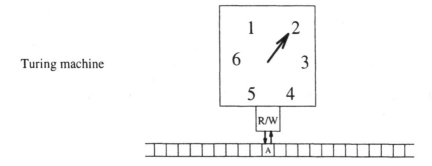

Turing machine

Turing table

State	x	Symbol	⟶	State	x	Symbol	x	Head move
1		A	⟶	2		A		L
1		B	⟶	3		A		R
1		C	⟶	6		D		R
.		.		.		.		.
.		.		.		.		.
.		.		.		.		.
.		.		.		.		.
6		D	⟶	3		B		L

Figure 10.1. The schema of a Turing machine and the respective Turing table.

with a set of axioms, formally given as certain strings of characters, and applies 'rules of inference' to some or all of the axioms. The result of each such application is a Theorem. Every string of characters that can be obtained by applying a sequence of 'inference steps' is a Theorem of the original axioms.

Post, on this basis, developed his *production rules*. Since production rules became popular in (symbolic) AI. Post's original conception is presented in this chapter.

A Post production system consists of the following:

– A finite alphabet $A = \{a_1, a_2, ..., a_r\}$.
– A finite set of axioms which are finite strings of the alphabet A.
– A finite set of 'inference rules' which are rules of the following form:

$$\underbrace{g_0 \$_1 g_2 \$_2 ... \$_n g_n}_{\text{antecedent}} \quad \rightarrow \quad \underbrace{h_0 \$_1' h_2 \$_2' ... \$_m' h_m}_{\text{consequence}},$$

where all g_i and h_i are fixed finite strings of A which includes the empty string. The $\$_i$ and $\$_i'$ are variables which can be replaced by any finite string of A including the empty string. All variables on the right side of the rule have to occur on the left side. A production rule p can be applied to all strings s which match with the left side of the rule. That is, the complete string s must be given on the left side of a rule by replacing the variables by suitable substrings of s. Applying a rule p to a string s results in the replacement of s by the the string given on the right side of the production rule p, where all variables have to be replaced by the substrings which have been assigned to them on the left side of the rule.

Example

- Alphabet $A = \{a, b, c, d\}$.
- Axioms:
  1. aab
  2. abc
  3. $ccdc$.
- Production rules:
  1. $aV_1 b \rightarrow baV_1$
  2. $aV_1 bV_2 \rightarrow V_2$.

Given this canonical system, the following productions can be performed:
Applying rule 1 to axiom 1:

$$aacb \rightarrow baac$$

Applying rule 2 to axiom 2:
$$abc \rightarrow c$$

None of the rules can be applied to axiom 3.

Post proved that any production system can be put into a 'Normal Form' where every production rule is of the simple form

$$g\$ \rightarrow \$h.$$

Post also proved that his production systems are computationally universal. Hence his Normal Form production systems with rules containing only a single constant string and a single variable on both sides, the antecedent and the consequence, are computationally universal too. For more details on that, see Minsky (1967).

10.1.3 Cellular Automata

Another computationally universal formalism are *cellular spaces* (or *cellular automata*), which are due to von Neumann (1966). Because cellular automata resemble in a sense the structure of regular (neural) networks, this formalism is presented as the second alternative to the Turing machine.[5] Although cellular

---

[5] Further recent universality proofs for types of neural networks can be found in Siegelmann and Sontag (1992) or Koiran, Cosnard, and Garzon (1994).

spaces may be of any dimension we will restrict our considerations to one and two-dimensional cellular spaces.

Intuitively speaking, a two-dimensional cellular space can be imagined as a chess board, infinite in all four directions. Each of the 'squares', represents a cell of the cellular space. Similarly, a one-dimensional cellular space amounts to a string or tape infinite in both directions. With each cell the following three items are associated:

- A neighbourhood
- A local transition function f
- A quiescent state.

Each cell is always in one of a finite number of internal states. The state of a cell c at time step $t + 1$ is given by the local state transition function f and depends on both its internal state at time t and the states at time t of c's neighbourhood. The neighbourhood of a cell c is a finite set of cells which are in fixed positions relative to c. If all cells in a given cellular space S have neighbourhoods of the same shape and all cells have the same state transition function, then it is said that the cellular space S is *uniform*.

All cells are changing their states synchronously. Thus, a global transition function F is determined by the local transition function f in each cell. A configuration of a cellular space S is the entirety of the local states of all cells. A cellular space starts its computation in a certain initial configuration c_0. Given an initial configuration, the subsequent configuration - after applying simultaneously the local transition function in all cells - is given by $F(c_0)$. Thus, a cellular space S is computing a sequence of configurations $c_0, c_1, c_2, ..., c_n, ...$

The following presents two Theorems along with proof sketches, which state certain types of cellular spaces to be computationally universal.

Theorem 10.1. *(Smith, 1971) For an arbitrary Turing machine T with m symbols and n states, there exists a two-dimensional cellular space S_T with at most $\max(2m + 1, 2n + 2)$ states and with a neighbourhood as given in Figure 10.3 (a) that simulates T in 3 times real-time.*

Proof: (Sketch)
The idea of the proof is basically to simulate the computation that any particular Turing machine may perform on its tape. For that purpose, one has to define a set of cells in the cellular space which correspond to the tape of the Turing machine, including the symbols which might be inscribed on some of the tapes. Further, the position of the read/write head and the internal state of the Turing machine have to be simulated.

To do so, one row in the two-dimensional cellular space is selected where each cell corresponds to a single square on the tape. The internal state of the cell has to correspond to the symbol being inscribed on the tape's square. Of course, for a blank square, there needs to be a special cell state representing it.

Similarly, in a second row (adjacent to the 'tape row') the internal state of the Turing machine can be represented along with the position of the read/write head. See Figure 10.2 for an illustration. Row n corresponds to the tape and row $n+1$ represents the Turing machine's internal state and head position. All other cells will stay in their quiescence state. A state transition function can be constructed that ensures that only that cell in row n immediately under the cell representing the state q in Figure 10.2 will change its state. Similarly, it can be ensured that the next state of the Turing machine is represented in the correct cell in row $n+1$. Thereby, the movement of the head is also observed. That is, depending on the head movement direction, either the cell on the left or the right of the cell q will represent the respective successor state of q. Since the successor state depends on both, the current state and the symbol under the read/write head, an additional symbol like '@' in Figure 10.2 is needed if the neighbourhood pattern in 10.3 (b) is used. That is, the cell which will represent the successor state has no access to the symbol under the read/write head. Therefore, a single step of the Turing machine is simulated by a sequence of three computation steps of the cellular space. For more details see Smith (1971).

□

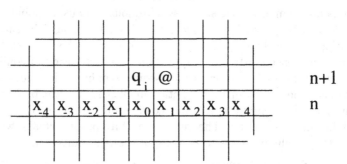

Figure 10.2. A Turing machine configuration represented in a two-dimensional cellular space. The row n is essentially representing the Turing machine's tape. The row $n+1$ is taking care of the Turing machine's read/write head position and the current state of the Turing machine.

Theorem 10.2. *(Smith, 1971) For an arbitrary Turing machine T with m symbols and n states, there exists a one-dimensional cellular space S_T with $m+2n$ states and with a neighbourhood as given in Figure 10.3 (b) that simulates T in at most 2 times real-time.*

Proof: (Sketch)
Every Turing machine configuration can be embedded into a one-dimensional cellular space as indicated in Figure 10.4. Here again, as in the proof idea of the previous Theorem, the one-dimensional space of cells represents mainly the content of the Turing machine's tape. At the current position of the read/write head, special symbols are inserted. These special symbols represent the current

(a) A one-dimensional neighbourhood template.

(b) A two-dimensional neighbourhood template.

Figure 10.3. Neighbourhood templates which allow computationally universal cellular spaces.

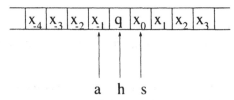

a   h   s

Figure 10.4. The a Turing machine configuration represented in a one-dimensional cellular space. The square h is storing the current state of the Turing machine. The square s right of that stores the symbol currently under the read/write head of the Turing machine.

state of the Turing machine and indicate the position of the read/write head. The transition function f of each cell only changes the state of those cells L, h, and R in Figure 10.4. The state transition function can be constructed in a way that a tape configuration like $\cdots x_0 q x_1 x_2 x_3 \cdots$ simulating a right move into the new state q' after changing symbol x_1 to x_1' looks as follows:

$$\cdots x_0 x_1 x_2 q x_3 \cdots$$

$$\cdots x_0 x_1 x_2 q' x_3' \cdots.$$

A left move would look like

$$\cdots x_0 x_1 x_2 q x_3 \cdots$$

$$\cdots x_0 x_1 x_2 q_L' x_3' \cdots$$

$$\cdots x_0 q' x_1' q' x_2 x_3' \cdots.$$

Thus, two states q and q_L are needed for each of the Turing machine states. It can be seen that using the template in Figure 10.3 the exact simulation of T's computation can be simulated.

□

10.2 Algorithmic Information Theory

It has been indicated above the notion of algorithm is very general, so general that it actually exceeds the power of physically possible machines. The following presents the notion of algorithmic information, which allows the consideration of suitably restricted classes of algorithms. In algorithmic information theory the amount of information necessary to construct a certain finite or infinite string s is considered. The amount of necessary information is measured as the minimal length of a program for a given universal Turing machine U that yields U to print exactly string s. Normally, only finite or infinite **binary** strings consisting of '0's and '1's not containing any blanks or other symbols are considered.

Note that only programs which do not receive any input are considered.[6] The length of a binary encoded program p for some universal Turing machine U is denoted by $|p|$.

Definition 10.3. *The length of the shortest program for constructing s is called its* **Kolmogorov complexity** $K(s)$.

According to the Invariance Theorem (see Li and Vitányi (1996)) the particular kind of considered universal Turing machine U only makes a difference for a certain constant c. Moreover, there are 2^n different binary strings of length n. Since each string requires another program there are strings s of length n whose Kolmogorov complexity $K(s)$ is at least n. Note: One program produces exactly one string, there is no input to the program. Moreover, *most* strings of length n have Kolmogorov complexity $K(s)$ of magnitude n.

Examples

> Strings as '11111111111111' or '00000000000' or '1010101010101010',
> etc. are presumably[7] simple strings, since their description by encoding a
> program which outputs the string under consideration is short. Mainly, only
> the length of the string itself is required, i.e. $\log_2(length\ of\ string)$ bits
> are sufficient. In addition, an indication whether '0's, '1's or alternating
> '1's and '0's should be printed is necessary. (This can be done with two
> further bits.)
> In contrast to the strings above, strings like '10110010011101100101111101010'
> are more complex, i.e. require a longer program for getting printed.

The length of an appropriate program depends on the primitive instructions of the program-interpreting machine. By the Invariance Theorem mentioned above, it is shown that this dependence on the program-interpreting machine

---

[6] Input can be simulated by a subprogram which prints the required input onto the tape.

[7] Of course, the exact complexity depends on the considered universal Turing machine U and may be different for a 'non-standard' universal Turing machine.

makes merely a difference in the program size of constant magnitude. This holds because there exists for every universal Turing machine U' a fixed program which can be run on a 'standard' universal Turing machine U and simulates U'.[8]

10.3 On the Algorithmic Information of Intelligence

According to Turing's test criterion for intelligence (Turing, 1950), mentioned earlier, we assume that for considering intelligent behaviour of agents our considerations can be restricted to agents which communicate with their environment through finite strings of symbols from a finite alphabet. In other words, we can say that an agent behaves intelligent, if it shows a certain appropriate output to the input supplied to it. Furthermore, all observable behaviour, intelligent or not, is a mapping from some finite input to some finite output. This may include control sequences to effectors of a robot as well as the input from visual, acoustic or other sensors. Note that only a single finite input or output stream is assumed for the complete lifetime of the intelligent agent. Learning behaviour fits into that framework as follows:

> To each part of the input stream there is a corresponding part in the output stream which can be viewed as the response to the input supplied. Thus, the response to the same pattern in the input stream may change or adapt over time.

It appears to be no restriction, if in addition, it is assumed that the length of the input to an agent through its lifetime is finite. However, there is a finite number of possible different inputs to such an agent. Thus, the required I/O-function that models the *intelligence* of any particular agent is simply some function from a finite number of input symbols to a finite number of output symbols. This implies that there definitely exists some TM that models the intelligent behaviour. Let us assume this I/O function is encoded as a binary string $s(f_{Int})$, e.g. the binary encoding of an appropriate TM table.

Therewith, f_{Int} has a certain Kolmogorov complexity $K(s(f_{Int}))$. In other words, the goal of AI is the development of a physical implementation of such a function f_{Int}.[9] It is clear that f_{Int} can be represented, e.g. as a binary string for feeding some universal Turing machine U. Assume the number of possible binary input symbols n_i is upper bounded by $n_i \leq 10^{25}$. The number of output symbols through the agents lifetime n_o may be upper bounded by $n_o \leq 10^{20}$.

---

[8] To add another technicality to the considerations, we may assume that the considered universal Turing machine has less than say 1000 lines in its Turing table. An example of such a universal Turing machine can be found in Minsky and Papert (1969). This would result in the fact that the Kolmogorov complexity depends only to a very limited extent on the respectively considered universal Turing machine.

[9] This holds at least for the engineering approach of AI.

Then the length $|s(f_{Int})|$ of the binary encoded function f_{Int} is upper bounded as follows.

$$|s(f_{Int})| \leq 2^{(10^{25})} \times 10^{20} \approx 10^{1,000,000,000,000,000,000,000,000}$$

Certainly $|s(f_{Int})|$ is astronomically large. However, the function f_{Int} may not be represented explicitly as a binary string. Instead it may be *compressed*, as much as possible, by describing the function by rules for entire classes of input strings or input substrings. The size of the most compressed form of *any* representation, whatsoever, is *lower bounded* by the Kolmogorov complexity $K(s(f_{Int}))$.

The algorithmic complexity of the human brain. The above calculation of an upper bound of the Kolmogorov complexity of human intelligent performance was based on a lifetime's interactions with the environment. The following calculation considers established neuro-physiological knowledge to give an impression in which order of magnitude the Kolmogorov complexity of human intelligence may lie.

As mentioned in section 6.2 the human brain has an estimated number of neurons in the order of 10 to 100 billion, i.e. 10^{10} to 10^{11} neurons. Each of these neurons has up to about $10,000$, i.e. 10^4, connections to other neurons. Furthermore, the topology of this huge network of neurons is believed to be highly irregular for most parts of the brain.

For assessing the potential Kolmogorov complexity of the human brain, we consider the combinatorial possibilities of connecting the given number of neurons to an arbitrary subset of 10,000 of these neurons.

That is, there are roughly $(10^{10})^{10,000} = 10^{100,000}$ different ways of connecting a single neuron to 10,000 other neurons in the brain. Thus, there are about $(10^{100,000})^{10,000,000,000} = 10^{1,000,000,000,000,000} = 10^{(10^{15})}$ different topologies for the entirety of the 10 billion neurons. This results in a potential Kolmogorov complexity of

$$\log_2 10^{(10^{15})} \approx 3.32 \times 10^{15} = 3,320,000,000,000,000.$$

This calculation does not take into account the fact that the different neurons vary in their appearance and functionality substantially. While the Kolmogorov complexity would not be greatly affected by encoding the information of which neuron is of what type, the precise functionality of the different types of neurons may add substantially to the complexity.

Even if we assume that the topological structure is highly redundant, e.g. that only a per cent of a per cent is necessary to ensure the proper functioning of the brain, there is still a descriptional complexity left of $322,000,000,000$ bits. This information could easily fill 100 million pages of an encyclopaedia! That is, if a scientist or engineer is going to read this description, and it takes one minute to read a single page, it would still take about 190 years of continuous reading 24 hours a day.

While the above calculations are speculative, it is important to note that the Kolmogorov complexity of $s(f_{Int})$ provides a *strict* lower bound on the representation size independently of the considered interpreting machine or mechanism. As the name 'algorithmic *information* theory' suggests, the particular kind of f_{Int} bears a certain amount of *information* in some absolute sense that is measured as the Kolmogorov complexity $K(s(f_{Int}))$. See also chapter 13, 14 and Hoffmann (1991c, 1992) for further implications of this descriptional complexity perspective for research in AI. Projects like, the CYC project (Lenat & Guha, 1990; Lenat, 1995) are also notable enterprises, attempting to build huge knowledge bases which contain all the relevant knowledge an adult has and uses to, for example, understand newspaper articles, encyclopaedia entries, etc.

11. Levels of Description

Processes can be described at different levels. For example, the physical movements of a car on a road can be described by merely describing how a certain reference point of the car's chassis is moving along what trajectory at what speed. Taking this description would enable an intelligent agent to reconstruct most or even all aspects of the car's movements which are visible to an observer on the road's kerb. Another possible description would be a sequence of pictures of the car on the road at different time points while the car is moving along. A third description could take the control actions into account which the driver is using to steer the car along the road. A further description would describe the movement of the car in terms of the forces which are applied to the car's tyres and which in turn are applied to the road via the tyres, etc. Yet another description could be even more detailed, by describing the complicated processes which make the engine turning by consuming fuel, etc. This process might even be described on an atomic or subatomic level, explaining what happens if a certain amount of fuel-air mixture is compressed including when and why it explodes, etc. Similarly, the actions of the driver could be described by taking his/her thoughts about where to go as the cause for the particular action the driver is taking, etc.

In fact, there seems to be an almost infinite number of possible descriptions of the car's movement along the road. Each of the possible descriptions would exhibit other aspects of the processes which are taking place besides the car's movement itself. Some descriptions may be reducible to others in the sense that one description implies another description. Usually a description which contains more details includes implicitly a less detailed description by simply allowing the derivation of the less detailed description. For example, a description which accounts for the driver's behaviour and the physics of the car may allow a description of the car's movement although it does not mention the movement of the car explicitly.

Similarly, one may argue that chemistry can be reduced to physics in that all chemical processes can be explained in physical terms of the involved atomic and subatomic processes. In contrast to that, it has been disputed whether psychological or mental processes can be reduced to physical processes.[1]

Computer Systems. Turning the considerations to computer systems, one usually distinguishes the following levels of description:

- Device level
- Circuit level
- Logic level
- Register transfer level
- Program level
  - Machine-level program
  - High-level program, e.g. Pascal, C, ...
- Knowledge level

Each of these levels has its own elementary entities. A behavioural description of each element is given along with the corresponding 'rules' or 'laws' of how these elements can be combined and what behaviour their combination has. At the device level the behaviour of the electrical devices like different types of transistors, resistors, and capacitors are described. By combining these devices a complex new behaviour will be generated. Since arbitrary combinations of these elements would lead to possibly very complex behaviour of the overall system, engineers developed an 'easy-to-use' way of building up functional units from the elements. These functional units are the elements of the next higher level of description and have a clearly defined functionality in terms of the next higher level. In the case of the device level, the next higher level is the circuit level, whose elements are simple electrical functions like logical gate functions such as NANDs, NORs, etc. or driver circuits etc. However, a NAND circuit is still considered as dealing with different voltages and currents. The next higher level, the logic level, would abstract from currents and voltages and would merely consider the function of a *logical* gate, e.g. a NAND gate as responding with a logical output signal depending on its logical input signals. (The exact voltages and the dynamics of changing electrical signals are ignored at the logic level.) Eventually, the program level allows one to deal with variables and program statements. The functionality of the program statements, however, are implemented by using units and respective behavioural laws of composition at the next lower level, whose elements in turn are provided by the next lower level of description.

Often, one is primarily interested in the behaviour of the computing system being described at the highest level, the *programming* or *symbol* level. At this level particular aspects of the lower levels are invisible and assumed to be irrelevant. For example, at the programming level the power dissipation of the computing system for executing the algorithm is completely invisible as well.

---

[1] This dispute, along with the problems of explaining the relation between mental processes and the physical processes in the human body, is known as the *Mind-Body problem* in philosophy.

Similarly, the actual execution time of the program on this particular computer system is usually invisible.

Cognitive Systems. For cognitive systems there have been other proposals of what types of different views of the system might be useful. For example, Pylyshyn (1984) proposes to distinguish the three levels of *neuronal, functional* and *intentional* level. At the *neuronal level* all the activities of the neurons are described without giving an explicit account of what overall function is performed. The *functional level* describes the performed function of the system in terms which abstract from the details of the system's neuronal implementation. The *intentional level* describes the system's function in terms of intentions, i.e. the system is said to intend to do or to accomplish certain things. That is, a chess player may be described as intending to win the game, to capture a certain piece, etc. To derive the actual behaviour from such intentions, it is assumed that the system behaves rationally, very similar to Newell's knowledge level. Similar to the chess player, a chess computer can also be said to intend to capture a pawn. It does not matter, whether the chess program does consciously intend anything, as long as *ascribing* intentions to the chess computer allows to predict its behaviour. Obviously, such a prediction can become much easier at the intentional level than at lower levels, if intentions are correctly ascribed in a way that the system behaves rationally. However, since the intentions are not programmed explicitly in natural cognitive systems, such as humans, it may not be obvious what intentions a system has and, hence, it cannot be easily judged whether the system behaves rationally.

Another distinction has been proposed by Marr (1982) to be suitable for cognitive systems in his highly influential book:

1. The *cognitive or functional level*. At this level the system's function is described in abstract terms.
2. The *algorithmic level*, where an actual algorithm for effectively computing the abstractly described function is specified.
3. The actual *implementation level*, where it is described how the function is actually computed in the given system, as opposed to how else it could be computed. That is, it is described how the algorithm is actually implemented, this includes the question whether or not the algorithm is implemented in a neuronal style and computed in a massively parallel and distributed fashion.

Marr's three levels of explanation are remarkably similar to Dennett's three stances, the *physical stance*, the *design stance*, and the *intentional stance* (Dennett, 1971, 1987).

This chapter is organised as follows: In section 11.1, the symbolic paradigm and its implied level of abstraction for describing processes is presented. Section 11.2 will discuss whether the symbolic level allows to describe all important aspects of the processes leading to intelligent behaviour. Section 11.3 will present the potential advantages of a connectionist paradigm compared to the symbolic paradigm. It will discuss the claims of Smolensky, one of the important and principled advocates of connectionism. This leads to section 11.4 in which the subsymbolic level is presented, which Smolensky considers the essence of connectionism. The chapter's conclusions are found in section 11.5.

11.1 The Symbolic Level

According to Newell and Simon, a physical symbol system is built from a set of elements, called symbols, which may be formed into symbol structures by means of a set of relations.

A symbol system has a memory capable of storing, retaining and retrieving symbols and symbol structures. It has a set of information processes that form symbol structures as a function of sensory stimuli. And it has a set of information processes which produce symbol structures that cause motor actions and modify symbol structures in memory in a variety of ways. A symbol system interacts with its environment in two different ways:

- It receives sensory stimuli from the environment which it converts into internal symbol structures.
- It acts upon the environment in ways determined by symbol structures that it produces by internal information processes.

Thus, its behaviour can be influenced by both: its current environment through its sensory inputs, and by previous environments through the information it has stored in memory from its experiences.

In general, both symbols and symbol structures are called 'symbols'. Here, symbols are *signs* or tokens which have a reference. Although it is not quite clear as to what kind of domain the symbols may refer, the idea is roughly that symbols correspond to the content of conscious thoughts. For example, symbols may refer to physical objects, like 'this house', 'the river over there', etc. Certainly, symbols may also refer to concepts which have no physical manifestation, like the general concept 'house', which refers rather to a *class* of objects (existing and non-existing in the physical world) than to a concrete physical object or group of objects. Further, symbols may even refer to completely abstract concepts, like mathematical concepts, e.g. 'number three' etc.

Symbols are thought as patterns which may be physically implemented in various ways. In today's computers they are usually patterns of electromagnetism, though their physical nature may differ radically in integrated circuits or vacuum tubes in the computers of the 1940s. Although it is unknown how patterns are represented in the human mind, it is generally assumed that they are represented as neuronal arrangements of some kind.

Newell and Simon's notion of symbol systems is extremely general, so general that symbol systems appear to be equivalent to the notion of the Turing machine (see section 10.1), i.e. equivalent to the notion of computation. Newell formulated the so-called *physical symbol system hypothesis* claiming that physical symbol systems may include symbols which correspond to those concepts, humans are usually using.

> ... It becomes a hypothesis that this notion of symbols includes symbols that we humans use everyday in our lives.[2]

The symbol level describes cognition by using symbols as the elementary units and by using rules to manipulate symbols for describing the behaviour of the system. The application of a rule to symbols depends entirely on symbols which are currently stored in the system.

A particularly strong version of a symbolic level of description allows to compose symbols to new symbol structures where the meaning, i.e. the reference, of the composed symbol structures can be derived from the way and the specific rules being used for composing the symbol structure. This requires a strong connection between the rules for composing symbol structures and the domain of reference.

11.1.1 Symbols in the Compositional Sense

The idea of symbols in the compositional sense has essentially been developed by modern logic, when the need for formal semantics of a logical language was recognised. The essential idea is that there is a set of primitive symbols with a fixed meaning, i.e. a fixed reference to certain objects. For a very simple version, see Figure 11.1. From such elementary symbols it is possible to

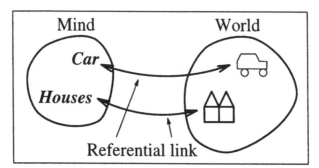

Figure 11.1. The basic idea of representation. Symbols in the mind represent objects in the world.

build more complex symbol structures according to a given set of syntactical rules. Compositionality means that the meaning of a composed complex symbol structure can be derived by following semantic rules which correspond one-to-one to the syntactic rules which have been used to build the compound

---

[2] In Newell (1980).

symbol structure. The typical example for symbol systems of this kind are logical languages with model-theoretic semantics.[3] The standard model-theoretic semantics are given by an interpretation function of the atomic syntactical symbols of a given language L into a domain of individuals D. Further, there may be functions among individuals which are interpreted as functions among the domain D. Finally, a predicate P is interpreted in an extensional way by the set of individuals to which the predicate P applies (in the case of P being a single-argument predicate). For multi-argument predicates the extension is given by the set of tuples of individuals to which the predicate applies. Based on the interpretations of these elementary syntactical units, the interpretation of complex syntactical expressions can be constructed from the interpretations of the involved elementary units.

Fodor and Pylyshyn (1988), Fodor and McLaughlin (1990) and Fodor (1997) argue that human cognition clearly exhibits essential features of such a compositional nature; namely, that mental representations have a *combinatorial syntax and semantics*[4] and that *structure sensitive processes* take place. What is meant by that is: It is clear that if people can think *John loves Mary* that one can also think *Mary loves John*, or *Mary loves Peter*, etc. This shows, according to Fodor and Pylyshn (1988), that people must employ a mental scheme, which allows to replace objects in propositions, and allows to invert relationships between objects etc. That is, both the subject and the object of the sentence can be mentally replaced by other persons, etc. Furthermore that 'loves' establishes a certain relationship between the first and the second person mentioned, etc. Structure sensitive operations would also take place, if logical connectives are accordingly interpreted where inferences are drawn from a set of propositions.

While the thrust of the critique of Fodor, Pylyshyn and McLaughlin is that current connectionist models have severe problems to handle the mentioned features, they cannot exclude the possibility of future more suitable connectionist architectures. Opposed to that type of argument, the analysis in this book will show a more general line of reasoning about symbolic and non-symbolic approaches.

Problems with the compositional symbol level. The idea of compositional symbol systems represents a convenient way for building AI systems. However, it is only applicable in domains where a clear-cut ontology[5] is available and deductive reasoning suffices for the tasks of the system.

However, the general applicability of the model-theoretic approach has been rejected by phenomenology as well as by the late Wittgenstein (1953) himself; who was once a strong advocate of the model-theoretic idea (Wittgenstein,

---

[3] See chapter 2 for more details of model-theoretic semantics of first-order predicate logic.

[4] See Fodor and Pylyshyn (1988):98.

[5] That is, where it is clear what objects are relevant to be considered and how to represent them in a system, i.e. what properties of those objects are described etc.

1961). Reason being the fact that there is knowledge beyond what can be expressed in model-theoretic terms. It is not enough to say all what is the case and all what is not the case. A static world description fails to give an account on how the world will change. It also fails to give an account on how a human being's knowledge or view of the world will change. The particular way, humans conduct non-deductive inferences cannot be described in purely model-theoretic terms. Hence, to describe such ways of reasoning, symbols are needed which do not refer merely to the physical world. Those symbols have to refer to abstract structures, like preference relations among a class of possible inferences which may be logically equally justified.

Not only a general intelligence needs to deal with descriptions beyond the model-theoretic approach. Also, many important practical AI applications require non-deductive reasoning. At least some inductive or analogical reasoning or reasoning under uncertainty and vagueness is required.[6] For example in inductive reasoning, there is usually an ambiguity among different hypotheses, when generalising inferences should be performed. Thus, there is a need for expressing some *preference relation* among competing hypotheses. However, any preference relation among a finite number of hypotheses can be represented by symbols, although these symbols do not refer to some 'natural' ontological entities, i.e. such symbols do not refer to the ontological entities of the domain of inductive reasoning. The same problem exists for reasoning under uncertainty: human reasoning incorporates a lot of interdependencies of subjective probabilities, when probability estimates of combined uncertain events are made. Compare the simplifying assumptions in Bayesian reasoning as outlined in section 2.3.

11.1.2 Non-Compositional Symbol Systems

Despite the appealing idea of compositionality, symbols do not need to be used in a system which has the feature of compositionality; they can still be used in less systematic ways. However, a symbolic description does not necessarily satisfy the conditions for the compositional symbol systems, where the reference of a complex symbol structure can be constructed systematically from the references of elementary symbols. In contrast to that, each symbol may just have its own reference without any systematic relation to the reference of other symbols. Such a description would still be a symbol level description.

---

[6] Although some reasoning models have been developed for such conditions, as outlined in part I, it is not clear in exactly what circumstances these models can be applied. A general difficulty is to account for the specifics of the current situation, which may be difficult or even impossible to express in the terms which the models make available. For example, decision tree learners do not allow to provide knowledge about how to classify or not to classify certain types of objects. Similarly, techniques such as Bayesian networks presume conditional independence of certain events, which do not necessarily hold. Fuzzy logic presumes that the defined operators of 'Min' and 'Max' for a logical 'and' and 'or' are appropriate.

However, the proper formulation of suitable symbol manipulation rules may become quite difficult in practice, due to the lack of systematicity of the meaning of the symbols involved. That is, systematic manipulation rules, such as resolution for logical inferences, cannot be easily developed.

11.2 Problems with the Symbolic Level

This section provides an outline of the most important reasons against the symbolic paradigm for describing and designing intelligent systems. These reasons have also been put forward as justification for connectionism as a model for cognition.

11.2.1 The Phenomenological Critique at Physical Symbol Systems

The following outlines the phenomenologically motivated critique at the possibility of AI put forward by Dreyfus (1972), Dreyfus and Dreyfus (1986), Dreyfus (1992), Winograd and Flores (1986), and others. The term *phenomenology* in philosophy means basically that the phenomena, i.e. the appearance of the world in us, while consciously experiencing it, are considered to form the basis of our access to 'the world' and thus the basis of all knowledge. Consequently, the phenomena must also be the basis of all further considerations. Hence, every analysis has to be grounded on the phenomena instead of an assumed outer world (or reality), which may exist independently of the consciousness. Edmund Husserl is usually considered to be the father of 20th century's *phenomenology*, although the term was already used earlier, e.g. by Hegel. Husserl promoted an analysis of the categories of the world and how it may appear to our consciousness. His goal was to ground all scientific investigations, including physics and mathematics, in the phenomena in order to give science a solid and sound basis.

However, his famous scholar Martin Heidegger criticised Husserl's approach to phenomenology as a rather artificial consideration. Husserl was looking at how phenomena of mathematical objects, for instance, could be analysed. This, so Heidegger, has almost nothing to do with the phenomena of ordinary people in their daily life. If the idea of phenomenology should be consequently pursued then as one that looks at how the world appears to ordinary people in their ordinary daily life. To illustrate the difference, consider the following plans for my activities of an ordinary day:

> *Today, I have to go to the optometrist to get another pair of eye glasses. After that I want to go to the library to search for books on phenomenology. Finally, I want to buy a pair of shoes for the approaching winter.*

When I take the subway in order to get to the city to the optometrist my thoughts may be as follows: Hopefully I will not have to wait very long at the optometrist in order to have enough time left to look for books on phenomenology without a hurry. In this example central notions like *care, concern, readiness-to-hand, present-at-hand, reference,* etc. of Heidegger's philosophical system can be explained.

Before my first activities of a new day, normally I already have certain concerns on mind, certain things I want to achieve, etc. That is, there are constantly some *concerns* which bother me. These will determine the phenomena which are coming up to my mind; they will guide the content of my conscious experiences. When considering the physical objects in these situations, I will realise that I am unaware of almost everything. I will not really think about how to enter the subway or how to open the door, etc. I will not think about where to leave the subway, I will just enter the subway and leave it as I did it and where I left it already so many times before. So, the subway is just *ready-to-hand* since I am not really aware of it and its detailed physical appearance.

Another remarkable point for Heidegger is the fact that all my experiences are shaped by the existence of the needs of other people and their similarity to my own needs. The subway stations are arranged in a manner that allows to fulfil the daily tasks, not only my tasks, but the tasks of the general population. Here is the exit, over there is the market place, with all the amenities to get the things of daily needs. This arrangement is not accidental, but because other people have the same or similar needs as I have. Therefore, the existence of other people shapes the world around me. Everything is arranged in a way that my own and other people's daily needs can easily be accommodated. When I go to the library, I will find the catalogues of all available items, there are librarians who can help me searching for books, there are places to study, etc. The fact that all these facilities are provided shapes my way of acting and, more importantly, it shapes the stream of phenomena which come up to my consciousness. The fact that all these facilities are designed to allow a meaningful flow of actions emphasises Heidegger; and he points out that they *refer* to each other. In the normal flow of actions every action, and this includes the use of specifically designed facilities, refers already to the next action in the sense that my thoughts connect both actions in my mind. Heidegger's notion of *breakdown* means that the human mind only starts reflecting about objects and their relations in an outer world in situations where the usual course of action cannot proceed as expected. For example, only when the catalogue (or the desk, the chair, etc.) in the library is missing and I cannot proceed as expected, I become aware of the fact that I was going to use it. When these objects become aware, their mode of appearance changes; in Heidegger's terminology the objects become *present-at-hand.*

What Heidegger really concerned was the following: The origin for an analysis of a philosophical ontology must be the everyday appearance of the world to our consciousness. This appearance is *totally different* from the ontological considerations which have been conducted through the past few thousand years of philosophy.

Interpreting Heidegger's Phenomenology in the Context of AI Although Heidegger's philosophy aimed at the analysis and understanding of the human *conscious experience* of life and the world, Dreyfus (1972), Dreyfus and Dreyfus (1986), Dreyfus (1992), and others took his considerations as evidence for the claim that even a *description* of the human *behaviour* has to be totally different from symbolic structures. It should be noted that Heidegger's concern was very different from that. He did not bother with a description of cognitive processes, but rather with the nature of phenomena and the constituting consciousness. However, even if the conclusion drawn by Dreyfus was not Heidegger's concern, it may still be valid or at least useful to assume its validity.[7]

Before proceeding, Dreyfus's interpretation of Heidegger's considerations in the context of AI will be presented in some more detail. Heidegger's emphasis on human's experiences as heavily shaped by the existence and the similarity of others is roughly summarised as follows: Human cognition and understanding is based on social interaction. As a consequence, intelligent systems have to be embedded in a context in order to assign proper meaning to symbols and to adapt to changes. The role of Heidegger's *breakdown* for determining when and what particular objects come to one's mind is used by Dreyfus. According to Dreyfus, this shows that human intelligence does not use a fixed representation of the agent's environment. Depending on what has happened, human intelligence 'creates on the spot' an appropriate representation of what might be relevant for the intended course of action. Related to this point is the argument that human values and goals are only *implicitly* contained in the way people act within their environment.

Accordingly, Dreyfus argued that sometimes people change completely their way to view the world, when their concerns change, e.g. when someone falls in love. The objects which constitutes the outer world can change along with their properties. The values which are only implicitly contained in the particular course of action of an individual can completely change as well. Dreyfus claims that such a kind of profound change which happens within the *ultimate context*, cannot be simulated by machines. The *ultimate context* as Dreyfus (1972) calls it, is the backbone on which the profound changes happen. The changes are only understandable on the basis of such a *ultimate context*, which is responsible for all the changes in behaviour, goals, intentions, values, etc., which human beings may encounter throughout their lives. But the *ultimate context* according to Dreyfus, is in some sense *infinite* which implies that it cannot be represented by symbols at all.[8] In contrast to all that - states Dreyfus - are computers, which *have* to represent values and goals as well as their 'view' of the world *explicitly* by symbols. Therefore, computers cannot behave like humans.

---

[7] Actually, there are also other considerations allowing similar conclusions. For example, Frixione, Spinelli, and Gaglio (1989) claim that intelligent systems must have a *subsymbolic* level of activity, because otherwise no link of symbols to what they refer could be established.

[8] At least, it cannot be represented by a finite number of symbols.

Promoted by Winograd and Flores (1986), this line of reasoning resulted in a new perspective on cognition and AI, the so-called *situated action* view, which has gained substantial popularity in recent years.

Situated action. The idea of situated action became popular in the late 1980's due to T. Winograd and F. Flores's book *Understanding Computers and Cognition* (1986). The very idea is that cognition cannot be properly understood, if considered independently of the context in which cognition occurs. The historical, cultural and social context of the interactions of a cognitive system are crucial to the understanding of the ongoing processes. It is claimed that any description of the processes inside a cognitive system is inadequate as long as the terms used for the description do not refer to the context in which the processes are embedded. The studies in situated action, focus on the outside world and how this world constrains and guides human behaviour. It is claimed that studying a 'disembodied' intelligence, an intelligence that is considered without the context and the constraints being imposed by a real 'living environment' is an artificial, unreal and most importantly an uncharacteristic consideration of intelligence. The crucial element of intelligence is the actual situation and the parts intelligent systems may play in it. It does not make sense to look just at the situation, or just at people or just at the environment. The very phenomena under study would be destroyed by such an approach. By that, the internal processing emphasised so much by the symbolic paradigm is essentially challenged. The situated action view downplays the importance of such internal representational issues. At its extreme, such internal representations and symbol manipulation processes are claimed to be irrelevant for the actual behaviour of a cognitive system. See Clark (1996), Menzies (1997), Slezak (1998a), or Feltovich, Ford, and Hoffman (1997) for recent work on situated action.

One of the prominent advocates of situated action, W. Clancey, rejected the hypothesis that the neurological processes and structures in the human brain resemble in kind the symbols humans create and use in their everyday's lives (Clancey, 1993). He claims that the symbolic approach confabulates *neurological structures and processes* with *physical representations* that humans use and manipulate, e.g. characters and character strings in creating texts, etc. Clancey calls it the confabulation of *first-person representations* and *third-person representations*. First-person representations are representations used by the person himself/herself which is the subject of the considerations. Opposed to that are *third-person representations* which may describe a person's thought processes viewed from outside, from a third person's perspective. The symbols used in such third-person representations may refer to the neurological activities inside another person's brain. The following will also use the terms *first-person symbols* and *third-person symbols* respectively.

11.2.2 Practical Experience in the Symbolic Paradigm

The practical experiences in AI so far were indicating rather severe difficulties in almost all areas of AI. The development of practically useful intelligent systems turned out to be much more difficult than expected in the beginning. While in the early years of AI, researchers hoped to succeed with developing general purpose heuristics which could deal with almost all types of problems, people realised in the late 1970s that systems need to be equipped with a substantial body of 'knowledge' to deal with a complex domain.

However, the process of knowledge acquisition again turned out to be much more difficult than initially expected. Domain experts showed substantial problems in articulating their knowledge. Describing their particular way of solving a given single problem with sufficient precision to be programmable proved to be very hard. These experiences supported the suggestion that the idea of symbol systems may be inappropriate after all.

11.2.3 Conclusions from the Critiques

Roughly speaking, the symbolic paradigm builds descriptions of cognitive processes from entities that are symbols in two senses: in the semantic sense of referring to external objects and in the syntactic sense of being operated upon by symbol manipulation. These manipulations are conceived to model fundamental psychological processes underlying cognition. As seen in the previous subsections, a number of arguments have been put forward, claiming that a symbolic description is by its very nature incapable to comprehensively account for cognition.

For a more detailed discussion, different types of cognitive processes can be distinguished. With respect to the question for which activities the symbol level provides an adequate account, Smolensky (1988)[9] as one of the main advocates of connectionism, distinguishes the following activities:

- *Cultural knowledge and conscious rule interpretation.* This means knowledge that is accessible to everyone belonging to the respective culture. That is basically the kind of knowledge that is being used in science. That is, propositions expressed in a more or less formalised language like predicate logic together with rules of how to interpret that knowledge, and how to infer further propositions from given knowledge, etc. The important point is that it is agreed throughout the scientific community on the particular way of interpreting such knowledge. This type of knowledge is opposed to the following type of *individual knowledge.*
- *Individual knowledge, skill, and intuition.* In practice, the articulated knowledge of an individual will be much less precise than it is required at the level of cultural knowledge. In fact, an expert will usually articulate their knowledge in a way which is at its best sufficient to give enough clues for themselves

---

[9] See for a further defence of his view also Smolensky (1990a).

or another expert with similar background and experience to determine appropriate interpretations and inferences from that knowledge. Consequently that kind of knowledge is *not* generally accessible. In other words, for the proper interpretation specialised 'skills' or 'intuition' are needed.

Smolensky admits the appropriateness of the symbolic paradigm to cope with *cultural knowledge and conscious rule interpretation*. However, he denies the symbolic paradigm being appropriate for the *individual knowledge, skill and intuition*. He claims that a connectionist paradigm is needed to treat the latter type of knowledge appropriately.

11.3 The Connectionist Alternative

Connectionist models are usually considered as large networks of simple computing units which act in parallel. Each computing unit carries a numerical *activation value* which is computed from the activation values of connected units in the network. The network's elements influence each other's values by connections of specific strengths. The strength of a connection may change over time. The change of a connection may depend on particular *training patterns* that are to be reflected in some sense by the overall network. The network's overall function is strongly dependent on the currently present connection strengths or *weights*. Hence, the weights of a network are also encoding the system's knowledge. Many of the connectionist models *program themselves*, i.e. the models have learning procedures for tuning their weights to implement a specific I/O-function for the overall network. At the heart of the following exposition of the connectionist claim lies the idea of *subsymbols*. According to Smolensky (1988) are subsymbols, roughly speaking, numerical values which cannot be interpreted in any sensible way individually. Only a large set of such subsymbols and only if they show certain patterns can be said to correspond to symbols. In other words, only certain patterns among a large number of subsymbolic values can be assigned any meaning. Hence, subsymbols differ in their interpretability substantially from the symbols of the symbolic paradigm, although numerical values may also appear in the symbolic paradigm.

11.3.1 The Connectionist Claim

The advocates of connectionism typically claim that a connectionist approach is *necessary* for an appropriate modelling of cognition and intelligent activities.[10]
To prove this seems a difficult task because of the fact that virtual machines can usually be implemented on another virtual machine. That is, it has to be shown that the subsymbolic level *cannot be reduced* to the symbolic level of

---

[10] See, e.g., Clark (1993) for a discussion of why a connectionist-style framework is needed for cognitive science.

description. One might say that a digital computer is some sort of dynamical system which simulates a von Neumann automaton. Furthermore that digital computers are used for simulating connectionist models. So, it seems plausible that both, the *symbolic* as well as the *subsymbolic* paradigm are correct - that they are two sides of the same coin.

Smolensky points out, that subsymbolic models are not equivalent to symbolic models, even if subsymbolic models are implemented on digital computers using a symbolic programming language. The crucial difference lies in the fact, that the symbols used to implement the subsymbolic models are merely some numbers used in the highly parallel and dynamical connectionist model. But the semantics of these numbers are very different from the semantics of the symbols in the symbolic paradigm. In the symbolic paradigm, the symbols refer to certain concepts which at least belong to a kind of *individual knowledge*. In the symbolic paradigm one would even prefer, if symbols referred to cultural knowledge. That is, to knowledge, which is generally accessible and can be precisely and systematically interpreted using generally agreed methods which will include classical logical inference rules. The known fact that von Neumann machines and certain connectionist models[11] can simulate each other has *no* impact on Smolensky's point. The crucial issue is not the possible reduction from one level to the other. The crucial issue is rather whether symbols can be used that refer to conceptual entities (as it is assumed in the symbolic paradigm) or whether the employed symbols cannot refer to anything more enlightening than a set of numbers, which essentially makes up the subsymbolic paradigm?

The very debate on an appropriate paradigm for cognitive science and AI cannot be discussed on a purely syntactical level. The debate rather takes place at a semantical level. Essentially the debate addresses the following question:

> What are the *conceptual entities* to which those syntactical entities refer, which are manipulated according to simple syntactical rules.

11.3.2 The Connectionist Research Program

As a consequence, substantial progress in subsymbolic cognitive science requires systematic commitments to vectorial representations for individual cognitive domains.

Smolensky believes that:

> ... powerful mathematical tools are needed for relating the overall behaviour of the network to the choice of representational vectors; ideally, these tools should allow us to *invert* the mapping from representations to behaviour so that by starting with a mass of data on human performance we can turn a mathematical crank and have representational vectors pop out. ... The subsymbolic paradigm needs tools such as a

---

[11] See section 10.1.3 for cellular spaces as an example of a 'connectionist' model which is computationally universal.

version of multidimensional scaling based on a connectionist model of the process of producing similarity judgements.[12]

Further he states that:

... systematic principles must be developed for adapting to the connectionist context, the featural analyses of domains that have emerged from traditional, non-connectionist paradigms. These principles must reflect fundamental properties of connectionist computation, for otherwise, the hypothesis of connectionist computation is doing no work in the study of mental representation.[13]

Similar considerations from a more technical point of view can, for example, be found in an article by Werbos (1993), who writes:

... that new developments in neurocontrol would permit a Newtonian revolution in our understanding of the human brain and the human mind, if we pursue these developments in the right way. ... to understand intelligence as it exists in the human brain, in the same way that we understand physics (since Newton), as a real science. If the brain itself – as a whole system – is a neurocontroller, then the mathematics which we need to use is neurocontrol.
People trained in conventional control theory are often skeptical of this idea. They are used to thinking of controllers as systems like glorified thermostats, designed to stabilise a chemical plant at some fixed equilibrium, or to make a robot arm follow a fixed path in space specified in advance, or the like.

The following quote from Smolensky goes into a similar direction:

Concepts from physics, from the theory of dynamical systems, are at least as likely to be important as concepts from the theory of digital computation.[14]

In other words, at least the strong proponents of connectionism believe that the analysis and understanding of the dynamic processes occurring in a complex network of a large number of neurons is essential in order to understand cognition and to successfully build intelligent systems.

Smolensky emphasises as a major advantage of connectionist models that there is no single 'rule' which can be considered and applied independently of all other 'rules' in the system. In connectionist models every 'rule' or connection between nodes can be 'overridden' by other 'rules'. Thus, always the entire system, and hence the entire knowledge and the entire context available, participates in deciding what kind of result the computation will have.

---

[12] Smolensky (1988):8.
[13] Ibid.
[14] Smolensky (1988):18.

To implement subsymbolic statistical inference, the correct connection strength between two units will typically depend on all the other connection strengths. The subsymbolic learning procedures that sort out this interdependence through simple, strictly local, computations and ultimately assign the correct strength to each connection are performing no trivial task.[15]

11.4 Characteristics of the Non-Symbolic Levels

In the previous section, the essentials of the connectionist idea were presented. The somewhat unclear term of *subsymbols* was used. This section attempts to clarify the notion of subsymbols, although no clear-cut definition can be expected. First of all, the question will be addressed to what extent *subsymbolic processes* can be identified with the physiological processes occurring in biological cognitive systems, like human brains. In other words the question is addressed, whether a detailed description of neuronal processes can be the appropriate description level for connectionism.

11.4.1 The Neural Level

The neural level considers merely the behaviour of single neurons and their interaction. The functionality of the entire brain is determined by the processes occurring at the neural level. The neural processes can be characterised in a variety of ways. The typical features considered to be specific for the neural level include the following:

- The overall system state is defined by continuous numerical variables like electrical potentials, synaptic areas, etc.
- The state variables change continuously over time.
- The interneuron interaction parameters are changeable. These parameters are controlling the particular dynamic interaction between neurons and consequently are also responsible for the overall emerging functionality of the entire system. Therefore, these parameters can also be considered to encode the 'knowledge' which a neural system captures.
- There is a huge number of state variables, each single neuron is characterised by a few state variables.
- The complexity of the interactions among the many neurons is very high.[16] It is also assumed that the interactions are quite inhomogeneous. That is, there is a large number of different characteristics governing the interaction between a group of neurons.

---

[15] Smolensky (1988):18.

[16] Here, the term complexity is to be understood in a rather intuitive way, as opposed to the formal treatment in section 13 using the notion of *Kolmogorov complexity*.

- There are complicated signal integration functions at a single neuron, which may vary from neuron to neuron.
- The signals emitted by neurons are quite diverse in their types. That is, continuous signals vs. 'almost discrete' vs. pulse coded signals.[17]

In other words, the neural level of description focuses on the physiology of the brain. This is opposed to the semantic bearing of the processes in the brain. The neural level considers only the 'syntactical aspects' of the processes; without any reference to the possible meaning of certain patterns of neural activity. The relation of the physiological processes to the semantics, usually associated with the cognitive processes, is beyond the scope of the neural level and hence ignored.

Smolensky believes that the neural level is incapable in practice of supporting the needs of the vast majority of cognitive models. Besides some knowledge about the brain's architecture used for special purpose processing, such as vision and spatial coordination, much too little is known about that part of the brain's architecture which is used for general problem solving, language processing and many other tasks.

Smolensky does not believe that the neural level of description is of much use, neither for understanding cognition at a symbolic level nor for understanding the principles at the subsymbolic level. Thus, he considers the details of the processes at the neural level as irrelevant for most aspects of cognition. He writes

(12) c. For most cognitive functions, neuroscience cannot provide the relevant information to specify a cognitive model at the neural level.[18]

In contrast to the neural level, Smolensky's *subsymbolic paradigm* is intended to suggest cognitive descriptions which are built up from entities that correspond to *constituents* of the symbols that would be used in the symbolic paradigm. These fine-grained constituents could be called *subsymbols*, and the activities of individual processing units in connectionist networks operate on.

11.4.2 The Subsymbolic Level

As an alternative to the neural level, the subsymbolic level of description was proposed by Smolensky (1988). The subsymbolic level is conceived to lie somewhere between the symbolic and the neural level. It is claimed that it allows a simple yet sufficiently detailed and complete connectionist model of cognition. Smolensky distinguishes carefully different possible levels of analysis. He believes that the principles of cognition being explored in the connectionist approach should not be constructed as the principles of the neural level. Instead he proposes a *subsymbolic* level of analysis.

---

[17] See Lynch and Granger (1989) for models of pulse-coded information transmission between neurons.
[18] Smolensky (1988):10.

Units	Micro-features
●	upright container
●	hot liquid
○	glass contacting wood
●	porcelain curved surface
●	burnt odour
●	brown liquid contacting porcelain
○	oblong silver object
●	finger-sized handle
●	brown liquid with curved sides and bottom

Figure 11.2. Representation of cup with coffee.

Smolensky suggests a *subsymbolic level* of description which may be approximately described by the following for the case of the intuitive processor:

> The intuitive processor has a certain kind of connectionist architecture which abstractly models a few of the most general features of neural networks.[19]

Entities that are typically represented in the symbolic paradigm by symbols are typically represented in the subsymbolic paradigm by a large number of subsymbols. For an illustration, let us consider the following example:[20]

> How can we represent concepts like *a cup*, *a cup with coffee*, and *coffee only*?

In the symbolic paradigm, this could possibly be represented in a language of first-order predicate logic as follows:

> Constants: *coffee, cup,...*
> Predicates: *with(.,.),...*
> Propositions: *with(cup,coffee)*[21], ...

In contrast to that, a distributed (subsymbolic) representation could look like it is shown in the Figures 11.2, 11.3, and 11.4.[22] The distributed representation would not assume, e.g. *coffee* to be an atomic entity. It rather depends on the context what is meant by 'coffee,' e.g. the 'hot brown liquid,' or 'coffee beans,' or a commodity in the stock market, etc. The figures show a possible representation of coffee in the context of being in a cup as hot brown liquid.

---

[19] In Smolensky (1988), page 3.

[20] The distributed representation is taken from Smolensky (1991).

[21] The two-place predicate *with* could also be a function, which would result in e.g. *with(cup,coffee)* representing the object *coffee* rather then a fact, as the proposition above does.

[22] The 'micro-features' in the tables give merely a rough idea of what suitable subsymbols might look like. Indeed, the idea of subsymbols is rather that they have no meaning which would be this easy to grasp.

The general point is that the distributed representation in all possible contexts would constitute the meaning of *coffee*, as opposed to have merely a single symbol standing for *coffee* regardless of the possible contexts.

Fodor and Pylyshyn (1988), Fodor and McLaughlin (1990) and Fodor (1997) criticised the distributed representation because, as proposed by connectionists so far, the connectionist models would not account for phenomena like systematicity or compositionality of language and thought.[23] They argue against connectionism, because it cannot handle apparent cognitive abilities which can be easily handled in the symbolic paradigm. These abilities are those of systematicity, compositionality and other structure-sensitive capabilities. They refer to abilities of understanding and constructing sentences like 'Paul loves Emma' and 'Emma loves Peter'. It seems that once one understands the relation 'loves' one can replace the subject and the object of the sentence by arbitrarily chosen persons. For processing natural language, it is a widely accepted assumption that humans are, in principle, able to parse sentences with an arbitrary structural depth.[24] Furthermore, the order of the persons matters. That is, whenever there is an internal representation of 'Paul' being used, there must also be a mechanism which ensures which role this representation will take in the relationship 'loves'. Fodor, Pylyshyn and McLaughlin call such properties of representations *structure-sensitive*. As a reply to that criticism, Smolensky proposed an integrated connectionist/symbolic architecture (Smolensky, 1995) whose basic idea was briefly sketched in 8.2. His architecture has, besides the features of the subsymbolic idea, also some special structure reflecting the features considered so important by Fodor, Pylyshyn and McLaughlin, such as systematicity and compositionality. However, for the reasoning in this book, Smolensky's more recent proposal for a new architecture as well as other proposals, such as the structured connectionist architecture by Shastri and Ajjanagadde (1993),

Units	Micro-features
•	upright container
○	hot liquid
○	glass contacting wood
•	porcelain curved surface
○	burnt odour
○	brown liquid contacting porcelain
○	oblong silver object
•	finger-sized handle
○	brown liquid with curved sides and bottom

Figure 11.3. Representation of cup without coffee.

---

[23] See section 11.1.1 for more details.

[24] While it is not clear what that 'in principle' exactly means, in practice it seems obvious that nobody will be able to parse a sentence correctly which contains, say, more than 5000 words.

Units	Micro-features
○	upright container
●	hot liquid
○	glass contacting wood
○	porcelain curved surface
●	burnt odour
●	brown liquid contacting porcelain
○	oblong silver object
○	finger-sized handle
●	brown liquid with curved sides and bottom

Figure 11.4. 'Representation of coffee', in the context of coffee being in a cup.

as sketched, in 8.1, will not be reviewed in further detail, as the discussion will not centre around any particular architecture which would need to be defended.

Along with this semantic distinction comes a syntactic distinction. Subsymbols are not operated upon by symbol manipulation: they participate in numerical, as opposed to symbolic, computation. Operations in the symbolic paradigm that consist of a single discrete operation (e.g. a memory fetch) are often achieved in the subsymbolic paradigm as the result of a large number of much finer-grained (numerical) operations.

The knowledge in a connectionist architecture is encoded in patterns of its connection strengths. Processing of that knowledge happens highly parallel. Smolensky phrases the following hypothesis

(8) a. The connectionist dynamical system hypothesis:
The state of the intuitive processor at any moment is precisely defined by a vector of numerical values (one for each unit). The dynamics of the intuitive processor are governed by a differential equation. The numerical parameters in this equation constitute the processor's program or knowledge. In learning systems, these parameters change according to another differential equation.[25]

Corresponding to that 'syntactical' vision of the processes on a subsymbolic level, Smolensky suggests the following hypothesis for the semantical level of those processes:

(8) b. The subconceptual unit hypothesis:
The entities in the intuitive processor with the semantics of conscious concepts of the task domain are complex patterns of activity over many units. Each unit participates in many such patterns.[26]

The basic idea is that the interactions between individual units are simple, but that these units do not have conceptual semantics as it is the case at the conceptual or symbolic level. From such simple interactions between a

---

[25] Smolensky (1988):6.
[26] Smolensky (1988), page 6.

large number of subconceptual units, complex interactions of the units at the conceptual level emerge. Smolensky believes that:

> ... Typically, these interactions can be computed only approximately. In other words, there will generally be no precisely valid, complete, computable formal principles at the conceptual level; such principles exist only at the level of individual units, *the subconceptual level.*[27]

Smolensky summarises his view as follows:

(8) c. The subconceptual level hypothesis:
Complete, formal, and precise descriptions of the intuitive processor are generally tractable not at the conceptual level, but only at the subconceptual level.[28]

The hypotheses 8a-8c are merged as follows, to formulate the cornerstone of Smolensky's *subsymbolic paradigm*:

(8) The subsymbolic hypothesis:
The intuitive processor is a subconceptual connectionist dynamical system that does not admit a complete, formal, and precise conceptual-level description.[29]

According to this conception, the context of a symbol is represented differently in different paradigms. Smolensky summarises that as follows:

(23) Symbols and context dependence:
In the symbolic paradigm, the context of a symbol is manifest around it and consists of other symbols; in the subsymbolic paradigm, the context of a symbol is manifest inside it and consist of subsymbols.[30]

Smolensky (1988) believes that the subsymbolic level should be treated as dealing essentially with *continuous values* which are changing continuously over time. The fact that virtually all subsymbolic computation models are simulated on digital computers does not contradict the claim that the subsymbolic paradigm is essentially continuous. This is since the emphasis is less on the mere possibility of an appropriate digital simulation, but much more on the concepts needed for *understanding* cognition. For understanding symbolic computations concepts from discrete mathematics are suitable. However, for understanding cognition, according to the claim, concepts from continuous mathematics are needed.

---

[27] Ibid.
[28] Ibid.
[29] Smolensky (1988):7.
[30] Smolensky (1988):17.

11.5 Conclusions

This chapter contrasted the essential points of both paradigms which are crucial to the debate about symbolism and connectionism.

While the symbolic approach attempts to describe cognition at the level of symbols which refer to human concepts, there have been a number of criticisms put forward, arguing that describing cognition at the symbolic level is bound to fail as there are no simple rules operating directly on symbols which could produce a simulation of (at least introspectively) observable cognitive behaviour.

Opposed to that, connectionism attempts to describe cognition by rules which do not operate directly on symbols, but rather on syntactical units (also called *subsymbols*) which are only constituents of symbols referring to conceptual entities. Only certain patterns among a large number of such subsymbols constitute symbols, which in turn represent conceptual entities.

The crucial point in the discussion was a *semantical* one, not a syntactical one! That is, while symbol systems, such as Turing machines, are computational universal, this does not imply that they really suffice for describing cognitive processes. It is not what paradigm allows to describe the functionality of a system. It is rather, what are the semantics of the units involved in the description of that functionality?! To stress this point a bit further:

> What would happen, if the processes at the subconceptual level are described at the conceptual level, e.g. by replacing the patterns of activity that have conceptual semantics by a single symbol referring to the respective conceptual entity?

According to the connectionist claim this will only work with sufficient accuracy, as long as the *processes* being described are of the type of *conscious rule application*.[31] As soon as the *intuitive processes* are being described at the conceptual level, it will be practically impossible to give a sufficiently accurate description of the subconceptual processes. This claim reflects manifold observations that the introspective descriptions of the way experts perform reasoning is usually by far too imprecise to be implemented in symbolic systems, such as expert systems.

A symbolic model uses symbols, where the symbols have *conceptual-level* semantics which refer to the task behaviour being explained. Considering a medical diagnostic expert system as an example, the program could be explained at the conceptual level as consisting of a number of modules, where each module's function is related to the task at hand, e.g. to gather information about the patient, such as asking for the performance of tests and obtaining the results of those, collecting evidence for a particular disease and comparing

---

[31] That is, processes where explicit rules known to a human are followed deliberately, such as performing arithmetic calculations, etc. This is opposed to other processes, where humans do not attempt to follow explicit rules, such as in most of personal decision making, creative activities, etc.

it against the evidence for alternative diagnoses, etc. Opposed to that are more intuitive processes, such as those resulting in asking for a particular test to be performed. The decision to do so may involve complex processes which cannot be explained in terms of the domain itself, in which a doctor is used to think and communicate. The doctor will normally be unaware of these processes, i.e. the doctor may be unable to explain each particular step they are taking.

Thus, there is a description of intuitive behaviour at the subconceptual level, which is opposed to the conceptual-level semantics. The elements in an explanation at that level, the units, *do not* have the semantics of the original behaviour. Their conceptual interpretation is not possible with reference to the task at hand. This difficulty is discussed further in the following chapters. In particular, in chapter 15, knowledge which is hard to explicate, and hard to verbalise in any form, is discussed in more depth.

12. The Notion of 'Symbols'

In this chapter the relation between symbolic and non-symbolic approaches to intelligent systems will be discussed. A new framework will be introduced within which the different views can be located, analysed and compared to each other.

Two different aspects of the various views will be considered. The first aspect is the understanding of the notion of *symbol*, i.e. what sort of reference is associated with it? It seems that both positions, the proponents of symbol systems as well as the proponents of connectionism, agree that symbols *refer* to something, as opposed to mere tokens, which are not assumed to have any particular meaning or reference. However, different conceptions of the notion of *symbol* can be distinguished with respect to the class of entities to which a symbol may refer.

The second aspect concerns the kind of processes which are assumed to manipulate the symbols. Usually, people from both parties, the connectionist as well as the symbolic proponents, accept the general notion of algorithm as the basis of all manipulation processes.[1] However, it is possible to diversify the general notion of algorithm by considering the Kolmogorov complexity of an algorithmic description of the manipulation procedures. That is, different views on the notion of *symbols* may require different complexities of the involved manipulation rules.

The chapter is organised as follows: section 12.1 discusses different conceptions of the notion of *symbol*. In section 12.2, the differences in the various conceptions of *symbol* are discussed with respect to the first aspect, i.e. to the kind of objects, symbols refer to. Section 12.3 analyses the complexity of the implied symbol manipulation in the various views on symbols. The final section 12.4 contains an extensive discussion on the points presented in this chapter.

---

[1] By *symbol* as opposed to *token* is meant that a particular interpretation is associated to the token. A numerical value in a connectionist model, for example, might be considered as mere token.

12.1 The Notion of *Symbol*

When taking a closer look at the notion of *symbol*, it seems a rather unclear issue. Do humans really use symbols with a fixed reference? Within the entire debate about the proper paradigm of AI, the question whether humans use symbols in thought has been surprisingly undisputed. Even in written or spoken language, it seems that the meaning of different terms can vary. The symbols, if any, which we might be using when thinking are presumably even less fixed in their meaning. To what kind of entities do symbols refer?

In the following, the notion of *symbols* will be investigated in more detail. Diverging views held by different parties in the debate about the two paradigms will be identified. It is interesting to note that there has been a centuries long discussion in philosophy about whether we humans use symbols in our thoughts and what the nature of these symbols is (see Slezak (1998b), Yolton (1996) for more details).

12.1.1 Types of Symbols

Generally, symbols are meant to bear a certain meaning. That is, symbols refer to something. To what kind of entities symbols refer, however, is rarely explicitly discussed. Obviously, symbols can be names for physical objects. But symbols sometimes refer also to more abstract entities, such as concepts, mathematical notions, etc. At least the following classes of entities to which symbols may refer can be distinguished:

- Physical objects.
  For example, a house, a particular person, or certain physical signals, e.g. a certain electrical voltage between two locations.
- Classes of physical objects.
  For example, the class of chairs, tables, human beings, computers, etc.
  Often it is difficult to exactly characterise what objects we actually subsume under a certain concept, which may be represented by a symbol.
- Abstract objects, e.g. mathematical objects including sets, numbers, or graphs.
  Such abstract objects are considered to have a special status as opposed to physical objects. Abstract objects do not have any physical property, i.e. they cannot be perceived via our (external) senses. They are rather objects of pure thought. Only in our thoughts they appear as objects at all. For example, the elements of a set do not have any particular property, though we think of them as being distinguishable entities.
- Complex abstract structures, including other symbol structures.
  Imagining elements of a set is a fairly simple cognitive task. However, much more complex abstract structures can be constructed from such elements by simple rules of composition leading to more complex abstract entities. In fact, the complexity of constructible entities is unlimited. Mathematical objects

like graphs, Turing machines, or programs belong to these complex entities, which are constructible by pure thought.

12.1.2 *Symbols* in the Different Views on AI

In the debates on whether the traditional symbolic approach to AI is appropriate, differences in the conceptions of the notion of *symbol* can be identified.

Symbols in *physical symbol systems*. Newell and Simon's symbol system approach has a broad view of the notion of *symbols*.[2] Their symbols can refer to a broad spectrum of entities: symbols are formed as the result of perception and symbols are used to control the system's actuators. Symbols are used for the internal processing of those symbols being involved in the interaction of the symbol system with the 'world'. For that purpose, symbols may refer to a memory location, where another symbol or symbol structure is stored.

Symbols are allowed to refer to physical objects in the environment, they may refer to abstract concepts used by humans, as well as to other symbol structures stored in a symbol system. In other words, the rules according to which symbols are manipulated can be built from symbolic structures and simpler manipulation rules. The most primitive level of manipulation rules are given by the Universal Turing machine. Thus, a symbol system in this sense is any algorithm executed on a Universal Turing machine. Roughly speaking, symbols also include everything which is part of a program code. This may be code of a high-level programming language as well as code for a universal Turing machine, which may be difficult to comprehend. The physical symbol system hypothesis claims that also those symbols are included which humans normally use:

> ... It becomes a hypothesis that this notion of symbols includes symbols that we humans use everyday in our lives.[3]

Symbols in the *phenomenological attack*. Dreyfus, the originator of the phenomenological attack on AI, argued strongly against the physical symbol system hypothesis. His main argument was the claim that in human cognition symbols do not have a fixed meaning. Instead, the meaning of symbols changes when the context of the thought processes involving those symbols changes. For example, symbols may change their meaning when the person's goals change, when unexpected events happen or when a new perspective is adopted on the domain the person is dealing with. Hence, there cannot be physical symbols that correspond to the symbols humans are using.

We come back to the distinction between 'first-person symbols' and 'third-person symbols', as in section 11.2.1, page 185. *First-person symbols* are those symbols which are used by the person whose thought processes are under

---

[2] See section 1.2.
[3] In Newell (1980).

consideration.[4] However, people certainly do manifest at least some of their thoughts in written or spoken language, which is an expression using symbols. Opposed to that are *third-person symbols* which are used by a third person observing from 'outside' the thought processes of the 'first person'.

Dreyfus addresses essentially the first-person symbols by his arguments from phenomenology. Opposed to that are Newell and Simon's physical symbol systems, which include also third-person symbols. Every programmer who attempts to write a program that simulates in some sense human cognition will also use third-person symbols. Dreyfus, however, extended the observations from phenomenology on thought processes from a 'first-person perspective' to the claim that even third-person symbols cannot provide an adequate account on human thought processes.

Symbols in the connectionist paradigm. The idea of connectionism offered an approach that does not need symbols at all, at least it does not use symbols which are 'comprehensibly' related to first-person symbols. That is, though a connectionist system deals with certain numerical signal values, these signals cannot be related to first-person symbols in a straightforward way. The idea is rather that certain patterns, which dynamically appear and disappear and which are distributed over a large number of computing units (or neurons) correspond to first-person symbols. The philosophical observations that the exact meaning of symbols in human thought is often rather gradually than abruptly changing, emerging and vanishing over time, is reflected by the connectionist paradigm:

> A connectionist system deals with a large set of numerical values, which, if appropriately combined, correspond in *their entirety* to symbols. These numerical values have virtually 'built-in' the property of gradual change and the possibility of sudden emergence of patterns which constitute a symbol.

12.2 The Semantics of Symbols

Although it is hardly possible to give a clear definition of the various conceptions of the nature of symbols, the following presents a rough description of the typical references of symbols in the different paradigms. To oppose those 'symbols' being used in a computational paradigm to the symbols being used by humans in speaking and thinking, the human symbols will be called *first-person symbols*. The symbols in the computational paradigms will be called *tokens* in order not to pre-suppose any particular interpretation of tokens as symbols or non-symbols.

---

[4] In what sense can it be said that a person actually uses symbols is quite unclear as can be seen by the centuries long discussion in philosophy on the topic as mentioned in the beginning of this section (see Yolton (1996), Slezak (1998b).

The following four levels at which the description of AI systems and cognition has been proposed will be distinguished: the *knowledge level*, the *physical symbol systems*, the *connectionist subsymbolic*, and *connectionist neuronal* systems. The knowledge level is considered here as a specific type of physical symbol system. Further aspects of the tokens and the associated manipulation processes in these four views will be discussed in the following subsections. First of all, however, the typical possible meaning of tokens in each of the four levels are characterised.

12.2.1 The Reference of Tokens

1. Knowledge level
   The tokens at the knowledge level represent exclusively *knowledge*, i.e., the tokens are first-person symbols. Since the term knowledge lacks a formal definition, this can only be taken as a coarse characterisation.
2. Physical symbol systems
   The tokens in physical symbol systems may refer to memory locations, i.e. to other tokens and strings of tokens as well as they may refer to locations within the program which is manipulating the tokens. According to the physical symbol system hypothesis, it is assumed that there are also certain tokens which correspond directly to the symbols humans use in their daily lives, i.e. to first-person symbols.
3. Connectionist *subsymbolic* systems
   The tokens in the connectionist subsymbolic paradigm are the individual numerical activation levels of a large number of interconnected computing units. A single token does not have an easily identifiable meaning. It is rather the entirety of a large number of such tokens which constitute, in a dynamically changing way, first-person symbols.
4. Connectionist *neuronal* systems
   The tokens in the connectionist neuronal paradigm are parts of models of biological neurons. The tokens will represent certain physical values, involving the chemo-electrical processes in the brain. As in the connectionist subsymbolic paradigm, it is difficult to assign any meaning to the tokens beyond their purely physical interpretation.

12.2.2 Tokens and Their Relation to First-Person Symbols

There is plenty of evidence, as indicated in the previous chapter, that the manipulation of first-person symbols in human thought takes place according to very complex rules[5] taking extensive context into account. This implies the following relation of tokens in the different views to first-person symbols.

---

[5] It has even been claimed that the complexity exceeds any finite number of rules, i.e. that no rules at all can be given, e.g. by Dreyfus (1972).

1. Knowledge level
   Tokens are only first-person symbols representing 'knowledge'. The manipulation rules derive all 'rational' consequences of the given knowledge.
2. Physical symbol systems
   Some tokens refer (hopefully) directly to first-person symbols. Additional
   tokens do not refer directly to first person-symbols. They rather ensure that
   the tokens referring to first person symbols are appropriately manipulated.
3. Connectionist subsymbolic systems
   The tokens, i.e. the subsymbols in connectionist subsymbolic systems, and
   their assumed uniform, simple, and local manipulation necessarily imply
   that the first-person symbols emerge as rather complex patterns of subsymbols. That is, the relation of a single token to a first-person symbol is
   highly dependent on the context, which is represented by a large number
   of further tokens.
4. Connectionist neuronal systems
   The tokens in the connectionist neuronal model represent the physical state
   of a biological system, e.g. a human brain. Since the tokens have to model
   the biological details of the neurons in addition to the cognitive processes,
   the complexity of the patterns of tokens which correspond to a first-person
   symbol will usually be higher than in connectionist subsymbolic systems.

12.3 Token Manipulation Processes

Different types of token manipulation processes are associated with each computational level. In particular, the complexity of manipulation rules varies.
We do not define complexity here, but roughly speaking, something like the
number of overall rules is meant, which could be formalised by the notion of
Kolmogorov complexity, i.e. the minimal description length of all such rules.

1. Knowledge level
   At the knowledge level, manipulation rules are needed, which generate
   suitable inferences. The generation of such inferences can be based only
   on the present knowledge, since no other information is available at the
   knowledge level. It seems obvious that this implies very complex rules,
   since not only deductive inferences have to be accommodated, but also
   non-demonstrative inferences, such as inductive, abductive, analogical and
   other types of inferences, which cannot properly be determined from the
   formal description of the given knowledge only. That is, the rules themselves
   have to contain the necessary information to disambiguate what inductive
   inference should be generated from the given knowledge. For example, two
   different rules are needed to infer from a few observed black ravens that all
   ravens are black and *not* to infer from a few observed non-black non-ravens
   that all non-black objects are non-ravens. The first inference could very
   roughly be formalised as follows:

	Knowledge Level	Symbol Systems
Tokens, e.g.,	'car', 'Peter', ...	'if x > y then a=3', 'car', 'ip=&a;' 'Peter'
Mapping to reference object (physical or abstract, e.g. car, number, $e = mc^2$)	immediate mapping	some symbols have immediate mapping
Complexity of mapping	minimal	minimal for respective symbols
Complexity of rules to produce subsequent state	extremely complex	very complex

	Subsymbolic	Neural Level
Tokens, e.g.,	1.2, 3.4, 0.5, 1.1,... (numerical activity values)	1,2, 0.4, 0.3, ... Neurotransmitter-level=0.5 (physiological activity values)
Mapping to reference object (physical or abstract, e.g. car, number, $e = mc^2$)	large set of specific numerical values altogether map to a reference object	large set of specific neurophysiological values map to a reference object
Complexity of mapping	very complex	very complex
Complexity of rules to produce subsequent state	simple	complex to extremely complex

Table 12.1. The complexity of mapping tokens to objects (including abstract objects like concepts, etc.) and the complexity of token manipulation in order to produce the next system state.

$$\frac{some\ x\ P(x) \to Q(x)}{forall\ x\ P(x) \to Q(x)}.$$

However, the second inference, which humans would not derive, fits into the same scheme by substituting P for non-black and Q for non-raven. The bottom line is that not only the form of the inference suffices, but also the content has to be taken into account by a rule. See chapter 15 for more details.

2. Physical symbol systems
   Each of the manipulation rules needs to take only a single token into account. This is due to the computational universality of the Turing machine. However, the resulting program may be very long, which can result in the a correspondingly complex manipulation of the entirety of tokens in the system. That is, arbitrarily complex manipulations of *token structures* can be built from simple manipulations of single tokens.[6]

---

[6] Opposed to physical symbol systems, at the knowledge level all tokens not directly corresponding to first-person symbols have to be hidden in the rules which manipulate the first-person symbols.

3. Connectionist subsymbolic systems

   The complexity of the manipulation rules of a single numerical activation level of a unit U is assumed to be very low. It merely depends on the current activation level of U and the activation level of the computing units connected to U. The set of connected computing units is determined by the connectionist architecture.

4. Connectionist neuronal systems

   The complexity of the manipulation rules of realistic neuronal activation levels and associated physiological processes is, according to current knowledge, at least for some types of neurons very high. However, the rules take physical specifics of the neuron N into account as well as of those neurons connected to N and the specifics of their interconnection.

Table 12.1 summarises the differences between the different views. The arguments supporting connectionism have largely attacked the first-person symbol view of symbol systems, mainly arguing that first-person symbols are not all there is in cognition. Dreyfus and others pointed out that certain tacit knowledge plays a central role in human intelligence and that such knowledge cannot be implemented in symbol systems.

While this claim is certainly too strong,[7] it nevertheless points to an important problem: there is knowledge which is very difficult to formalise. To a large extent it is difficult because it is virtually impossible to verbalise it. This 'knowledge' is reflected in the particular sequence of conscious thoughts that we encounter, but it does not become explicit. It seems that we cannot access this knowledge itself introspectively. We just experience how our thoughts are guided, but we cannot give a satisfactory and precise description of what thought will follow in a given state of mind. The next section and chapter 15 discuss the nature of such 'tacit' knowledge further.

12.4 Discussion

As has been seen, there are different views of the central notion of *symbol*. In the connectionist view the first-person perspective prevails. First-person symbols, however, are of little importance for the engineering view of AI. For developing intelligently behaving systems, it does not matter whether the system manipulates internally symbols which can or cannot be interpreted as first-person symbols.

The crucial issue is rather the difficulty of the actual engineering process and the verifiability of a system design. The difficulty of the engineering process seems to depend essentially on the possibility to express an engineer's understanding of the system functionality which has to be implemented. The

---

[7] Even Dreyfus himself apparently lost his strong conviction to a certain degree (Dreyfus, 1992).

functionality of an intelligent system may be described by using first-person symbols. However, this is by far not the only possibility. A description in terms of third-person symbols is possible as well and it is even the more flexible approach, as it allows to use a superset of first-person symbols. However, the use of first-person symbols in designing intelligent systems may be convenient as it may facilitate, e.g the knowledge acquisition from experts, who tend to express their knowledge using first-person symbols.

It should be noted that the philosophical arguments from phenomenology which have been put forward to support connectionism, merely imply that the complete functional description of an intelligent system in terms of first-person symbols is a very difficult, if not even an impossible task. Hence, these arguments are only an objection to a *first-person* symbol system. In fact, the complex activity patterns claimed to be unique for connectionist systems can be claimed in all kinds of systems, including physical symbol systems as it is demonstrated in the following.

12.4.1 Explicit versus Implicit Symbol Processing

In human cognition, symbols seem to be used in ways which are difficult to explain exactly. A certain thought, represented by certain (first-person) symbols, may cause quite different subsequent thoughts, depending on the entire context in which the original thought occurred. Hence, the connectionist argument appears plausible that symbols in human cognition have a rather dynamically emerging behaviour, which is very different from a systematic manipulation of symbols[8] according to fixed rules and the systematic construction of symbol structures.

Although the connectionist objection to (a fairly narrow view of) the classical physical symbol systems seems valid, it is not valid as a reason for adopting a connectionist computing model. This is because the account of first-person symbols in connectionist models is much too vague. Essentially, it is roughly claimed that some patterns of neural or subsymbolic activity will indicate that the current overall system state corresponds to a cognitive state involving particular first-person symbols. No reasonably precise explanation is given on *what* first-person symbol is represented by *which* activity patterns. This is rather left to an observer who may consider the connectionist system as a black box, assuming that its processes correspond to some sort of cognitive processes which may lead to the same overall behaviour. This feature is supposed to make the computational processes in connectionist systems more authentic than the processes in a physical symbol system. As Smolensky and others emphasise, the crucial feature which makes a system fit for a connectionist subsymbolic system, is the fact that symbols correspond to patterns of a large number of numerical (continuous) values carried by different computing units in a con-

---

[8] The emphasis lies on (physical) symbols with a fixed graspable meaning.

nectionist network. Recall also the following quote from subsection 11.4.2 by
Smolensky:

> (8) b. The subconceptual unit hypothesis: The entities in the intuitive
> processor with the semantics of conscious concepts of the task domain
> are complex patterns of activity over many units. Each unit participates
> in many such patterns.[9]

Opposed to that are physical symbol systems normally considered to account for a first-person symbol by using and manipulating internally a certain
symbol or symbol structure, which is assumed to correspond directly and constantly over time to the first-person symbol in question. Once the claim of
a direct and constant correspondence of a single symbol used in a physical
symbol system to first-person symbols is abandoned, there is no reason why a
physical symbol system should not at least be equally able to perform computational processes which, if properly interpreted, do correspond to the use of
first-person symbols in human cognition. To oppose the connectionist claim, a
claim as paraphrased in the following can be made of physical symbol systems:

> Physical symbol systems are manipulating symbols according to simple
> rules. A group of symbols may form a more complex symbol structure.
> Certain symbol structures correspond to first-person symbols in the
> following sense: They are formed in exactly those system states which
> functionally correspond to the conscious use of the first-person symbol
> in the cognitive system being modelled. These compound symbol struc-
> tures may dynamically appear and disappear, due to the manipulation
> of some or all of their elements.

This characterisation is not more vague than the connectionist account on
first-person symbols. But it does not commit the system engineer to using a
connectionist architecture. Instead, the system engineer is free in choosing design steps as they like and feel comfortable with. It is convincing that under
such circumstances physical symbol systems are at least as appropriate as connectionist systems. One should remember that in principle, one may simply
simulate a connectionist system by a physical symbol system on a serial computer using the connectionist subsymbols (continuous numerical values) as the
symbols in the physical symbol system. Of course, the connectionist subsymbols
of first-person symbols might be considered as mere tokens which can hardly
be related individually to the emerging first-person symbols, but rather, a large
group of such tokens can be related to emerging first-person symbols.

12.4.2 Understanding a Symbol's Meaning

A much more pressing problem is the question of the cognitive feasibility to
make sense out of tokens in a given paradigm. That is, which tokens can be

---

[9] See Smolensky (1988):6.

interpreted or understood by a cognitive scientist or an engineer of intelligent systems. How easy, or how feasible is it to understand a description made up of tokens of a certain type? From that perspective, the fundamental problem with the physical symbol system approach seems to be a rather practical one: both the meaning of first-person symbols and their manipulation are very difficult to explain. By introspection, usually only a certain aspect of a symbol's meaning and/or its appropriate manipulation is explicated. Thus, the explication may hold for a particular behaviour, but it does not allow a generalisation to a larger class of similar cases. Sometimes even incorrect explanations are given, which seem to be rather oriented on what the social environment of a person expects or approves, than on the actual reasons.[10] The well-known fact that people often rationalise their own behaviour by giving false explanations to themselves which sound more logical or sensical than a more accurate explanation goes into a similar direction.

The distributed connectionism, however, goes one step too far: Since a design in terms of first-person symbols is impractical, it abandons entirely the symbolic approach, including the use of third-person symbols. Designing a complex intelligent system without using any symbols at all means to specify a complex functionality without having any means to tie the system specification to the engineer's understanding of the desired functionality. The understanding of an engineer needs to be expressed by symbols which can be interpreted by the engineer, i.e. the understanding needs to be expressed by third-person symbols. Thus, the connectionist approach, in its radical version, seems to fail to fulfill its promise!

12.4.3 Operationalising First-Person Symbols by Third-Person Symbols

First-person symbols in an AI system need to be operationalised, i.e. to be defined in terms with a clear meaning. This needs to be done for its effective use to a varying degree depending on the purpose of the AI system. An operationalisation, at least in the symbolic paradigm, will use third-person symbols, which are understood by the system engineer, in order to define first-person symbols. While those first-person symbols may be understood by an expert without any further comments, for the proper use in an AI system, an operationalisation of these symbols may require an extensive description in terms which the machine can relate to its other knowledge, data, inputs and outputs.

Unfortunately, such first-person symbols referring to human concepts are often difficult to define. This has been widely recognised in philosophy. To name one term which was introduced by Wittgenstein,[11] a quote follows on

---

[10] See Nisbett and DeCamp Wilson (1977) for empirical psychological studies showing the existence of this phenomenon.

[11] Ludwig Wittgenstein (1889–1953) is one of the most important and original philosophers of the twentieth century. In his early work, the Tractatus-Logico

the term of *family resemblance* among objects which are subsumed under the same concept:

> 66. Consider for example the proceedings that we call 'games'. I mean board-games, card-games, ball-games, Olympic games and so on. What is common to them all? ... Are they all 'amusing'? ... Or is there always winning and losing, or competition between players? Think of patience. In ball games there is winning and losing; but when a child throws his ball at the wall ... this feature disappeared. Look at the parts played by skills and luck; and at the difference between skill in chess and skill in tennis. Think now of games like ring-a-ring-a-roses; here is the element of amusement, but how many other characteristic features have disappeared! ...
> And the result of this examination is: we see a complicated network of similarities overlapping and criss-crossing ...
> 67. I can think of no better expression to characterise these similarities than 'family resemblances' ...[12]

The observation by Wittgenstein is important for the symbolic AI, since it indicates that an operationalisation of 'every-day' concepts like *games* is anything other than straightforward. While one may have a symbol which refers to the first-person symbol of *games* its operationalisation seems still a long way to go. Concepts which have traditionally been mentioned by the Fuzzy[13] community, like *a heap of sand, baldness*, etc., are other examples. It is also interesting to note that Wittgenstein discussed fuzzy concepts as well. Another quote follows:

> 75. What does it mean to know what a game is? What does it mean, to know it and not be able to say it? Is this knowledge somehow equivalent to an unformulated definition? So that if it were formulated I should be able to recognise it as the expression of my knowledge? Isn't my knowledge, my concept of a game, completely expressed in the explanations that I give? That is, in my describing examples of various kinds of game, showing how all sorts of other games can be constructed on the analogy of these; saying that I should scarcely include this or this among games; and so on.

Philosophicus (Wittgenstein, 1961), he advocated a model-theoretic interpretation of language and made important contributions to the development of formal logic. In his later years he developed a view which strongly opposed his early view of language. He developed many very convincing arguments for his later view of language, which roughly meant that linguistic terms have no simple and fixed meaning at all. His late philosophy was as ground-breaking as his early work and prompted a substantial re-orientation of contemporary philosophy.

[12] In Wittgenstein (1953).

[13] The term goes back to Zadeh (1965). See Zimmermann (1991) or Pedrycz (1995) for introductions to Fuzzy sets and fields of their application.

76. If someone were to draw a sharp boundary I could not acknowledge it as the one that I too always wanted to draw, or had drawn in my mind. For I did not want to draw one at all. His concept can then be said to be not the same as mine, but akin to it. The kinship is that of two pictures, one of which consists of colour patches with vague contours, and the other of patches similarly shaped and distributed, but with clear contours. The kinship is just as undeniable as the difference.

77. And if we carry this comparison still further it is clear that the degree to which the sharp picture *can* resemble the blurred one depends on the latter's degree of vagueness. For imagining having to sketch a sharply defined picture 'corresponding' to a blurred one. In the latter there is a blurred red rectangle: for it you put down a sharply defined one. Of course - several such sharply defined rectangles can be drawn to correspond to the indefinite one. - But if the colours in the original merge without a hint of any outline won't it become a hopeless task to draw a sharp picture corresponding to the blurred one? Won't you then have to say: "Here I might just as well draw a circle or heart as a rectangle, for all the colours merge. Anything - and nothing - is right." - And this is the position you are in if you look for definitions corresponding to our concepts in aesthetics or ethics.

In such a difficulty always ask yourself: How did we *learn* the meaning of this word ("good" for instance)? From what sort of examples? In what language-games? Then it will be easier for you to see that the word must have a family of meanings.[14]

In these paragraphs Wittgenstein uses drawing pictures as a metaphor for defining concepts. His observations here and in other paragraphs suggest, that humans do not have exact or complete concept definitions readily available. They are rather creating the boundaries of their concepts when there is a demand for it. (As seen quite clearly in paragraph 76: "For I did not want to draw one at all.") They decide on single cases and shape the partial boundaries of their concepts by doing so. Wittgenstein's investigations also suggest, that his 'blurred' concepts cannot easily be operationalised by defining something like a gradual membership function, as it is done with Fuzzy sets,[15] because such a gradual membership function would still need to be specified very carefully for each 'part' of the concept, i.e. each part of the blurred picture may be blurred in a different way.

We see that the operationalisation of first-person symbols is often very difficult. In fact, many concepts seem to have a rather 'generic' definition which

---

[14] From Wittgenstein (1953).

[15] The basic idea of Fuzzy sets is to define sets, where the membership function for the domain of objects is not a binary function but a continuous one. That is, an object may be a member of the set of *bald head* to a degree of 0.3. Also a set of operations are defined on such gradual membership values in order to account for the usual set-theoretic operations, such as union, intersection, etc. (See Zimmermann (1991) or Pedrycz (1995) for more details.

shapes up by instantiating the concepts with concrete objects. That is, our concepts do not have sharp boundaries initially, and that the boundaries are drawn incrementally during use of the concept and probably also during use of other more or less related concepts.

This observation actually suggests something like a 'patchwork approach' as an effective way to the acquisition of conceptual expert knowledge. The meaning of a first-person symbol, e.g. the concept of 'table', can be explicated step by step. When asking an expert for a characterisation of such a concept, their answer will reflect their imagination of the concept within a certain context. For example, they may remember their own dinner table. Because of the context dependency, the characterisation will be incomplete, overly general, or both. However, by recalling different contexts the characterisation can be extended by including alternative characteristics or it can be restricted by adding further conditions or exception rules. Thus, the given characterisation can grow and become more and more precise by 'patching' the current concept description in new contexts where it proves insufficient.[16]

Another issue which has not been addressed by the discussion so far, is the fact that apparently a substantial part of human reasoning seems to be based on visual images including diagrams. That is, the treatment of respective contents as singular first-person symbols is presumably not appropriate. Although the field of visual reasoning is only little explored so far, it seems unlikely that the general arguments in this book about the symbolic and connectionist paradigm will be affected by further progress in this field. However, the interested reader may be referred to texts on the subject, such as (Osherson, Kosslyn, & Hollerbach, 1990; Glasgow, Narayanan, & Chandrasekaran, 1995) or (Stenning & Yule, 1997).

---

[16] See Compton and Jansen (1990), Edwards et. al. (1993), Richards and Compton (1997), Beydoun and Hoffmann (1997), Kaspar and Hoffmann (1997) for an actual implementation of such an approach as knowledge acquisition method or see also section 3.3 for more references.

13. Computational Limitations of Connectionist Architectures

As discussed in Part II, many attempts have been made to develop neural network architectures which are capable of intelligent behaviour. Although analysing the exact behaviour of a large number of interconnected computing units appears to be very hard, there is the hope that the right type of large neural networks will show intelligent behaviour and good learning capabilities, since human brains consist of a very large number of neurons.

Thorough analyses of two-layer networks have been provided in the past; a particularly well-known study is Minsky and Papert's book *Perceptrons* (1969). The analysis of even such a restricted class of networks turned out to be extremely difficult, as Papert (1988) himself reports. Consequently, analyses of the computational abilities of more complex networks have been suffering from their inherent complexity of interaction.

This chapter introduces a powerful method for analysing the computational abilities of connectionist systems, here also used synonymously of neural networks, which is based on algorithmic information theory or, synonymously, on Kolmogorov complexity, as presented in section 10.2. The method shows that the idea of many interacting computing units, as in connectionist systems, does not essentially ease the task of constructing intelligent systems or intelligent learning systems. Results are obtained which strongly suggest that building intelligent systems as well as powerful learning systems cannot essentially be simplified by the use of massively parallel and distributed computing systems, such as connectionist systems.[1]

The idea was originally introduced by Hoffmann (1990b). Further results presented in this chapter have been previously published in Hoffmann (1991b, 1993, 1997a) and Hoffmann (1997b). With regard to learning capabilities similar results for general learning algorithms were published in Hoffmann (1990a) and Hoffmann (1991a).

This chapter does not provide all the technical details of the proofs. It rather provides an intuitive exposition of the results along with important assumptions and consequences of them. The technical details of the proofs and exact

---

[1] These results do not address the issue of computing time. Note that the computational complexity of reasoning as well as of learning is often a hindrance to use certain techniques in practice. Hence, the inherent parallelism of connectionist systems may help here.

definitions of involved mathematical concepts are deferred to appendix B to allow an easier grasp of the main ideas and implications. The organisation of the
current chapter is as follows: In section 13.1 the complexity measure for neural
network architectures is introduced. Section 13.2 indicates how this complexity
measure can be applied to analyse the limitations of the computing abilities of
particular network structures as well as their learning capabilities. Section 13.3
provides an outline of the analyses of the potential and limitations of unsupervised learning, which is performed by systems such as self-organising networks,
as presented in section 7.7. In section 13.4 the significance and consequences of
the obtained results are discussed.

13.1 The Complexity of Connectionist Architectures

In this section a descriptional complexity measure for neural computation models is defined. The notion of *algorithmic information theory* or, synonymously,
Kolmogorov complexity will be used for the following considerations. The reason for this is: it is often claimed that connectionist networks or self-organising
systems are capable of acquiring complex functions. Thereby, it is usually not
discussed what exactly is meant by this intuitive notion of 'complex'. Algorithmic information theory is a notion of complexity that refers to the most
compact description possible. That is, whatever is called complex in the sense
of Kolmogorov complexity is also complex[2] with respect to any other encoding scheme. Hence, Kolmogorov complexity can be used to distinguish between
seemingly complicated functions,[3] distributed over the entire network, and really complex functions[4] that have been learned. A 'really complex function',
with respect to Kolmogorov complexity, requires a long description, regardless
of the chosen representation. For this purpose, it is shown how every particular
neural network can be described in a simple and unified way. Different possible
learning mechanisms are covered by the description scheme as well. After that
the complexity measure will be defined.

Describing Neural Computation Models. There are many different approaches to construct neural network architectures. For a general description
of neural networks we can distinguish the following two aspects.

a) The functionality of a single neuron. Often a certain threshold function of
   the sum of the weighted inputs to the neuron is proposed (see part II).
b) The topological organisation of a complete network consisting of a large
   number of neurons. Often networks are organised in layers (see Figure 13.2).

---

[2] That is, it requires a long description.
[3] ... those functions that have a much shorter description if a more suitable repre-
    sentation is chosen.
[4] ... those functions which do not have a shorter description in any other represen-
    tation scheme.

Thus, networks can be distinguished depending on their number of layers. For example, whether they contain hidden units, i.e. units which are neither connected to the input signals nor to the output signals of the network. See also part II.

It will be shown that the different approaches to both aspects a) and b) play only a minor role for building intelligent and/or powerful learning machines. In this chapter, only discrete networks are considered. All synapses of such networks carry a discrete signal and the neural activities are synchronised. Hence, all neurons change their output signals only in discrete time steps. Clearly, such neural networks can be simulated by a Turing machine. Without loss of generality, it can be assumed that there are only *binary* input/output signals to a single neuron. Consequently, any discrete neural network can be described using the following items:

1. The set Σ_N of all neurons, of which the following subsets are marked as such:
   - The subset σ_I of input nodes, appropriately indexed.
   - The subset σ_O of output nodes, appropriately indexed.

Each node $\nu \in \Sigma_N \setminus \sigma_I$ of a neural network N can be described by the following items:

2. The number i of input signals of the particular node together with the nodes in the network whose output signals are connected to each input of ν.
3. The specification of the I/O behaviour of ν: ν may be in different internal states. Let the set of all possible internal states of ν be denoted by S_ν. The number of internal states may be potentially infinite. For each computation step of the network, ν computes a function $f : \{0,1\}^i \times S_\nu \to \{0,1\}$ as output value of ν. Thus, f depends on the current input values and the current internal state of ν. Furthermore, ν possibly changes its internal state determined by a function $g : \{0,1\}^i \times S_\nu \to S_\nu$. Both functions f and g are encoded as programs p_f, p_g of minimal length for a universal Turing machine U. If $|S_\nu| = 1$ for all nodes ν, we say that the network N is static.

   There is one particular state $s_0 \in S_\nu$, which is the initial state of ν, when processing in the overall network is started. Note: ν may store all input values which are given to it during the complete operation time of the network. Thus, ν may compute the output values depending on former input values; i.e. the network may learn locally. However, global learning mechanisms, which modify the function of a single neuron depending on other factors than the immediately connected neurons can be modelled as well: then the architecture needs to be amended by additional connections to the individual neurons for communicating the desired effect of the global strategy. The additional complexity of these connections and the 'global

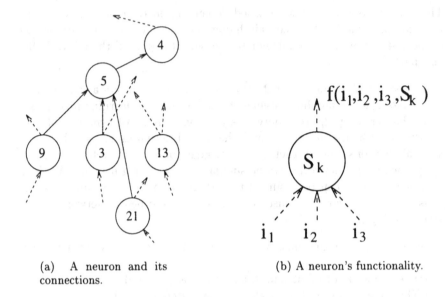

(a) A neuron and its connections.

(b) A neuron's functionality.

Figure 13.1. Describing a single neuron in the network.

learning controller' will be proportional to the complexity of the global learning strategy.

Figure 13.1 illustrates the description of each of a network's neurons. The complete network N can be described by concatenating the descriptions of all its single nodes. The description may be preceded by the overall number of nodes in N.

It may be noted that within a binary string there are no delimiting symbols which could indicate the end of a substring; e.g. the end of the description of a single neuron. Thus, each substring s_j should be preceded by the number of symbols of which s_j consists. The number is given as a binary number, where all digits are separated by a single '0'. Behind the last digit follows a '1' indicating the end of the preceding number.

Example

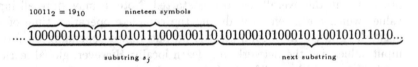

As identification of each node can its relative position within the concatenation of all nodes be used.

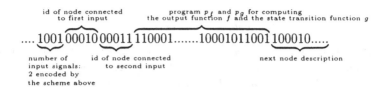

In this way, each particular neural network architecture can be represented by an individual binary string s. For our purposes we need not give more details of the possible description of a neural network by a binary string. Figure 13.2

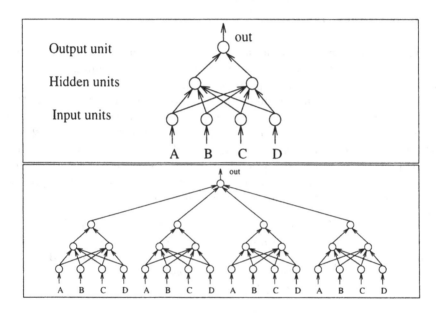

Figure 13.2. Two neural networks with a similar structure.

shows two different networks. One small and one large network, where both networks have a similar topology. In this chapter we show that a regular topology means that the output function *out* is also a rather regular function of the input values. Assuming all the nodes have the same functionality, this implies that the computed function is of similar complexity in both networks, although the networks are of significantly different size. This sort of regularity is well reflected in the following neural network complexity measure. Using the notion of Kolmogorov complexity, as presented in section 10.2, the complexity of a neural network N can be defined as follows:

Definition 13.1. *Let descr(N) be the binary encoded description of an arbitrary discrete neural network N as described in section 13.1. Then, the complexity of N **comp(N)** as the Kolmogorov complexity of descr(N) is defined* *as*

$$comp(N) = K(descr(N)).$$

It is worth noting that $comp(N)$ reflects the minimal amount of engineering work necessary for designing the network N. That means, there is no way of substantially shortening a description of the neural network N of length $comp(N)$ by using tools, repetitive structures in the design, loops or recursive functions, etc. in order to describe the design.

13.2 Limitations of Functions Computable by Connectionist Systems

Using the defined complexity measure of a neural network, it can be shown that the maximal descriptional complexity of the function computed by a neural network is limited by the description of that network itself!

This is illustrated in the following: A network will output either a '1' or a '0' to every possible input vector. All possible input vectors with a vector length of i can simply be enumerated by binary counting from '0' up to '$2^i - 1$'. Hence, all possible reactions of a static network upon a binary vector applied to its input nodes can be described by a binary sequence s of length 2^i. In s to each input vector the output of the network is given at the corresponding position according to the binary enumeration scheme.

Definition 13.2. *Let N be a static discrete neural network with i binary input signals $s_1, ..., s_i$ and one binary output signal. Then the output behaviour of N **is in accordance with a binary string** s of length 2^i, **if and only if** for any binary number b of the i digits applied as binary input values to N, N outputs exactly the value at the bth position in s.*

Based on that definition, the following Theorem states the limitations on the output behaviour of neural networks.

Theorem 13.3. *Let N be an arbitrary static discrete neural network. Then, N's output behaviour must be in accordance with a binary sequence s of a Kolmogorov complexity $K(s) \leq comp(N) + \text{const}$ for a small constant* const.[5]

For a proof see appendix B. Theorem 13.3 reflects a fundamental issue in neural computing. Assuming that intelligent behaviour presupposes a rather complex output behaviour, it shows that we cannot expect to obtain intelligent networks, if the networks have a simple structure. Intelligent behaviour does not rest on a large number of interacting computing units. It rests rather on an **adequate structure and function** of a not necessarily large number of

---

[5] The size of the constant 'const' is only as large as it takes to accommodate an interpreter for the provided description.

computing units. That is, if uniform computing units are used, then intelligence rests only on the adequate structure, i.e. the topology, of the network.

Furthermore, it should be noted that there is no way of obtaining a complex topology by simple principles. That is, there is no simple[6] algorithm for constructing a complex network structure with respect to Kolmogorov complexity. A complex network simply requires a long description. For illustration, in Figure 13.2 both networks are of similar structure, and hence of similar complexity. From Theorem 13.3 it follows, that the larger network cannot compute a significantly more complex function than the smaller one.

While it has been shown that in large neural networks, the capability of computing complex functions cannot come from the fact that many computing units interact in a complicated way with each other, it may be argued that nevertheless large networks may be capable of *learning* complex functions from training data. The following subsection investigates the capabilities of neural networks to learn complex functions.

13.2.1 Neural Networks and Their Learning Capabilities

In the following, the learning capabilities of neural networks are investigated. For assessing the learning capabilities of neural networks, it is necessary to make appropriate assumptions about the learning target and about the conditions under which the learning should take place. More specifically, what sort and how much training data can be expected and how does that relate to the function that should be learned? Furthermore, if the target function is not exactly learned by the neural network, would it still be useful to learn a similar function, which approximates in a useful way the target function?

While the formal description of respective assumptions are presented in the appendix B, the following presents an intuitive idea of the involved assumptions and the results.

The learning task. In this section, only the task to learn a binary classification function from classified examples is considered. There are many more learning tasks conceivable, such as learning multiple classes, learning continuous functions, learning decision making under uncertain circumstances etc., or learning from unclassified examples as it is investigated later in this chapter. However, classification learning is of substantial importance as it occurs as an important task itself or as subtask of other learning tasks. For example, it occurs in the task to learn a network of concepts as it is involved in the human acquisition of language competence.

For the learning of a binary classification function, it is assumed that all objects are described by a fixed number of binary attributes. This, however, represents no loss of generality, as other object representations can be mapped into binary representations. Furthermore, it is assumed that there is a fixed target classification function which is to be found during the learning process.

---

[6] ... that means short ... .

Furthermore, a similar classification function is considered as acceptable, if its probability to misclassify a randomly chosen object is less than some specifiable error ε. To assess the probability of choosing an object for which the neural network may be asked to determine its class, it is assumed that some unknown but fixed probability distribution exists, according to which the objects are chosen.

As an example, imagine the task of diagnosing patients as having or not having a certain disease D. There will be different types of patients, each type showing a different pattern of symptoms. A classifier may be able to recognise most of the possible symptom patterns. Only on a few patterns will it fail to diagnose correctly. However, each pattern of symptoms will occur with a certain frequency. The order in which the types of patients come along for diagnosis may well be considered as random. Then, each pattern of symptoms can be considered to occur with a certain probability, though it is unknown how large this probability is. Then, a classifier which fails on a certain possibly very small percentage, e.g. on 0.1% of the cases, may still be acceptable though it is not perfect.

The next issue concerns how the training data is obtained. If, for example, all possible symptom patterns are provided as well as a number of cases, where the disease D is not present, then learning will be relatively simple. This, however, will normally only be possible if there is some kind of teacher, which prepares the training data on purpose. On the other hand, if some symptom patterns are never provided in the training data, we cannot expect the learner to know about it. One assumption which is made in most theoretical studies of such probabilistic learning is that which goes back originally to Valiant (1984b) and is generally known as the *probably approximately correct learning model*, or shorter, the pac-model. There it is assumed that the training examples are also chosen randomly according to the same but still unknown probability distribution according to which the objects are chosen for classification. That is, if there are some frequently occurring symptom patterns which the learner needs to know about to avoid a large classification error, then the probability to have those patterns included in the training examples is also correspondingly high. Furthermore, if a particular symptom pattern is very rare, so that it does not occur among the training examples, then the error which may be caused by not knowing about it would also be relatively small. Overall, these probabilistic assumptions allow successful learning, at least if the concept space of the learning task is not too large. Compare also chapter 4 for a more detailed discussion of the issue.

What is proved in appendix B in Theorem B.6 for neural networks, is the following: Under the sketched probabilistic assumptions, any network of negligible complexity, which is able to learn a function of Kolmogorov complexity k, requires a number of training examples randomly chosen which grows roughly linearly in the complexity k as well as in the inverse of the tolerable error ε, i.e. it grows also linearly in $\frac{1}{\varepsilon}$. The complexity of the network can, in the best case, be subtracted from the complexity k of the target function. The difference has still to be learned from a number of examples which again grows roughly linearly in the complexity difference as well as in $\frac{1}{\varepsilon}$. A numerical example follows:

Example

> Consider a Multi-Layer Perceptron (MLP) with, say, 1000 binary or continuous input nodes and 100 nodes on a single hidden layer. If each weight is encoded as 10 bits and one assumes that each weight is relevant, i.e. each possible weight combination results in another overall function one looks already at some 10x100x1000=1,000,000 bits of Kolmogorov complexity for the most complex concept.
>
> The above assumption that there are this many different overall functions is presumably not true. However, one may think of another (regularly structured) network architecture where, in fact, 100,000 or more different weights can be combined in a respective number of different combinations resulting indeed in this many different overall network functions.

While it is often not clear, what the Kolmogorov complexity of a particular concept might be, it is clear from the theoretical studies detailed in appendix B that the use of a large network for massively parallel and distributed processing does not reduce the number of examples needed for learning. That is, other learning approaches which allow to learn the target function at all and which bear the same amount of algorithmic information towards the learning target, will similarly be able to learn from the same set of examples. Clearly, there may be differences between a learning system that learns smooth continuous functions, such as most neural network models, opposed to a learner that learns discrete decision surfaces, such as decision tree learners. However, in terms of (descriptional) complexity of the learned function, the neural network is not superior to any other learner. Furthermore, whether or not a large number of units participate in the learning process in a massively parallel fashion has no impact on the learning result. Which type of learner is more successful depends on the task domain; e.g., whether it requires smooth continuous functions or rather discrete axis-parallel decision functions.

The following subsection considers the potential use of developing more sophisticated models of neurons, which may or may not resemble closely biological neurons in animal and human brains.

13.2.2 On Modelling Biological Neuronal Functionalities

Research activities in biology and neuroscience stimulate the development of new functional models of the involved computing units (see Gray, Konig, Engel, and Singer (1989), Grzywacz and Koch (1987), Marr (1982), Ryckebusch, Bower, and Mead (1989), Selverston (1985), or Erwin, Obermayer, and Schulten (1995) or Sejnowski and Ritz (1997)). The following and appendix B prove that the particular functionality of the involved computing units in a network plays only a *negligible role on the emergent intelligent behaviour* of large networks. In particular, it is shown that the influence of a particular connectionist functionality on the overall network behaviour steadily decreases[7] when the topological complexity of the network increases. This implies that the particular functionality of the used computing units in complex connectionist networks plays a negligible role for the emergent overall behaviour of large networks. This effect is the same for the learning behaviour in connectionist networks.

The complexity of connectionist networks Recalling the description scheme for neural networks as given in section 13.1 the description of the following two parts can easily be separated:

a. The functionality of all the types of involved computing units.
b. The topological organisation of all computing units.

That is, we split the description of the network into two parts as illustrated in Figure 13.3. Based on that distinction, we can define the complexity of both

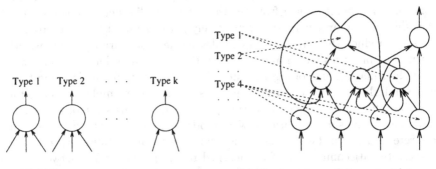

(a) Different types of neurons in a network.

(b) The topology of the network.

Figure 13.3. Two aspects of a connectionist network which can be described separately. The functionalities of the neurons in a network N are described by $descr_{func}(N)$ (part (a)), while the topology of a network N is described by $descr_{top}(N)$ (part (b)).

aspects of a connectionist network N:

Definition 13.4. *Let $descr_{top}(N)$ be the binarily encoded description of the topology of an arbitrary discrete connectionist network N as indicated above. Then, we define the topological complexity of N, $\mathbf{comp}_{top}(N)$ as the Kolmogorov complexity of $descr_{top}(N)$, i.e.*

$$comp_{top}(N) = K(descr_{top}(N)).$$

---

[7] Even asymptotically to zero.

Similarly, the complexity of the functionality of the set of types of computing units $\mathbf{comp}_{func}(N)$ *used throughout the network is defined as:*

$$comp_{func}(N) = K(descr_{func}(N)).$$

Finally, the complexity of the complete network $\mathbf{comp}_{all}(N)$ *is given by:*

$$comp_{all}(N) = comp_{func}(N) + comp_{top}(N).$$

Based on that, it can easily be shown that the learning power of a large neural network cannot be substantially enhanced by providing sophisticated models of the function of an individual neuron. This is essentially due to the fact that a model of a single neuron will contain relatively little information. In contrast to that, the specific topological organisation of a large network may have a much larger contribution to allow a neural network to perform the desired complex target function. This holds, regardless of whether a learning process is involved or not. See Theorem B.10 in appendix B for more technical details. This theoretical study also shows that the following fact holds in the case, where the order of magnitude of the number of required examples should be smaller than the complexity of the concept to learn: The influence of a particular functionality of the involved computing units on the complete network design is asymptotically zero.

All the presented results hold, no matter what particular learning mechanism is used, as long as it is counted in the complexity measure of the neural network in question. The results hold even for the case, where the computing units show an *optimal adaptation behaviour*, i.e. no example has to be presented twice.[8]

13.3 Unsupervised Learning and Self-Organising Systems

The idea of self-organisation has attracted considerable interest from scientists in different disciplines, including computer science, neuroscience, cognitive science, and philosophy. Processes of self-organisation are often believed to be capable to capture complex environmental conditions by allowing complex structures to emerge within the self-organising system itself. See Grossberg (1976), Carpenter and Grossberg (1987b), Carpenter and Grossberg (1990), Kohonen (1984), Kangas et al. (1990), Ritter, Martinetz, and Schulten (1992), Mao and Jain (1996), or Bégin and Proulx (1996) for recent work on self-organising systems and compare part II for an introduction into basic models.

The basic idea is to have a system which learns to behave usefully in a given domain in a certain sense by just observing a set of *unclassified* objects

---

[8] In most of the popular network models, such as MLPs trained by backpropagation, the adaptation behaviour is by far not optimal. That is, the particular examples have to be presented many times in order to train the network for classifying the examples correctly.

of the respective domain. The system receives *no* feedback whether its learning approach is correct or not. That is, self-organisation is a kind of unsupervised learning. This contrasts supervised approaches, where the system is confronted with pre-classified objects or feedback whether its predictions have been correct. Besides clustering for classification, self-organising systems are also used for learning the distribution of objects in the object space. In the following, we concentrate on learning classification functions.

However, as a consequence in self-organisation the only source of information for the system is the fact that not all possible objects will be presented, but only a certain 'meaningful' subset. This subset is assumed to show some 'natural' clusters which are supposed to be recognised by the self-organising system. Figure 13.4 shows the 'data perspective'. In Figure 13.6 the 'system perspective' of the self-organisation process is shown. In neural networks it is assumed that the system reorganises itself internally according to certain (self-organising) principles reflecting in a certain way the outside world being perceived by the system. A possible application of self-organisation is to extract compound features for (high level) symbolic learning approaches.

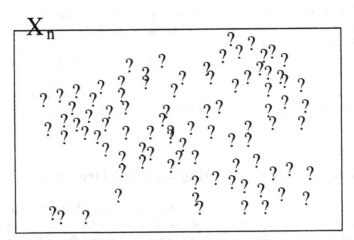

Figure 13.4. The subset Y_n which is supposed to provide the information necessary in order to find the two shaded regions in Figure B.2 (in appendix B) is merely indicated by a set of unclassified examples. Here it becomes fairly obvious that finding the target classification of these question-marks is by far not a trivial task.

As opposed to unsupervised learning, for supervised learning objects are presented with a class label associated to them. This allows a fairly simple learning process to take place which eventually may result in very complex classification functions. See Figure 13.5. Unsupervised learning can also be considered as a clustering process. The similarity measure being used is, however, not necessarily explicitly given. That is, it can be hidden in the used algorithm. Further, a similarity measure may not only depend on a given pair of

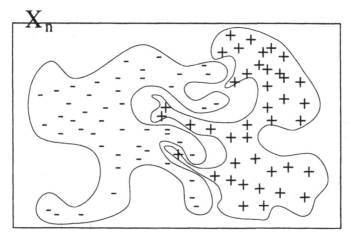

Figure 13.5. The subset Y_n (indicated by both of the enclosed areas) of the basic set X_n provides the available information. Opposed to unsupervised learning, in supervised learning a class label comes with each presented example.

objects but may also take the entire set of presented objects into account. However, for unsupervised learning objects are presented without any indication of how they should be classified, as is illustrated in Figure 13.4. This fact poses the question of how a self-organising system can know, which of all possible classification functions it should learn? Certainly, to assist the system, data is presented. But what kind of information can unclassified examples really provide? To what degree does the eventual construction of a classification function rest essentially on the strong bias the learning system has built in beforehand as opposed to the provided unclassified training data? Usually, such a system may effectively use some simple distance measure, which indicates the degree of similarity of a pair of objects. This may be used to find a certain number of clusters among the presented objects. Self-organising systems are usually considered to learn in an incremental setting; i.e. to modify their classification function continuously as the system sees new data. To what extent does the result of the self-organisation process depend on the particular order in which the system sees the data? Certainly, it would be desirable, if the self-organisation process would eventually arrive at the same classification function, regardless in which order the unclassified examples are actually provided to the system. Is there a natural limit up to what degree of complexity a system can learn a classification function from unclassified data only?

This section addresses some of these questions by providing first rigorous theoretical results on the general computational abilities of self-organising systems. By the use of algorithmic information theory (Kolmogorov complexity) an analysis of the possibly complex system dynamics becomes feasible. Earlier results on self-organising systems were published in Hoffmann (1993) and Hoffmann (1997b).

The following presents, again, a rather intuitive exposition of the theoretical results. For more technical details of the used mathematical notions, theorems and proofs, see appendix B.

13.3.1 Preliminaries

This subsection provides the formal definition of a self-organising system as it is used throughout this section.

Object space and natural objects. Most learning systems, whether supervised or unsupervised learners, whether neural network type learners or other learning systems, use a feature vector representation for the objects being presented to them in a training sample. Therefore, the following general considerations assume a feature vector representation for both the objects to be classified by the self-organising system and for the representation of the training data.

It is a well recognised fact that the choice of the particular representation has a major impact on the success or failure of the learning system. With respect to supervised versus unsupervised learning, however, there are significant differences in the role the choice of a representation plays.

While in supervised learning, it can often be guaranteed that the system will learn a classification function that classifies correctly at least a major fraction of those objects which have been in the training sample, in unsupervised learning things are more subtle. Suppose a sample of objects is chosen for training, which is just randomly chosen by picking a number of objects as they occur in nature. Suppose further, an unsupervised learning system uses a feature representation such that every possible feature vector occurs with equal probability in the given environment. For example, assume objects being represented by feature vectors consisting of 20 boolean attributes: then each particular combination of 20 boolean values has equal probability to be included in the sample. There are $2^{20} \approx 1,000,000$ different vectors, each having a probability of $\approx \frac{1}{1,000,000}$ to occur in a sample of only one object. What does that mean for the classification function being learned by an unsupervised learning system from a sample of say $5,000$ randomly chosen objects? The only clue given for determining a classification function is the fact that these particular $5,000$ feature vectors are contained in the sample as opposed to any other possible combination. That is, the absence of the remaining $995,000$ objects provides information for choosing a classification function. In the setting above, that means that the classification function being chosen by the unsupervised learning system depends entirely on this random collection of objects. Consequently, the chosen classification function will be the product of a meaningless random process and can in no sense reflect some 'natural clusters' existing in nature.

The task of self-organisation. The following two modes of operation of a self-organising system S will be distinguished in the subsequent considerations:

1. **The learning mode:** A sequence of unclassified objects is presented to the system. Based on that input, S modifies itself such that it will classify objects according to a certain classification function $f : X_n \to \{0,1\}$.
2. **The classification mode:** The system receives as input some object $x \in X_n$. It outputs the value of the learned function $f(x)$.

In principle, a self-organising system may change its mode of operation from learning mode to classification mode and vice versa as often as desired. For the

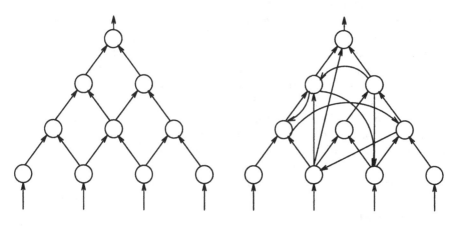

(a) Initial network structure.

(b) Network structure after the process of self-organisation.

Figure 13.6. A network before and after the self-organisation process. The new network structure should compute a desired classification function f.

sake of completeness and reference to the popular idea of self-organising neural networks, the following definition is specific to neural network style learning systems. However, the theoretical results detailed in appendix B hold for any computational system, whatsoever.

Definition 13.5. *A* **self-organising system** *S is a network whose functionality can be completely described by the following items:*

a) *The functionality of each single neuron. Often a certain threshold function of the sum of the weighted inputs to the neuron is proposed.*

b) *The topological organisation of a complete network consisting of a possibly large number of neurons.*

c) *The algorithm which controls the self-organisation process while the system is in learning mode.*

The complete system S can be described by concatenating the descriptions of all its parts. Let the description of S be denoted by $descr(S)$. In classification mode, the behaviour of the system can directly be derived from a) and b).

Figure 13.6(a) shows a simple network structure and similar system is shown in Figure 13.6(b) which may be the result of a self-organisation process.

13.3.2 Computational Limitations of Self-Organisation

An interesting question is, under exactly what circumstances can such a self-organising system develop a more meaningful structure with respect to certain purposes? What sort of training data need to be available to allow the development of a meaningful system function?

The following investigations make similar assumptions as those mentioned before: essentially that there is some unknown but fixed probability distribution according to which unclassified objects occur. During the learning phase, such randomly chosen objects are shown to the self-organising system to help it to develop a suitable classification function. During classification, such randomly chosen objects are to be classified by the system and a sensible error measure of the system's classification performance is the probability of misclassifying the next randomly chosen object. This is the same error measure as used in subsection 13.2.1 (with more details in the appendix B.1.1), i.e. the error measure of Valiant's notion of probably approximately correct learning (see Valiant (1984b), Natarajan (1991) or Anthony and Biggs (1992)).

However, the nice relationship between training data and learning performance no longer holds in the case of self-organising systems, i.e. for unsupervised learning. Since the training examples are unclassified, the actual clue the system receives about how to classify a particular object, is the entire set of objects it has seen. As a consequence, if a particular object x has a high probability of occurrence, there is no guarantee that during the learning phase, the system received appropriate information, i.e. the right set of examples, to infer x's correct class. This sharply contrasts the situation of supervised learning.

In fact, as detailed in appendix B, it can be proved that under the above mentioned probabilistic conditions of obtaining training data and measuring the classification accuracy of the system, a self-organising system S cannot be guaranteed to develop a target function of substantially higher algorithmic information than that which S contains before training, regardless of the number of randomly drawn training examples!

Theorem B.17 (in the appendix B) indicates that the complexity of 'meaningful' classification functions, which can emerge based only on unclassified examples, is rather limited. It is remarkable as well as unusual that the Theorem holds for any choice of the allowed classification error ε and any choice of the confidence level δ within the specified range, although neither of the two variables, nor the sample size occurs in the complexity bound given in the Theorem. This again is very different to the typical Theorems proved in Valiant's framework for supervised PAC-learning.

The reason for the validity of Theorem B.17 is the fact that the probability of misclassifying a given object x cannot directly be linked to the probability that enough information for determining the correct classification of x is provided in a random sample of a given size.

13.4 Implications for Artificial Intelligence and Cognitive Science

This chapter studied the computational limitations of massively parallel and distributed processing systems. Such systems may comprise a huge number of computing units which interact with each other and perform computations which are difficult to analyse due to the sheer mass of computing that is going on and the complex sequences of interactions that may emerge.

This chapter used the notion of algorithmic information theory to get a handle on the possible results of such massively parallel computing processes. It has essentially been shown that such large-scale parallel and distributed systems cannot compute functions which are more complex than the description of the distributed computing system itself. While this result is fairly obvious from a technical perspective of the theory of computing, it appears nevertheless counter-intuitive from the perspective of a huge parallel and distributed computing system: there are so many computations, which may possibly go on in such a system. The complexity limitations become even less intuitive, when the potential learning capabilities are taken into account. That is, there are so many ways a large neural network or another parallel and distributed computing system can change its computations, by storing locally in each of its units certain information which reflects the overall system's past exposition to input data.

In fact, with regard to the potential of learning it has been shown that the task of learning a complex function is not supported by using a large parallel and distributed computing model per se. In case of supervised learning, under probabilistic assumptions according to Valiant's notion of probably approximately correct learning (Valiant, 1984a, 1984b), the number of required examples grows essentially linear in the Kolmogorov complexity of the function to be learned.[9] This holds, regardless of the particular learning algorithm in use whether symbolic or connectionist. In the case of unsupervised learning, it was even proved that under similar probabilistic conditions as above, it cannot be guaranteed that *any* unsupervised learning system, such as self-organising neural networks, are capable to evolve to a useful structure which is substantially more complex than the system's structure before any training data was presented.

The learning task can only be simplified by providing a substantial part of the required algorithmic information in the specific structure of the used distributed computing model. For the case of connectionist-style computing mod-

---

[9] A numerical example for a relatively small Multi-Layer Perceptron was given in section 13.2.

els with a large number of the same type of computing units, that means that specific structure has to be provided by the topology of the interconnections of the many computing units. That is, a regularly structured topology, such as Multi-Layer Perceptrons, cannot ease the task of learning a complex function. One consequence of that is that refined models of the individual neuron cannot be expected to result in more intelligent networks or in superior learning capabilities of large networks composed of units which function according to the same refined model of biological neurons. To substantially increase the complexity the complexity of an artificial neural network (i.e. to capture more information), a large number of different functionalities of individual neurons would be needed and/or a complex (i.e. an irregular) topology of the network.

This result is coherent with the neuro-biological findings about the human brain, with regard to the large variety in the functionality of the individual neurons as well as with regard to the irregular interconnection patterns of the neurons in the human brain, each neuron being connected with up to 10,000 other neurons. Compare also chapter 6 for a rough picture on the biological findings on the human brain.

An important consequence of these investigations is the fact that a simple generic structure of a large neural network does not assist at all in reducing the difficulty of learning a complex function, as it does not provide any specific information with regard to the function to be learned. That is, even an automatic generation of a large neural network structure, e.g. by computer-aided design techniques, would not improve the situation. To alleviate the problem, one has to 'hand-craft' a structure into the computing system, which already contains part of the algorithmic information of the function to be learned by the system.

This, however, poses the question of how the appropriate structure can in practice be provided by designing a connectionist computing model. If the connectionist model is dealing with subsymbols in the sense of Smolensky, how is it possible that engineers or scientists can grasp a proper way of encoding a meaningful structure into the system?[10] What, then, is the advantage of a connectionist approach, if a substantial part of the system has to be pre-structured and it is particularly difficult to provide this structure, owing to the philosophy behind the connectionist paradigm?

One may argue that providing the appropriate structure and to encode it using symbol structures will result in a vastly longer description than the minimal length encoding. In other words, in order to find an encoding that is close to the shortest possible encoding, one cannot refer to symbols at all. Hence, a connectionist computing model may indeed offer just the right framework

---

[10] See chapter 8 for research on integrating symbols into connectionist systems. However, these approaches do not fit well into the widespread philosophical assumptions of connectionism as they have been explicated in Smolensky (1988).

for encoding the needed information succinctly.[11] However, the question still remains, whether finding the short encoding of the information in a connectionist framework is more feasible in practice than a longer encoding of the same information using symbolic structures which are much more amenable to a sensible interpretation, and hence, allowing a more feasible conceptualisation of the encoded information.

While the proved theorems show the limitations of learning classification functions from classified or unclassified data in connectionist systems, it should be borne in mind that the limitations apply equally to both the symbolic as well as to the connectionist paradigm. However, the theorems show, opposed to manifold claims, that there is no specific advantage of connectionist systems over symbolic systems in the sense that connectionist systems are per se more suitable for acquiring complex functions by learning. Furthermore, they show that the claim that all required knowledge can simply be trained into a network is overly optimistic. This holds, regardless of what sort of neural network models will be developed and regardless of how sophisticated future learning techniques might be.

Despite the discussed results, it should also be noted that the provided analysis does not cover all important types of learning which take place in humans. Humans learn the greatest fraction about their environment not by direct interaction with the environment but rather by communicating with their fellows. Their language communicates ontologies,[12] i.e. what sort of things exist, what conceptual hierarchies about the world can be used for reasoning, etc. That is, there is not a direct feedback mechanism, like in supervised learning, where the learner receives the class of an object, etc. How exactly humans learn their language, and how much structure to understand natural language is innate is still largely unknown.[13] Furthermore, it should be noted that classification learning, in particular from classified examples, seems much easier than other types of learning, such as the acquisition of language competency mentioned above. In chapter 15, a special type of knowledge, *non-factual knowledge*, will be discussed for which not even suitable models of learning have been developed so far. Not to mention that satisfying technical analyses of such models are missing. But it is very clear that learning such knowledge faces significantly greater difficulties than learning simple classification functions, because the straight feedback for whether the learning process was successful or not is missing.

While it has not been proved that a substantial amount of algorithmic information is really needed for a truly intelligent system, if it has learning capabilities which allow the system to enhance its performance, there is plenty of

---

[11] While there is some plausibility that a short encoding may be based on some sorts of subsymbols, it is not at all clear, why subsymbols in the connectionist sense should be optimal for a short encoding.

[12] This happens merely by the language's structure, i.e. its terms and their relation to each other, as opposed to the specific content which is communicated as well.

[13] See Chomsky (1975) for arguments for the innateness of the structure of language.

evidence that humans do indeed have much information innate. Such evidence can be gathered from the biological findings about the physiology of the human brain as well as from the linguistic studies on language acquisition from psychological and philosophical studies on concept formation or similar cognitive tasks.

The next chapter discusses the consequences of the presumed need to encode a substantial amount of algorithmic information into a system, in order to provide the system with sufficient learning capabilities so that it can develop to a truly intelligent system by learning, regardless whether it is a symbolic or a connectionist system.

14. Methodological Discussion

Method and *methodology* are terms frequently used in AI. Generally speaking, a methodology is the study of methods, and more practically speaking, a methodology represents the principles according to which methods are developed or employed. This chapter concerns largely with the *research methods* used in AI and cognitive science. It discusses principles according to which research methods should be developed and used to ensure validity of the findings and progress in the discipline. Since those research methods are meant to lead to methods in the sense of techniques, the methodological discussion in this chapter concerns principles of both the techniques to be developed and the research methods employed for developing those techniques.

How to develop and evaluate techniques or theories in AI and cognitive science is rarely discussed, although there is clearly a need to do so, as the field is relatively young and has not yet established a generally accepted set of research methods. Researchers come from different disciplines, ranging from philosophy and psychology, to physics, mathematics and electrical engineering. Each discipline has its own research methods which are often specific for the discipline and are not adequate for other fields of study.

Among other things, this chapter points out that the commonly used criteria to assess success and failure of new ideas are inappropriate. It provides a methodological guideline to rectify that situation.

The following line of argument will involve terms like *feasible, cognitive feasibility*, and similar terms which demand, a *cognitively feasible* description that can be used, understood and manipulated by human beings, such as engineers and scientists. Overall, these terms will refer to the requirement that a human can actually handle such descriptions, which implies that descriptions are not too complex or inaccessible due to the lack of interpretable symbols. However, it should be kept in mind that in the following, *cognitive feasibility* and similar terms will only apply to the observer, scientist or engineer, not to the cognitive system being described.

This chapter is organised as follows: The first section 14.1 discusses the methodological search for general principles, those principles create implicitly or explicitly abstraction levels at which the overall system has to be described. It will be argued in section 14.2 that the appropriate description levels are much less determined by the nature of intelligent systems themselves but rather by the human, i.e. by the *subject*, who attempts to build or to understand such systems. The following section 14.3 argues that it is not enough for a suitable paradigm to resemble the human brain metaphorically. Section 14.4 presents a new explanation for why it is so often observed that new approaches to model aspects of intelligence turn out to fail on larger scale domains after they were successful in initial studies on toy-domains. In section 14.5, some alternatives to connectionism are discussed with respect to their potential as a general paradigm for AI.

14.1 Choosing Abstract Description Levels for Complex Systems

This section summarises the thrust of the previous chapters with regard to the problem of dealing with complex systems. In accordance with section 10.3, assume there is a system with a very large Kolmogorov complexity of, say, more than 10^{10} bits. As long as a paradigm offers a computationally universal framework, it is obvious that there is no significant advantage for any particular paradigm with regard to the minimum length for encoding the desired functionality. That is, the minimum encoding length is given by the Kolmogorov complexity and is not significantly reduced by a particular paradigm.

A complex system can be described in many different ways and at different levels of abstraction as has already been discussed in section 1.3 and chapter 11. Furthermore, there is no right or wrong way of creating levels of abstraction. Since *abstraction* means essentially to disregard certain aspects, different choices of which aspects of a system to disregard can be made.

In engineering, different levels of abstraction of a complex system are created in order to make the entire system design (cognitively) more feasible for the engineer. For example, in the case of computer systems, there is a level of most elementary building blocks such as transistors or logic gates. Using these building blocks, other more abstract building blocks are assembled. However, these more abstract building blocks have again a functionality which is fairly simple to describe. When determining which more abstract building blocks should be constructed at the next higher system level, the objective is to keep the cognitive complexity of dealing with the building blocks reasonably low. Similarly, in software engineering, we organise our programs in a collection of procedures or in objects, as in object-oriented programming.

A similar observation can be made in other engineering disciplines, e.g. in civil engineering. A high-rise building is designed at a fairly abstract level, disregarding the particular specifics of lower levels of the design, such as the material properties of the screws being used for fitting the blinds on the 43rd floor in office number 4302. However, at some stage, it has to be determined even which screw to choose, etc. But these details do not need to be taken into account when designing the structure of the high-rise building. It is merely known that by using certain standard concrete for the walls, blinds can be fitted and suitable screws can be found. It is likely that the overall design of a high-rise building could be optimised if such a strict hierarchy of conceptual building blocks and their description at different levels of abstraction would not be used.

The guideline to determine suitable levels of abstraction is not so much some intrinsic property of the objects to be designed. It is rather the cognitive capacities of the system engineer what determines the suitability of a given way of abstraction. In other words, suitable levels of abstraction reflect the engineer's cognitive capacities in the first place. The question of the system's actual 'nature' takes a second rank. This effect that the actual object to be described plays a minor role on the way of structuring its description, is due to the complexity of the object. The larger the complexity, in terms of Kolmogorov complexity or a similar descriptional complexity measure, the more important becomes the cognitive capacities of the human to comprehend a given description in determining its suitability. The larger the complexity of a system, the more different ways of structuring a description exist and the more freedom one has to choose a suitable abstraction level.

14.2 Key Factors Determining the Suitability of a Description Level

As indicated above, *the subject*, i.e. the human engineer or scientist who needs to understand the description of an intelligent system is the crucial factor. The human subject determines the appropriateness or inappropriateness of a level of description or an entire hierarchical structure of description levels.

The actual *object* of the description, e.g. the intelligent system to be described, determines the content of the description at the level chosen. Since the chosen description level needs to be suitable to express the system's functionality, the system itself may well have a certain impact on which description level is appropriate, though this impact is certainly limited. The role of the subject, the human engineer or scientist, is stressed in this chapter. It is remarkable that in the literature on the debate between symbolism and connectionism, the *subject*, the human component, is largely ignored.

What are the consequences of that point for the controversy between symbolism and connectionism? Engineers as well as scientists are communicating through symbols; i.e. a design needs to be written down or drawn and can be understood by other engineers which participate in the project. Similarly, scientists attempt to formalise their knowledge, i.e. they try to write down a theory which should unambiguously explain the phenomena in question.

In other words, the *human subject*, as the engineer or the understanding seeking scientist, requires that symbols are used for describing intelligent systems. It is not the nature of intelligence or cognition itself, which dictates the paradigm. It is rather the nature and the resulting needs of those who want to understand intelligence or cognition within a certain paradigm! Hence, what is required in descriptions, are *third-person symbols*. This implies that the *first-person symbols*, i.e. those symbols whose role in cognition is to be explained, are to be explained by using any sort of other symbols, as long as the description is understandable and allows an engineer or a scientist to do their job.

The claim of connectionism was essentially that there are simple manipulation rules only at the subsymbolic level, which govern the cognitive processes at the symbolic level. Complex patterns of subsymbols constitute symbols in a dynamical way, where the mapping of patterns of subsymbols to the symbols being constituted is everything else than straightforward. The 'knowledge' of such a subsymbolic system is encoded in a distributed way in those numerical vectors, each number representing a subsymbol.

As a consequence, the possibility of an understanding of the knowledge which is encoded in the system is largely abandoned. Instead, it is hoped that 'mathematical cranks' can be developed, which allow a mapping from (desired) behaviour of the overall system to representational vectors at the subsymbolic level. That is, learning mechanisms are required which automatically encode the knowledge of the system, as it would be impossible for an engineer to do it 'manually'. This knowledge can only be derived from samples of desired behaviour, as the connectionist paradigm presumes that it is impossible to express the required knowledge in symbols.

Unfortunately, as has been seen in chapter 13, such learning approaches are inherently limited. In order to avoid the need for excessive training data, the learning system has to have part of the knowledge beforehand. Hence, a successful learning system would require substantial structure built into it a priori, in order to learn effectively complex functions. Encoding this a priori knowledge faces the same practical problems as discussed above; i.e. owing to its claimed 'unrelatedness' to symbols, there is no way for an engineer to encode such knowledge other than by some sort of blind trial-and-error.

While the arguments used by connectionist proponents *against* the symbolic paradigm seem largely valid, they are *not* conclusive arguments *for* the connectionist paradigm.

14.3 The Connectionist Metaphor

Connectionism represents an approach for building intelligent systems and understanding cognition on the basis of a metaphorical resemblance to the human brain. Connectionism at the subsymbolic level does not attempt to reflect the neuro-physiological details of the human brain, but rather focuses on a particular aspect of what is suspected or even known about the biological functioning of the human brain: some massively distributed processing is taking place, such that the overall behaviour of the system depends on the entirety of the neural network. Furthermore, the elementary processing units are working on rather continuous operands than discrete ones.[1]

While these features of the biological function of the human brain are very appealing and reflect a number of aspects which have been found in cognition, as outlined in chapter 11, the essential ideas of connectionism are merely small parts of a system description, where a very essential part is missing:[2] namely, *what* is the particular knowledge that has to be encoded in subsymbolic vector representations in order to make the overall system work. The implicit hope is that this missing part will be found in due course, once the proper computational paradigm has been developed far enough. This implicit hope, however, is unfortunately poorly justified. Since the human subject, as engineer or scientist, is the crucial measure of a paradigm, the question is, whether the missing knowledge can be encoded in any cognitively feasible way.

When a new computational paradigm is to be adopted, the critical question to be raised should always be: what are the advantages of the new paradigm for the practical development of intelligent systems? A metaphorical similarity to, e.g., the natural role-model, is not good enough, since the main difficulty in the more traditional symbolic paradigm lies in providing the right 'knowledge', or structure to the system. That is, if a new paradigm does not substantially contribute to the alleviation of this difficulty, it is hard to see what its merits should be for the engineering approach to AI. An abstract similarity to certain aspects of intelligence, a similarity which abstracts from the difficulty of providing the right knowledge and structure, simply misses the point!

In the following chapter, a special type of knowledge, called *non-factual knowledge*, is discussed which seems virtually inaccessible in an introspective way. The critiques of the symbolic paradigm seem to have had this sort of knowledge in mind, which the symbolic paradigm has problems to cover. However, it will be indicated that so far connectionism has, just as the symbolic paradigm, by and large failed to even attempt to deal with that knowledge in any systematic way.[3]

14.4 The Fallacy of Empirical Validations of AI Techniques

The euphorical reception of connectionism in the late 1980s was strongly driven by early successes of training connectionist computing models, such as the Multi-Layer Perceptron, in simple domains, where they had been tested. (See Rumelhart et al. (1986) for a collection of such examples.) In the following

---

[1] It is unknown, to what degree the neural activation levels can safely be approximated by a limited number of discrete values.

[2] One can even argue that *the* essential part is missing.

[3] There are a few notable exceptions such as Thrun and O'Sullivan (1996), though in general the problem has not received much attention yet.

years, many people were surprised by the apparent difficulty to scale-up the early successes of neural networks to more demanding, more complex problems. Nowadays, connectionism seems to have lost some of its appeal due to the spent efforts to overcome these difficulties, which had rather disappointing results.

Similar difficulties have been seen regularly in the development of AI during the past decades, such as the General Problem Solver (Newell & Simon, 1963), SHRDLU (Winograd, 1972), or expert systems. In the light of the massive algorithmic information which cognition seems to require for a complete description, these difficulties have a simple explanation:

> The techniques did not represent the keys to success at all. They were just one of the essential parts of a working system. The techniques could be proved successful for toy-domains because the remaining (algorithmic) information needed, was either tacitly provided in the actual implementation or was supplied in a problem-specific component of the system. However, for the toy-domain the information needed to complement the proposed technique was very small and the effort to provide that information was neglected.
>
> Only when the technique is tried for more complex problems, difficulties emerge, as the actual problem of supplying suitable domain-specific information has not been tested in the experiments. The practical problem of supplying this domain-specific information is usually not even addressed by the proposed technique. This domain-specific information is sometimes extremely difficult to provide, as it will often contain tacit knowledge, i.e., an expert is not even aware of that knowledge, let alone that the knowledge could easily be verbalised. This issue is discussed in more depth in chapter 15.

The problem is twofold:

1. The techniques *do not address the feasibility* of providing the necessary domain-specific information. Furthermore, for the toy-domain, the effort to supply the needed domain-specific information is very limited because of the low complexity of the domain. When using the approach for a more complex domain, the effort for providing the domain-specific information grows tremendously and results in a failure of the approach to deliver the promised advantages. In particular, in the simple toy-domain, part of the necessary information for the system functionality will be hidden in the new approach. Only little additional information about the domain needs to be added. However, when the required algorithmic information increases due to a more complex domain, the information contained in the approach remains constant, while the information required to be supplied grows more than proportional with the increase in the domains complexity. Besides the sheer amount of required domain-specific information is the fact that it is often very difficult to provide at all, as it involves tacit, non-factual knowledge. See also chapter 15 on this issue.

2. The claim that a technique is generally applicable, contains a hidden assumption about the exact shape of the general class of problems which constitute that aspect of human intelligence for which the technique is claimed to be a valid model.

The second point needs some more explanation: for example, the development of classical logical inference techniques for modelling a central part of human cognition assumes that humans do exactly that job of logical inference, which includes also that they can infer all logical consequences from a set of propositions.

However, this assumption is highly questionable, as most people will agree that humans are often not very good in logical reasoning at all. Even mathematicians or logicians would certainly have their limitations when it comes to really involved logical arguments. However, the typical answer to this objection would normally be something like:

While it is true that humans make mistakes in logical reasoning, they could figure out the correct conclusion at least in principle, i.e. if they had only enough time, memory, patience, etc.

Can we really know that this 'in principle' argument is valid? Can we know that humans could really find the correct conclusions from any number of arbitrarily involved propositions? We cannot possibly know it from observation. It is rather a generalisation from a number of observations together with introspective insights into the process of our own cognition. However, it seems very optimistic to believe that this constitutes a sufficiently solid basis for the claim. How do we know that our limitations in such situations are due to some coincidental imperfections rather than due to the very nature of cognition?!

The crucial point here is that human logical inferences may actually work according to completely different principles than those of formal logic. The results of both the formal and the human logical reasoning process may coincide for a certain class of tasks, but they may differ on others. We do not have any empirical evidence for either of the cases. We have even empirical evidence for the opposite, but we use some argument to defend our view against the empirical facts![4]

If we are so convinced that logical reasoning needs to be modelled along the lines of formal logic, we may miss out on more appropriate techniques, which may be capable of taking care of other problems as well, such as the computational complexity in logical inference.

---

[4] Indeed indicate psychological findings, such as the experiments reported by Krause and Wysotzki (1983), that human subjects, when presented with a number of facts, tend to create an internal structure from which logical inferences of those facts can immediately be obtained when needed. This is opposed to memorising the given facts and inferring logical conclusions from these facts only when required. In the context of visual reasoning, the inadequacy of logical derivation processes for human thinking has also been pointed out by Waltz and Bogess (1979) and Waltz (1981).

The fact that a researcher has certain prejudices about what the principles behind certain cognitive phenomena are, which they wish to model, causes the following methodological problem: the experimental domains in which the new approach is to be tested will often already serve as a conceptual model while developing the approach. That is, by showing that the approach works for the toy-domains, nothing is shown about the general applicability of the approach. It is merely shown that it works for the toy-domain for which it was designed. The debt to explain why the new approach should work for a wider class of problems remains unpaid.

Further conclusions along with a summary of this chapter are presented in chapter 16. The following discusses some alternative approaches to AI.

14.5 Alternative Approaches to Understanding Cognition and Intelligence

Besides connectionism there have been a number of other proposals for frameworks which are claimed to be better suited to model and understand cognition than the symbolic paradigm. These alternative frameworks include genetic algorithms (Holland, 1975; Goldberg, 1989) or (Rosca & Ballard, 1994), as well as dynamical systems (see van Gelder (1995), van Gelder and Port (1995), or Thelen and Smith (1994), Garson (1996) or Eliasmith (1996)). Dynamical systems are systems which evolve over time in a quite complex way. They show features of chaotic behaviour, i.e. small differences in input signals may have a major effect soon after. It has been speculated that such systems could behave quite differently than traditional symbolic systems. Indeed, assuming that they take some continuous (irrational) numbers into account, their overall behaviour may be non-computable in the sense of a Turing-machine. This non-computability, however, would only be due to the fact that a corresponding Turing machine would not be given the corresponding infinite stream of input containing the relevant information about the irrational continuous numbers involved in the evolving dynamic system. It is clearly possible to create any sequence of discrete behaviour by a Turing machine if there is only a corresponding (possibly infinite) code as input.[5] Another well-known approach are Brooks' *subsumption architectures* (Maes & Brooks, 1990; Brooks, 1991, 1996). Brooks implemented his idea in the form of crawling many-legged small and simple robots. The robots have simple learning capabilities. The hope is that they have the potential to bootstrap to high levels of intelligence due to their exposure to the physical world. Brooks calls his approach *intelligence without reason* (see e.g. Brooks (1991)). One of the reasons of the hope for success is that the environment is thought to provide stimulating signals which may be of very high complexity; thus allowing such a learning system to potentially acquire

---

[5] This infinite input stream cannot be part of the program as a Turing machine program needs to be of *finite* length by definition.

knowledge of high complexity without symbolically encoding that knowledge. (See Steels and Brooks (1995) for more work in that direction.) Compare also the results of chapter 13 on limitations of self-organisation, as these simple robots do not learn in a supervised way. In principle, they may receive some occasional feedback, such as that they found a power point to re-charge their batteries, etc. However, for higher cognitive capacities, there is virtually no feedback in their horizon of experiences. For comparisons, humans get plenty of feedback and high-level information through the use of their language and exchange with fellows at fairly abstract levels.

So far, Brooks's robots did not manage to get significantly beyond simple crawling behaviour. The shortcoming of these alternative approaches to AI and cognitive science are very similar to the problems already discussed in this chapter: while the alternative approaches may have metaphorical appeal, they do not give a precise account on the processes to be modelled. To obtain an exact descriptive or even predictive model of human-level intelligence, additional information is needed regarding, e.g., inductive bias for learning. Unfortunately, there is no obvious way of encoding the needed additional information using third-person symbols. That is, there seems to be no comprehensible way of expressing the required additional knowledge.[6] In other words, the encoding of the missing details for a proper model of cognition appears infeasible, because the details cannot be encoded neither by using first-person symbols nor by using third-person symbols.

In summary, it is important to note that we cannot expect a 'scientific revolution' by adopting a new computing model. The adoption of a new paradigm cannot completely change the situation from a framework that is supposedly limited in principle, to a new framework which allows to solve the problem of building truly intelligent systems. The notion of Turing computability is not merely the current theoretical framework of computing, it is, much more importantly in this context, the most powerful formalism to describe *effectively*[7] computable functions. We do not have a better way to define a (mathematical) function in a precise way that allows to determine, i.e. to compute, the function value for any given argument of the function. As a consequence, the limitations of Turing computability are not that much the limitations of computers specifically, but also the limitations of us humans to effectively describe functional dependencies.

Thus, the problem is not that the notion of Turing computability is insufficient, but rather the question of how to write the proper program, or how to conceptualise the functionality of an intelligent system or a cognitive theory. The question of a suitable conceptualisation, however, is not addressed by

---

[6] Compare also the following chapter 15 for a deeper discussion on the nature of such knowledge.

[7] The question of a function being *effectively computable* becomes only non-trivial for functions which are defined over an infinite domain. This, however, is primarily of interest to mathematicians, as for AI, a meaningful restriction of functions to be defined over finite domains is in principle possible.

defining a new framework which has merely some metaphorical resemblances with certain aspects of cognition. A truly promising framework has to explain why a conceptualisation is supposed to be *more feasible* than in a paradigm that is already in use, i.e. the symbolic paradigm. Unless this question is addressed by the new framework and there is a potential to provide a positive answer, possibly after additional research, there is no reason to adopt a new framework.

15. Non-Factual Knowledge

This chapter discusses a type of knowledge which clearly plays a major role in human cognition and intelligent behaviour, although most humans are hardly aware of its existence, not to mention that they have great difficulty in articulating that knowledge. Furthermore, AI systems so far, whether connectionist or symbolic, deal to a very limited extent with non-factual knowledge explicitly. After an introduction in section 15.1, a discussion on the difficulty of acquiring non-factual knowledge is presented in section 15.2. Section 15.3 present a discussion on the difficulties and potential ways of integrating such knowledge into machines.

15.1 Introduction

Suppose we know that something is the case or is not the case, such as Fred is in his house and that the neighbour on the left has a red house and the neighbour on the right has a green house.

Then it is easy for us to articulate the knowledge we have with regard to, say, spatial relationships between the mentioned objects and persons. In principle, it seems that if we only know what physical objects are located at what place, we can make all sorts of inferences about these *facts*, and articulate all sorts of more or less complex statements concerning what is the case and what is not the case.[1] Similarly, we can juggle with abstract objects like mathematical entities and concepts and again, in principle, we can articulate what is the case and what is not the case. This sort of knowledge refers to observable facts, either observable via our sense organs or observable by introspection, by 'looking' into the realm of abstract ideas which are the objects of our mathematical reasoning. However, when we make judgements or reason about the empirical world, there is typically some sort of *projection* involved. That is, we project certain aspects of a situation A to another situation B.

For example, we may not know whether Fred's neighbour on the left is in his house at this point in time? However, we may still make a

---

[1] Limitations of formal reasoning procedures, such as those incompleteness results proved by Gödel (Gödel, 1931) are ignored here for the sake of simplicity. They occur only if sufficiently powerful general statements are involved in the knowledge we want to deal with.

statement which we deem likely to be true. For example, we may say the neighbour is at home because his car is in front of the house, and Fred is always in his house, if his car is in front of it, etc.

To arrive at such a statement, we project previous experiences of our own or with, e.g. Fred, to the neighbour of Fred. Since the situation is similar in some respect to previously encountered situations, we assume this or that.

However, in nature there are no exact repetitions; between two different situations, there is always a difference,[2] such as the time or location will differ at least. Thus, every projection involves some judgement about the appropriateness of the projection. The knowledge which governs our projections, does not concern the factual world. It concerns rather relationships between possible situations.

Such projections could also be viewed as abstractions from those details of a situation, which are not characteristic with respect to the proposition we want to make.

For example, when we are interested to know whether Fred's neighbour is in his house, it seems irrelevant whether Fred's car is parked on the street or not. However, it may well be relevant, whether the trees in the neighbour's garden blossom.

A complicated network of relationships between possible situations is apparently involved, as the projectability depends strongly on what particular aspect of a situation we are interested in. Under certain circumstances, the trees blossom matters, but more often it does not ... Our judgement will often be amazingly accurate, even for questions about which we never thought before.

The sort of projection discussed above is essentially an inductive inference. Moreover, there are other types of non-demonstrative reasoning going on in human cognition, which are equally guided by non-factual knowledge, such as analogical reasoning.

A procedure which derives all the generalisations, the projection from some observed situations to other new situations captures knowledge which does not refer directly to any facts. It is rather knowledge which describes what should be done with available knowledge about facts. Hence, it can be said that such general reasoning is guided by non-factual knowledge, which does not refer to the facts but to the knowledge about the facts; so it is knowledge at the meta-level of the factual knowledge.

Analogical reasoning. Analogical reasoning uses analogies between different situations and assumes that certain aspects of a known situation also applies to the analogical situation.

For example, suppose we know that Fred's neighbour on the right runs around the block every morning at 7am. Then we could derive by

---

[2] Otherwise we could not talk about *two different* situations!

analogy that the neighbour across the street is not in her house at 7am in the morning, although her car is in front of the house. Or, maybe we can again, by analogy, derive that she is in her house, analogical to Fred's neighbour on the left?

Analogical reasoning involves an abstraction from one case to a more general statement, such as that all people run around the block at 7am, or all people are in their houses if their car is in front of the house. A second step is the instantiation of the general statement with respect to the new situation for whose assessment the analogy is to be derived. This more general statement is not explicitly made, but it is implied by the result of the analogy. Again, the difficulty in analogical reasoning is to find a suitable abstraction. To perform sensible analogical inferences requires a good judgement about what aspects of a situation can safely be ignored and which aspects may make a difference.

Abductive reasoning. Abductive reasoning concerns the causes of a particular situation. For example, the diagnosis of a certain disease which causes the observed symptoms, is typical for abductive inference. Again, our abductive reasoning capabilities are very impressive, as there is typically a virtual infinity of coincidences, all being potential causes, but we will often find the correct one.

> For example, a patient may come on a Tuesday morning to the doctor and may wear a green jacket, etc. The doctor would never assume a causal link between the jacket or the fact that the patient comes on a Tuesday morning and the disease, etc. A psychiatrist, however, may possibly consider the colour of the jacket, or even the Tuesday morning ...

In abductive reasoning, we face a similar difficulty as in induction. It is generally unclear, what aspects of a situation bear a potential causal relationship to the effect in question and which aspects are just meaningless coincidences. Again with abductive reasoning there is a similar difficulty as with inductive reasoning and analogical reasoning: How do we know which of the many coinciding observations are the cause of the event in question? How do we know which of the many aspects of a situation are relevant for causal relationships?

Since, the knowledge which guides us in reasoning does not refer to facts, we cannot possibly have learned it directly from experience. Later on in this chapter, we will see that this sort of non-factual knowledge even shapes our experiences in the first place! However, before that, a few more examples of problematic inductive inferences will be presented to emphasise the point.

One well-known example is Hempel's paradox,[3] which demonstrates that their is no simple statistical approach possible to determine the degree of confirmation of a general statement:

---

[3] See Hempel (1965).

- Consider the sentence "*All ravens are black*" as a hypothesis which we want to confirm by gathering empirical data.
  - Assume we have seen 1000 ravens which were all black, no non-black raven has been experienced.
  - Then the sentence "*All ravens are black*" appears fairly well confirmed and we may want to accept it as a general statement.
- Now assume the logically equivalent sentence "*All non-black objects are non-ravens*", which is just the contraposition of the original sentence.
  - Assume further that we have again gathered 1000 cases of non-black objects which all turned out to be non-ravens.
  - This will not provide us with sufficient evidence to believe in the original sentence "*All ravens are black*".

In other words, the question is, why instances of the first sentence give us, at least subjectively, more evidence for "*All ravens are black*", than instances for the logically equivalent contraposition?! There have been a number of proposals to dissolve this paradox such as taking into account the overall frequency of the occurrence of an object in question. A less frequently occurring object should be weighted more than a more frequently occurring object. Based on that, a raven that turns out to be black would provide more reason to believe in "*All ravens are black*", than a non-raven which turns out to be non-black for believing "*All non-black objects are non-ravens*".[4]

This is essentially a discussion on a formalism which would allow to account for supporting and non-supporting evidence for a collection of hypotheses, as the philosopher Carnap (1950) attempted to develop it. However, the following demonstrates that the actual problem of induction lies much deeper and, hence, we will see that there is indeed an intricate body of non-factual knowledge involved in our human non-demonstrative reasoning and judgement.

As mentioned before, one of the great riddles of how humans manage to generalise correctly, is how they choose the attributes they consider to be characteristic for a situation or object. These characteristic attributes then allow the generalisation by simply assuming all objects showing the characteristic attributes belong to the same class or kind as the initially observed ones. Consider, for example, the following induction problem. Suppose the following propositions are known:

1. All observed people who spoke at the Capitol in Washington D.C. gave their speech in English.
2. All observed people who cannot speak English, did not learn English in one day.
Furthermore, assume, Mr X cannot speak English and is going to give a (free) speech at the capitol in Washington D.C. tomorrow.
Will the speech be in English? 'Yes' and 'No' are equally supported by experience.

---

[4] See Watanabe (1969) for more details.

Without hesitation will most people answer 'No', though it is not as clear on what basis they pick the right answer. The point is that the evidence reported in sentence 1. and 2. above, strongly suggests the following two generalisations:

1. All speeches given at the Capitol in Washington D.C. will be in English.
2. Anybody who cannot speak English on day y will not speak English on day $y + 1$.

If we take the two generalisations as true statements, we have contradictory predictions for the language in which the speech of Mr X will be. The first generalisation suggests that the speech will be in English as all speeches have been in English at that place so far. However, the second generalisation suggests that the speech will not be in English, as nobody has yet managed to learn English within a single day.

There seems no answer in a purely formal sense. To make the problem clearer, another rather extreme example follows, which is due to the philosopher Goodman (1955). Goodman gave the following nice example in order to illustrate the deep principled problems with induction. It shows that there is no purely formal ground on which human induction can be justified or explained.

Consider the following hypothesis H_1:

$$H_1 : All\ emeralds\ are\ green.$$

This statement is to be evaluated empirically by observing emeralds and finding out whether they are green or not. Each emerald found to be green supports the hypothesis H_1. Each emerald found to be, e.g. blue, does refute the hypothesis H_1. By finding more and more emeralds being green, the hypothesis H_1 is more and more confirmed. Furthermore, H_1 is predicting that all further investigations of emeralds will lead to the finding that they are green.

Consider next the following predicate *grue*, which means, all objects being considered *before* some time t are found to be green and all objects considered *after* t are found *blue*. I.e. the predicate is defined as:

$$grue = \begin{cases} \text{if observed } \underline{before} \text{ time } t \text{ and found to be } \underline{green}. \\ \text{if observed } \underline{after} \text{ time } t \text{ and found to be } \underline{blue}. \end{cases}$$

The new predicate leads to the following problematic hypothesis H_2:

$$H_2 : All\ emeralds\ are\ grue.$$

Before time t, hypothesis H_2 is exactly equally confirmed by each green emerald which confirms hypothesis H_1! However, hypothesis H_1 and H_2 predict contradicting findings for those emeralds which are examined after t. In other words, the pure fact that confirming evidences for a particular hypothesis have been found does not represent a sufficient basis for accepting a hypothesis as a justified proposition or predictor. Besides the evidence, for us it is obvious that hypothesis H_2 should not be considered at all. But we do not have any *formal* criterion to distinguish hypothesis H_1 from hypothesis H_2. The fact that the predicate *grue* is defined in a time-dependent way cannot be used as a criterion to exclude *grue* as a sensible predicate. This is, since the standard predicate *green* can also be defined in a time-dependent way by using *grue* and a complementing predicate *bleen* as ground predicates. Let *bleen* be defined as follows:

$$bleen = \begin{cases} \text{if observed } \underline{\text{before}} \text{ time } t \text{ and found to be } \underline{\text{blue}}. \\ \text{if observed } \underline{\text{after}} \text{ time } t \text{ and found to be } \underline{\text{green}}. \end{cases}$$

Using the two predicates *grue* and *bleen*, the predicate *green* can be defined as follows:

$$green = \begin{cases} \text{if observed } \underline{\text{before}} \text{ time } t \text{ and found to be } \underline{\text{grue}}. \\ \text{if observed } \underline{\text{after}} \text{ time } t \text{ and found to be } \underline{\text{bleen}}. \end{cases}$$

This definition leaves *green* to have exactly the same meaning as usual, although *green* is now defined in a time-dependent way. This shows that we cannot simply solve the problem of choosing suitable predicates for hypotheses on purely formal grounds. If the predicates used in the general statement G are sufficiently irrelevant and reflect just spurious aspects, then there is no confirming effect for G associated with the empirically observed facts. The underlying deeper problem is really that of *projection*: From what situation can we project what aspects to a new situation? Our assumptions about this question is implicit in the choice of predicates we choose to describe a situation. If we choose the predicate *green*, we assume implicitly that the colour will remain largely stable over time. If we choose *grue* we assume, implicitly, that the colour will change at time t. Whatever predicates we choose to describe a situation, those predicates impose a structure on all possible situations and restricts the possible inferences. If the choice of predicates is poor, and we choose, e.g. the predicate, *grue*, no formal method for induction will be able to correct it!

15.2 How to Acquire Non-Factual Knowledge?

It is evident that humans also acquire and shape their 'non-factual' knowledge. This is seen, for example, by the fact that an expert usually performs better inductive inferences than a layperson based on the same empirical data. The expert performs 'educated guesses' as opposed to a layperson who 'just guesses'. The expert acquires non-factual knowledge by learning about a domain. The learning process involves the acquisition of an appropriate domain ontology.[5]

---

[5] An ontology is the kind of substances or objects which make up the world. In this context, it is the kind of objects which are relevant for the domain.

An expert knows what kind of objects and attributes are useful to consider in a domain. This includes not only a selection of physical objects and attributes which appear relevant. Mental constructions of useful theoretical objects, such as diseases in medicine, are included as well.[6] Such knowledge is normally at least partly conveyed by the use of a respective domain language.

Further, it seems that something like priorities among different attributes make an expert believe in inductive generalizations which are based on those attributes which are considered to be more 'relevant', i.e. which have a higher priority. But where can such priorities possibly come from?

Such non-factual knowledge seems to be conveyed in a number of forms, most of them are more or less indirect. For example, by using a certain domain language, a certain ontology is implied. By indicating that certain attributes values are changing over time to various degrees, etc., some conclusions on the attributes' potential use for generalizations may be drawn. That is, the easier or more likely an attribute's value changes the less characteristic may be the attribute for the respective object. However, there are exceptions as well. It has to be conceded that the process of acquiring such non-factual knowledge is very poorly understood. Goodman's proposal for a theory is outlined below. He made the proposal more than 40 years ago. No convincing proposal has been made to date.

A proposal for a solution. Goodman (1955) offered a notion which he proposed as an explanation for the way humans perform inductive reasoning. He developed his notion of *entrenchment* of a predicate as an explanation for why humans use that particular predicate for their generalisation. So, in the case of the green emeralds, humans do not generalise on the basis of the artificial predicates *grue* or *bleen* because those predicates are predicates which are not used in normal human practice.

Goodman proposed to consider for each predicate a particular degree of entrenchment, which increases when a predicate is used in daily practice. The most *entrenched* predicates are considered to be the predicates on which an inductive generalisation is most likely to be successful.

However, this idea does not account for the problem that different predicates may be used in different contexts at different frequencies. Thus, the degree of entrenchment of a predicate depends on the particular context in which it is used. If for every context the use of a predicate is counted independently, then this poses a new problem of distinguishing properly between different and same contexts! This problem does not seem to be much easier than the problem of determining the right degree of entrenchment in the first place.

---

[6] A disease is typically a mental construction as it is not directly observed but rather constructed from current symptoms and subsequent symptoms patients have shown in the past. The symptoms are either directly observed or results of certain measurement procedures.

15.3 Discussion: Non-Factual Knowledge in AI Systems

In AI systems, the problem of making non-factual knowledge explicit is twofold: Firstly, current AI systems of relatively limited competence are provided with a domain terminology, a set of predicates to characterise and distinguish different objects and situations. Hence, the responsibility remains with the user or system developer to ensure that sensible predicates are chosen. Secondly, given a user-provided domain terminology, the system will still have to make choices among different predicates which appear all equally qualified for conducting, e.g., an inductive inference on their basis. Then some preferably explicitly encoded non-factual knowledge should arbitrate among the competing candidates of an inductive generalisation.

Work on making such non-factual knowledge explicit has been fairly limited so far. There are a number of approaches to declaratively specify to a certain degree inductive bias,[7] but this seems still a long way to go to have a comprehensive systematic treatment of non-factual knowledge at a larger scale. One problem is again to allow a *comprehensible* way of specifying that knowledge. Furthermore, it needs to be well integrated with other bodies of knowledge in order to become applicable at a larger scale for general intelligent agents. Since humans acquire and sharpen such knowledge, a general intelligent agent would need a similar capability.

The problem of learning non-factual knowledge has not been largely addressed, neither in the connectionist nor in the symbolic paradigm.

The current state of both connectionist and symbolic learning models focuses largely on learning a certain I/O-function. Learning approaches, such as back-propagation, ensure merely that the trained network's I/O-function will eventually comply with the data points presented to the network being trained. The convergence considerations, e.g. for back-propagation, ensure merely that a particular I/O-function is being learned. They do not endeavour to learn any non-factual knowledge which would add to a deeper understanding of the domain in order to improve the performance in the next learning task. Neither do most of the current symbolic learning approaches, such as decision-tree learners, address this problem.

There are a few notable exceptions, which address the problem of learning to learn, i.e. of learning non-factual knowledge which will assist in the next learning task, such as Thrun (1995), Thrun and O'Sullivan (1996), Thrun and

---

[7] For example, in C4.5 (Quinlan, 1993a) there are a few user-specifiable parameters which influence the size of the resulting decision tree. Other systems, such as Grendel (Cohen, 1992) or MOBAL (Morik et al., 1993) allow to explicitly constrain the hypothesis space. In inductive logic programming (ILP) systems generally, background knowledge can be provided to assist the search for a generalisation. More recently, people started studying approaches to an automatic model selection, i.e. that different sub-hypothesis spaces are provided to the system and the system decides on its own in which of the sub-hypothesis spaces to search for a solution, see e.g. Kearns et al. (1997) or Kohavi and John (1997).

Pratt (1997) or the work on model selection, e.g. Kearns et al. (1997), Kohavi and John (1997).

A major difficulty for the automatic acquisition of non-factual knowledge which guides human non-demonstrative reasoning, is the fact that no feedback is easily available that tells whether the correct knowledge was acquired or not. This differs dramatically from the situation of learning factual knowledge, e.g. knowledge about the correct classification of objects. There, it is usually relatively easy, at least in principle, to determine empirically for every classified object, whether it was correctly classified or not. In principle, it is possible to observe the convergence speed of inductive learning of factual knowledge. For learning classifications, as an example, forming feedback could take place on the following basis:

> The faster the correct classification was found by the system, the better
> is the acquired non-factual knowledge which is guiding the inductive
> inference process.

However, this would still be opposed to human learning which often takes substantial leaps towards accelerating learning by acquiring and understanding certain relations in the domain. Thus, an important area of study to advance current techniques is the integration of learning techniques with a larger body of factual and non-factual knowledge about a domain. However, as acquiring a large body of such non-factual knowledge 'from scratch' will be very difficult, means have to be developed that alleviate the existing difficulty of expressing non-factual knowledge. The difficulty is twofold: on the one hand, introspection seems not to give sufficient access to the human non-factual knowledge. On the other hand, even if there are ways of reconstructing such knowledge, e.g. by non-introspective means, suitable languages are required to express that knowledge.[8]

Since humans have further knowledge which guides them, e.g. in choosing a particular hypothesis in inductive inference, or in many other situations of non-demonstrative reasoning, and since they also acquire such non-factual knowledge during their lives, it is obvious that a comprehensive approach to intelligent systems needs to address this problem.

---

[8] Some work has been done towards the 'manual' acquisition of non-factual knowledge, where the human is queried how he or she would handle a particular situation and is asked to provide an explanation, which would be more generally applicable. Subsequently, this more general statement can be refined by the human if cases occur, where the general statement turns out not to coincide with the human's way of handling that case. See Beydoun and Hoffmann (1997) or Beydoun and Hoffmann (1998) for more details on how that can work for the acquisition of search control knowledge, which is another type of such non-factual knowledge.

16. Conclusions

Since its very beginning, (symbolic) AI has had its strong advocates, which were not shy of making bold claims and predictions. For long, there were harsh critiques, claiming either the general impossibility of AI or the inappropriateness of the symbolic paradigm. The fact that this debate is still not settled, served as motivation to write this book, which reflected on the assumptions and implications of the two major paradigms of AI.

The major points of the book will be briefly summarised in this chapter and some further general conclusions derived. The first two parts presented the essence of both of the two competing paradigms of AI. The third part provided a comparative analysis of the paradigms.

This final chapter is organised as follows. Section 16.1 provides a very brief summary of the main points of the book. This is followed by section 16.2 which summarises and concludes the discussion on a research methodology for AI. Section 16.3 concludes the discussion on non-factual knowledge and proposes some ideas of how to address this issue. The final section presents an outlook of how the paradigms of AI should develop and how the enterprise of AI as a whole may benefit.

16.1 Brief Summary of the Book

16.1.1 Symbolic AI

The symbolic approach to AI is largely characterised by the idea of the *knowledge level* as is indicated by terms such as *knowledge representation*, *knowledge-based systems*, etc. The knowledge level can be viewed as an extension of the classical hierarchy of system description levels, which include the *device level*, the *circuit level*, the *logical gate level*, the *computer architecture level*, the *machine program level*, and the *symbolic programming language level*, as detailed in chapter 1.

16.1.2 Connectionism

Connectionism represents a non-symbolic approach to AI. On the one hand, it was motivated by its architectural resemblance to the human brain. On the other hand, it was argued that in human thought symbolic (conceptual) structures dynamically emerge and vanish.[1] In connectionist systems, structures which correspond to symbols which humans use,[2] are implemented as dynamically emerging patterns of activity in a distributed computing system. While the elementary level of processing units can be described at least at the computer architecture level[3] and at the levels beneath that, a higher level description becomes very difficult. In fact, it is the very essence of the connectionist paradigm that it does not provide a functional description level which allows to use *symbols*![4]

16.1.3 Comparative Analysis of Both Paradigms

Since connectionism was generally denying the adequacy of symbols, a useful distinction between *first-person symbols* and *third-person symbols* was made in chapter 11. The idea of first-person symbols is roughly to represent the knowledge an expert uses. Opposed to that are third-person symbols, which may represent whatever the system's engineers decide they should represent. Third-person symbols represent what a third person, i.e. a person observing the cognitive system to be modelled from outside, may think of what is happening inside the cognitive system. This may reflect the neuro-physiological processes to a certain degree of precision or it may describe the resulting functionality at a more abstract conceptual level. When analysing the current and potential roles of the two rivalling paradigms of AI, both paradigms were viewed as different ways of describing the required overall functionality of the intelligent system.

The philosophical motivation[5] for the connectionist paradigm has been discussed and appreciated. While the philosophical arguments have been accepted, the connectionist conclusion from these points have been rejected. The reason being that the connectionist approach[6] completely abandons the option to specify in a symbolic form, at least partly, the knowledge which, e.g., a human expert uses for solving problems.[7] There seems to be no way around a symbolic description level for specifying the knowledge a person has. The epistemological problem as claimed by connectionism is that symbolic structures are not capable of fully representing human knowledge. The point being made in this book

---

[1] This is assumed to be due to unconscious processes.

[2] That is, structures which correspond to the knowledge, concepts, etc. an expert may use.

[3] Where the functionality of each neuron is described.

[4] That is, it does not allow a description using symbols, which are comprehensible to humans.

[5] The main reason was evidence for the point that in human thought symbols generally have no fixed meaning. The symbols humans use in communication change their meaning with the context in which they are used. See section 11.2 for more details.

[6] ... in its strict form according to Smolensky (1988).

[7] Or, more generally, for exhibiting intelligent behaviour.

is as follows: even if it were not possible to fully capture all human knowledge symbolically, symbols are still required to approximately capture such knowledge in a *feasible* way. Not using symbols means simply, to use a description whose components cannot be interpreted by humans, neither by the system builders, nor by a scientist seeking an understanding of the description, nor by an expert, whose expertise is to be modelled.

In the following section, this objection is discussed in more detail. Conclusions are drawn for a research methodology for both AI in general and research on learning in particular.

16.2 On a Research Methodology for AI

In chapter 14, general methodological problems have been discussed which emerge when increasingly complex systems are to be designed. With increasing complexity, the role of the paradigm of the underlying computational system on which the entire system is to be implemented becomes less and less important. As a consequence, the potential advantage of a connectionist architecture in resembling the physical structure of the brain is decreasing with an increasing overall system complexity. In fact, it has been argued in chapter 14 that due to the (assumed) high functional complexity of intelligent systems, the question of the metaphorical or possibly even literal resemblance of the underlying computational architecture to the brain becomes virtually a non-issue.

Much more important is the intuitive comprehensibility of a given description level, which is moving into the foreground as another consequence. Instead of the system's functionality, the cognitive capabilities of the system engineer to deal with the means of system specification becomes the most influential factor for the overall effort of designing complex intelligent systems. This brings the engineer much more into perspective than the actual functionality of the system to be designed. In chapter 14, it has been concluded that the *subject*, i.e. the person who designs the system has to be the most important measure for determining the appropriateness of a paradigm. This opposes the widespread belief that the *object*, i.e. the system to be designed, developed, engineered, or 'merely' to be understood as in cognitive science is the crucial factor for choosing the proper paradigm.

16.2.1 The Human Subject Must Be the Measure

With increasing complexity and with the given diversity of functions, which intelligent systems are supposed to fulfill, the human dealing with a computational paradigm becomes the measure of the paradigm's usefulness.

In the following, two aspects are distinguished: *developing* an AI system on the one hand and *understanding* a given intelligent cognitive system on the other hand.

Paradigms for systems engineering. So far, many approaches to AI as well as more general approaches in computer science, including connectionism, genetic algorithms, simulated annealing, etc. have been considered as promising general frameworks for the development of systems which proved difficult to develop by 'conventional' means. As evidence, successful experiments on a small scale have been conducted. These experiments were considered to show the new framework's potential to allow the easy development of systems. In practice, however, it turned out later that these hopes for a generally applicable framework were unjustified: the approaches showed an unexpectedly poor scale-up behaviour.

The analyses in Part III suggest that this is a typical phenomenon, which is due to the fact that an *inappropriate criterion* was used for assessing the potential of such approaches in the first place. Since the crucial issue is the time and effort required for engineering a system, there are two factors involved: on the one hand, there is the *engineer* who is conducts the design; on the other hand, there is the *functionality* of the system to be designed. A general framework has to be useful for all kinds of functional requirements; at least within a certain class of systems. Further, such frameworks are of particular interest for complex functionalities. For the design of complex systems by 'conventional' means, the necessary effort is much larger so that the impact of a more suitable paradigm is hoped to be a major advantage. This is opposed to simple systems which can be built with limited effort in any case.[8]

Since the required functionality can vary so much, the engineer and their cognitive capabilities are the more important and the more constant factors. Due to the varying functionalities, it is impossible to have a major part of the functional design already included in the general framework. Consequently, a general framework cannot greatly be tailored towards a single system. Hence, a general framework has be tailored to the engineer's needs and cognitive capabilities.

This implies also that for evaluating a new approach, it is fairly irrelevant, whether a working system has been designed. The important point is the (cognitive) effort needed for developing the system and how this effort compares to alternative approaches. Learning methods, for example, can assist in the development of systems only if they are well-chosen for the task and if appropriately represented data is available. Thus, the effort for choosing and employing a suitable learning method and supplying the data also has to be taken into account.

Paradigms for scientific explanations. An *explanation* of a phenomenon has essentially to serve two ends. On the one hand, it has to give an account on

---

[8] A low descriptional complexity (low Kolmogorov complexity) is roughly meant by 'simple systems'. This is only roughly true since the encoding of a given function f_1 may take much more effort in some cases than the encoding another function f_2, whose minimal encoding length may be much larger. Thus, the measure of minimal encoding length in this context should rather be taken as a heuristic measure, which will probably correlate to a certain degree with the actual effort required.

the phenomenon in question which meets the required accuracy. On the other hand, the explanation has to be reasonably comprehensible for the 'consumer', such as a scientist.

A typical means in describing complex systems is to put some, often hierarchical, structure into the description which makes the understanding of the overall system easier. That means, to break the entire system into parts, each part being of cognitively feasible complexity. The well-known top-down or bottom-up design of software is an example for that.

In any case, a comprehensible description has to use symbols. At the lowest system level,[9] the complexity of the description using tokens at that level may easily exceed the cognitive capacity of the 'consumer'. Hence, an overall description at this level will be incomprehensible. Consequently, in more complex systems, the use of symbols for describing abstractions of the functionality at the lowest system level is inevitable.

In other words, any description of a sufficiently complex system needs layers of abstraction. Thus, even if a non-symbolic approach uses tokens at its base level which cannot be reasonably interpreted, there still needs to be a more abstract level of description. The role of such a more abstract description level is to provide cognitive access to the functionality of the system or parts thereof. In complex systems, there is no unique way of introducing abstract levels of functional descriptions. In fact, such description levels are artifacts which can be chosen on purpose. Since, the purpose is to make the description comprehensible, these abstract description levels have to use interpretable symbols. Those symbols, however, may largely be third-person symbols as opposed to first-person symbols.

16.2.2 General Methodological Objectives

Accepting the necessary engineering effort for developing a system as quality measure of an approach has the following consequence. A methodology for AI research has to ensure progress on the following questions:

> How to design a functional specification of an intelligent system to perform tasks of type x? The design may include the incorporation of:
> a) (expert) knowledge which is easily accessible in practice by introspective or similar means.
> b) tacit knowledge which experts have great difficulties to become aware of and to express. This includes 'non-factual knowledge' as discussed in chapter 15.

It has been recognised in AI that the knowledge of type a) is rather limited and that substantial system engineering efforts have to complement the provided knowledge in order to successfully build intelligent systems.

---

[9] What constitutes the lowest system level depends on the system being described. For example, it might be the device level in an electronic computer, the neurophysiological level in a brain, etc.

The knowledge of type b) is crucial in many cases but it is not clear how it can systematically be obtained. In fact, the philosophical motivation for connectionism and for the rejection of symbolically encoded knowledge includes the observation that humans have severe difficulties to explicate the way they use symbols in conscious reasoning.[10] Philosophy provided a case for the point that human cognition involves a large part of unconscious processing which is inaccessible by introspection. Besides the philosophical reasons, this conclusion is also supported by empirical studies in psychology through the past decades.[11]

While connectionism does not deal with symbolic descriptions of knowledge, connectionist's advocates did not consider this as a severe problem.[12] The way to put knowledge into a connectionist system is by letting the system learn and organise its knowledge representation itself. Thus, the idea of learning in a connectionist system is intimately connected to the very idea of connectionism as an alternative paradigm for AI in general. Hence, an important issue is a research methodology for learning systems.

Methodological Questions for Research on Learning Systems. Chapter 13 presents computational limitations of learning systems to learn complex functions from data with no or limited prior knowledge. From these results the general need for exploiting knowledge to assist in the process of learning from training data has been derived. The limitations hold regardless of the particular learning mechanism and regardless of the particular paradigm in which a learning mechanism is employed. Hence, whether learning takes place in a connectionist or in a symbolic system does not make a major difference with respect to the need of additional knowledge for building complex intelligent systems. As a consequence, research on learning has to ensure progress on the following questions:

- How to choose a representation for the training data and how to choose a suitable learning algorithm?
- How to provide inductive bias to a learning system by exploiting expert knowledge which might be both difficult to express and difficult to access introspectively?
- How to process effectively the provided inductive bias along with the training data?
- How to integrate learning into large bodies of various kinds of factual and non-factual knowledge?

These questions are largely qualitative ones, where we do not expect precise quantifications. Possible answers to these questions may be of the type that certain guidelines are given and intuitive arguments are presented for or against a particular approach. This contrasts the objective of many recent evaluation

---

[10] That is, to provide parts of their tacit knowledge.

[11] See Berry and Bienes (1993) or Nisbett and DeCamp Wilson (1977).

[12] The specification of symbolic rules would be unsuccessful anyway. So the reasoning of connectionist's advocates.

studies in machine learning which are of a quantitative statistical nature. Furthermore, it should be noted that these questions are phrased independently of a particular paradigm. A good paradigm, however, has to support progress on these questions.

16.3 Non-Factual Knowledge

Another consequence from the presented analyses of part III concerns the question of knowledge acquisition, representation and processing. While substantial progress has been made for treating 'factual' knowledge, i.e. knowledge that describes a world state, e.g. by using a logical language, Bayesian networks,[13] etc, the symbolic paradigm gave comparably little attention to the declarative treatment of non-factual knowledge. However, as discussed in chapter 15, non-factual knowledge need to be handled. While the current state of the art allows already a wide variety of knowledge types to be represented and processed, there are still more types of knowledge which await proper formalisations. This includes even certain types of factual knowledge, such as knowledge about the character of sequential processes, e.g. time series, knowledge about spatial relationships, etc. In particular, for all topics for which knowledge may be available, humans will often provide only incomplete descriptions, which abstract from some details while they contain other details. Here exists a large variety of possibilities to exploit such incomplete knowledge, which have not yet been exhausted by currently available techniques.

Another reason, which is particularly emphasised in this book, are the practical limitations of humans to access their non-factual knowledge by introspection. Dreyfus (1972, 1992) uses the term *tacit knowledge* for such knowledge, which humans are rarely even aware that they have it. It seems that humans have a certain ability to 'circumscribe' their knowledge, e.g., by excluding certain possible 'world states', or by recognising certain generalizations from data as implausible, etc., rather than by stating possibly a particular 'world state.'[14] Qualitative reasoning is a good example of a formalism that handles incomplete knowledge, by abstracting from numerical details.[15] (See e.g. (Forbus, 1993; Kleer, 1994) or (Hoffmann, 1994) for integrating qualitative descriptions into learning.)

---

[13] Note that the treatment of uncertainty falls still under 'factual knowledge' according to chapter 15, as long as the (uncertain) proposition describes facts.

[14] One important difference between world state and knowledge state is that a world state includes a description of all possible objects in the world and their relations among each other. This is opposed to knowledge which may include classification rules which apply not only to all objects currently in the world but also to objects which are non-existent in the current world state.

[15] Qualitative reasoning reasons about qualitative knowledge as opposed to quantitative knowledge. For example, instead of describing the speed of a falling object by a numerical function of time, it may merely be stated that the speed increases monotonically.

Two important dimensions according to which knowledge can generally be distinguished are:

- Knowledge that describes an *individual* world state or 'knowledge state' of an intelligent system versus knowledge that describes *a set of possible* world states or 'knowledge states' of an intelligent system.
- Knowledge that describes a static world or 'knowledge state' of an intelligent system versus knowledge that describes the dynamic change of a world state or the knowledge state of an intelligent system.

The first type of knowledge excludes merely a set of possible world states or knowledge states while it does not positively determine a particular state. It concerns the degree of precision of the description the knowledge provides. This spans from describing exactly an individual state up to not knowing anything about the world, i.e. assuming everything to be possible.[16]

The second dimension of knowledge concerns the dynamic aspect of the world and/or the knowledge about the world. Thus, the second dimension may be considered as 'procedural knowledge' for a simulator of the world or the 'procedural knowledge' describing the dynamic development of knowledge structures in an intelligent system. The following indicates different degrees along this scale.

1. A description of a particular world state or knowledge state of an intelligent system.
2. A description of the *change* of a world state into a temporally subsequent world state[17] or a change of a knowledge state into a temporally subsequent knowledge state. This includes rules that guide generalising reasoning, analogical reasoning, and other types of non-deductive reasoning.
3. A description of the change of the previous type of knowledge. This includes the change of inductive bias due to the acquisition of new data, or the new formation and/or change of knowledge structures which represent knowledge with a dynamic character as explained above.

While in principle, such knowledge can be represented within a connectionist system, at least if the connectionist system is computationally universal,[18] so far not all of the mentioned types of knowledge have been systematically

---

[16] ... in the space of all possible descriptions as defined by the used description language. Every computational system uses a basic language in which the system's knowledge, information, data, or however it may be called, is represented. For example, in the case of the Turing machine there is an alphabet which provides tokens, which are manipulated by the Turing machine's program. Depending on that program, the Turing machine's behaviour may or may not be easily derivable from the arrangements of the tokens used.

[17] While the dynamic behaviour of closed physical systems is relatively well understood, the situation for open systems as we have to deal with in our daily life is very different.

[18] See subsection 10.1.3 for an example of such a model.

addressed by connectionist systems. For example, the representation and acquisition of knowledge describing the change of knowledge states has received
relatively little attention.

It has been pointed out in chapter 15 that humans also acquire knowledge
that is not directly reflected in their intelligent *behaviour* but in their way of
acquiring new knowledge. Such knowledge[19] cannot be acquired and/or verified
in a straightforward way by using positive and negative examples, which is
the basis of most learning in connectionist systems to date. It is generally
unclear what type of methods could and should be employed to deal with the
acquisition of such knowledge. Simply to try a second order induction process
is not justifiable from an epistemological point of view. It will run into similar
difficulties as those of ordinary induction as discussed in chapter 15.

Despite this ignorance, it can be noted that the connectionist paradigm
seems to give away an important handle to utilise human-provided knowledge
that could assist a learning system.

On the other hand, the symbolic paradigm keeps all options open for constructing a possible way to incorporate any type of knowledge which a human
is able to express. This may, for example, be procedures which deal with the
acquisition of non-factual knowledge. Or it may be knowledge which provides
some indirect guidance, by e.g., characterising certain ways of generalisation as
being invalid or at least implausible. The specification of that sort of guidance
may be possible for an expert, although it may be impossible for the expert to
fully articulate the precise mechanisms involved in their own cognitive processes
including their learning processes.

16.4 Perspectives

It seems logical to study computer architectures, which are in accordance with
our understanding of the human brain and its organisation and function. After
all, the human brain seems[20] to prove the existence of a solution to our problems
in building intelligent systems. As a consequence it may appear sensible to
emulate the working system in order to duplicate its marvellous performance.
However, the history of human attempts in engineering, for example to build
flying machines, would rather suggest that one has to look into alternative
approaches. Only after man stopped trying to imitate the moving wings and
feathers of birds, did he manage to get off the ground!

In this book, I argued that there are good reasons not to attempt to follow
too closely the lines of the biological role-model for building intelligent systems.
I argued that due to the enormous complexity of the human brain as well as
the cognitive processes going on, a shift in the emphasis takes place: it is not

---

[19] ... which may be viewed as providing inductive bias for further learning.

[20] I say *seems*, because one could still claim that intelligence is not due to the physical
nature of the brain but rather to the mind's spirit, etc.

an accurate or metaphorical modelling of the biological role model that serves as a guideline, but much more the human capacity to understand and handle complex systems in general. While for simple systems, it may be feasible to describe them accurately using our tools of natural science, this is very different for the case of highly complex systems.

The cognitive feasibility of a description becomes the major issue with increasing system complexity. This makes it mandatory that suitable abstractions are found which allow an engineer or a scientist to understand a description and to design systems, while having a grip on what the result will be. Hence, it will not so much be the brain or the cognitive processes that will have a say in how a sensible description must look like. It is rather the human capacity to understand certain types of abstractions better than other abstractions, which has to dictate what kind of description to choose. This implies, as I argued in this book that there needs still to be a symbolic level of system description.[21] However, it has also been recognised that in human intelligence, certain knowledge plays an indispensable role, which is probably not representable by first-person symbols.[22] While the numerical, i.e. non-symbolic, aspects of neural networks is clearly a useful and important asset of today's technological landscape, the idea of building connectionist systems, which resemble the human brain in the proposed metaphorical sense, seems to go one step too far.

It is conceivable, though, that the encoding of intelligence is substantially shorter in a connectionist-style system than a symbolic description. The latter one being cognitively much more feasible for us to understand. However, even if that were true, it is hard to see how such an encoding of intelligence can be found. More or less random guessing of a suitable connectionist architecture does not look likely to be a successful approach. What needs to be done, is to push the boundary of what is described by *first-person* symbols further and to leave the rest to a subsymbolic style of computation. That is, to develop formalisms to handle further types of knowledge expressed in first-person symbols. This will be complemented by subsymbolic computation, which may not be of the style of connectionist systems, but rather some computational mechanism described in *third-person* symbols.

---

[21] Although it may and it will be a third-person symbol level.

[22] Symbols, which do neither directly correspond to human concepts nor to linguistic expressions. That human cognition can form new concepts covering such symbols, and hence, those symbols may become first-person symbols seems highly unlikely.

Appendix

A. More Details on Logic

The following provides the technical details of the resolution procedure as well as additional theoretical foundations to understand why it works. This appendix is to be used as a supplement to chapter 2 for interested readers.

In appendix A.1 the notion of models in formal logic is presented. Based on that notion a special class of interpretations and associated models is presented in A.2, so-called Herbrand interpretations and Herbrand models. These are the only interpretations, which need to be considered when developing a sound proof procedure, although there exists an infinity of other interpretations of a predicate logical language. Based on that presents appendix A.3 all the technical details of the resolution proof procedure including the theorem on its completeness.

A.1 Models

The first notion concerns the idea of models. These are the 'worlds' that are possible, given a set of formulas S is true. These worlds are called *models* of S and are discussed below.

Given a set of formulas, the interpretations for which these formulas are true are of particular interest. Those interpretations are called **models**. Models are particularly interesting for the development and verification of 'laws of logic'. This is because the laws of logic are supposed to work for any set of propositions, or formulas. Hence, no particular assumptions about the world being described by the formulas can be made. The 'laws of logic' are required to hold for *any possible world* being described. Thus, assuming that a set of formulas S is true leads directly to the set of models of S. If a formula f derived from S by some 'laws of logic' is true in all models of S, it can be said that f is in fact a *logical* consequence of S. However, first a few more definitions will be introduced to allow the formal considerations concerning the validity of the 'laws of logic' in the remainder of this section. Usually, the following types of formulas S of a predicate logic language are distinguished:

Definition A.1. *Let S be a set of closed formulas of a first order predicate logic language L.*

– *We say S is* **satisfiable** *if L has an interpretation which is a model for S.*

– We say S is **valid** (or **tautological**) if <u>every</u> interpretation of L is a model for S.
– We say S is **unsatisfiable** (or **contradictory**) if <u>no</u> interpretation of L is a model for S.
– We say S is **non-valid** if L has <u>an</u> interpretation which is <u>not</u> a model for S.

Particularly interesting formulas with respect to a given set of formulas S are called *theorems* of S:

Definition A.2. *Given a set of formulas S, a further formula $t \notin S$ is called a* **theorem** *of S, if and only if t is true in all models of the given set of formulas S. t is also called a* **logical consequence** *of S.*

Respectively, the following definition concerns the complete set of theorems of a given set of formulas:

Definition A.3. *Let S be a set of formulas of first order predicate logic. The set of formulas T is called the* **Theory** *of S, if and only if T is the set of all formulas, which are true in all models of S. The formulas of S are also called* **axioms** *of T. If T has a model, we say T is* **consistent**.

It may be noted that T is **not** consistent, if and only if neither T nor the set of axioms S has a model. The relation between the theory of a set of axioms and the axioms themselves can be described as follows in terms of models:

Definition A.4. *Let T be a theory and let L be the language of T. A* **model** *for T is an interpretation for L which is a model for each axiom of T.*

The following definition gives the rules according to which the truth value of a formula can be determined under a given interpretation I for a language L.

Definition A.5. *If I is an* **interpretation** *of L, and D the* **domain** *of I, then for every constant in A_L, I determines an object in D, i.e. $I(c) \in D$. Then V_I, the* **valuation** *V based on I, is defined as follows:*

(i)   if $P(a_1, \ldots, a_n)$ is   an atomic sentence in L,

then
$V_I(P(a_1, \ldots, a_n)) = true$ iff $\langle I(a_1), \ldots, I(a_n) \rangle \in I(P)$.

(ii) $V_I(\neg\phi) = true$ iff $V_I(\phi) = false$;

(iii) $V_I(\phi \wedge \psi) = true$ iff $V_I(\phi) = true$ and $V_I(\psi) = true$;

(iv) $V_I(\phi \vee \psi) = true$ iff $V_I(\phi) = true$ or $V_I(\psi) = true$;

(v) $V_I(\phi \rightarrow \psi) = true$ iff $V_I(\phi) = false$ or $V_I(\psi) = true$;

(vi) $V_I(\phi \leftrightarrow \psi) = true$ iff $V_I(\phi) = V_I(\psi)$;

(vii) $V_I(\forall x \phi) = true$ iff $V_{I_d}(\phi) = true$ for all possible $d \in D$. (where the interpretation I_d equals I, except that $I_d(x) = d$.)

(viii) $V_I(\exists x \phi) = true$ iff $V_I(\phi) = true$ for at least one $d \in D$. (where the interpretation I_d equals I, except that $I_d(x) = d$.)

Interpretations of predicate logic languages can be very different and numerous. More precisely, there is an infinite number of different interpretations for each language L. This is simply due to the fact that it is possible to create an infinite number of different domains of objects, e.g. some subset of the set of integers. In fact, this results even in an uncountable number of different interpretations. This poses severe technical problems for dealing with notions like 'theorem', since an uncountably infinite number of different interpretations, and also often an uncountably infinite number of different models has to be considered. That is, since rules for deriving logical consequences have to hold for any possible interpretation, we have to take *all* possible interpretations into account, when establishing 'laws of logic.' To circumvent these technical difficulties, a particularly significant kind of interpretations, so-called Herbrand interpretations, are introduced in the following subsection.

A.2 Herbrand Interpretations

This subsection presents the notion of Herbrand interpretations, which will be used as a kind of 'reference interpretations' in the remainder of this section. To understand the construction of Herbrand interpretations, a few more technical definitions are needed.

Two phases in constructing an Herbrand interpretation are distinguished: The Herbrand pre-interpretation assigns objects to terms in L. Based on that, the Herbrand interpretation assigns meanings to all predicates by listing for each n-ary predicate P the set of all n-tuples of objects for which P is true.

Definition A.6. *An **atom** is a formula in L (closed or not), which consists only of a predicate applied to the respective number of terms. That is, an atom is a formula generated by rule 2 in Definition 2.2 in chapter 2.*

Example

$P(a, b)$ and $Q(x, f(a))$ are atoms, while $\neg P(a, b)$ or $(P(a, x) \vee \neg Q(a, a))$ are not.

As mentioned earlier, terms are either constants, variables or functions of terms in a predicate logic language L. An important type of terms are so-called ground terms.

Definition A.7. *A **ground term** is a term, not containing any variable. Similarly, a **ground atom** is an atom not containing any variable.*

Example

a, $f(a)$, and $g(b, f(a))$ are ground terms, while x or $g(a, x))$ are not. Respectively, are $P(a, b)$ and $Q(b, f(a))$ ground atoms, while $P(x, b)$ or $R(f(g(a, f(g(b, x)))))$ are not.

Using these notions, the set of objects considered in the Herbrand interpretation can be defined:

Definition A.8. *The domain of an Herbrand interpretation is called the* **Herbrand universe** *and defined as the set of all ground terms.*

This definition may be confusing, since it defines a universe as a set of terms. That is, the definition says that objects are a set of syntactical expressions. It equals syntactical and semantical units! It should be noted, however, that the Herbrand universe is a mathematical notion. That is, the objects of the universe are elements of a mathematical set. While this set is to be distinguished strictly from the logical language to be interpreted, the objects needs to be named to allow proper treatment in a mathematical way.

For convenience, the objects in the Herbrand universe are named according to some terms of the language to be interpreted. However, it should be emphasised that conceptually, the Herbrand universe is still distinct from the set of terms of the language to be interpreted.

Definition A.9. *Let L be a first order language. The pre-interpretation given by the following is called the* **Herbrand pre-interpretation** *for L:*

a) *The domain of the pre-interpretation is the Herbrand universe U_L.*
b) *Constants in L are assigned to themselves in U_L.*
c) *If f is an n-ary function symbol in L, then the mapping from $(U_L)^n$ into U_L defined by $(t_1, \ldots, t_n) \to f(t_1, \ldots, t_n)$ is assigned to f.*

An **Herbrand interpretation** *for L is any interpretation based on the Herbrand pre-interpretation for L.*

Example

Assume the predicate logic language L_1 contains only the constants a, b, c, the variables x and y and no function symbols. Then the Herbrand universe of the language L_1 is given by $U_{L_1} = \{a, b, c\}$. Since the Herbrand universe contains only *ground terms* the number of variables of the language are irrelevant for the construction of U_{L_1}.

Opposed to that, consider the language L_2, which contains the same constants and variables as L_1 and additionally the single-argument function $f(.)$ and another two-argument function $g(.,.)$.

Then the Herbrand universe of the language L_2 is given by
$U_{L_2} = \{a, b, c, f(a), f(b), f(c), g(a, a), g(a, b), \ldots, g(c, c), g(f(a), a),$
$g(f(a), b), \ldots, g(g(a, a), f(g(a, f(b)))), \ldots\}$.

Going further in constructing the Herbrand interpretation, an account on the possible meaning of the predicates of the considered language has to be given. Therefore, the second step is the construction of the so-called Herbrand base.

Definition A.10. *The **Herbrand base** is the set of all ground atoms.*

Example

Assume the predicate logic language L_1 as above which contains only the two-argument predicate $P(.,.)$. Then the Herbrand base is given by
$B_{L_1} = \{P(a,a), P(a,b), P(a,c), ..., P(c,b), P(c,c)\}$.
Assuming the predicate logic language L_2 as in the example above which contains only the single-argument predicate $Q(.)$, the Herbrand base of L_2 is given by
$B_{L_2} = \{Q(a), Q(b), Q(c), Q(f(a)), ..., Q(g(a,b)), ..., Q(g(c,c)),$
$..., Q(f(g(a, f(b)))), ...\}$.

The Herbrand base contains all possible ground atoms. Thus, the Herbrand base contains all facts which may be either true or false in a possible world being described by formulas of the respective predicate logic language. It is important to note that each ground atom may be true or false completely independent of the truth value of all the other ground atoms. Consequently, an interpretation assuming a subset of the ground atoms as true is defined as follows:

Definition A.11. *An **Herbrand interpretation** is a subset of the Herbrand base.*

The Herbrand interpretation states simply all ground atoms which are true in the interpretation. The missing ground atoms are interpreted as being false.

Example

Assume the predicate logic language L_1 as in the example above which contains only the two-argument predicate $P(.,.)$. Then a possible Herbrand interpretation is given by
$I_{L_1}^1 = \{P(a,a), P(a,c), P(c,c)\}$.
Another Herbrand interpretation is given by
$I_{L_1}^2 = \{P(a,a), P(a,b), P(a,c), P(b,a), P(b,b), P(c,c)\}$.
Yet another Herbrand interpretation is given by
$I_{L_1}^3 = \{\}$.

Consistent with the previously defined notion of a *model*, we define an Herbrand model as follows:

Definition A.12. *Let L be a language of first order predicate logic and S a set of closed formulas of L. An **Herbrand model** for S is an Herbrand interpretation for L which is a model for S.*

Now, we are ready to establish the significance of the presented way of constructing interpretations, i.e. constructing Herbrand interpretations of a language. The following proposition has been proved:

Proposition A.13. *Let S be a set of closed formulas and suppose S has a model. Then S has an Herbrand model.*

This proposition is complemented by the following statement:

Proposition A.14. *Let S be a set of closed formulas. Then S is unsatisfiable if and only if S has no Herbrand models.*

These propositions establish an important shortcut in analysing interpretations and models of a set of formulas. It is stated that instead of considering all possible interpretations in order to determine whether a set of formulas S has a model or not, it is equivalent to determine whether S has an Herbrand model. Thus, only the Herbrand interpretations have to be checked for being a model of S, when the validity of logical derivation rules are proved.

Equipped with the notion of Herbrand interpretations and Herbrand models the reader is prepared to understand why the 'law of logic', the resolution principle, is a valid strategy to draw conclusions from a given set of formulas of a predicate logic language.

A.3 Resolution

This subsection provides the details of the resolution procedure. Resolution is a technique for proving theorems introduced by Robinson (1965), which is particularly well-suited for computers. It is a uniform procedure performing a single *resolution step* at a time. Resolution is a complete proof procedure. That is, it will find a proof of a theorem if a proof exists. Moreover, resolution is *sound*, i.e. it will never say, a proposition θ is a theorem of a set of sentences S, if in fact θ is not a theorem of S.

Resolution proves theorems by detecting contradictions. In fact, the only thing the resolution procedure attempts to do is to find a contradiction in a set of formulas. Although, normally the existence of a contradiction in a set of formulas is a rather undesirable fact, the detection of a contradiction can also be exploited in a very useful way. The existence of a contradiction in a set of formulas S implies that S has no model, i.e. there exists no interpretation of the underlying language, in which all formulas in S are simultaneously true. How can a detector for contradictions be used for proving theorems?

Let us recall the definition of the notion of *theorem*: A formula θ is a theorem of a set of formulas S, if and only if all models of S are also models of θ. Moreover, the following observation is important. According to the rules of valuation of a formula under a given interpretation, as given in definition A.5 the following holds: For every interpretation I a formula $\neg\theta$ is false if and only if the formula θ is true under I. Therefore, every interpretation which is a model of θ is not a model of $\neg\theta$ and vice versa.

This observation leads to the following idea. Suppose a formula θ is in fact a theorem of a set of formulas S. That is, all interpretations of the underlying language L which are models of S are also models of θ. This implies that exactly all models of S are not models of $\neg\theta$. Hence, the set of models of S and the set of models of $\neg\theta$ are mutually disjoint, provided θ is in fact a theorem of S. In other words, the conjunction of the formulas in S and the formula $\neg\theta$ have no common model if and only if θ is a theorem of S.

As a consequence, in order to prove that θ is a theorem of S, it is sufficient to prove that $S \cup \{\neg\theta\}$ has no model, which means that $S \cup \{\neg\theta\}$ is a contradiction. Moreover, due to proposition A.14, to prove that a set of formulas has no model, it is sufficient to prove that S has no Herbrand model. The following definitions prepare the way to the simple technique of *resolution*, which determines whether or not there exists an Herbrand model for a set of (closed) formulas of a predicate logic language.

Definition A.15. *A* **literal** *is either an atomic formula or its negation.*

A canonical form for all possible formulas of first order predicate logic is defined as follows:

Definition A.16. *A formula is in* **prenex conjunctive normal form** *if it has the form*

$$Qx_1 \ldots Qx_k((L_{11} \vee \ldots \vee L_{1m_1}) \wedge \ldots \wedge (L_{n1} \vee \ldots \vee L_{nm_n}))$$

where each Q is an existential or universal quantifier and each L_{ij} is a literal.

It can be shown that every formula can be transformed into its *prenex conjunctive normal form*. That is, using the following definition the subsequent proposition can be proved.

Definition A.17. *We say two formulas are logically equivalent, if they have the same truth values for any interpretation of L and any variable assignment.*

Proposition A.18. *For each formula ϕ there is a formula ψ, logically equivalent to ϕ, such that ψ is in prenex conjunctive normal form.*

Figure A.1 shows an algorithm which transforms any formula ϕ into a logically equivalent formula in prenex conjunctive normal form. However, the proof that the resulting formula is, in fact logically equivalent, is left to the reader.

1. Eliminate $\rightarrow$ and $\leftrightarrow$ symbols.
   a) Replace every occurrence in ϕ of the form $(\psi_1 \leftrightarrow \psi_2)$
      by $((\psi_1 \rightarrow \psi_2) \wedge (\psi_2 \rightarrow \psi_1))$.
   b) Replace every occurrence in ϕ of the form $(\psi_1 \rightarrow \psi_2)$ by $(\neg\psi_1 \vee \psi_2)$.
2. Move negation symbols from compound formulas to the atoms, i.e.
   a) Replace every occurrence in ϕ of the form $\neg(\psi_1 \vee \psi_2)$ by $(\neg\psi_1 \wedge \neg\psi_2)$.
   b) Similarly, replace every occurrence in ϕ of the form $\neg(\psi_1 \wedge \psi_2)$ by
      $(\neg\psi_1 \vee \neg\psi_2)$.
   c) Replace every occurrence in ϕ of the form $\neg\exists v\psi$ by $\forall v\neg\psi$. Similarly,
      replace every occurrence in ϕ of the form $\neg\forall v\psi$ by $\exists v\neg\psi$.
3. Resolve disjunctions of conjunctions and double negations, i.e.
   a) Replace every occurrence in ϕ of the form $(\psi_1 \vee (\psi_2 \wedge \psi_3))$ or of the
      form $((\psi_2 \wedge (\psi_3) \vee \psi_1)$ by $((\psi_1 \vee \psi_2) \wedge (\psi_1 \vee \psi_3))$.
   b) Replace every occurrence in ϕ of the form $\neg\neg\psi$ by ψ.
4. Move quantifiers in front of the entire formula, i.e.
   a) Rename all quantified variables such that no two quantified variables
      have the same name. (Replace every occurrence of a quantified variable throughout its scope by the new name.)
   b) Move all quantifiers in front of the entire formula by preserving the
      order of the quantifiers.

Figure A.1. Algorithm for transforming a predicate logical formula into an equivalent formula in prenex conjunctive normal form.

Example

Consider the following formula:
$(P(a) \vee \neg\forall x(Q(x) \rightarrow (P(a) \vee \exists xQ(x))))$.
After executing step 1, we obtain:
$(P(a) \vee \neg\forall x(\neg Q(x) \vee (P(a) \vee \exists xQ(x))))$.
After executing step 2c, we obtain:
$(P(a) \vee \exists x\neg(\neg Q(x) \vee (P(a) \vee \exists Q(x))))$.
After executing step 2a, we obtain:
$(P(a) \vee \exists x(\neg\neg Q(x) \wedge \neg(P(a) \vee \exists Q(x))))$.
After executing step 2b, we obtain:
$(P(a) \vee \exists x(\neg\neg Q(x) \wedge (\neg P(a) \wedge \neg\exists Q(x))))$.
After executing step 2c, (step 2 completed) we obtain:
$(P(a) \vee \exists x(\neg\neg Q(x) \wedge (\neg P(a) \wedge \forall x\neg Q(x))))$.
After executing step 3b, we obtain:
$(P(a) \vee \exists x(Q(x) \wedge (\neg P(a) \wedge \forall x\neg Q(x))))$.
After executing step 4a, we obtain:
$(P(a) \vee \exists x_1(Q(x_1) \wedge (\neg P(a) \wedge \forall x_2\neg Q(x_2))))$.
After executing step 4b, we obtain:
$\exists x_1\forall x_2(P(a) \vee (Q(x_1) \wedge (\neg P(a) \wedge \neg Q(x_2))))$.

After a formula has been transformed into prenex conjunctive normal form, there may be variables which are existentially-quantified. Since the following considerations presuppose that all variables are *all*-quantified, the existentially-quantified variables have to be eliminated. This is done by replacing each of the existentially-quantified variables by a new function f_S. f_S is a function of all all-quantified variables in whose scope the existential quantifier lies. This process is called *Skolemisation* according to the logician 'T. Skolem'.

Definition A.19. *Let ϕ be a formula and $\exists y \psi$ be a sub-formula of ϕ. Let $x_1, ..., x_n$ be the all-quantified variables, whose scope contains ψ. Then the* **Skolemisation** *of the existentially-quantified variable y is the replacement of every occurrence of y in ψ by a the function $f_s(x_1, ..., x_n)$, where f_s is a newly introduced function symbol. The existential quantifier $\exists y$' is removed as well.*

Example

Consider the formula
$F = \exists y_1 \forall x_1 \forall x_2 \exists y_2 (P(x_1, y_2) \wedge (\neg Q(x_2) \vee R(f(y_1), f(g(a, y_2)))))$. The variables y_1 and y_2 are to be substituted by newly created function symbols.
By Skolemisation the formula is transformed into
$\forall x_1 \forall x_2 (P(x_1, f_2(x_1, x_2)) \wedge (\neg Q(x_2) \vee R(f(f_1), f(g(a, f_2(x_1, x_2))))))$.
The existentially-quantified variable y_1 in front of the formula claims that there is at least one value for y_1 such that the entire formula is true.

The idea behind Skolemisation is to denote this variable concretely. Since it is a priori unknown whether a suitable choice for y_1 is a given constant c, a new constant c_n is simply introduced. If a respective interpretation would require that the new constant would be equivalent to an already known constant, the interpretation can 'take care of that', by assigning all the properties assigned to c to the new constant c_n as well. Thus, c and c_n would become 'semantically equivalent'.

In the example, the variable y_1 is replaced by a constant f_1 (f_1 is chosen for better of Skolemisation) since no all-quantified variables are on the left of the quantifier of y_1. The formula claims that for all possible values of x_1, x_2 there exists a suitable value for y_2 such that the formula is true. Hence, we have to substitute y_2 by a function of these variables allowing to choose the value for y_2 depending on the values of x_1 and x_2 respectively.

After Skolemisation of the prenex conjunctive normal form formula the formula can be broken up into a set of all-quantified disjunctions. That is, every disjunction of the conjunctive normal form is separated from each other. The variables in each disjunction are consistently renamed such that no variables in two different disjunctions have the same name. We call the disjunctions of literals in a Skolemised prenex conjunctive normal form *clauses*. Clauses are the units, which are used to determine possible resolution steps. If a formula in prenex conjunctive normal form has a model, then there must be at least one Herbrand interpretation I of the underlying predicate logic language such that each of the clauses of the prenex conjunctive normal form is true under that Herbrand interpretation I. However, if in two clauses the same predicate occurs, in one of the clauses negated and in the other clause as atom, it is clear that either the atomic predicate is false or the negated predicate. Thus, it follows that at least one of the remaining literals in either of the clauses must be true as well. Otherwise, the two clauses would not have a common model.

Example

> Consider the following two clauses: $C_1 = (P(a) \vee Q(b) \vee \neg R(a, b))$ and $C_2 = (\neg Q(b) \vee R(b, a))$. Suppose the interpretation I is a model of both clauses. Each clause is true under a given interpretation I if and only if at least one of its literals is true under I. Since $Q(b)$ occurs in the first clause and its negation in the second clause, it is impossible that both $Q(b)$ and $\neg Q(b)$ is simultaneously true under any interpretation I. Thus, either at least one of the remaining literals in the first clause must be true under I or at least one of the remaining literals in the second clause must be true under I. Therefore, a third clause $C_3 = (P(a) \vee \neg R(a, b) \vee R(b, a))$. can be created comprising the mentioned remaining literals of both clauses. From the reasoning above it is clear that at least one of the literals of C_3 must be true under I. Hence, C_3 is a theorem of C_1 and C_2 since every interpretation which is a model of both clauses C_1 and C_2 is also a model of C_3. Note that $\neg R(a, b)$ in the first clause does not match $R(b, a)$ in the second clause because both predicates have different constants as their first respectively their second argument.

In the example given above, the literals in both clauses were ground literals. However, literals may contain variables which would not allow an immediate matching of literals as in the example. Nevertheless, since the meaning of an all-quantified variable is that the formula holds for any possible value of the variable, the variable would 'semantically' match any constant or another all-quantified variable. The process to determine, whether the terms of two literals match 'semantically' is known as *unification*.

A.3.1 Unification

This subsection provides the technical details for the understanding of the *unification algorithm* given at the end of the subsection.

In predicate logic, the resolution step cannot be applied to every pair of clauses, where in one clause a predicate P appears negated and in the other clause P appears positively. This is, since the predicates may be applied to different objects, and hence, the reasoning for the validity of the resolvent as outlined above may not be applicable. In fact, the resolution is only applicable if the matching literals apply to the same object or to the same set of objects. Literals may involve variables which normally implies that the respective predicate applies to a set of objects, since we are generally dealing with all-quantified variables, To determine, whether two literals are in fact matching, it has to be determined, whether the set of objects over which each of the two literals ranges, are mutually disjoint or not. If the intersection of the two sets is non-empty, then the resolution step can be applied. Although, the resolvent is **only** valid for the set of objects in the intersection set. The following presents a syntactical procedure for determining whether the ranges of two literals have a non-empty intersection. Therefore, all-quantified variables are *substituted* by less general terms. That is, an all-quantified variable x may be substituted by a constant a or a function $f(x')$. Note that both substitutions range over a subset of the range of the initial all-quantified variable. The general idea of the unification procedure is to substitute one or more variables in one or in both of the literals, such that the two predicates have exactly the same terms as their corresponding arguments. Hence, the name *unification*. Since the substitutes are less general than the original terms, the stated propositions hold for the substitutes as they hold for the original terms. The *most general unifier* will exactly describe the intersection set of two given literals ranging over their original terms.

In other words, the goal of the unification algorithm is to apply semantically valid syntactic operations on two terms in order to obtain two syntactically equal terms. The basic operation of the unification algorithm is to substitute one or more variables in the one or the other term by appropriate new terms such that both of the terms to be unified are transformed into the same syntactical form. Therefore, first we will define what is understood by *substitution*.

Definition A.20. *A substitution θ is a finite set of the form $\{v_1/t_1, ..., v_n/t_n\}$, where each v_i is a variable, each t_i is a term distinct from v_i and the variables $v_1, ..., v_n$ are distinct. Each element v_i/t_i is called a binding for v_i. θ is called a ground substitution if the t_i are all ground terms. θ is called a variable-pure substitution if the t_i are all variables.*

Definition A.21. *An expression is either a term, a literal or conjunction or disjunction of literals. A simple expression is either a term or an atom.*

If variables in an expression are replaced by other terms, the resulting expression is called an *instance* of the original expression. That is,

Definition A.22. *Let $\theta = \{v_1/t_1, ..., v_n/t_n\}$ be a substitution and E be an expression. Then $E\theta$, the instance of E by θ, is the expression obtained from E by simultaneously replacing each occurrence of the variable v_i in E by the term t_i for all $i = 1, ..., n$. If $E\theta$ is ground, then $E\theta$ is called a ground instance of E.*

Example

Consider the expression $E = P(f(g(x,a), f(y)), \theta_1 = \{x/a, y/f(y)\}$ and $\theta_2 = \{z/b\}$. Then, $E\theta_1 = P(f(g(a,a), f(f(y))))$ and $E\theta_2 = P((f(g(x,a), f(y)))$.

Definition A.23. *The substitution given by the empty set is called the* **identity substitution** *and is denoted by* ε.

Definition A.24. *Let* $\theta = \{u_1/s_1, \ldots, u_m/s_m\}$ *and* $\sigma = \{v_1/t_1, \ldots, v_n/t_n\}$ *be substitutions. Then the* **composition** $\theta\sigma$ *of* θ *and* σ *is the substitution obtained from the set*

$$\{u_1/s_1\sigma, \ldots, u_m/s_m\sigma, v_1/t_1, \ldots, v_n/t_n\}$$

by deleting any binding $u_i/s_i\sigma$ *for which* $u_i = s_i\sigma$ *and deleting any binding* v_i/t_i *for which* $v_i \in \{u_1, \ldots, u_m\}$.

Example

Consider the expression $E = Q(f(g(x, a), f(y), z)$.
Let $\theta_1 = \{x/a, y/f(y), x_1/z\}$ and $\theta_2 = \{y/a, z/c\}$.
Then, $E\theta_1\theta_2 = Q(f(g(a, a), f(f(y)), z)\theta 2 = Q(f(g(a, a), f(f(a)), c)$.

Proposition A.25. *Let* θ, σ *and* γ *be substitutions. Then*

a) $\theta\varepsilon = \varepsilon\theta = \theta$.
b) $(E\theta)\sigma = E(\theta\sigma)$.
c) $(\theta\sigma)\gamma = \theta(\sigma\gamma)$.

Definition A.26. *Let* E *and* F *be expressions. We say* E *and* F *are* **variants** *if there exist substitutions* θ *and* σ *such that* $E = F\theta$ *and* $F = E\sigma$. *We also say* E *is a variant of* F *or* F *is a variant of* E.

The intuition behind the notion of *variants* is that two expressions are semantically equivalent but syntactically different.

Example

$Q(f(g(x, a), f(y), z)$ and $Q(f(g(z, a), f(x), y)$ are variants of each other.
Opposed to that are $P(x, x)$ and $P(x, y)$ <u>not</u> variants of each other.

Definition A.27. *Let* E *be an expression and* V *be the set of variables occurring in* E. *A* **renaming substitution** *for* E *is a variable-pure substitution* $\{x_1/y_1, \ldots, x_n/y_n\}$ *such that* $\{x_1, \ldots, x_n\} \subseteq V$, $\{y_1, \ldots, y_n\}$ *are all distinct variables and* $(V \setminus \{x_1, \ldots, x_n\}) \cap \{y_1, \ldots, y_n\} = \emptyset$.

Proposition A.28. *Let* E *and* F *be expressions which are variants. Then there exist substitutions* θ *and* σ *such that* $E = F\theta$ *and* $F = E\sigma$, *where* σ *is a renaming substitution for* F *and* σ *a renaming substitution for* E.

Definition A.29. *Let* S *be a finite set of simple expressions. A substitution* θ *is called* **unifier** *for* S *if* $S\theta$ *is a singleton. A unifier* θ *for* S *is called a* **most general unifier** *(mgu) for* S *if, for each unifier* σ *of* S, *there exists a substitution* γ *such that* $\sigma = \theta\gamma$.

Example

Consider the finite set of simple expressions $S = \{P(a, f(x)), P(y, z)\}$ and the substitution $\theta_1 = \{x/a, y/a, z/a\}$. Applying θ_1 to S results in $S\theta = \{P(a, f(a)), P(a, a)\}$.

However, the substitution $\theta_2 = \{x/f(a), y/a, z/f(f(a))\}$ is a unifier since $S\theta = \{P(a, f(f(a)))\}$, i.e. applying the substitution of θ_2 results in two times the same syntactical expression. Hence the resulting set of expressions contains only a single element, i.e. the resulting set is a singleton. Is θ_2 a most general unifier?

Consider the substitution $\sigma = \{y/a, z/f(x)\}$. $S\sigma = \{P(a, f(x_1))\}$; hence σ is a unifier. However, there exists no substitution γ such that $\sigma = \theta_2\gamma$. This is easily seen, because only *variables* can be substituted and after applying θ_2 there are no variables left for being substituted. However, there is a substitution $\delta = \{x/f(a)\}$ such that $\theta_2 = \sigma\delta$. Moreover, σ is in fact the most general unifier for S.

Definition A.30. *Let S be a finite set of simple expressions. The* **disagreement set** *of S is defined as follows. Locate the leftmost symbol position at which not all expressions in S have the same symbol and extract from each expression in S the subexpression beginning at that symbol position. The set of all such subexpressions is the disagreement set.*

We are interested in finding pairs of matching literals in two different clauses. For simplicity, let a clause be described just as a set of l;literals of whose disjunction it is made of. For example, a clause $C = (L_1 \vee (l_2 \vee L_3))$ is described by $C = \{L_1, L_2, L_3\}$.

Definition A.31. *Two clauses $C_1 = (L_{11}\vee, ..., \vee L_{1n})$, $C_2 = (L_{21}\vee, ..., \vee L_{2n})$ contain a* **pair of matching literals** *if and only if there exists a literal $L_1 \in C_1$ and a literal $L_2 \in C_2$ such that either $L_1 = \neg L_2$ or $L_2 = \neg L_1$.*

If the pair of matching literals can be unified, a resolution step can be performed which creates another clause $C_3 = (C_1 \cup C_2) \setminus \{L_1, L_2\}$. That is, the resolution step creates a new clause which contains all literals of the two clauses C_1 and C_2 except the two matching literals.

A.3.2 The Unification Algorithm

The unification algorithm in Figure A.2 finds the most general unifier for any set of expressions, if a unifier exists. In fact, the following theorem can be stated:

Theorem A.32. The Unification Theorem *(See e.g. Lloyd (1987))*

   Let S be a finite set of simple expressions. If S is unifiable, then the unification algorithm terminates with the most general unifier for S. Otherwise, the unification algorithm terminates and reports this fact.

1. Put $k = 0$ and $\sigma_0 = \varepsilon$.
2. If $S\sigma_k$ is a singleton, then stop; σ_k is an mgu of S. Otherwise, find the disagreement set D_k of $S\sigma_k$.
3. If there exist v and t in D_k such that v is a variable that does not occur in t, then put $\sigma_{k+1} = \sigma_k\{v/t\}$, increment k and goto step 2. Otherwise, stop; S is not unifiable.

Figure A.2. The unification algorithm

Examples

Let $S = \{P(a, f(a, y)), P(x, f(a, g(c)))\}$. $\sigma_0 = \varepsilon$, thus $S\sigma_0 = S$.
Step 2: $D_0 = \{a, x\}$.
According to step 3: $\sigma_1 = \{x/a\}$.
Step 2: $S\sigma_1 = \{P(a, f(a, y)), P(a, f(a, g(c)))\}$ is not a singleton. Thus, $D_1 = \{y, g(c)\}$.
According to step 3: $\sigma_2 = \sigma_1\{y/g(c)\} = \{x/a, y/g(c)\}$.
Step 2: $S\sigma_2 = \{P(a, f(a, g(c))), P(a, f(a, g(c)))\}$ is a singleton, hence $\sigma_2 = \{x/a, y/g(c)\}$ is the *most general unifier* (mgu) of S.

As second example, consider $S = \{Q(a), Q(g(y))\}$. The disagreement set $D_0 = \{a, g(y)\}$ contains no *variable*. Since only variables are allowed to be substituted by other terms there is no unifier to unify the disagreement set and therefore there is no unifier for S.

A.3.3 The Resolution Process

The process of detecting a contradiction in a set of clauses S by resolution works as follows:

1. Find a pair of clauses C_1 and C_2 which contain matching literals that can be unified. Let θ be the mgu of this pair of literals L_1 and L_2.
   Form the new clause $C_n = ((C_1 \cup C_2) \setminus \{L_1, L_2\})\theta$ and add it to S.
   If $C_n = \square$ (the empty clause), then stop and report a contradiction.
2. Goto step 1.

Definition A.33. *A **resolution derivation** from a set of clauses C is a sequence of derivation steps applied to C and the emerging resolvents. That is, let R_i denote the ith resolvent resolution step. Then, R_i is a resolvent obtained from two clauses in $C \cup \{R_1, ..., R_{i-1}\}$.*

Definition A.34. *A **refutation** of a set of clauses C is a finite derivation $\{R_1, ..., R_n\}$ from C which has the empty clause $\square$ as the last resolvent. If $R_n = \square$, we say the refutation has **length** n.*

Theorem A.35. Completeness of Resolution *(See e.g. Lloyd (1987).) If a set C of clauses is unsatisfiable, then there is a resolution derivation of the empty clause $\square$ from C of finite length. I.e. there is a refutation of C.*

More details on the resolution proof procedure can be found in Lloyd (1987).

B. Technical Details and Proofs for Chapter 13

The headings in this part of the appendix correspond to the headings of chapter 13.

B.1 Limitations of Functions Computable by Neural Networks

The context of the following theorem is found in section 13.2.

Theorem 13.3. *Let N be an arbitrary static discrete neural network. Then, N's output behaviour must be in accordance with a binary sequence s of a Kolmogorov complexity $K(s) \leq comp(N) + \text{const}$ for a small constant* const.

Proof: We prove the Theorem by contradiction. Assume there is a neural network N whose output behaviour is in accordance with a binary sequence s of Kolmogorov complexity $K(s) > comp(N) + \text{const}$. Then, there is a program p for a universal Turing machine U of length $comp(N) + \text{const} = K(descr(N)) + \text{const}$, which computes the same string s. The program p contains mainly a subroutine p' of length $comp(N)$ which prints the network description, $descr(N)$ on the working tape of U. Subsequently, another subroutine p'' prints the binary numbers from '0' up to '$2^i - 1$' on the working tape and calls for each number another subroutine p'''. p''' is a neural network simulator which simulates N based on N's description on the working tape. p''' prints the output signal of N on the output tape. Hence, p prints s on the output tape. But this is a contradiction, since by the definition of Kolmogorov complexity there exists **no** program of length less than $K(s)$ which outputs exactly s. Thus, the Theorem holds.

$\square$

B.1.1 Neural Networks and Their Learning Capabilities

The following considers *learning* with the objective of correctly classifying a set of objects. That is, the formal setting, as given in section 4.2.3 can be used. Thus, we consider a set of objects $X_i = \{0,1\}^i$ as being a set of binary vectors of a certain length i. The classification task is assumed to be binary, i.e. for object in X_i belongs either to class '0' or '1'. A classification is given by a concept c which is understood as a subset of X_i. c classifies all objects as *positive* ('1'), which belong to c and all remaining objects in X_i as *negative* ('0'). An initially unknown *target concept* c_t classifies all objects in X_i correctly. The learning system tries to find this particular c_t.

In neural networks, this is achieved by acquiring a representation of the target concept somewhere in the network. The acquisition may happen for example by adjusting certain threshold values for each node of the network. The representation of a concept is either local, within a single node, or distributed, i.e. a larger part of the network is involved in storing the concept (Hinton, McClelland, & Rumelhart, 1986). In the distributed variant it is usually hard to get a clear picture of what is really going on in the network while it is learning.

For illustration, in pattern classification X_i may be the set of all possible pixel matrices. A concept c may be the set of all pixel matrices representing a straight line of a certain orientation. C may be the set of all possible concepts c representing straight lines of arbitrary orientation.

For any learning system L, whether a network or not, there is exactly one concept class $C \subseteq 2^{X_i}$ as follows: For all $c \in C$ there is some appropriate input to L such that L will eventually learn c. On the other hand, L will never learn to classify objects according to a concept $c \notin C$. Then, we say C **is the concept class underlying** L. C may also be called the *a priori* knowledge of L. (See Figure B.1 for illustration.) The *a priori* knowledge enables L to exclude all subsets of X_i not contained in C without any empirical data.

Sets of objects used for learning in neural networks or in machine learning are usually rather large. For example, assume the objects to classify are described by 30 boolean attributes. Then X_{30} contains all possible attribute-value combinations over 30 attributes. That means $|X_{30}| = 2^{30} > 1\,000\,000\,000$.

Let n be the number of objects in X_i. Then there are 2^n subsets, or concepts of X_i. There are 2^{2^n} different concept classes on X_i since there exist 2^{2^n} different sets of subsets of X_i. Thus, to encode an arbitrary concept class on X_i, we need at least a description of $\log_2 2^{2^n} = 2^n$ bits. Since $n = 2^i$, this encoding length is astronomically, even for small i. For example, looking at binary input vectors of length 10, most concept classes on X_{10} have a Kolmogorov complexity of $2^{2^{10}} = 2^{1024} \approx 10^{350}$.

Of course, in most practical cases learning networks are of much lower complexity. That implies, the concept classes underlying such networks have to be rather regularly structured in a certain sense.[1]

Definition B.1. *Let each object in X be denoted by a binary number from '0' up to $|X| - 1$. Let $c \subseteq X$ be an arbitrary concept. Let $s(c)$ be a binary string of length $|X|$. To each position of the string $s(c)$ there is a correspondingly*

---

[1] 'Regularly structured' with respect to the notion of Kolmogorov complexity. That is, in the sense that all concepts in C can be enumerated by a short program.

Let be $X = \{1, 2, 3, 4, 5, 6, 7, 8, 9\}$,
$c_1 = \{1, 4, 8, 9\}$,
$c_2 = \{1, 4, 6, 7\}$,
$c_3 = \{1, 3, 5, 8, 9\}$,
$c_4 = \{2, 4, 8, 9\}$ and finally

$C = \{c_1, c_2, c_3, c_4\}$.

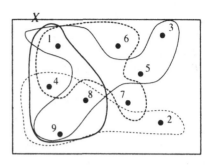

The *a priori* knowledge in this case is:
(1) C contains not all possible subsets of X, but only four concepts.
(2) These four concepts are in particular c_1, c_2, c_3 and c_4.

Figure B.1. An example for a concept class and the implied *a priori* knowledge.

numbered object in X for which a '1' in $s(c)$ indicates $x \in c$ while a '0' indicates $x \notin c$ respectively. Then **the string $s(c)$ is called the representation of the concept c.**

In the example of Figure B.1 there are nine objects in X. According to definition B.1 we obtain: $s(c_1) =$ '100100011', $s(c_2) =$ '100101100', $s(c_3) =$ '101010011' and $s(c_4) =$ '010100011'.

Concept classes containing complex concepts. In this way, for each concept $c \in C$ we can speak of its Kolmogorov complexity, $K(s(c))$. Based on that, we define the complexity of a concept class C with respect to the task of learning a concept from C, as opposed to C's description, by the complexity of the most complex concept in C. That is,

Definition B.2. *The complexity $K_{max}(C)$ of a concept class C is defined as*

$$K_{max}(C) = \max_{c \in C} K(s(c))$$

The following considers the learning abilities of neural networks with respect to the definitions above. It may be interesting to note again that for most of the existing concept classes C, $K_{max}(C) \approx |X|$ holds. However, in practice one may be rather interested in relatively simple concepts. That means, that the complexity of concept classes used in practice may be substantially lower.

A lower bound on examples needed for PAC-learning complex concepts. For learning from examples there may be different ways the examples will be chosen. Here, we adopt the notion of probably approximately correctly PAC-learning as introduced by Valiant (1984b) in its slightly modified version of Ehrenfeucht, Haussler, Kearns, and Valiant (1989).

We assume that there is an arbitrary unknown but fixed probability distribution P on X. Each $x \in X$ appears with a fixed probability given by P. Based on this probability distribution, we define the error of a concept as follows:

Definition B.3. *Let X be a set of objects and P a probability distribution on X. Let $c_t \subseteq X$ be the target concept, i.e. all objects $x \in c_t$ belong to class 1 and all objects $x \in X \setminus c_t$ belong to class 0. Let $c \subseteq X$ be some concept.*

Then, the error of c (with respect to the target concept c_t is given by

$$error(c) = \sum_{x \in (c \setminus c_t) \cup (c_t \setminus c)} P(x).$$

That is, $error(c)$ is the probability of finding an object in a random drawing that will be misclassified by c.

During the learning phase the objects in X appear along with an indication whether or not they belong to the target concept. After the learning phase the system receives objects according to P which are to be classified by the system. The goal is to minimise the error in the system's classification of objects after the learning phase. Furthermore, a small classification error should be achieved with high probability. Again, *classification error* is measured as the probability to misclassify an object which is randomly drawn according to the fixed probability distribution P.

Definition B.4. *Let C be a class of concepts over a set of objects X. P is the probability distribution on X and c_t denotes the target concept according to which all presented examples are classified. We say algorithm L probably approximately correctly learns (PAC-learns) C if and only if*

$$(\forall c_t \in C)(\forall P)(\forall \varepsilon > 0)(\forall \delta > 0)$$

with probability of at least $1 - \delta$ algorithm L will classify an object x randomly chosen according to P with error of at most ε.

In other words, the examples given are not chosen to be particularly helpful for the learning algorithm being used. The examples are rather randomly chosen according to their natural relative frequency of occurrence. For this conception of successful learning, we can state the following lower bound on the number of required examples:

Now we can state our first Theorem on learning capabilities in neural networks.

Theorem B.5. *Let N be a neural network and $comp(N)$ its complexity according to definition 13.1. Let C be the concept class underlying N. If $K_{max}(C) \geq comp(N) + \text{const}$ then there are at least*

$$2^{K_{max}(C) - comp(N) - \text{const}}$$

concepts in C, where const *is a small constant integer.*

Proof: $K_{max}(C)$ is the number of bits necessary for any program running on a universal Turing machine U for constructing a binary-string representation $s(c)$

of the most complex concept c in C. The learning network N learns to classify the presented objects $x \in X$ consistent with c. Let us consider a program p which uses a program p' as a subroutine, where $|p'| = comp(N)$ such that p' prints the description of N on the working tape of U. A second subroutine p'' simulates the neural network N described on the working tape. Subsequently, after N's learning phase a third subroutine p''' of p is started which uses the network simulator in the following way:

p''' produces binary numbers starting with zero up to the binary string representing $|X| - 1$ and gives each number as input to p''. p''' writes the binary output value of p'', i.e. the learned classification, on the output tape. Thus, p''' produces the binary representation $s(c)$ of the concept c learned by the network N which in turn is simulated by p''. The relation $|p|=comp(N)+$const holds for a small integer 'const', where 'const' only depends on U. Since $|p|$ is less or equal to $K_{max}(C)$, p is not of a sufficient size in order to output $s(c)$. In particular, at least there are $d = K_{max}(C) - |p|$ additional bits necessary in order to construct $s(c)$. These d further bits have to be provided by the interaction with the environment of p during N's learning phase. Assume in contradiction to the Theorem that $|C| < 2^{K_{max}(C)-|p|-1}$. Suppose, the concepts in C are arbitrarily ordered. Then for optimal learning conditions (optimal with respect to the coding length of information) $d - 1$ bits to transmit to p would suffice (e.g. the binary encoded ordering number of the target concept in C). But the $d - 1$ bits of information transmitted to p cannot enable p to output $s(c)$. This is due to the fact that the shortest program for outputting $s(c)$ is of length $|p| + d$ bits. (Instead of reading the $d - 1$ bits from the input tape, p could read a part of its own description, but this part of its description has to be at least of length d.) Hence, from this contradiction follows the Theorem.

$\square$

Theorem B.5 shows that attempts to design learning networks which are capable of learning complex concepts involve a dilemma. One either has to construct an approximately equally complex network, or one has to provide the network with a huge amount of information during its learning phase. In other words, this result shows that if a rather regular network N is able to learn complex concepts, then C must also contain a large number of further concepts. This also implies that for implementing a small concept class C containing a few complex concepts one has to put a respective amount of information into the network, i.e. N has to be complex in the sense of definition 13.1. The implications of that for the task of learning are illuminated in more depth in the following Theorem.

Theorem B.6. *Let N be a neural network and let C be the concept class underlying N. Let be $0 < \varepsilon \le \frac{1}{4}$; $0 < \delta \le \frac{1}{100}$. If $K_{max}(C) \ge comp(N) + const$ then for pac-learning a target concept $c \in C$ the network N requires at least*

$$\max[\frac{K_{max}(C) - comp(N) - \text{const}}{32\varepsilon \, \log_2 |X|}, \frac{1 - \varepsilon}{\varepsilon} \ln \frac{1}{\delta}]$$

examples randomly chosen according to P. The small constant const *only depends on the type of the universal Turing machine U for determining comp(N).*

Proof: For the proof we need the Vapnik-Chervonenkis Dimension of sets of subsets, i.e. of concept classes, well known in computational learning theory. The following recalls the notion of the **Vapnik-Chervonenkis dimension** (Vapnik & Chervonenkis, 1971) (in short VC-dimension) as it was introduced in the context of learning theory in Blumer, Ehrenfeucht, Haussler, and Warmuth (1986).

Definition B.7. *We say a set $S \subseteq X$ is shattered by C iff $\{S \cap c | c \in C\} = 2^S$. The Vapnik-Chervonenkis dimension of C, $VCdim(C)$ is the cardinality of the greatest set $S \subseteq X$ shattered by C, i.e.*

$$VCdim(C) = \max_{S \in \{S | S \subseteq X \wedge \{S \cap c | c \in C\} = 2^S\}} |S|$$

Lemma B.8. *Any concept class C of k concepts on a set X of size n has a $VCdim(C)$ of at least $\log_n k = \frac{\log_2 k}{\log_2 n}$ for $n > 3$; $\log_n k > 3$.*

Proof: Let be $d = \log_n k$. A set of size n has $\binom{n}{d}$ different subsets of size d. For any two different concepts $c_1, c_2 \in C$ on X there is at least one subset S of X of size d such that $(S \cap c_1) \neq (S \cap c_2)$. Furthermore, for each subset $S \subset X$ of size d the set $\{S \cap c | c \in C\}$ must be of size less than 2^d for S not being shattered by C. Thus, in C there must be less than $2^d \binom{n}{d}$ different concepts. That means,

$$|C| < 2^d \frac{n!}{(n - d)! \, d!} = \frac{2^d}{d!} \frac{n!}{(n - d)!} \leq \frac{n!}{(n - d)!} \leq n^d$$

But this is a contradiction to $d = \log_n |C|$.

□

For the proof of Theorem B.6 we still need the following Theorem B.9, which has been proved by Ehrenfeucht et al. (1989). The Theorem states the relationship between the Vapnik-Chervonenkis dimension of a concept class C and the minimal number of necessary examples for *pac*-learning.

Theorem B.9. *(Ehrenfeucht et al., 1989)*
Let be $VCdim(C) \geq 2$; $0 < \varepsilon \leq \frac{1}{4}$; $0 < \delta \leq \frac{1}{100}$. Any learning algorithm L requires at least

$$\max[\frac{VCdim(C) - 1}{32\varepsilon}, \frac{1-\varepsilon}{\varepsilon} \ln \frac{1}{\delta}]$$

examples for learning probably approximately correctly with parameters ε and δ as defined in definition B.4 for an arbitrary probability distribution P on X.

For a proof of Theorem B.9 (see Ehrenfeucht et al. (1989)). Theorem B.6 follows from Theorem B.5, Lemma B.8 and Theorem B.9 together.

B.1.2 On Modelling Biological Neuronal Functionalities

Setting for asymptotic considerations. The following discusses in networks that compute complex functions. Therefore, a sequence of networks will be considered which compute functions of steadily increasing complexity. This allows asymptotic considerations of the role of the topology versus the functionality of the various types of neurons in a network.

Consider an infinite sequence $N_\infty = \{N_1, N_2, \ldots\}$ of discrete networks constructed from a fixed set of types of computing units U_{typ}. Each network N_j has j input signals. Assume further that for all j the output behaviour of network N_j is in accordance with the string s_j, where $|s_j| = 2^j$. Let $S_\infty = \{s_1, s_2, \ldots\}$ be the set of strings describing the output behaviour of N_∞ respectively. Furthermore, assume for all $i \in \mathbf{N}$ that $K(s_i) < K(s_{i+1})$. That is, for all i the network $N_i + 1$ computes a more complex function than the network N_i in terms of Kolmogorov complexity.

Learning Neural Networks. For asymptotic considerations of learning in neural networks, the following further assumptions are made:

Consider an infinite sequence $N_\infty = \{N_1, N_2, \ldots\}$ of discrete networks constructed from a fixed set of types of computing units U_{typ}. Each network N_i has i binary input signals. Let $C_\infty = \{C_1, C_2, \ldots\}$ be a family of concept classes such that for all i the concept class C_i is underlying the network N_i, and that $K_{max}(C_{i+1}) > K_{max}(C_i)$.

Considering the learning abilities of the networks N_∞, we can state the following Theorem on the role of particular functionalities of the involved computing units. The Theorem addresses the case that the number of required examples should be lower bounded for *pac*-learning.

Theorem B.10. *Let $C_\infty = \{C_1, C_2, ...\}$ be a family of concept classes. Let N_∞ be an infinite set of discrete networks, where for all i, the concept class C_i underlies the network N_i. Let $n(i, \varepsilon, \delta)$ be the number of examples required for pac-learning the concept class C_i with error ε and confidence $1 - \delta$ by the network N_i. Let be $\varepsilon \leq \frac{1}{4}$, $0 < \delta \leq \frac{1}{100}$.*

If there is an i_0 such that $\forall j > i_0$

$$n(j, \varepsilon, \delta) < \frac{c_0 K_{max}(C_j)}{j\varepsilon} \ln \frac{1}{\delta}$$

for some suitable constant $c_0 > 0$, then

$$\lim_{i \to \infty} \frac{\mathbf{comp}_{func}(N_i)}{\mathbf{comp}_{top}(N_i)} = 0$$

That is, if the number of required examples is always lower than $c_0 K_{max}(C_j)/j$ for $j > i_0$ for some i_0, then the limes holds. Note that $K_{max}(C_j) \geq j$ for all j.

Proof: The Theorem is proved by contradiction. Assume

$$\lim_{i \to \infty} \frac{\mathbf{comp}_{func}(N_i)}{\mathbf{comp}_{top}(N_i)} > 0. \qquad (B.1)$$

Since $comp_{func}(N_i)$ is the same constant for all i, inequality B.1 is only true, if for all , i $comp_{top}(N_i) < c_1$ for some constant $c_1 \in \mathbf{N}$. Since $K_{max}(C_i)$ is strictly growing in i, the difference $K_{max}(C_i) - comp_{all}(N_i)$ is growing infinitely in i. From Theorem B.5 it is known that this implies that $|C_i|$ grows exponentially in i. This together with Theorem B.9 completes the proof in analogy to the proof of Theorem B.6.

□

B.2 Unsupervised Learning and Self-Organising Systems

B.2.1 Preliminaries

A set of possible feature vectors X is assumed for a given learning system. Both, the objects in the training sample as well as the objects being presented later for classification are represented by feature vectors in X. Further, in order to emphasise the specific difficulty in unsupervised learning, it is assumed that there is a particular subset $Y \subseteq X$, which is normally significantly smaller than X, which covers all representations of those objects which actually occur in practice. Of course, this distinction can also be made for supervised learning. However, it emphasises the fundamental dependence of unsupervised learning on the chosen representation and on those 'gaps' in the feature space X, i.e. the set $X \setminus Y$, which will never occur in any training sample presented to the system. This is the basis for the system to find clusters among the given objects and group those together which seem more related to each other than the remaining objects. Such a grouping is based on some sort of similarity measure which the system applies. This measure may be explicitly given or it may be merely implicitly hidden somewhere in the unsupervised learning algorithm which eventually comes up with a grouping.

For the sake of simplicity, the following considerations assume binary feature representations throughout this section. Note that this can be done without loss of generality since non-binary features can easily be converted into binary features with a corresponding adjustment of the sets X and Y.

Let n be an arbitrary positive integer. The set of binary feature vectors of length n will be denoted by X_n. The subset of X_n from which the training vectors my be chosen is denoted by Y_n. Note that under the given assumptions, it is irrelevant, how the classification function being eventually learned by the self-organising system behaves on those feature vectors $X_n \setminus Y_n$, which never occur in practice. The self-organising system is expected to determine a classification of the objects in Y_n (see Figure B.2).

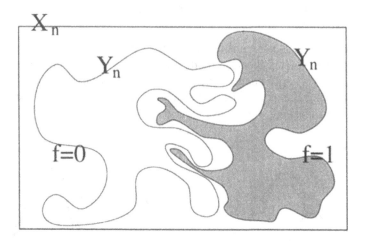

Figure B.2. The subset Y_n (both of the shaded areas) of the basic set X_n and a classification function f.

Choosing training samples and probabilistic assumptions. For giving an account of the normally somewhat arbitrary choice of training samples, the following probabilistic setting is assumed: Given a set $Y_n \subseteq X_n$ of feature vectors which may occur in practice, a fixed probability distribution P_n on X_n is assumed. Since objects are only allowed to be chosen from Y_n, $P_n(X_n \setminus Y_n)$ is obviously 0. Moreover the following conditions hold:

$$\forall x \in Y_n \; P_n(x) > 0$$

and

$$\sum_{x \in Y_n} (P_n(x)) = 1.$$

Thus, the probability distribution P_n reflects the idea of Y_n representing the set of 'naturally' appearing objects. This fixed probability distribution allows on the one hand to investigate the probability for a sample that provides sufficient information for learning. On the other hand, it will also be used as a measure of classification accuracy and approximation for the classification function being learned. This is in analogy to the setting in the well-known framework of *Probably Approximately Correct* Learning for supervised learning tasks as introduced by Valiant (1984b).[2]

The task of self-organisation. The following two steps in the activities of a self-organising system S will be distinguished in the subsequent considerations:

1. **The learning mode:** A sequence of unclassified objects is presented to the system. Based on that input, S modifies itself such that it will classify objects according to a certain classification function $f : X_n \to \{0, 1\}$.
2. **The classification mode:** The system gets as input some object $x \in X_n$. It outputs the value of the learned function $f(x)$.

In principle, a self-organising system may change its mode of operation from learning mode to classification mode and vice versa as often as desired.

Let $S[x_1, \ldots, x_i](x)$ denote the value of the function f that was formed in S after providing S exactly with the sequence $x_1, \ldots, x_i$ of unclassified examples while S is in learning mode.

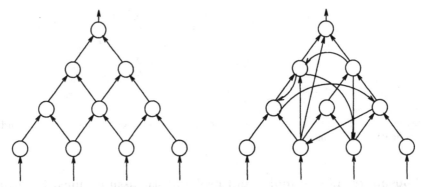

Figure B.3. The left figure shows the initial network structure of a self-organising neural network. After learning the network has reorganised its internal structure as shown in the right figure. The new network structure should compute a desired classification function f.

For the sake of completeness and reference to the popular idea of self-organising neural networks, the following definition is specific to neural network

---

[2] Valiant introduced the idea to assume a fixed probability distribution P on the set of objects X being considered for learning: Objects are chosen from X according to P to be classified by the learned function f. The error of f is thereby measured as the probability to misclassify a randomly chosen object. Similarly, for supervised learning, training examples are chosen from X according to P and are complemented by a class label indicating how a given object x is correctly classified.

style learning systems. However, the theoretical results in this section hold for any computational system, whatsoever.

Definition B.11. *A* **self-organising system** *S is a network which functionality can be completely described by the following items:*

a) *the functionality of a single neuron. Often a certain threshold function of the sum of the weighted inputs to the neuron is proposed.*

b) *the topological organisation of a complete network consisting of a large number of neurons.*

c) *The algorithm which controls the self-organisation process through learning.*

The complete system S can be described by concatenating the descriptions of all its parts. Let the description of S be denoted by descr(S).

Figure B.3 shows a simple network structure. In the following similar to section 13.1, the notion of *algorithmic information theory*, or synonymously, the notion of *Kolmogorov complexity* is used. Kolmogorov complexity will be used to shed more light on the relation between the information a self-organising system holds already before learning and the information it can possibly gain from being exposed to a set of unclassified training examples.

Measuring the complexity of emerging structures. For measuring the complexity of emerging system structures, again the notion of Kolmogorov complexity will be used. The following Theorems involving the Kolmogorov complexity of particular strings and functions are conceived to provide a general understanding of the relationships between the complexity of the self-organising system, the data, and the classification function being acquired. However, the Theorems are not supposed to provide directly applicable numbers or numerical bounds for whose application the Kolmogorov complexity of certain strings has to be determined. The purpose of the Theorems is to advance the general understanding of the occurring processes, as opposed to the numbers which, nevertheless, occur in the formulas and proofs.

Freivalds and Hoffmann (1994) used also Kolmogorov complexity in a very similar context to investigate the relation between clustering and inductive inference. In that work, the possibility of partial functions which do not compute a value for the elements in $X_n \setminus Y_n$ has also been considered. In contrast to that, in the following it is generally assumed that a self-organising system will always compute a total function on its domain of possible input values. Thus, the function f computed by a network can also be described by a respective string $s(f)$ containing the function value of f for all possible input values.

Following the notion of Kolmogorov complexity as recalled above, the complexity $comp(S)$ of the self-organising system S is therefore defined as the Kolmogorov complexity of its description. That is,

$$comp(S) = K(descr(S)).$$

Thus, $comp(S)$ measures the minimal encoding length of the system's functionality. By that, $comp(S)$ also measures, implicitly, the complexity of the similarity measure being used by the self-organising system S. The following investigates possible classifications of the subset Y_n. For the purpose of measuring the complexity of a classification of Y_n, for each possible classification function f, the class F_{f,Y_n} of classification functions will be considered, which are equivalent in their values on Y_n. That is,

$$F_{f,Y_n} = \{g | (\forall x \in Y_n) \; f(x) = g(x)\}.$$

Let $K_{Y_n}(f)$ denote the minimal Kolmogorov complexity among all classification functions in F_{f,Y_n}, i.e.

$$K_{Y_n}(f) = \min_{f' \in F_{f,Y_n}} K(s(f')).$$

Thus, $K_{Y_n}(f)$ denotes the Kolmogorov complexity of the least complex description of the classification of the subset Y_n according to f. See Figure B.4.

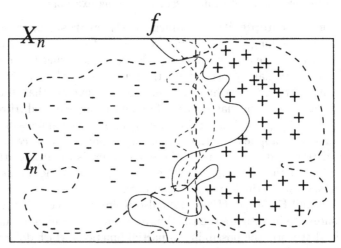

Figure B.4. For every function f on X_n, there is a family of functions F_{f,Y_n}, which all classify the subset Y_n equally to f. However, the functions differ in their values on those feature vectors, which are assumed to never occur throughout the use of the self-organising system. The value $K_{Y_n}(f)$ measures the Kolmogorov complexity of the least complex function in F_{f,Y_n}.

Using the presented definitions, the following section will provide Theorems on the limitations and capabilities of computational systems to acquire substantial amounts of algorithmic information from unclassified training examples only. Some of the proofs of the Theorems will be particularly revealing for improving the understanding of the differences between supervised and unsupervised learning. Thus, the reader is encouraged to not only studying the Theorems but also to study some of the proofs provided.

B.2.2 Computational Limitations of Self-Organisation

This subsection investigates the *complexity* of classification functions that can possibly emerge in self-organising networks.

To provide more insight into the particularities of self-organising systems initially a very strong assumption is made on the behaviour of the self-organising system. This is followed by investigations into the capabilities and limitations of successively less restricted classes of self-organising systems.

Monotonicly growing classification competence. Monotonicly classifying self-organising systems are considered first. While these systems are very restricted in their allowed behaviour, they still provide insight into the specific difficulties unsupervised learning approaches face in general.

The following requires a self-organising system S not to change its 'mind' about the classification of those objects it has a classification once made. It is assumed that S classifies each object being presented 'on the spot'. By *classifying* an object x it is meant that S computes a function value for x. That is, all objects once being presented to S are classified immediately and the function being acquired later in S has to comply with the classification being made for all presented objects at the time of their first presentation.

Definition B.12. *A* **monotonicly classifying self-organising system** S *classifies incrementally the presented objects and never changes the classification of previously classified objects. That is, S is* **monotonicly classifying,** *if*

$$(\forall k)(\forall j \leq k)\ S[y_1, \ldots, y_k](y_j) = S[y_1, \ldots, y_{k+1}](y_j).$$

Clearly, the requirement of being monotonicly classifying is very strong. Practical systems will at least have some freedom to change their mind to a certain extent. However, one will still expect a self-organising system to converge on a certain classification function after a sufficient number of examples has been presented. After convergence, it will usually be much less or even completely unacceptable to change that part of the classification function which concerns those objects which have already been presented.

At next let us define our notion of convergence as follows:

Definition B.13. *Let S be a self-organising system and F be the set of functions that can be learned by S. Then for every function $f \in F$ there is a set of k examples Y_f and an ordering $o_{Y_f} = \{y_{f,1}, y_{f,2}, \ldots, y_{f,k}\}$ of the examples in Y_f such that S will learn f upon presenting Y_f in a suitable ordering, i.e. $S[o_{Y_f}] = f$. The self-organising system S is called* **converging** *if and only if for all $f \in F$ there is a set $Y_{f,conv}$ which can be presented in any order to S*

and S will learn f. That is, for π_j being the jth ordering (permutation) of the elements of $Y_{f,conv}$, S is converging if for all $f \in F$

$$S[\pi_j(Y_{f,conv})] = f,$$

for all $j \in \{1, ..., |Y_{f,conv}|!\}$.

That is, a self-organising system S converges, if for any learnable function f, the 'triggering set of objects' can be presented in any order and S learns always the same function f. While the following Theorem considers the very restricted class of monotonicly classifying systems, it allows the derivation of a Corollary which is much more applicable to practically interesting learning systems.

Theorem B.14. *Assume an arbitrary but fixed $Y_n \subseteq X_n$ and a fixed probability distribution P_n on Y_n for arbitrary n. Then, for any converging and monotonicly classifying self-organising system S the following holds: Let f_t be the target function, S will eventually learn after being provided with the set Y_n in an arbitrary order. Then the Kolmogorov complexity of f_t, or another function $f' \in F_{f_t,Y_n}$ which is equivalent to f_t on Y_n, is upper bounded as follows:*

$$K_{Y_n}(f_t) \leq comp(S) + n.$$

Proof: The Theorem is proved by contradiction. Assume S determines a classification function f_t with $K_{Y_n}(f_t) > comp(S) + n$. ($n$ is the amount of information necessary for describing a single object of X_n.) Then, there must be an object $y_1 \in Y_n$ as follows. Provide y_1 as the first element of a 'randomly' drawn sequence to S. Further, there must be another object $y_2 \in Y_n$, which cannot be classified according to f_t. This is since the amount of information provided so far ($comp(S) + n$) does not suffice for determining the function f_t. Since $K_{Y_n}(f_t)$ is by definition the smallest amount of information in order to compute all values of f_t on Y_n, there must be a $y_2 \in Y_n$ for which $f_t(y_2)$ differs from $S[y_1](y_2)$ for at least one appropriate y_1.

□

While the definition of *monotonicly classifying* is obviously quite rigid for a system that has not seen many objects at all, it appears to be a more realistic assumption for a system that has already seen a reasonable number of objects and will not greatly change its 'conception of the world' after seeing some further objects.

Corollary B.15. *Assume an arbitrary but fixed $Y_n \subseteq X_n$ and a fixed probability distribution P_n on Y_n for arbitrary n. Then, Let S be a converging self-organising system to which a sample of k randomly drawn examples are presented (in some fixed but arbitrary order). Upon these k examples S determines a classification function f_k. Let the S' denote the self-organising system*

S after being presented these k examples. If S' behaves monotonicly classifying after that, then the Kolmogorov complexity $K_{Y_n}(f_t)$ is upper bounded as follows:

$$K_{Y_n}(f_t) \leq comp(S) + i(k+1)n \leq comp(S') + n \leq K_{Y_n}(f_k) + n.$$

Proof: The proof is analogously to the proof of Theorem B.14, except that the self-organising system S in the proof of Theorem B.14 is to be replaced by the self-organising system S' of the Corollary.

□

In the extreme case, the self-organising system S stores all presented examples as they are, i.e. the complexity of S' may by up to $comp(S) + kn$ for k presented examples. However, in general it is rather assumed that the self-organising system incorporates the given examples in some 'processed' form, i.e. that S transforms into a new system S' where the complexity of S' is rather strongly related to the complexity of the classification function S' is computing. Then, however, a monotonicly classifying behaviour would limit the complexity of the function target function much stronger.

One may argue, in particular, that the property of being *monotonicly classifying* in the sense of Theorem B.14, i.e. assuming that the learning system has not seen any training data so far, is too restricted to apply to practically useful self-organising systems. However, assuming that in practice, self-organising learning systems are not monotonicly classifying has an important implication: It means essentially that for classifying the initially presented examples properly, the unsupervised learning system relies crucially on the presentation of further, more informative examples. The following subsection addresses a more realistic setting which reflects exactly the critical fact, that the classification of some objects cannot properly be determined unless further examples are presented.

Approximating a classification function. In the following, more realistic and more general self-organising learning systems are investigated. Since monotonicly classifying systems are so limited, it is natural to ask for the conditions under which a general self-organising system[3] can reliably acquire a given level of correct classification accuracy. That is, given the fact that more powerful learning systems have to rely on information, which is provided by further training examples in order to correctly classify an initial set of training examples, it is not obvious how to ensure that exactly those informative examples are actually presented to the learner.

If it is not guaranteed with certainty that such further informative examples are presented to the system, one will be interested in investigating the capabilities of self-organising systems to at least approximate the correct classification

---

[3] That is, a self-organising system which may change 'its mind' as often as it seems suitable.

with a high probability. Therefore, it follows a definition of the notion of *approximation* as it seems appropriate in the given context in order to allow the assertion of the following Theorems.

The following definition measures the error ε of a function f' approximating a target function f_t by equating ε with the probability to misclassify an object $x \in Y_n$ which is randomly drawn according to the fixed probability distribution P_n.

Definition B.16. *Let n be an arbitrary positive integer. Assume a $Y_n \subseteq X_n$ and a fixed probability distribution P_n on Y_n. Then, it is said a function f ε-approximates a target function f_t, if*

$$\sum_{x \in \{x | x \in Y_n \wedge (f(x) \neq f_t(x))\}} P_n(x) \leq \varepsilon$$

This definition of approximation is comparable to the definition of approximation and *error* in the Probably Approximately Correct-learning model (the PAC model) which is a popular framework for theoretical investigations of supervised learning (see Valiant (1984b) or Natarajan (1991)). This notion of approximation in the PAC model allows to ensure convergence of a supervised learner since every object, which has a significant probability to occur for classification, has the equal probability to occur in the training sample. That is, in supervised learning, the random character of the training sample is directly reflected in the concept of approximation error.

This, however, is very different in the case of unsupervised learning as the following Theorem shows by providing a strong upper bounds of the complexity of classification functions, which can be ε-approximated with a reasonable probability of success.

Theorem B.17. *For all $0 < \varepsilon < \frac{1}{2}$ and $0 < \delta < 1$, for an arbitrary self-organising system S, an arbitrary but fixed sample size s and a target classification function f_t with a complexity*

$$K_{Y_n}(f_t) > comp(S) + 2n + const,$$

the following holds: If providing S with a sample of size s randomly drawn according to an arbitrary probability distribution P_n on X_n, the emerging classification function f in S will with probability of at least δ be no ε-approximation of f_t.

Proof: A suitable probability distribution P_n on Y_n for which the Theorem holds can be constructed as follows: First of all, note that $|Y_n| > 2$. Moreover, the following proposition holds:

Proposition B.18. *Given the conditions hold which are stated in the Theorem B.17 above, then there are two objects $y_1, y_2 \in Y_n$, a positive integer m, and a subset $Z = \{z_1, \ldots, z_m\} \subseteq (Y_n \setminus \{y_1, y_2\})$ with the following property:*

$$S[y_1, y_2](y_1) \neq S[y_1, y_2, z_1, \ldots, z_m](y_1)$$

Proof: Assume, the proposition is false. Then, there exists a function f'_t which is equivalent to f_t on the set Y_n with $K_{Y_n}(f_t) \leq comp(S) + 2n + const$. Hence, a contradiction.

$\square$

Proposition B.18 states that if the complexity of the target classification function is greater than the provided bound in the Theorem, there exist two examples y_1 and y_2 in Y_n, such that the self-organising system must classify at least one of them non-monotonicly if y_1 and $_y2$ are presented as the two first examples to the system. That is, after a set of further examples (the examples $z_1, \ldots, z_m$) is provided, the self-organising system must change its classification of the initial two examples in order to allow the formation of a complex classification function! See Figure B.5.

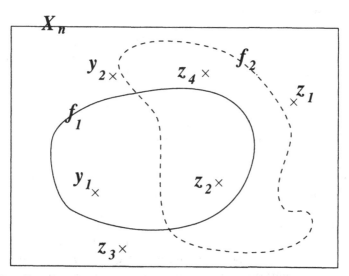

Figure B.5. Function f_1 is determined by S after seeing only the two examples y_1 and y_2. After the self-organising system S has seen $z_1, \ldots, z_4$, it changes its classification function from f_1 to f_2.

That is, the Proposition shows that there is an element $y_1 \in Y_n$, whose classification changes, when S gets the elements of the set Z as input. This fact is due to the complexity of f_t. That is, $2n$ is the amount of information for describing y_1 and y_2. Let P_n be given by $P_n(y_1) = P_n(y_2) = \frac{1-\gamma}{2}$ and $\forall i \in \{1, \ldots, m\}$ let $P_n(z_i) = \frac{\gamma}{m}$ for some $0 < \gamma < 1$. γ can be chosen arbitrarily close to 0. Hence, for all δ there is an appropriate γ as follows: The probability that the complete set Z occurs in a sample of size s randomly drawn according to P_n is less than $1 - \delta$. That is, y_1 will be misclassified with probability greater than $1 - \delta$, since it will be classified according to $S[y_1, y_2]$.

□

Theorem B.17 indicates that the complexity of 'meaningful' classification functions, which can emerge based on unclassified examples only is rather limited. It is remarkable as well as unusual that the Theorem holds for any choice of the allowed classification error ε and any choice of the confidence level δ within the specified range, although neither of the two variables, nor the sample size occurs in the complexity bound given in the Theorem! This again is very different to the typical Theorems proved in Valiant's framework for supervised PAC-learning.

The reason for the validity of Theorem B.17 is the fact that the probability of misclassifying a given object y cannot directly be linked to the probability that enough information for determining the correct classification of y is provided in a random sample of a given size.

One may argue that this is an unfair consideration that an example whose classification will change after a number of further examples have been seen by the learning system may have a high probability, while the probability that the required further examples occur may be very low. However, while this consideration is certainly not very supportive for unsupervised learning, it illustrates one of the fundamental issues in unsupervised learning: If only a large number of examples considered as a whole allows to acquire useful classifications, how can we ensure that enough sufficiently informative examples are actually provided?

On the minimal sample size. The following Theorem gives a minimal number of randomly drawn examples necessary in order to allow the emergence of a complex and desired structure in a self-organising system. This is a best case consideration in both, the possible probability distribution and in the assumed information provided by the particular encoding of the examples.

The limitations on a possible information gain of m bits can directly be translated into limitations on the complexity of an emerging function in S, which would be bound to the complexity of S plus m bits, i.e. the Kolmogorov complexity of the function f being computed by S upon seeing the examples is limited by $comp(S) + m$.

Theorem B.19. *Let n be a positive integer, $X_n = \{0,1\}^n$ and Y_n be an arbitrary subset of X_n. Let S be an arbitrary self-organising system. Given a uniform probability distribution P_n on $Y_n \subseteq X_n$. Let be $m > n^2$. Then, for all δ, $0 \geq \delta \leq \frac{1}{2}$, for S to achieve an information gain of m bits with probability of at least $1 - \delta$ from a sample randomly drawn according to P_n requires a sample size of at least*

$$(\frac{m}{n} + \frac{1}{2}\log_2 \frac{m}{n})\frac{9}{10}\log \frac{1}{\delta}.$$

Proof: The idea of the proof is to show that there are at least k different objects which need to be presented in order to single out the particular target function f_t which is associated to the actually given Y_n. As a second step, it is shown that to obtain those k objects in a random sample from a uniform distribution over Y_n implies the lower bound on the sample size given in the Theorem.

Addressing the first point, note that any self-organising system S that determines a certain classification function f upon being provided with a sample of objects from X_n obviously implements a certain mapping from subsets of X_n to the set of classification functions it can possibly learn.

Let F denote the class of functions the self-organising system S can possibly learn (if appropriate data is provided). In other words, we may assign to each possible function $f \in F$ a certain subset $Y_{n,f} \subseteq X_n$ upon whose presentation as a sample, S determines exactly f. In general, it can be assumed that even a suitable subset of $Y_{n,f}$ will suffice to let S unambiguously determine f. That is, a subset $Z \subset Y_{n,f}$ is suitable if there is no function $f' \in F$ such that Z is also a subset of $Y_{n,f'}$.

Note that these set theoretic considerations already imply that S ignores the particular order in which a sample may be successively presented to the self-organising system. Here, we are only concerned with the function, which S determines eventually, as opposed to the functions it may determine through the incremental intake of examples. That is, each possible function f which may be the outcome of the self-organisation process is related to a certain set $Y_{n,f}$ as follows: Given a sample which is a (sufficient) subset of $Y_{n,f}$, the self-organising system S will classify objects according to f.

However, the following proposition is proved first, which establishes a minimum number of examples being necessary to let S determine unambiguously a particular function $f \in F$. That is, we are considering, how many examples are at least needed, to rule out all but one possible set $Y_{n,f}$ as the set which is underlying the presented sample. (Remember that the actual Y_n is unknown to S. S must rather hypothesise that any $Y_{n,f}$ might underlie the data as long as no contradicting examples are provided.)

Proposition B.20. *Let n and m be any positive integer, where $m \leq 2^n$. Given a set X_n of 2^n elements and a set Z of 2^{mn} subsets of X_n, i.e. $Z \subseteq 2^{X_n}$ and $|Z| = 2^{mn}$. Set $k = \frac{m}{n} + \frac{1}{2}\log_2 \frac{m}{n}$. Then, there exists a set $z_0 \in Z$ with at least k elements as follows: There are subsets $z_1, ..., z_k \in Z$ which 'partially overlap' with z_0 such that $(z_i \setminus (\bigcup_{j \neq i} z_j) \cap z_0) \neq \emptyset$ for all $i, j \in \{1, ..., k\}$. In other words, considering only the 'overlap' of the sets $z_1, ..., z_k$ with z_0, none of the sets $z_1, ..., z_k$ are completely covered by the union of all the remaining sets. That is, each set z_i has its individual elements in its intersection with z_0. (See Figure B.6.)*

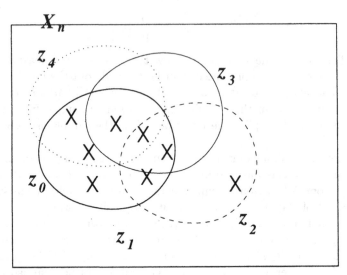

Figure B.6. Consider the sets $z_0, z_1, ..., z_j$. Assume a sample s of objects is drawn from z_0. However, for a self-organising system in order to identify unambiguously from which of the sets $z_0, z_1, ..., z_j$ the sample s is drawn, s has to contain for each of the sets $z_i \in \{z_1, ..., z_j\}$ at least one object x_i which is not contained in z_i. The above Proposition considers $|X_n|$ being 2^n and a set of 2^{kn} subsets of X_n. Upon that, it states how many 'overlapping' subsets $z_1, ..., z_j$ there may be.

Proof: (By contradiction) Let us first denote the set of individual elements of z_i in the intersection with z_0 by c_i. That is, $c_i = (z_0 \cap z_i) \setminus (\bigcup_{j \neq i} z_j)$. for all $i, j \in \{1, ..., k\}$.

Assume there were no more than $k-1$ subsets $z_1, ..., z_{k-1}$ with the properties as stated in the proposition above. Consider a sample set s' containing exactly one of the individual elements in c_i of each set $z_i \in \{z_1, ..., z_{k-1}\}$ in their intersection with z_0. Then, the only set in Z which would cover the complete sample s' were z_0. In other words, a set of $k-1$ examples would suffice to single out the set z_0 as the only one in Z which is 'consistent' with the sample. (Since no class labels are given with examples, 'consistent' means here to contain the complete sample.) This is since for any other set $z \in Z$ an element is given which is not contained in z. Since every example is described by not more than n bits, the amount of $n(k-1)$ bits of information would suffice to identify any set in Z. This, however, allows for not more than $2^{n(k-1)}$ different combinations. Further, since the order of the examples given is ignored, a set of $k-1$ objects can only provide the information of

$$\log_2 \frac{2^{n(k-1)}}{(k-1)!} = n(k-1) - \log_2((k-1)!) \leq n(k-1) - \log_2(k^{\frac{k-1}{2}})$$

For right-hand expression the following equivalence holds:

$$n(k-1) - \log_2(k^{\frac{k-1}{2}}) = n(k-1) - \frac{k-1}{2} \log_2 k \tag{B.2}$$

We replace k by $\frac{m}{n} + \frac{1}{2}\log_2 \frac{m}{n}$ (which is the bracket expression of the Theorem's bound) and obtain from the expression in (B.2) on the right-hand side:

$$n(\frac{m}{n} + \frac{1}{2}\log_2 \frac{m}{n} - 1) - \frac{\frac{m}{n} + \frac{1}{2}\log_2 \frac{m}{n} - 1}{2}\log_2(\frac{m}{n} + \frac{1}{2}\log_2 \frac{m}{n})$$

$$\leq n(\frac{m}{n} + \frac{1}{2}\log_2 \frac{m}{n} - 1) - \frac{\frac{m}{n} + \frac{1}{2}\log_2 \frac{m}{n} - 1}{2}\log_2 \frac{m}{n}$$

$$= (\frac{nm}{n} + \frac{n}{2}\log_2 \frac{m}{n} - n) - (\frac{m}{2n} + \frac{1}{4}\log_2 \frac{m}{n} - \frac{1}{2})\log_2 \frac{m}{n}$$

$$\leq m - n + \frac{n}{2}\log_2 \frac{m}{n} - \frac{m}{2n}\log_2 \frac{m}{n}$$

$$= m - n + \log_2 \frac{m}{n}(\frac{n}{2} - \frac{m}{2n})$$

This is less than $m - n$, since m is greater than n^2 according to the Theorem's precondition. As a consequence, for setting k to the bracket expression of the Theorem's bound $\frac{m}{n} + \frac{1}{2}\log_2 \frac{m}{n}$, providing a set of k different examples still provides less than m bits of overall information. Thus, the Proposition follows.

□

Using the Proposition, it remains to show that obtaining $k = \frac{m}{n} + \frac{1}{2}\log_2 \frac{m}{n}$, examples with probability of at least $1 - \delta$ requires at least a sample size of $\frac{9k}{10}\log_2 \frac{1}{\delta}$. Clearly, the probability for obtaining a sample of k examples as described in the Proposition is maximum if the probability of c_i, $p(c_i) = \frac{1}{k}$ for all $i \in \{1, ..., k\}$. Hence, the probability of not obtaining any example from c_i for an arbitrary i in a sequence of r random drawings according to P_n is $(1 - \frac{1}{k})^r$. Thus, for $r = \frac{9k}{10}\log_e \frac{1}{\delta}$ the probability of not drawing an example from c_i is at least δ.

□

Theorem B.19 gives a minimal bound on the number of examples needed which are drawn from an unknown but fixed probability distribution. Note that for this bound again, it is assumed that the complete encoding of the examples provided can be exploited for acquiring a complex classification function.

By comparison, in the supervised model of probably approximately correct learning, it is known that a number of examples suffices which is essentially linear in the amount of information to be acquired. See the previous sections or Hoffmann (1997a, 1990a) for a respective proof of such a bound.[4] That is, even in the worst case an essentially linear number of random examples suffices. For unsupervised learning, however, the almost linear bound is merely a best-case consideration.

---

[4] In these papers there is also a bound on the *Vapnik-Chervonenkis dimension* of a function class F, a well-known and important combinatorial measure for PAC learning, which is linear in the Kolmogorov complexity of the most complex function in F.

However, in many practical situations it is presumably not possible to completely exploit the encoding of the examples provided. This is because it implies that the description of unclassified examples can essentially be used as minimal length program code for the target classification function. This would be an extremely advantageous setting, which cannot be assumed to occur in practice. As Theorem B.19 already indicated, it is not at all clear that a self-organising system can reliably acquire a substantial amount of information from unclassified examples only. Consequently, in practice the given bounds will be significantly exceeded.

Theorem B.19 assumes indirectly that the necessary information for encoding the target function f_t is 'literally' contained in the representation of some particular examples. That is, that the particular encoding of the objects can be used as part of a program which computes the function of the self-organising system. This is certainly a rather optimistic assumption. See Figure B.7 for illustration.

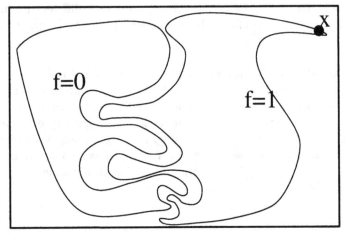

Figure B.7. The shape of an appropriate function f separating the right from the left area is actually encoded by the particular location of the informative object x.

Bibliography

Abeles, M. (1982). *Local cortical circuits: Studies of brain function*. Springer-Verlag. Vol. 6.

Abeles, M. (1991). *Corticonics: Neural circuits of the cerebral cortex*. Cambridge University Press.

Aha, D. (1997). Lazy learning. *Artificial Intelligence Review*, (11):7–10. Editorial Introduction to Special Issue on Lazy Learning.

Alexander, J. A. and Mozer, M. C. (1995). Template-based algorithms for connectionist rule extraction. In Tesauro, G., Touretzky, D., and Leen, T., editors, *Advances in Neural Information Processing Systems (vol. 7)*, Cambridge, MA. MIT Press.

Alspector, J. and Allen, R. B. (1987). A neuromorphic VLSI learning system. In Losleben, P., editor, *Advanced Research in VLSI: Proceedings of the 1987 Stanford Conference*. MIT Press, Cambridge, MA.

Andrews, R. and Diederich, J., editors (1996). *Proceedings of the NIPS'96 Rule Extraction From Trained Artificial Neural Networks Workshop*. Available from Queensland University of Technology, Neurocomputing Research Centre, GPO Box 2434, Brisbane, Queensland 4001, Australia.

Anthony, M. and Biggs, N. (1992). *Computational Learning Theory*. Cambridge University Press.

Appel, K. and Haken, W. (1977). The solution of the four-color-map problem. *Scientific American*, pages 108–121.

Arbib, M. A. (1989). *The Metaphorical Brain II*. Wiley.

Arbib, M. A., editor (1995). *The Handbook of Brain Theory and Neural Networks*. MIT Press.

Arbib, M. A., Erdi, P., and Szentagothai, J., editors (1997). *Neural Organization: Structure, Function, and Dynamics*. MIT Press.

Aussenac, N., Frontin, J., Riviere, M.-H., and Soubie, J.-L. (1989). A mediating representation to assist knowledge acquisition with MACAO. In *Proceedings of the European Knowledge Acquisition Workshop*, pages 516–529. Springer-Verlag.

Bartlett, F. (1932). *Remembering*. Cambridge University Press, Cambridge, UK.

Bégin, J. and Proulx, R. (1996). Categorization in unsupervised neural networks: The Eidos model. *IEEE Transactions on Neural Networks*, 7(1):147–154.

Berry, D. C. and Bienes, Z. (1993). *Implicit Learning: Theoretical and Empirical Issues*. Lawrence Erlbaum Associates, Ltd.

Beydoun, G. and Hoffmann, A. (1997). Acquisition of search knowledge. In *Proceedings of the European Knowledge Acquisition Workshop*, pages 1–16, Spain. Springer-Verlag.

Beydoun, G. and Hoffmann, A. (1998). Building problem solvers based on search control knowledge. In *Proceedings of the 11th Workshop on Knowledge Acquisition, Modeling and Management*, Banff, Canada. to appear.

Blumer, A., Ehrenfeucht, A., Haussler, D., and Warmuth, M. (1986). Classifying learnable geometric concepts with the Vapnik-Chervonenkis dimension. In *Proceedings of the 18th Symposium on Theory of Computing*, pages 273–282.

Boring, E. (1933). *The Physical Dimensions of Consciousness*. Watkins Glen, N.Y.

Bower, J. M., editor (1997). *Computational Neuroscience: Trends in Research, 1997*. Plenum Publishing Corporation.

Bratko, I. (1990). *PROLOG - Programming for Artificial Intelligence*. Addison Wesley. second edition.

Bratko, I., Mozetič, I., and Lavrač, N. (1989). *KARDIO: A study in Deep and Qualitative Knowledge for Expert Systems*. MIT Press, Cambridge, MA.

Breiman, L. (1996). Bagging predictors. *Machine Learning*, 2(24):123–140.

Breiman, L., Friedman, J. H., Olshen, R. A., and Stone, C. J. (1984). *Classification and Regression Trees*. Wadsworth.

Brooks, R. A. (1991). Intelligence without reason. In *Proceedings of the 12th International Joint Conference on Artificial Intelligence*, pages 569–595.

Brooks, R. A. (1996). Prospects for human level intelligence for humanoid robots. In *Proceedings of the First International Symposium on Humanoid Robots*, Tokyo, Japan.

Bryson, A. and Ho, Y.-C. (1969). *Applied Optimal Control*. Blaisdell, New York.

Buchanan, B. G. and Shortliffe, E. H. (1984). *Rule-Based Expert Systems*. Addison-Wesley.

Buntine, W. (1989). A critique of the Valiant model. In *Proceedings of the 11th IJCAI*, pages 837–842.

Cameron-Jones, M. and Quinlan, J. R. (1993). Avoiding pitfalls when learning recursive theories. In *Proceedings of IJCAI-93*. Kaufmann.

Carnap, R. (1950). *Logical Foundations of Probability*.

Carpenter, G. and Grossberg, S. (1987a). ART2: self-organization of stable category recognition codes for analog input patterns. *Applied Optics*, 26(3):4919–4930. Reprinted in Anderson, Pellionisz, & Rosenfeld[1990], pp. 151–162.

Carpenter, G. and Grossberg, S. (1987b). A massively parallel architecture for a self-organizing neural pattern recognition machine. *Computer Vision, Graphics and Image Processing*, 37:54–115.

Carpenter, G. and Grossberg, S. (1990). ART3: hierarchical search using chemical transmitters in self-organizing pattern recognition architectures. *Neural Networks*, 3(4):129–152.

Cestnik, B., Kononenko, I., and Bratko, I. (1987). ASSISTANT86: A knowledge-elicitation tool for sophisticated users. In Bratko, I. and Lavrac, N., editors, *Progress in Machine Learning*. Sigma Press, Wilmslow, UK.

Chandrasekaran, B. (1986). Generic tasks in knowledge-based reasoning: High-level building blocks for expert system design. *IEEE Expert*, pages 23–30.

Chomsky, N. (1975). *Reflections on Language*. Pantheon, New York.

Church, A. (1936). An unsolvable problem of elementary number theory. *American Journal of Mathematics*, 58.

Clancey, W. (1983). The epistemology of a rule-based expert system: A framework for explanation. *Artificial Intelligence*, 3(20):215–251.

Clancey, W. (1993). Situated action: A neuropsychological interpretation. *Cognitive Science*, 17:87–116.

Clark, A. (1993). *Associative Engines*. MIT Press/Bradford, Cambridge, MA.

Clark, A. (1996). *Being There*. MIT Press, Cambridge, MA.

Clark, P. and Boswell, R. (1991). Rule induction with CN2: Some recent improvements. In Kodratoff, Y., editor, *Machine Learning EWSL-91*, pages 151–163. Springer-Verlag.

Clark, P. and Niblett, T. (1989). The CN2 induction algorithm. *Machine Learning*, 3(4):261–283.

Cohen, W. W. (1992). Compiling prior knowledge into an explicit bias. In *Proceedings of the 9th International Conference on Machine Learning*, pages 102–110. Kaufmann.

Compton, P. and Jansen, R. (1990). A philosophical basis for knowledge acquisition. *Knowledge Acquisition*, 2:241–257.

Compton, P., Kang, B., Preston, P., and Mulholland, M. (1993). Knowledge acquisition without knowledge analysis. In *Proceedings of the European Knowledge Acquisition Workshop*, pages 277–299. Springer-Verlag.

Craven, M. and Shavlik, J. (1993). Learning symbolic rules using neural networks. In *10th International Conference on Machine Learning*, pages 73–80. Kaufmann Publishers.

Craven, M. W. and Shavlik, J. (1997). Understanding time-series networks: A case study in rule extraction. *International Journal of Neural Networks*. In Special Issue on *Noisy Time Series*; in press.

Da Ruan (1997). *Intelligent Hybrid Systems: Fuzzy Logic, Neural Networks, & Genetic Algorithms*. Kluwer Academic Publishers.

David, J.-M., Krivine, J.-P., and Simmons, R., editors (1993). *Second Generation Expert Systems*. Springer-Verlag.

Davis, M. (1982a). Why Gödel didn't have Church's thesis. *Information and Control*, 54.

Davis, R. (1982b). Expert systems: Where we are? and where do we go from here? *AI Magazine*, 2(3):3–22.

Davis et al., R. (1971). The DIPmeter advisor: Interpretation of geological signals. In *Proceedings IJCAI'71*, Vancouver, Canada. Morgan Kaufmann.

de Groot, A. (1946). *Het Denken van den Schaker*. North-Holland, Amsterdam.

de Kleer, J. (1986). An assumption-based TMS. *Artificial Intelligence*, 28:127–162.

de Kleer, J., editor (1994). *Readings in Qualitative Reasoning*. Morgan Kaufmann Publishers.

De Raedt, L. (1992). *Interactive Theory Revision: An Inductive Logic Programming Approach*. Academic Press, London, UK.

De Raedt, L. and Bruynooghe, M. (1989). Interactive concept learning and constructive induction by analogy. In *Proceedings of IJCAI-89*, pages 849–854. Kaufmann.

De Raedt, L. and Bruynooghe, M. (1992). Interactive concept learning and constructive induction by analogy. *Machine Learning*, 2(8):107–150.

Dennett, D. C. (1971). Intentional systems. *Journal of Philosophy*, 68:87–106.

Dennett, D. C. (1987). *The Intentional Stance*. MIT Press.

Dieng, R., Giboin, A., Tourtier, P.-A., and Corby, O. (1992). Knowledge acquisition for explainable, multi-expert, knowledge-based system design. In *Proceedings of the European Knowledge Acquisition Workshop*, pages 298–317. Springer-Verlag.

Doyle, J. (1979). A truth maintenance system. *Artificial Intelligence*, 3(12):231–272.

Dreyfus, H. L. (1965). Alchemy and artificial intelligence. Technical Report P3244, RAND Corporation, Santa Monica, CA.

Dreyfus, H. L. (1972). *What Computers Can't do - The Limits of Artificial Intelligence*. Harper & Row.

Dreyfus, H. L. (1992). *What Computers Still Can't do*. MIT Press.

Dreyfus, H. L. and Dreyfus, S. E. (1986). *Mind over Machine - The Power of Human Intuition and Expertise in the Era of the Computer*. Free Press.

Duda, R., Gaschnig, J., and Hart, P. (1979). Model design in the Prospector consultant system for mineral exploration. In Michie, D., editor, *Expert Systems in the Microelectronic Age*. Edinburgh University Press, Edinburgh, Scotland.

Duda, R. O. and Hart, P. E. (1973). *Pattern Recognition and Scene Analysis*. John Wiley and Sons, New York.

Duncker, K. (1945). On problem solving. *Psychological Monographs*, 58(5):Whole No.

Džeroski, S. and Bratko, I. (1992). Handling noise in inductive logic programming. In *Proceedings of the 2nd International Workshop on Inductive Logic Programming*, Tokyo, Japan. ICOT.

Džeroski, S. and Lavrač, N. (1991). Learning relations from noise examples: An empirical comparison of LINUS and FOIL. In *Proceedings of the 8th International Conference on Machine Learning*, pages 399–402. Kaufmann.

Edwards et. al., G. (1993). Peirs: a pathologist maintained expert system for the interpretation of chemical pathology reports. *Pathology*, (25):27–34.

Ehrenfeucht, A., Haussler, D., Kearns, M., and Valiant, L. (1989). A general lower bound on the number of examples needed for learning. *Information and Computation*, 82:247–261.

Eliasmith, C. (1996). The third contender: a critical examination of the dynamicist theory of cognition. *Philosophical Psychology*, 9(4):441–463.

Elman, J. (1990). Finding structure in time. *Cognitive Science*, 14:179–211.

Emde, W., Habel, C., and Rollinger, C. (1983). The discovery of the equator or concept driven learning. In *Proceedings of the 8th IJCAI*, pages 455–458.

Erwin, E., Obermayer, K., and Schulten, K. (1995). Models of orientation and ocular dominance columns in the visual cortex: A critical comparison. *Neural Computation*, 7:425–468.

Fagin et al., R. (1995). *Reasoning about Knowledge*. MIT Press, Cambridge, Massachusetts.

Fayyad, U., Piatetsky-Shapiro, G., Smyth, P., and Uthurusamy, R., editors (1996). *Advances in Knowledge Discovery and Data Mining*. MIT Press.

Feldman, J. (1993). Structured connectionist models and language learning. *Artificial Intelligence Review*, (7):301–312.

Feltovich, P., Ford, K., and Hoffman, R., editors (1997). *Expertise in Context*. AAAI Press/The MIT Press.

Fiesler, E. and Beale, R., editors (1997). *Handbook of Neural Computation*. Jointly published by Institute of Physics and Oxford University Press.

Fikes, R. E. and Nilsson, N. J. (1971). STRIPS: A new approach to the application of theorem proving to problem solving. *Artificial Intelligence*, 2:189–208.

Findler, N. V. (1979). *Associative Networks: Representation and Use of Knowledge by Computer*. Academic Press, New York.

Fodor, J. (1997). Connectionism and the problem of systematicity (continued): why Smolensky's solution still doesn't work. *Cognition*, 62:109–119.

Fodor, J. A. and McLaughlin, B. P. (1990). Connectionism and the problem of systematicity: Why Smolensky's solution doesn't work. *Cognition*, 35:183–204. Reprinted in C. Macdonald and G. Macdonald: *Connectionism - Debates on the Psychological Explanation*, pp. 199–222, Basil Blackwell Ltd, 1995.

Fodor, J. A. and Pylyshyn, Z. W. (1988). Connectionism and cognitive architecture: a critical analysis. *Cognition*, 28:3–71. Reprinted in C. Macdonald and G. Macdonald: *Connectionism - Debates on the Psychological Explanation*, pp. 90–163, Basil Blackwell Ltd, 1995.

Forbus, K. (1993). Qualitative process theory: Twelve years after. *Artificial Intelligence*, 59:115–123.

Frasconi, P., Gori, M., Maggini, M., and Soda, G. (1995a). Unified integration of explicit knowledge and learning by example in recurrent networks. *IEEE Transactions on Knowledge and Data Engineering*, 7(2):340-346.

Frasconi, P., Gori, M., and Soda, G. (1995b). Recurrent neural networks and prior knowledge for sequence processing: A constrained nondeterministic approach. *Knowledge-Based Systems*, 8(6):313-332.

Frege, G. (1879). *Begriffsschrift, eine der arithmetischen nachgebildeten Formelsprache des reinen Denkens*. Halle. (Neudr. in: K. Berka & L. Kreiser (eds.) Logik-Texte, Berlin (Ost), 1971).

Freivalds, R. and Hoffmann, A. (1994). An inductive inference approach to classification. *Journal of Experimental and Theoretical Artificial Intelligence*, 6(1):63-72.

Frixione, M., Spinelli, G., and Gaglio, S. (1989). Symbols and subsymbols for representing knowledge: a catalogue raisonné. In *Proceedings of the 11th International Joint Conference of Artificial Intelligence*, pages 3-7.

Fu, L. (1992). A neural network model for learning rule-based systems. In *International Joint Conference on Neural Networks*, pages 343-348.

Fu, L. (1994). Rule generation from neural networks. *IEEE Transactions on Man, Systems & Cybernetics*, 8(24):1114-1124.

Gallant, S. (1988). Connectionist expert systems. *Communications of the ACM*, 31(2):152-169.

Gardenförs, P. and Rott, H. (1995). Belief revision. In Gabbay, D. M., Hogger, C. J., and Robinson, J. A., editors, *Handbook of Logic in AI and LP, Vol.4: Epistemic and temporal reasoning*, pages 35-132. Press.

Garey, M. R. and Johnson, D. S. (1979). *Computers and Intractability*. Freeman, San Francisco, CA.

Garson, J. W. (1996). Cognition poised at the edge of chaos: a complex alternative to a symbolic mind. *Philosophical Psychology*, 9(3):301-322.

Gedeon, T. D. (1997). Measuring the significance and contributions of inputs in back-propagation neural networks for rule-extraction and data mining. In *Brain-like Computing and Intelligent Information Systems*. Springer-Verlag.

Gedeon, T. D., Ramer, A., Padet, C., and Padet, J. (1995). Abstracting uncertain knowledge: Case for neural nets application. *International Journal on Intelligent Automation and Soft Computing*, 1(4):365-377. Special Issue on Fuzzy Information Processing and Neural Networks.

Gero, J. and Sudweeks, F., editors (1996). *Artificial Intelligence in Design*. Kluwer Academic Press.

Glasgow, J., Narayanan, N., and Chandrasekaran, B., editors (1995). *Diagrammatic Reasoning: Cognitive and Computational Perspectives*. AAAI Press and MIT Press.

Gödel, K. (1931). Über formal unentscheidbare Sätze der Principia Mathematica und verwandter Systeme I. *Monatshefte für Mathematik und Physik*, 39.

Goldberg, D. E. (1989). *Genetic Algorithms in Search, Optimization, and Machine Learning*. Addison-Wesley.

Good, I. J. and Card, W. I. (1971). The diagnostic process with special reference to errors. *Methods of Information in Medicine*, 3(10):176–188.

Goodman, N. (1955). *Fact, Fiction and Forecast*. Cambridge, MA.

Gray, C., Konig, P., Engel, A. K., and Singer, W. (1989). Oscillatory responses in cat visual cortex exhibit intercolumnar sychronization which reflects global stimulus properties. *Nature*, 338:334–337.

Grobelnik, M. (1992). MARKUS: an optimized model inference system. In *Proceedings of Workshop on Logical Approaches to Machine Learning at 10th European Conference on Artificial Intelligence*.

Grossberg, S. (1976). Adaptive pattern classification and universal recoding I & II. *Biological Cybernetics*, 23:121–134 & 187–202.

Grzywacz, N. M. and Koch, C. (1987). Functional properties of models for direction selectively in the retina. *Synapse*, 1:417–434.

Hebb, D. O. (1949). *The organization of behavior*. Wiley & Sons.

Heckerman, D., Geiger, D., and Chickering, D. M. (1995a). Learning Bayesian networks: the combination of knowledge and statistical data. *Machine Learning*, 20(3):197–243.

Heckerman, D., Mannila, H., Pregibon, D., and Uthurusamy, R., editors (1997). *Proceedings of the 3rd International Conference on Knowledge Discovery and Data Mining (KDD-96)*. AAAI.

Heckerman, D. E. (1991). *Probabilistic Similarity Networks*. MIT Press, Cambridge, MA.

Heckerman, D. E., Breese, J., and Rommelse, K. (1995b). Decision-theoretic troubleshooting. *cacm*, 38(3):49–57.

Heijenoort, J. v. (1967). *From Frege to Gödel. A Source Book in Mathematical Logic*. Harvard University Press, Cambridge, Massachusetts.

Heimer, L. (1994). *The human brain and spinal cord : functional neuroanatomy and dissection guide*. Springer-Verlag, New York. 2nd edition.

Hempel, C. (1965). *Aspects of Scientific Explanation and Other Essays in the Philosophy of Science*. Free Press.

Hilbert, D. and Bernays, P. (1968). *Grundlagen der Mathematik*. Springer-Verlag. 2. Auflage.

Hillis, D. W. (1985). *The Connection Machine*. MIT Press, Cambridge, Massachusetts.

Hillis, D. W. (1987). The connection machine. *Scientific American*, 256:108–115.

Hinton, G. E. and Anderson, J. (1981). *Parallel Models of Associative Memory*. Lawrence Erlbaum Associates, Potomac, Maryland.

Hinton, G. E., McClelland, J. L., and Rumelhart, D. E. (1986). Distributed representations. In Rumelhart, D. E., McClelland, J. L., and the PDP Research Group, editors, *Parallel Distributed Processing: Explorations in the Microstructure of Cognition, I: Foundations.* MIT Press, Cambridge, MA.

Hoffmann, A. (1990a). General limitations on machine learning. In *Proceedings of the 9th European Conference on Artificial Intelligence*, pages 345–347, Stockholm, Sweden.

Hoffmann, A. (1990b). On computational limitations of neural network architectures. In *Proceedings of the 2nd IEEE Symposium on Parallel and Distributed Processing*, pages 818–825, Dallas, Texas, USA. IEEE.

Hoffmann, A. (1991a). Asymptotic performance of learning algorithms. In *Proceedings of the World Conference on the Fundamentals of Artificial Intelligence*, pages 247–256, Paris, France.

Hoffmann, A. (1991b). Connectionist functionality and the emergent network behavior. *Neurocomputing*, 2(2):161–172.

Hoffmann, A. (1991c). On the principles of intelligence. In *Proceedings of the World Conference on the Fundamentals of Artificial Intelligence*, pages 257–266, Paris, France.

Hoffmann, A. (1992). Phenomenology, representations and complexity. In *Proceedings of the 10th European Conference on Artificial Intelligence*, pages 610–614, Vienna, Austria. Wiley & Sons.

Hoffmann, A. (1993). Complexity bounds of emerging structures in self-organizing networks. In *Proceedings of the International Joint Conference on Neural Networks '93*, pages 475–478, Nagoya, Japan.

Hoffmann, A. (1994). Exploiting causal domain knowledge for learning to control dynamic systems. In *Proceedings of the 11th European Conference on Artificial Intelligence*, pages 433–437, Amsterdam, The Netherlands. Wiley & Sons.

Hoffmann, A. (1997a). Complex connectionist dynamics and the limited complexity of the network function. *Connection Science*, 9(2):201–215.

Hoffmann, A. (1997b). On computational limitations of self-organization. *Neurocomputing*, (15):69–87.

Holland, J. (1975). *Adaptation in Natural and Artificial Systems.* University of Michigan Press, Ann Arbor.

Hopfield, J. J. (1982). Neural networks and physical systems with emergent collective computational abilities. *Proceedings of the National Academy of Sciences*, 79:2554–2558. (Biophysics).

Hopfield, J. J. (1984). Neurons with graded response have collective computational properties like those of two-state neurons. *Proceedings of the National Academy of Sciences*, 81:3088–3092. (Biophysics).

Hopfield, J. J. and Tank, D. W. (1985). Neural computation of decisions in optimization problems. *Biological Cybernetics*, 52:141–152.

Hopfield, J. J. and Tank, D. W. (1986). Computing with neural circuits. *Science*, 233:625–633.

Hunt, E. B., Mairn, J., and Stone, P. J. (1966). *Experiments in Induction.* Academic Press, New York.

Jochem, T. and Pomerleau, D. (1996). Life in the fast lane: The evolution of an adaptive vehicle control system. *AI Magazine*, 2, (Summer)(17):11–50.

Jordan, M. and Jacobs, R. (1994). Hierarchical mixtures of experts and the EM algorithm. *Neural Computation*, 6(2):181–214.

Kaelbling, L. P., editor (1996). *Recent Advances in Reinforcement Learning*. Kluwer Academic Publishers.

Kang, B., Compton, P., and Preston, P. (1995). Multiple classification ripple down rules: Evaluation and possibilities. In *Proceedings of the 9th AAAI-sponsored Banff Knowledge Acquisition for Knowledge Based Systems Workshop*, pages 17.1–17.20.

Kangas, J. A., Kohonen, T. K., and Laaksonen, J. T. (1990). Variants of self-organizing feature maps. *IEEE Transactions on Neural Networks*, 1(1):93–99.

Kaspar, S. and Hoffmann, A. (1997). Using knowledge acquisition to build spoken language systems. In *Proceedings of the European Knowledge Acquisition Workshop*, pages 353–358, Spain. Springer-Verlag.

Kearns, M., Mansour, Y., Ng, A., and Ron, D. (1997). An experimental and theoretical comparison of model selection methods. *Machine Learning*, 7:7–50.

Kietz, J. and Wrobel, S. (1992). Controlling the complexity of learning in logic through syntactic and task-oriented models. In Muggleton, S., editor, *Inductive Logic Programming*, London, UK. Academic Press.

Kim, S., Kim, J., and Kim, H. (1996). On-line recognition of cursive Korean characters using neural networks. *Neurocomputing*, 3(10):291–305.

Kischell, E., Kehtarnavaz, N., Hillman, G., Levin, H., Lilly, M., and Kent, T. (1995). Classification of brain compartments and head injury lesions by neural networks applied to MRI. *Neuroradiology*, 7(37):535–541.

Kohavi, R. and John, G. (1997). Wrappers for feature subset selection. *Artificial Intelligence*, 1–2(97):245–271.

Kohonen, T. (1982a). Analysis of a simple self-organizing system. *Biological Cybernetics*, 44:135–140.

Kohonen, T. (1982b). Self-organized formation of topologically correct feature maps. *Biological Cybernetics*, 43:59–69.

Kohonen, T. (1984). *Self-Organization and Associative Memory*. Springer-Verlag, Heidelberg, West-Germany.

Kohonen, T. (1987). Adaptive, associative and self-organizing functions in neural computing. *Applied Optics*, 26(3):4910–4918.

Kohonen, T. (1997). *Self-Organizing Maps*. Springer-Verlag, Heidelberg, Germany. 2nd Edition, Series in Information Sciences, 30.

Koiran, P., Cosnard, M., and Garzon, M. (1994). Computability with low-dimensional dynamical systems. *Theoretical Computer Science*, 1–2(132):113–128.

Kolodner, J. L. (1993). *Case-Based Reasoning*. Morgan Kaufmann.

Krause, W. and Wysotzki, F. (1983). Three-dimensional orderings and text representation. In Geissler, H.-G., editor, *Modern Issues in Perception*, pages 149–165. VEB Deutscher Verlag der Wissenschaften, Berlin.

Kripke, S. A. (1959). A completeness theorem in modal logic. *Journal of Symbolic Logic*, 24:1–14.

Kuhn, T. S. (1962). *The Structure of Scientific Revolutions*. University of Chicago Press, Chicago; London.

Lavrač, N. and Džeroski, S. (1994). *Inductive Logic Programming*. Ellis Horwood.

Lavrač, N. and Džeroski, S., editors (1997). *Proceedings of the European Inductive Logic Programming Workshop 1997*. Springer-Verlag. Lecture Notes in Computer Science.

Lavrač, N., Džeroski, S., Pirnat, V., and Križman, V. (1993). The utility of background knowledge in learning medical diagnostic rules. *Applied Artificial Intelligence*, 7:273–293.

Lavrač, N., Džeroski, S., and Grobelnik, M. (1991). Learning nonrecursive definitions of relations with LINUS. In Kodratoff, Y., editor, *Machine Learning EWSL-91*, pages 265–281. Springer-Verlag.

Leake, D. B., editor (1996). *Case-Based Reasoning - Experiences, Lessons, & Future Directions*. AAAI Press/MIT Press.

Lenat, D. (1995). CYC: A large-scale investment into knowledge infrastructure. *Communications of the ACM*, 11(38):33–38.

Lenat, D. and Guha, R. (1990). *Building Large Knowledge-Based Systems: Representation and Inference in the CYC Project*. Addison-Wesley.

Li, M. and Vitányi, P. (1996). *An Introduction to Kolmogorov Complexity and Its Applications*. Text and Monographs in Computer Science. Springer-Verlag. Second edition.

Lloyd, J. W. (1987). *Foundations of Logic Programming*. Springer-Verlag.

Lucas, J. R. (1961). Minds, machines, and Gödel. *Philosophy*, 36:112–117. (rpt. in: *Minds and Machines*, ed. Alan R. Anderson, Englewood Cliffs, N.J., Prentice-Hall, 1964.).

Lucey, K. G. (1996). *On Knowledge and the Known: Introductory Readings in Epistemology*. Prometheus Books.

Luckman, A., Allinson, N., Ellis, A., and Flude, B. (1995). Familiar face recognition - a comparative study of a connectionist model and human performance. *Neurocomputing*, 1(7):3–27.

Lynch, G. and Granger, R. (1989). Simulation and analysis of a simple cortical network. In Hawkins, R. and Bower, G., editors, *Computational models of learning in simple Neural systems*, pages 205–241. Academic Press, Orlando, Florida. Vol. 23 of: The Psychology of Learning and Motivation.

Macq, D., Verleysen, M., Jespers, P., and Legat, J. (1993). Analog implementation of a Kohonen map with on-chip learning. *IEEE Transactions on Neural Networks*, 3(4):456–461.

Maes, P. and Brooks, R. A. (1990). Learning to coordinate behaviors. In *Proceedings of AAAI-90*, volume 2, pages 796–802, Boston, MA. AAAI Press/The MIT Press.

Manhaeghe, C., Lemahieu, I., Vogelaers, D., and Colardyn, F. (1994). Automatic initial estimation of the left ventricular myocardial midwall inemission tomograms using Kohonen maps. *IEEE Transactions on Pattern Analysis and Machine Intelligence*, 3(16):259–266.

Mao, J. and Jain, A. K. (1996). A self-organizing network for hyperellipsoidal clustering (HEC). *IEEE Transactions on Neural Networks*, 7(1):16–29.

Marr, D. (1982). *Vision: A computational investigation into the human representation and processing of visual information*. Freeman.

Martinez-Bejar, R., Shiraz, G., and Compton, P. (1998). Using ripple-down rules-based systems for acquiring fuzzy domain knowledge. In *Eleventh Workshop on Knowledge Acquisition, Modeling and Management (KAW'98)*, Banff, Alberta, Canada.

McCulloch, W. S. and Pitts, W. (1943). A logical calculus for the ideas immanent in nervous activity. *Bulletin of Mathematical Biophysics*, 5:115–143.

McDermott, J. (1982). R1: A rule-based configurer of computer systems. *Artificial Intelligence*, 19:39–88.

McDougall, W. (1912). *Psychology. The Study of Behaviour*. London, UK.

Mead, C. (1989). *Analog VLSI and Neural Systems*. Addison & Wesley.

Menzies, T. J. (1997). Is knowledge maintenance an adequate response to the challenge of situated cognition for symbolic knowledge based systems? *Journal of Human Computer Studies*. Special issue: "The Challenge of Situated Cognition for Symbolic Knowledge Based Systems".

Michalski, R. S. (1969). On the quasi-minimal solution of the general covering problem. In *Proceedings of the 5th International Symposium on Information Processing (FCIP 69)*, volume A3, pages 125–128. Liphhok.

Michalski, R. S. (1983a). A theory and methodology of inductive learning. In Michalski, R. S., Carbonell, J. G., and Mitchell, T. M., editors, *Machine Learning: An Artificial Intelligence Approach*, volume I, pages 83–134. Morgan Kaufmann Publishers.

Michalski, R. S. (1983b). A theory and methodology of machine learning. *Artificial Intelligence*, 20:111–161.

Michalski, R. S. and Larson, J. (1983). Incremental generation of vl_1 hypotheses: the underlying methodology and the description of program AQ11. Technical Report ISG 83-5, Dept. of Computer Science, University of Illinois at Urbana-Champaign, Urbana, IN.

Miller, A. and Coe, M. (1996). Star galaxy classification using Kohonen self-organizing maps. *Monthly Notices of the Royal Astronomical Society*, 1(279):293–300.

Minsky, M. (1954). *Neural Nets and the Brain Model Problem*. PhD thesis, Princeton University.

Minsky, M. (1967). *Computation: Finite and Infinite Machines.* Prentice-Hall, Englewood Cliffs, NJ.

Minsky, M. (1975). A framework for representing knowledge. In Winston, P. H., editor, *The Psychology of Computer Vision.* McGraw-Hill, New York.

Minsky, M. and Papert, S. (1969). *Perceptrons: An Introduction to Computational Geometry.* MIT Press, Cambridge, MA.

Mitchell, T. (1997). *Machine Learning.* McGraw Hill.

Mitchell, T. M. (1982). Generalization as search. *Artificial Intelligence,* (18):203–226.

Morik, K. (1989). Sloppy modelling. In Morik, K., editor, *Knowledge Representation and Organization in Machine Learning.* Springer-Verlag.

Morik, K. (1991). Balanced cooperative modelling. In *Proceedings of first International Workshop on Multistrategy Learning,* pages 65–80.

Morik, K., Wrobel, S., Kietz, J., and Emde, W. (1993). *Knowledge Acquisition and Machine Learning - Theory, Methods, and Applications.* Academic Press, London.

Mozer, M. C. (1992). *Induction of multi-scale temporal structure.* Morgan Kaufmann.

Muggleton, S. (1991). Inductive logic programming. *New Generation Computing,* 4(8):295–318.

Muggleton, S. (1995). Inverse entailment and progol. *New Generation Computing Journal,* 13:245–286.

Muggleton, S. and Buntine, W. (1988). Machine invention of first-order predicates by inverting resolution. In *Proceedings of International Workshop on Machine Learning,* pages 339–352. Kaufmann.

Muggleton, S. and Feng, C. (1990). Efficient induction of logic programs. In *Proceedings of 1st Conference on Algorithmic Learning Theory,* pages 268–381. Ohmsha, Tokyo.

Müller, W. and Wysotzki, F. (1996). The decision tree algorithm CAL5 based on a statistical approach to its splitting algorithm. In *Machine Learning and Statistics.* Wiley & Sons. to appear.

Musgrave, A. (1993). *Common Sense, Science and Scepticism: A Historical Introduction to the Theory of Knowledge.* Cambridge University Press, Cambridge, UK.

Natarajan, B. K. (1991). *Machine Learning - A Theoretical Approach.* Morgan Kaufmann Publishers.

Nebel, B. (1990). *Reasoning and Revision in Hybrid Representation Systems.* Springer-Verlag. Lecture Notes in Artificial Intelligence 422.

Newell, A. (1980). Physical symbol systems. *Cognitive Science,* 4:135–183.

Newell, A. (1982). The knowledge level. *Artificial Intelligence,* 18:87–127.

Newell, A., editor (1990). *Unified Theories of Cognition.* Harvard University Press, Cambridge, MA.

Newell, A. and Simon, H. (1963). GPS, a program that simulates human thought. In Feigenbaum, E. and Feldman, J., editors, *Computers and Thought*, pages 279–293. McGraw Hill, New York.

Newell, A. and Simon, H. A. (1972). *Human problem solving*. Prentice-Hall, Englewood Cliffs, N.

Newell, A. and Simon, H. A. (1976). Computer science as empirical inquiry: Symbols and search. *Communications of the Association for Computing Machinery*, 19:113–126.

Nienhuys-Cheng, S.-H. and Wolf, R., editors (1997). *Foundations of Inductive Logic Programming*. Springer-Verlag. LNCS 1228.

Nilsson, N. (1965). *Learning Machines: Foundations of Trainable Pattern-Classifying Systems*. McGraw-Hill, New York.

Nilsson, N. (1995). Eye on the prize. *AI Magazine*, (Summer).

Nilsson, N. and Genesereth, M. R. (1987). *Logical Foundations of Artificial Intelligence*. Springer-Verlag.

Nisbett, R. E. and DeCamp Wilson, T. (1977). Telling more than we can know: Verbal reports on mental processes. *Psychological review*, 84(3):231–259.

Osherson, D. N., Kosslyn, S. M., and Hollerbach, J. M., editors (1990). *Invitation to cognitive science: Visual cognition and action*. Bradford.

Papert, S. (1988). One AI or many. In Graubard, S. R., editor, *The Artificial Intelligence Debate*. MIT Press.

Parker, D. (1985). Learning logic. Technical Report TR-47, Center for Computational Research in Economics and Management Science, Massachusetts Institute of Technology, Cambridge, Massachusetts.

Parks, R. W., Levine, D. S., and Long, D. L., editors (1998). *Fundamentals of Neural Network Modeling: Neuropsychology and Cognitive Neuroscience*. Bradford Books.

Pazzani, M., Brunk, C., and Silverstein, G. (1991). A knowledge-intensive approach to learning relational concepts. In *Proceedings of International Workshop on Machine Learning*, pages 432–436. Kaufmann.

Pearl, J. (1988). *Probabilistic Reasoning in Intelligent Systems: Networks of Plausible Inference*. Morgan Kaufmann Publishers.

Pearson, D. W., Albrecht, . R. F., and Steele, N. C. (1995). *Artificial Neural Nets and Genetic Algorithms*. University of Michigan Press, Ann Arbor.

Pedrycz, W. (1995). *Fuzzy Sets Engineering*. CRC Press.

Piaget, J. (1929). *The child's conception of the world*. Harcourt, Brace and company, London, New York.

Plotkin, G. (1969). A note on inductive generalization. In Meltzer, B. and Michie, D., editors, *Machine Intelligence 5*, pages 153–163. Edinburgh: Edinburgh University Press.

Pomerleau, D. A. (1993). *Neural Network Perception for Mobile Robot Guidance*. Kluwer Academic Publishers, Dordrecht, The Netherlands.

Post, E. L. (1943). Formal reduction of the general combinatorial decision problem. *American Journal of Mathematics*, 65.

Puppe, F. (1993). *Systematic Introduction to Expert Systems*. Springer-Verlag.

Pylyshyn, Z. W. (1984). *Computation and cognition: Toward a foundation for cognitive science*. MIT Press/Bradford Books.

Quine, W. v. O. (1951). Two dogmas of empiricism. *Philosophical Review*, (60):20–43.

Quine, W. v. O. (1953). *From a Logical Point of View*. Harvard University Press, Cambridge, MA.

Quinlan, J. R. (1979). Discovering rules by induction from large collections of examples. In Michie, D., editor, *Expert systems in the microelectronic age*. Edinburgh University Press.

Quinlan, J. R. (1986). The effect of noise on concept learning. In Michalski, R. S., Carbonell, J. G., and Mitchell, T. M., editors, *Machine Learning: An Artificial Intelligence Approach*, volume 2. Morgan Kaufmann Publishers.

Quinlan, J. R. (1987). Simplifying decision trees. *International Journal on Man-Machine Studies*, 27:221–234.

Quinlan, J. R. (1990). Learning logical definitions from relations. *Machine Learning*, 3(5):239–266.

Quinlan, J. R. (1991). Knowledge acquisition from structured data - using determinate literals to assist search. *IEEE Expert*, 6(6):32–37.

Quinlan, J. R. (1993a). *C4.5: Programs for Machine Learning*. Morgan Kaufmann Publishers.

Quinlan, J. R. (1993b). Combining instance-based and model-based learning. In *Proceedings of the 10th International Workshop on Machine Learning*, pages 236–243. Kaufmann.

Quinlan, J. R. (1996a). Bagging, boosting, and C4.5. In *Proceedings of the 14th National Conference of Artificial Intelligence*.

Quinlan, J. R. (1996b). Improved use of continuous attributes in C4.5. *Journal of Artificial Intelligence Research*, 4:77–90.

Reiter, R. (1980). A logic for default reasoning. *Artificial Intelligence*, 13:81–132.

Reiter, R. (1987). A theory of diagnosis from first principles. *Artificial Intelligence*, 32:57–95.

Richards, D. and Compton, P. (1997). Knowledge acquisition first, modelling later. In *Proceedings of the 10th European Knowledge Acquisition Workshop*. Springer-Verlag.

Ritter, H., Martinetz, T., and Schulten, K. (1992). *Neural Computation and Self-organizing Maps*. Addison & Wesley.

Robinson, J. A. (1965). A machine-oriented logic based on the resolution principle. *Journal of the ACM*, 12.

Rosca, J. P. and Ballard, D. H. (1994). Hierarchical self-organization in genetic programming. In *Proc. 11th International Conference on Machine Learning*, pages 251–258. Morgan Kaufmann.

Rosenblatt, F. (1957). The perceptron: A perceiving and recognizing automaton. Technical report, Cornell Aeronautical Laboratory, Ithaca, New York. Report 85-460-1, Project PARA.

Rosenblatt, F. (1959). Two theorems of statistical separability in the perceptron. In *Proceedings of the Symposium on the Mechanization of thought*, pages 421–456, London. Her Majesty's Stationary Office.

Rosenblatt, F. (1962). *Principles of Neurodynamics*. Spartan, Chicago, Illinois.

Rosenbloom, P., Laird, J., and Newell, A., editors (1993). *The Soar Papers: Readings on Integrated Intelligence*. MIT Press, Cambridge, MA.

Rouveirol, C. (1991). Completeness for inductive procedures. In *Proceedings of International Workshop on Machine Learning*, pages 452–456. Kaufmann.

Rumelhart, D. E., Hinton, G. E., and Williams, R. J. (1986a). Learning internal representations by error propagations. In Rumelhart, D. E., McClelland, J. L., and the PDP Research Group, editors, *Parallel Distributed Processing: Explorations in the Microstructure of Cognition, I: Foundations*. MIT Press, Cambridge, MA.

Rumelhart, D. E., McClelland, J. L., and the PDP Research Group (1986b). *Parallel Distributed Processing: Explorations in the Microstructure of Cognition,I & II*. MIT Press, Cambridge, MA.

Russell, S. and Norvig, P. (1995). *Artificial intelligence: A modern approach*. Prentice Hall, Englewood Cliffs.

Ryckebusch, S., Bower, J. M., and Mead, C. (1989). Modelling small biological oscillating networks in VLSI. In Touretzky, D., editor, *Advances in neural network information processing systems*. Kaufmann, Cambridge, MA.

Sammut, C. and Banerji, R. (1986). Learning concepts by asking questions. In Michalski, R. S., Carbonell, J. G., and Mitchell, T. M., editors, *Machine Learning: An Artificial Intelligence Approach*, volume 2, pages 167–191. Morgan Kaufmann Publishers.

Sarkar, S., editor (1996). *Logical empiricism at its peak : Schlick, Carnap, and Neurath*. Garland Publishers.

Schank, R. and Abelson, R. (1977). *Scripts, plans, goals and understanding*. Lawrence Erlbaum Associates, Hillsdale, NJ.

Schreiber, G., Wielinga, B., and Breuker, J. (1993). *KADS A Principled Approach to Knowledge-Based System Development*. Academic Press.

Schreiber, T., Wielinga, B., Akkermans, J., van de Velde, W., and de Hoog, R. (1994). CommonKADS: A comprehensive methodology for KBS. *IEEE Expert*, 9(6):28–37.

Sejnowski, T. J. and Ritz, R. (1997). Synchronous oscillatory activity in sensory systems: New vistas on mechanisms. *Current Opinion in Neurobiology*, 7:536–546.

Sejnowski, T. J. and Rosenberg, C. R. (1987). Parallel networks that learn to pronounce english:text. *Journal of Complex Systems*, 1(1):145–168.

Selverston, A. I. (1985). *Model neural networks and behavior*. Plenum, New York.

Selz, O. (1924). *Die Gesetze der Produktiven und Reproduktiven Geis-testätigkeit.* Bonn, Germany.

Senator, T., Goldberg, H. G., Wooton, J., Cottini, M. A., Khan, A., Klinger, C., Llamas, W., Marrone, M., and Wong, R. (1995). The financial crimes enforcement network AI system (FAIS): Identifying potential money laundering from reports of large cash transactions. *AI Magazine*, (Winter):21–39.

Servan-Schreiber, D., Cleeremans, A., and McClelland, J. (1989). Learning sequential structure in simple recurrent networks. In Touretzky, D., editor, *Advances in neural network information processing systems*, pages 643–652. Kaufmann, Cambridge, MA.

Shadbolt, N. R. and Wielinga, B. (1990). Knowledge-based knowledge acquisition: The next generation of support tools. In *Proceedings of the European Knowledge Acquisition Workshop*, pages 98–317. IOS Press.

Shannon, C. E. and Weaver, W. (1949). *The Mathematical Theory of Communication.* University of Illinois Press, Urbana, Illinois.

Shapiro, E. (1983). *Algorithmic Program Debugging.* MIT Press, Cambridge, MA.

Shastri, L. and Ajjanagadde, V. (1993). From simple associations to systematic reasoning: A connectionist representation of rules, variables and dynamic bindings using temporal synchrony. *Behavioral and Brain Sciences*, 16:417–494. (Includes peer commentaries.).

Shaw, M. L. and Gaines, B. R. (1993). Personal construct psychology foundations for knowledge acquisition and representation. In *Proceedings of the European Knowledge Acquisition Workshop*, pages 256–276. Springer-Verlag.

Siegelmann, H. and Sontag, E. (1992). On the computational power of neural nets. In *Proceedings of the 5th ACM Workshop on Computational Learning Theory*, pages 440–449.

Simon, H. A. and Newell, A. (1958). Heuristic Problem Solver: The Next Advance in Operations Research. *Operations Research*, 6.

Simoudis, E., Han, J. W., and Fayyad, U., editors (1996). *Proceedings of the 2nd International Conference on Knowledge Discovery and Data Mining (KDD-96).* AAAI.

Singh, M. and Provan, G. M. (1996). Efficient learning of selective Bayesian network classifiers. In *Proc. 13th International Conference on Machine Learning*, pages 453–461. Morgan Kaufmann.

Skinner, B. (1953). *Science and Human Behavior.* New York.

Slezak, P. (1998a). The 'idea' idea. Unpublished.

Slezak, P. (1998b). Situated cognition: Empirical issue, 'paradigm shift' or conceptual confusion. In *Perspectives on Cognitive Science, Vol. 2.* Norwood, Ablex Publishing, New Jersey, USA.

Smith, A. R. (1971). Simple computation-universal cellular spaces. *Journal of the ACM*, 18(3):339–353.

Smith, D., Parra, E., and Westfold, S. (1996). Synthesis of planning and scheduling software. In *Advanced Planning Technology*, pages 226–234. AAAI.

Smolensky, P. (1988). On the proper treatment of connectionism. *Behavioral and Brain Sciences*, 11:1–74. (Includes peer commentaries).

Smolensky, P. (1990a). In defence of PTC. *Behavioral and Brain Sciences*, 13(2):407–412.

Smolensky, P. (1990b). Tensor product variable binding and the representation of symbolic structures in connectionist systems. *Artificial Intelligence*, (46):159–216.

Smolensky, P. (1991). Connectionism, constituency and the language of thought. In Loewer, B. and Rey, G., editors, *Meaning in Mind: Fodor and his Critics*. Reprinted in C. Macdonald and G. Macdonald: *Connectionism - Debates on the Psychological Explanation*, pp. 164–198, Basil Blackwell Ltd, 1995.

Smolensky, P. (1995). Reply: Constituent structure and explanation in an integrated connectionist/symbolic cognitive architecture. In Macdonald, C. and Macdonald, G., editors, *Connectionism - Debates on the Psychological Explanation*, pages 223–290. Basil Blackwell Ltd.

Soloway, E., Bachant, J., and Jensen, K. (1987). Assessing the maintainability of XCON-in-RIME: Coping with the problems of a VERY large rule=base. In *Proceedings of AAAI'87*. Morgan Kaufmann.

Steels, L. and Brooks, R. A., editors (1995). *The Artificial Life Route to Artificial Intelligence: Building Embodied Situated Agents*. Lawrence Erlbaum Associates, Inc., Hillsdale, NJ.

Stefik, M. (1981). Planning and meta-planning. *Artificial Intelligence*, (16):141–170.

Stenning, K. and Yule, P. (1997). Image and language in human reasoning: a syllogistic illustration. *Cognitive Psychology*, 34(2):109–159.

Sutton, R. S. (1988). Learning to predict by the methods of temporal difference. *Machine Learning*, 3(1):9–44.

Sutton, R. S. and Barto, A. G. (1998). *Reinforcement Learning: An Introduction*. MIT Press.

Suzuki, J. (1996). Learning Bayesian belief networks based on the minimum description length principle: an efficient algorithm using the B & B technique. In *Proc. 13th International Conference on Machine Learning*, pages 462–470. Morgan Kaufmann.

Swartout, W. R. and Moore, J. D. (1993). Explanation in second generation expert systems. In David, J.-M., Krivine, J.-P., and Simmons, R., editors, *Second Generation Expert Systems*, pages 543–585. Springer-Verlag.

Tesauro, G. (1995). Temporal difference learning and TD-gammon. *Communications of the ACM*, 3(38):58–68.

Thelen, E. and Smith, L. (1994). *A dynamic systems approach to the development of cognition and action*. MIT Press, Cambridge, MA.

Thiel, T. (1994). *The Design of the Connection Machine*, volume 10. MIT Press, Cambridge, Massachusetts.

Thrun, S. (1995). Is learning the n-th thing any easier than learning the first? In Touretzky, D., Mozer, M. C., and Hasselmo, M., editors, *Advances in Neural Information Processing Systems 8*. San Mateo, California: Morgan Kaufmann.

Thrun, S., editor (1996). *Explanation-Based Neural Network Learning: A Lifelong Learning Approach.* Kluwer Academic Publishers, The Netherlands.

Thrun, S. and O'Sullivan, J. (1996). Discovering structure in multiple learning tasks: The TC algorithm. In *Proceedings of the 13th International Conference on Machine Learning.* Kaufmann.

Thrun, S. and Pratt, L. Y., editors (1997). *Learning to Learn.* Kluwer Academic Publishers, The Netherlands.

Tickle, A. B., Andrews, R., Golea, M., and Diederich, J. (1998). The truth will come to light: directions and challenges in extracting the knowledge embedded within trained artificial neural networks. *IEEE Transactions on Neural Networks*, 9.

Tolman, E. (1932). *Purposive Behavior in Animals and Men.* Watkins Glen, N.Y.

Tolman, E. and Brunswik, F. (1935). The organism and the causal texture of the environment. *Psychological Review*, 42:43–77.

Towell, G. and Shavlik, J. (1993). Extracting refined rules from knowledge-based neural networks. *Machine Learning*, 1(13):71–101.

Towell, G. and Shavlik, J. (1994). Knowledge-based artificial neural networks. *Artificial Intelligence*, (70):119–165.

Turing, A. M. (1937). On computable numbers, with an application to the Entscheidungsproblem. *Proceedings of the London Mathematical Society*, 2(42):230–265 and (43) 544–546.

Turing, A. M. (1950). Computing machinery and intelligence. *Mind*, 59:433–460.

Utgoff, P. E. and Mitchell, T. M. (1982). Acquisition of appropriate bias for inductive concept learning. In *Proceedings of the AAAI*, pages 414–417.

Valiant, L. (1984a). Deductive learning. *Philosophical Transactions of the Royal Society of London*, 312.

Valiant, L. (1984b). A theory of the learnable. *Communications of the ACM*, 27:1134–1142.

van Gelder, T. (1995). What might cognition be, if not computation? *Journal of Philosophy*, (91):345–381.

van Gelder, T. and Port, R. (1995). It's about time: an overview of the dynamical approach to cognition. In *Mind as motion: explorations in the dynamics of cognition.* MIT Press, Cambridge, MA.

Vapnik, V. N. and Chervonenkis, A. Y. (1971). On the uniform convergence of relative frequencies of events to their probabilities. *Theory of Probability and its Applications*, 16(2):264–280.

von der Malsburg, C. (1981). The correlation theory of brain function. Technical report, Max-Planck Institute for Biophysical Chemistry, Göttingen. Internal Report 81-2.

von der Malsburg, C. (1986). Am I thinking assemblies? In Palm, G. and Aertsen, A., editors, *Brain theory*. Springer-Verlag.

von der Malsburg, C. and Schneider, W. (1986). A neural cocktail-party processor. *Biological Cybernetics*, 29:29–40.

von Neumann, J. (1966). *The Theory of Self-Reproducing Automata*. University of Illinois Press.

Waibel, A. (1989). Modular construction of time-delay neural networks for speech recognition. *Neural Computation*, (1):39–46.

Waltz, D. L. (1981). Toward a detailed model of processing for language describing the physical world. In *Proceedings of the 7th International Joint Conference on Artificial Intelligence*.

Waltz, D. L. and Bogess, L. (1979). Visual analog representations for natural language understanding. In *Proceedings of the 6th International Joint Conference on Artificial Intelligence*.

Watanabe, S. (1969). *Knowing and Guessing*. John Wiley & Sons.

Watkins, C. J. (1989). *Learning from delayed rewards*. PhD thesis, King's College, Cambridge, UK.

Watson, J. (1913). Psychology as the behaviorist views it. *Psychological Review*, 20:158–177.

Wei, G.-Q. and Hirzinger, G. (1997). Parametric shape-from-shading by radial basis functions. *IEEE Transactions on Pattern Recognition and Machine Intelligence*, 19(4).

Weiss, S. and Indurkhya, N. (1994). Decision tree pruning: Biased or optimal? In *Proceedings of the 12th National Conference of Artificial Intelligence*, pages 626–632.

Weiss, S. and Indurkhya, N. (1997). *Predictive Data Mining: A Practical Guide*. Morgan Kaufmann Publishers, Inc.

Weiss, S. and Kulikowski, C. (1991). *Computer Systems that Learn*. Morgan Kaufmann, San Mateo, CA.

Werbos, P. J. (1974). *Beyond regression: New tools for prediction and analysis in the behavioral sciences*. PhD thesis, Harvard University.

Werbos, P. J. (1993). Brain-like intelligence in artificial models: How can we really get there? *INNS Above Threshold*. A publication of the International Neural Network Society.

Wertheimer, M. (1945). *Productive Thinking*. Harper & Row, New York.

Werthner, H. (1994). *Qualitative Reasoning*. Springer-Verlag.

Widrow, B. (1962). Generalization and information storage in networks of adaline "neurons". In Yovits, M., Jacobi, G., and Goldstein, G., editors, *Self-Organizing Systems*, pages 435–461. Spartan, Chicago, Illinois.

Widrow, B. and Hoff, M. (1960). Adaptive switching circuits. In *1960 IRE WESCON Convention record*, pages 96–104.

Wiener, N. (1948). *Cybernetics.* Wiley, New York.

Winograd, T. (1972). *Understanding Natural Language.* Academic Press, New York.

Winograd, T. and Flores, F. (1986). *Understanding Computers and Cognition: A new Foundation for Design.* Norwood Publisher.

Wittgenstein, L. (1953). *Philosophical Investigations.* Macmillan, Oxford.

Wittgenstein, L. (1961). *Tractatus logico-philosophicus.* Routledge & K. Paul, London, UK. First German edition in *Annalen der Naturphilosophie*, 1921.

Xu, L. and Jordan, M. (1996). On convergence properties of the EM algorithm for Gaussian mixtures. *Neural Computation*, 8(1):129–151.

Yolton, J. (1996). *Perception and Reality: A History from Descartes to Kant.* Cornell University Press, Ithaca.

Zadeh, L. (1965). Fuzzy sets and systems. In *Proceedings of the Symposium on System Theory*, pages 29–37, Polytechnic Institute, Brooklyn, NY.

Zimmermann, H.-J. (1991). *Fuzzy Set Theory - And Its Applications.* Kluwer, Dordrecht, Netherlands.

Authors Index

Subject Index